ACADEMIC AND DEVELOPMENTAL LEARNING DISABILITIES

Samuel A. Kirk and James C. Chalfant
University of Arizona

LOVE PUBLISHING COMPANY
Denver · London

Editing and typesetting by Special Press, Columbus, Ohio.

Copyright © 1984 Love Publishing Company
Printed in the United States of America
ISBN 0-89108-124-0
Library of Congress Catalog Card Number 83-82702

10   9   8   7   6   5   4   3   2   1

Preface

For more than 20 years the term *learning disabilities* has been used by different people to describe a heterogenous group of children. The diversity of theories and concepts applied to the term is the result of interest in this area by members of a number of disciplines, including neurology, psychology, education, psychiatry, pediatrics, and others. In addition, parents' interest in seeking educational services for their underachieving children has markedly increased the enrollment in programs for learning disabled children. Today the largest group of exceptional children enrolled in all special education classes (approximately 40% of the total) is the learning disabled.

The purposes of this book are two-fold. The first is to provide a basis for classifying children who can legitimately be included under the rubric of learning disabilities. The second is to help teachers diagnose and remediate those children who have major disabilities in the learning process. This book is addressed to teachers in the regular grades as well as to special teachers in programs for the learning disabled. School psychologists and educational diagnosticians also should find the concepts in this text of value in their work in diagnosing learning disabled children.

We hope that the readers will appreciate the emphasis we place on observation and informal assessment without reliance solely on formal testing. Throughout the book, directions for informal diagnosis and remediation have been outlined for the teacher or diagnostician. The reason for this emphasis is our reaction against the practice of assessing children by relying primarily on scaled or standard scores, IQs, percentile ranks, stanines, and other statistical measures. We trust that this emphasis will tend to increase the importance of the clinical judgment of teachers and diagnosticians.

Thus the suggestion of this text is that before a teacher refers a child for formal diagnosis by a team of diagnosticians, he or she will use the guidelines for observation and informal assessment. In this way, when test scores are obtained, they can be used as aids or as corroboration or denial of assumptions made through careful repeated observations.

The contents of the text are divided into four parts. The first part, *background considerations,* includes a description of the learning disabled child, the historical background of the field, causes and contributing factors, and general diagnostic and remedial procedures. The second part discusses the *developmental disabilities* of memory, attention, perception, thinking, and language. The third part discusses the *academic disabilities* of reading, handwriting, spelling and written expression, and arithmetic. The fourth part comments on *major issues* of social behavior, educational services, and the relationship between developmental and academic disabilities.

We are indebted to many keen minds who, over the past century, have laid the foundation for the current discussion of developmental and academic learning disabilities. We wish to express deep appreciation to our colleagues Dr. John McLeod, Dr. Esther Minskoff, and Dr. Eugene Ensminger for their critical and useful review of the first draft of the original manuscript. Their suggestions for deletions and inclusions were extremely valuable. We also wish to acknowledge the contributions of two doctoral fellows at the University of Arizona. Nancy Mather read many of the chapters and made helpful contributions, as well as contributing to the information in chapter 16. Lynne Jaffe spent many hours in the library searching for elusive books and articles and checking on the accuracy of references.

We also wish to express our appreciation to Winifred Day Kirk for her thorough and detailed review of each chapter. Her insightful comments and her ability to detect the kernel of a thought were most helpful. Janet Rauchut, our secretary, was of priceless help and assistance in preparing the manuscript for publication.

Finally, we wish to thank the many learning disabled children and their parents with whom we have worked over the years. Our efforts in trying to assess and remediate problems of these learning disabled children and adults were the key factor in our development of the concepts, principles, and diagnostic and remedial practices included in this volume.

Samuel A. Kirk
James C. Chalfant

Contents

3 Causes and contributing factors, 38

4 Educational diagnostic and remedial procedures, 54

part 2 developmental learning disabilities, 73

5 Attentional disabilities, 74

6   Memory disabilities, 94

7   Perceptual disabilities, 108

8 Thinking disabilities, 124

11 Handwriting disabilities, 196

12   Spelling and written expression disabilities, 212

13   Arithmetic disabilities, 236

part 1

background considerations

1
The learning disabled child

Until relatively recently, special education was involved primarily with children who were having problems in learning because of hearing or vision impairments, mental retardation, speech and language handicaps, serious emotional disturbance, or crippling and other health conditions. Institutions, special schools, and special classes were organized to educate these obviously handicapped children. The states formulated rules and regulations to identify and classify these children, and schools developed a variety of curricula to educate these different groups differentially. Children who were not learning in school but who were not deaf or blind or mentally retarded did not receive special services because no programs were available for them.

Because of this situation and the urging of parents, educators have come to recognize that there are a substantial number of children who show delays in learning to talk, to use language well, to develop normal visual or auditory perception, or to read, spell, write, or calculate. Some of these children do not understand language but are not deaf; some are not able to perceive visually but are not blind; and some cannot learn by ordinary methods of instruction though they are *not* mentally retarded. This is the group of children who now come under the rubric of *specific learning disability*.

Learning disabilities has become an accepted term that encompasses many kinds of problems not included in traditional categories of exceptionality—blindness, deafness, mental retardation, and other well-known disabilities.

Three examples

The following vignettes portray some of the puzzling problems encountered in learning disabled children. Each of these three children had normal vision and hearing, and the estimated level of intellectual functioning was in the normal range. They were able to learn and perform many tasks at their chronological age or grade level. Yet each of these children had a specific kind of learning disability that required special help.

A disability in oral language

Many years ago one of the authors was playing golf with some friends who were complaining that their daughter refused to send her 4-year-old mentally retarded child to the state institution. They were afraid that the retarded child, Sally, might interfere with the social development of her older sister. They wanted the mother (their daughter) counselled, hoping that she would allow Sally to be institutionalized (which was the common action for retarded children at that time).

A conference with the mother revealed that Sally was still not talking. As an infant she had had trouble eating and had become undernourished. At the age of 7 months, she had had an operation performed on the cord beneath her tongue. It gave more mobility to the tongue and allowed Sally to eat more normally. Subsequent examinations in medical and psychological clinics had resulted in a working diagnosis of mental retardation as an explanation for the lack of speech and language development.

After this conference, Sally was given a more complete developmental evaluation. Tests and observations revealed that she was developing normally in some areas, including visual memory, understanding language, understanding what she saw, and communicating through gestures. She was, however, very retarded in speech and related areas requiring verbal expression. In fact, she was making only a few sounds. Because of these deviations, the earlier diagnosis of mental retardation was questioned.

During the following 2 years, Sally received special tutoring in language and speech development. She learned to respond to questions orally, and because of her superior visual memory, she learned to read words and phrases. When she entered school at the age of 6½, she was examined by the school psychologist, who concluded that Sally was not mentally retarded. Consequently she was placed in the regular grades. She progressed through school at a low average rate. Upon graduation from high school, she enrolled in a course in bookkeeping in the local community college.

Sally was a girl with no auditory or visual handicaps who had been erroneously diagnosed as mentally retarded. The psychoeducational evaluation at the age of 4 indicated wide discrepancies in development, with a specific disability in verbal expression. She was remediated as a learning disabled child rather than as a child with mental retardation.

A disability in reading

Johnny entered first grade at the age of 6 and was promoted each year. At the age of 14 he was in the eighth grade, even though he had not learned to read. At that time he was assigned to a prevocational school, since it was believed that he could not survive in a more academic high school.

A psychoeducational examination at this time revealed that Johnny was a boy of average intelligence who scored at the eighth-grade level in arithmetic computation, but at the lower first-grade level in reading. He was given intensive remedial training in reading by means of a systematic phonic method for a year and a half. After this training he succeeded in scoring at the fifth-grade level on reading tests.

Johnny was a child who was not sensorially handicapped, not emotionally disturbed, and not mentally retarded. He was learning disabled with a specific disability in reading. Special training in reading resulted in rapid progress in that academic area.

A disability in arithmetic

In contrast to Johnny, Sampson, age 12, was referred to a learning disability clinic because he seemed unable to learn arithmetic. Educational tests revealed a boy who could read at the sixth-grade level, but who was unable to perform on arithmetic tests beyond the second-grade level.

According to his father, Sampson had developed normally up to the age of 8, when he suffered a brain concussion in an auto accident. In intelligence, in reading, and in most situations he appeared to recover normally, but he seemed unable to think quantitatively. He learned to add and subtract simple numbers but could not understand the significance of place value nor could he multiply or divide.

Instruction in mathematics consisted of practical mathematics problems during his apprenticeship in a garage. Sampson was a boy who was learning disabled with a specific disability in mathematics.

Definitions

The recognition of specific learning disabilities as a type of handicap was relatively recent. The term became popular in 1963 when representatives of several parent organizations dealing with brain-injured and perceptually handicapped children met in Chicago to discuss their mutual problems and to establish a national organization. At this meeting they decided to use the term *specific learning disability*. The resulting organization adopted the title Association for Children with Learning Disabilities (ACLD). The concept and label were introduced to encompass a large group of children who did not fit into other categories of handicapped children but who did definitely need help in acquiring school skills. The term was preferable to the general categories of *brain injured* or *minimal brain dysfunction (MBD)*, or the specific labels of *aphasia* or *dysphasia* (language disorder), *alexia* or *dyslexia* (reading disability), *acalculia* or *dyscalculia* (arithmetic disability), *agraphia* or *dysgraphia* (writing disability), and a host of others.

In the years since 1963, many people have tried to define *learning disabilities* but no one has produced a definition acceptable to everyone. The situation is reminiscent of the three blind men who felt different parts of an elephant and described the elephant as a rope, a wall, and a tree, respectively. Similarly, professionals working with learning disabled children tend to define *learning disabilities* from their own professional points of view. Hence a variety of definitions have been proposed by different professionals.

In 1968 the National Advisory Committee for the Handicapped in the U.S. Office of Education formulated a definition which, with minor revisions, was later included in the 1975 *Education for All Handicapped Children Act,* Public Law 94-142. This definition reads:

> The term "children with specific learning disabilities" means those children who have a disorder in one or more of the basic psychological processes involved in understanding or in using language, spoken or written, which disorder may manifest itself in imperfect ability to listen, speak, read, write, spell, or do mathematical calculations. Such disorders include such conditions as perceptual handicaps, brain injury, minimal brain dysfunction, dyslexia, and

developmental aphasia. Such term does not include children who have learning problems which are primarily the result of visual, hearing, or motor handicaps, of mental retardation, of emotional disturbance, or of environmental, cultural, or economic disadvantage.

The 1968 federal definition has enjoyed wide acceptance among the states. Gillespie, Miller, and Fielder (1975), summarizing the state definitions, assert that the states have accepted the federal definition or made slight modifications of it.

Although the federal definition has been accepted by many, it has been criticized by others. The major criticisms revolve around (1) the ambiguous nature of the phrase "psychological disorders"; (2) the omission of reference to the central nervous system, which results in perceptual-motor involvement, which in turn affects academic progress (Cruickshank, 1981b); and (3) the exclusion of other handicaps, since some experts believe that children with sensory handicaps or mild mental retardation (or other handicaps) can also have a learning disability and thus could be considered multiply handicapped.

As a result of these criticisms, many professionals have offered substitute definitions, none of which substantially improve the federal definition. In the last few years, however, a joint committee* of six professional associations has been working to refine the term. They have finally agreed on a definition which they believe circumvents the major criticisms of the federal definition. This definition is as follows:

> *Learning disabilities* is a generic term that refers to a heterogeneous group of disorders manifested by significant difficulties in the acquisition and use of listening, speaking, reading, writing, reasoning or mathematical abilities. These disorders are intrinsic to the individual and presumed to be due to central nervous system dysfunction. Even though a learning disability may occur concomitantly with other handicapping conditions (e.g., sensory impairment, mental retardation, social and emotional disturbance) or environmental influences (e.g., cultural differences, insufficient/inappropriate instruction, psychogenic factors), it is not the direct result of those conditions or influences. (Hammill, Leigh, McNutt, & Larsen, 1981, p. 336)

In concluding their discussion of why that definition was offered and agreed upon, the committee acknowledged that the definition is not perfect, but that it is an improvement over previous definitions. According to the committee, in the future it, too, may be replaced by a better definition.

The definitions that have been proposed have attempted to differentiate learning disabilities from other conditions that influence academic under-

*The National Joint Committee for Learning Disabilities (NJCLD) consisted of representatives of The American Speech-Language-Hearing Association, The Association for Children and Adults with Learning Disabilities, The Council for Learning Disabilities, The Division for Children with Communication Disorders, The International Reading Association, and the Orton Dyslexia Society.

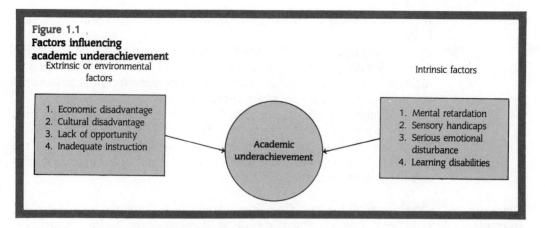

Figure 1.1
Factors influencing academic underachievement

Extrinsic or environmental factors

1. Economic disadvantage
2. Cultural disadvantage
3. Lack of opportunity
4. Inadequate instruction

Academic underachievement

Intrinsic factors

1. Mental retardation
2. Sensory handicaps
3. Serious emotional disturbance
4. Learning disabilities

achievement. In any school system 10 to 20% of the children are seriously underachieving for one reason or another. Figure 1.1 presents the major contributing factors to underachievement in school children. Two major types of factors are listed: extrinsic and intrinsic.

Extrinsic conditions refer to contributing factors in the environment, including socioeconomic conditions, cultural factors, lack of opportunity to learn, and inadequate or inappropriate instruction that interferes with or inhibits the child's ability to learn. These factors are referred to in the federal definition as "environmental, cultural or economic disadvantage, and inadequate instruction" and in the NJCLD definition as "environmental influences."

Intrinsic refers to conditions within the child. These include mental retardation, sensory handicaps (severe auditory or visual impairments), serious emotional disturbances, and learning disabilities. The latter, the subject of this book, is considered intrinsic in the NJCLD definition. It is referred to in the federal definition as "psychological disorders."

Classification of learning disabilities

Since specific learning disabilities in children constitute a wide variety of conditions, it is important to delineate the kinds of problems children with learning disabilities exhibit. Some professionals emphasize reading and language problems as the core of learning disabilities. To other professionals, difficulty in attending is the major consideration; to still others, different "psychological disorders" such as memory, figure-ground recognition, or other visual or auditory perceptual problems are central. The federal regulations (*Federal Register,* 1977c) list three kinds of problems: (1) language problems (oral expression and listening comprehension), (2) reading and writing problems (written expression and reading skills), and (3) mathematics problems (calculation and reasoning).

The organization of this book recognizes specific learning disabilities from a broader perspective than does the federal definition. Our taxonomy includes both the learning disabilities listed in the federal regulations and developmental disabilities occurring at the preschool level and beyond.

Learning disabilities can be classified into two groups: (1) developmental learning disabilities, referred to in the federal definition as "basic psychological processes" and (2) academic learning disabilities encountered at the school-age level. Figure 1.2 illustrates these two kinds of learning disabilities and the subsets of each.

Developmental learning disabilities

Developmental learning disabilities involve those prerequisite skills that the child needs in order to achieve in the academic subjects. To learn to write his or her name, a child must have developed many prerequisite skills in perception, motor and eye-hand coordination, sequencing, memory, and so forth. To learn to read, a child must have developed adequate visual and auditory discrimination, visual and auditory memory, language, and other operations. Fortunately, these functions are sufficiently developed in most children to enable them to learn the academic subjects. It is only when these functions are significantly disordered and the child cannot compensate through other functions that he or she has difficulty learning to write or read or spell or calculate.

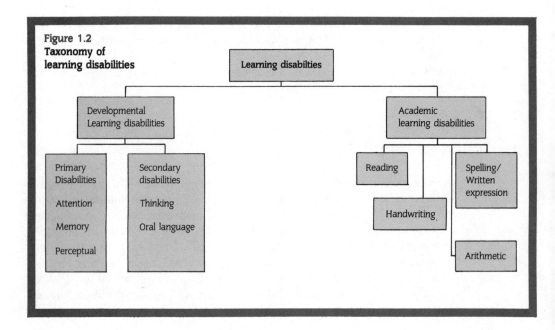

Figure 1.2
Taxonomy of learning disabilities

The left-hand half of figure 1.2 presents the more common developmental learning disabilities found in children with learning disabilities. Many of these are manifested before the child enters school; they may also be identified when a child begins to fail to learn in school.

In figure 1.2 attention, memory, and perceptual-motor disabilities have been grouped under primary disabilities. These appear to be basic interrelated mental operations that, when disordered, influence thinking and oral language. We have labelled thinking and language disabilities as secondary disabilities since they are markedly influenced by the primary disabilities and are often related to difficulties of attending, remembering, and being aware of concepts, objects, and spatial relations. Let us elucidate further.

Attention is the ability to select appropriate or pertinent factors from among numerous competing stimuli (auditory, tactile, visual, kinesthetic) that impinge on the organism at any time. When a child tries to attend and respond to too many stimuli, we consider the child distractible. It is difficult for children to learn if they cannot focus attention on the task at hand.

Memory is the ability to recall what has been seen or heard or experienced. Children with *marked* visual or auditory memory problems may have difficulty in learning to read or spell or write or calculate.

Perceptual disabilities include impairments in visual-motor coordination; visual, auditory, and haptic discrimination; spatial relations; and other perceptual attributes.

Thinking disorders consist of problems with any of a number of kinds of mental operations including judgment, comparison, calculation, inquiry, reasoning, evaluation, critical thinking, problem solving, and decision making.

Oral language disorders refers to the difficulty children might have in understanding language, integrating inner language, and expressing ideas verbally.

Chapters 5, 6, 7, 8, and 9 are devoted to an explanation of these developmental disabilities, their assessment, and their remediation.

Academic learning disabilities

As shown in the right-hand section of figure 1.2, academic learning disabilities are problems primarily experienced by school-aged children. The term includes: (1) reading disabilities, (2) handwriting disabilities, (3) spelling and written expression disabilities, and (4) arithmetic disabilities. When a child appears to have the *potential* to learn, has had the opportunity to learn in school, and fails to learn after adequate instruction, he or she can be considered learning disabled in reading, or handwriting, or spelling or written expression, or arithmetic. Techniques of identification, evaluation, and remediation will be discussed in the chapters for each of these subjects.

Relationship of developmental to academic learning disabilities

To explain further the relationship of academic to developmental learning disabilities, we will present another case study.

Tony, at age 9 and in the fourth grade, was referred for examination because he was not learning to read. Inability to read can be caused by mental retardation, severe auditory impairment, or a marked visual defect. To exclude these possibilities, Tony was examined in all these areas. His visual acuity was reported as average. His audiometric test showed normal auditory acuity. On an intelligence test, he obtained a mental age of about 10. Tony had attended school regularly since the age of 6. His arithmetic computation achievement was at the fourth-grade level but he scored at the lower end of the first grade in reading. It was obvious that there was a significant discrepancy between his intelligence, language ability, and arithmetic performance and his inadequate reading ability.

The major question with Tony was why, after regular schooling for 3 years and with average intelligence and intact sensory acuity, he was unable to decode words or sentences. The question was, What developmental learning ability or abilities were lacking or delayed, or what skills (prerequisite to learning to read) had not developed or were not functioning adequately? What had inhibited Tony's learning to read with ordinary instruction?

The examination revealed two deficient developmental abilities. The first was a disability in sound blending. Three-sound words, such as *c-a-t,* were presented. Tony was unable to blend these three sounds into a word. The second developmental disability was in visual memory. He was unable to reproduce a visually presented word from memory. The word *horse,* for example, was written on the board. He was told that the word was *horse.* The word was erased and he was asked to write the word on the board from memory. Seven repetitions were required before he was able to reproduce the word from memory. It was hypothesized that these two developmental learning disabilities, poor sound blending (auditory perception) and poor visualization (visual memory), were inhibiting Tony's learning to read. It was also discovered that, though he had normal visual acuity, Tony did have significant eye muscle imbalance. This may have contributed to poor visual fusion and subsequent visual memory difficulties. With extensive tutoring, Tony was taught to use sound blending in a phonic approach to reading and also to develop visualization in recognizing sight words. By developing these two abilities in a reading task, Tony learned to read.

Three criteria for identifying learning disabled children

To differentiate learning disabilities from other handicapping conditions or from other forms of educational retardation, it is necessary to describe or define the conditions that differentiate these groups of children. There are three conditions or criteria that must be present before we can say that a child has a specific learning disability. These three criteria are: (1) a discrepancy criterion, (2) an exclusion criterion, and (3) a special education criterion.

The discrepancy criterion

Children with learning disabilities show disparity in one of two ways, or in both: (1) a significant discrepancy in the development of various psychological behaviors (attention, discrimination, language, seeing relationships, visual-motor ability, memory, and so forth); (2) discrepancies between general or specialized intellectual development and academic achievement. At the preschool level, the developmental imbalances are noted, while at the school-aged level, academic retardation is observed.

Disparities in development

Disparities in development in psychological and linguistic functions are noted in some children at the preschool age level. In these instances, the child develops normally in some functions and is delayed in development in other functions. For example, a child of 4 who has developed adequately in language but who is delayed in walking, motor coordination, and visual-motor abilities would be a child with a discrepancy in development.

An example of a preschool child with a developmental learning disability is Andy. At the age of 4, Andy was erroneously assigned to a preschool for trainable mentally retarded children because of a chromosomal translocation, an invalid IQ below 50, and very little verbal expression. As an aid to assessing the child's performance, a test of different developmental abilities (the ITPA) (Kirk, McCarthy, & Kirk, 1968) was administered. The results are shown in figure 1.3. Five of the 10 subtests deal with visual-motor factors (visual reception, visual association, motor expression, visual closure, and visual memory). The other five subtests evaluate language (auditory reception, auditory association, verbal expression, grammatic closure, and auditory memory). Figure 1.3 shows that this 4-year-old child scored like a 5- or 6-year-old child on the visual-motor tests and like a 1- or 2-year-old child on the auditory-vocal tests that are more closely related to language. The disparity between visual-motor scores and auditory-vocal scores indicates a significant discrepancy between developmental abilities. The behaviors indicated by the test scores were also borne out by observation. Andy played with toys like a 5- or 6-year-old child but could not talk or respond to auditory stimuli. It was obvious from his behavior and from scores on nonverbal tests that he had an oral language learning disability.

Many other kinds of developmental learning disabilities are found in children. One 6-year-old child had difficulty identifying objects seen, even her classmates, though she had normal visual acuity. She recognized her classmates when they talked but not by sight. In this case, her visual perceptual abilities were low while her auditory perceptual abilities were average. Other children, especially those who are born with or acquire (through disease or accident) some brain disability such as cerebral palsy, may have developmental learning disabilities. In these cases some functions are normal while other functions are significantly defective.

Figure 1.3
A profile of a child with a
developmental learning disability

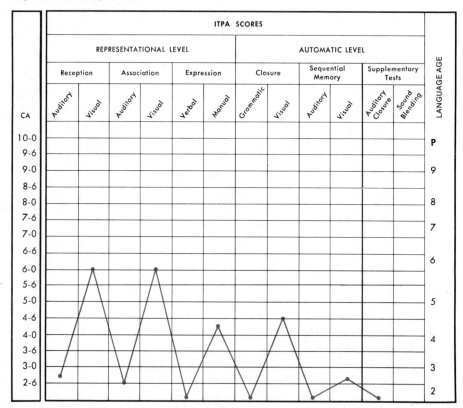

Source: Adapted from S.A. Kirk and W.D. Kirk, "Uses and Abuses of the ITPA," *Journal of Speech and Hearing Disorders,* 1978, *43,* 71.

Disparity between academic achievement and expectancy

When a school-aged child gives evidence of relatively average mental ability, has made normal or near normal progress in arithmetic and in language, but has not learned to read after adequate schooling, that child can be considered learning disabled in reading. Similarly, a child may have learned to read but be markedly retarded in mathematics.

The profile of Tony, the 9-year-old discussed earlier who had failed to read, is presented in figure 1.4. Note that Tony's intelligence was above average, with a mental age of 10 years. His arithmetic computation was at fourth-grade level, similar to an "average" child of 9, and his language comprehension was estimated to be at the 10-year level, as represented by his understanding of a fifth-grade textbook that was read to him. But his reading was at grade 1.2 on an oral reading test and 1.5 on a silent reading test. Tony's potential ability (as measured by mental age, arithmetic computation, and language age) is 3 or more years above his achievement in reading. This represents a substantial disparity of several years between reading achievement and reading expectancy. Thus Tony is considered to be learning disabled in reading. As indicated in the case report, Tony was found to have two developmental learning disabilities.

**The
exclusion
criterion**

Numerous surveys on the prevalence of academic retardation in the schools have found that 10 to 20% of school children perform below their chronological age in one or all of the academic subjects of reading, spelling, arithmetic, and writing. However, a child may be retarded academically or developmentally and yet not be considered learning disabled.

It should be recalled that the definitions of *learning disability* exclude those difficulties in learning that can be explained by general mental retardation, auditory or visual impairment, emotional disturbance, or lack of opportunity to learn. The reason for excluding these conditions may be obvious. A child who is deaf does not naturally develop language, yet his or her visual and intellectual abilities may be normal. The fact that there is a discrepancy between language learning and other achievements can be explained by deafness. That child would require an educational program for the deaf, rather

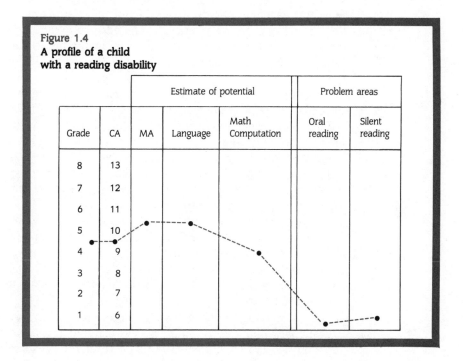

Figure 1.4
**A profile of a child
with a reading disability**

than a program for the learning disabled. Similarly, a child who has not developed in language, in visual perception, in social adjustment, or in self-help skills requires a general program of development organized for children with mental retardation. On the other hand, a blind child who has finger agnosia (lack of feeling in the fingers) will have difficulty learning Braille. He or she would be considered multiply handicapped (blind and learning disabled).

In classifying children for instructional purposes, considerable care must be taken to avoid mistaken diagnoses and misclassifications. As shown in figure 1.1, several conditions result in educational retardation that can be mistaken for learning disabilities. These conditions include (1) mental retardation, (2) sensory handicaps, (3) serious emotional disturbances, and (4) lack of opportunity to learn.

Mental retardation can often explain a child's slow achievement in academic subjects. A child who is mentally retarded has great difficulty in learning to read, to spell, or to calculate at his or her age level. Many such children do not begin to read, for example, until the age of 8 or 10 and then progress more slowly than the average child. Kirk, Kliebhan, and Lerner (1978) have reviewed the research on the effects of mental retardation on academic achievement. They concluded that "regardless of age, slow learning children tend to read below their mental age" (p. 229). A child whose IQ is 50 to 60 or 70 has a mental level of 3 to 4 years at the age of 6. This means that the child will be 9 to 12 years old before he or she has the prerequisite skills for reading. Since the academic retardation is due to mental retardation, the child's education should be general and practical and adapted to the slower rate of development. Such a child does not have a discrepancy between achievement and expectancy as determined by mental ability, language, and arithmetic computation.

Sensory handicaps, notably hearing and visual impairments, also affect the ability to learn. Deaf children are retarded in reading because deafness interferes with the development of language. It is also impossible for blind children to learn to read print, though they can learn to read Braille. We do not consider sensory handicapped children learning disabled because we have special progams designed specifically for deaf or blind children. Some sensory handicapped children may also have a learning disability; they would be considered multiply handicapped.

Serious emotional disturbances can also affect academic achievement. Studies have shown that seriously maladjusted and emotionally disturbed children are retarded educationally. It is important to analyze those children to determine whether or not a learning disability has influenced the social or emotional maladjustment, or whether the emotional disturbance has affected educational progress.

Lack of opportunity to learn is another reason why some children are educationally retarded. A child who has matured at a normal rate socially, vocationally, and linguistically, but who is retarded academically, may not have had an opportunity to learn. Although there is a disparity between his or her potential and achievement, the child is not considered learning disabled. Picture a 10-year-old child coming into the city from some isolated area where he had never attended school or had attended school only sporadically. The child may be of average intelligence, may have normal hearing and vision, but be unable to read or spell or calculate. The child may not have any developmental disabilities. Although this child has the required discrepancy between potential and achievement and is not mentally retarded or seriously handicapped, he does not qualify as learning disabled. He does not meet the third criterion, namely, needing special education. Such a child will learn if given an opportunity with developmental reading, spelling, and arithmetic methods, beginning at his level of competence. No special remedial method is needed. What is needed is a regular reading program.

Economic and cultural disadvantage sometimes negatively affects motivation for learning. Some children are not motivated to learn. Their home environment may not have put a premium on schooling. There may be a discrepancy between potential and achievement, but the lack of achievement is due to negative attitudes toward school. Some children from economically underprivileged areas are not motivated to learn because of frustration and lack of examples and encouragement.

The special education criterion

Children with learning disabilities are those children who require a special method of instruction designed specifically for that child's problem. In other words, children who have not had an opportunity to learn and therefore are retarded educationally will generally learn if they are exposed to ordinary methods of instruction used for the majority of children. Children who are educationally retarded because they have not attended school or have attended sporadically will learn by the developmental methods used for all children. On the other hand, if a child is retarded educationally and also has a developmental learning disability, that child will require special education, that is, a unique or atypical method not ordinarily used with all children. A good example of a special education method is speech reading (lip reading) taught to hearing impaired children. It is considered a special method since it is an atypical or unique method not used with the ordinary child. Another example is the use of the kinesthetic method (writing words and phrases from memory) for children with reading disabilities.

The need for a special method because of some developmental disorder that has inhibited the child's ability to learn is an important and often neglected criterion. This criterion is necessary since it requires that, following a diagnosis of discrepancy and exclusions, the diagnostician must specify a special remedial program needed. Special methods of instruction will be discussed in detail in the chapters dealing with specific academic and developmental learning disabilities.

Using the three criteria for identifying learning disabled children, Kirk and Gallagher (1983) formulated the following description:

> *A learning disability is a psychological or neurological impediment to spoken or written language or perceptual, cognitive, or motor behavior. The impediment (1) is manifested by discrepancies among specific behaviors and achievements, or between evidenced ability and academic achievements; (2) is of such nature and extent that the child does not learn by the instructional methods and materials appropriate for the majority of children and requires specialized procedures for development; and (3) is not primarily due to severe mental retardation, sensory handicaps, emotional problems, or lack of opportunity to learn.* (p. 368)

This description can serve as a guide in diagnosing a learning disabled child by determining (1) that a significant discrepancy exists, (2) that the educational retardation is not due to other handicaps, and (3) that the child has not learned by ordinary methods and requires a special method of instruction.

Learning disability vs. educational retardation

The problem posed by the dichotomy of educational retardation vs. learning disability is of concern to educators. All children are entitled to be educated to the maximum of their ability. A child who is educationally retarded is entitled to educational service regardless of the "cause" of the problem.

Again, children who have been labelled *learning disabled* should meet the three criteria: (1) demonstrate a disparity between academic achievement and expectancy or a disparity in areas of development; (2) show no intellectual, sensory, instructional, or emotional disorders that could explain the retardation; and (3) require special educational procedures. Many professionals, as well as writers of definitions cited earlier, do not consider an educationally retarded child to be learning disabled unless that child has an intrinsic neurological or psychological impediment to learning.

In contrast, children who are educationally retarded may have any one of many other conditions, such as mental retardation, sensory handicaps, emotional disturbance, lack of opportunity to learn, inadequate instruction, economic or cultural disadvantage, and lack of motivation. This is not to suggest that children who are mentally retarded or seriously emotionally disturbed or who have sensory handicaps could not also have a learning disability. Those children would be considered multiply handicapped and remediated as such.

It is important to distinguish between learning disabled children and educationally retarded children because the type of instruction needed depends upon the nature of the difficulty. The child with a learning disability will require a special method of training, including the remediation of the academic disability and the prerequisite developmental skills or developmental disabilities in the same program. The child who is educationally retarded because of mental retardation, deafness, blindness, emotional disturbance, lack of adequate instruction, and so forth will need a different kind of instructional program, as will be discussed in chapter 4.

Prevalence

When learning disabilities as a category of exceptional children was accepted by federal, state, and local officials, the first question asked was, How many learning disabled children are there? To this question we still do not have an adequate answer. We cannot answer this question accurately because different researchers use different criteria. Myklebust and Boshes (1969) used one criterion and obtained a 15% figure, but when they used another criterion they obtained a 7% figure. Likewise Meier (1971), who studied 2,400 school-aged children in Colorado, found 4.7% to be learning disabled. Wissink, Kass, and Ferrell (1975) found that different experts in the field estimated from 2 to 20% of the school population as learning disabled.

Another approach to a study of prevalence of learning disabled children is to note the enrollment in classes or services for such children. In recent years, states have been required to report figures on enrollment in classes for exceptional children. Table 1.1 presents the enrollment for children with learning disabilities, speech impairments, and mental retardation for the 5 years from 1978 to 1983.

As the table shows, there has been a slight decrease in enrollment for the mildly retarded and speech impaired, but a gradual increase in enrollment for the learning disabled (from 2.3% of the school population in 1978–79 to

Table 1.1

Handicapped children receiving special education and related services under P.L. 94-142 and P.L. 89-313

	1978–79		1980–81		1982–83	
	Total	% of Population	Total	% of Population	Total	% of Population
Speech Impaired	1,214,994	2.42	1,117,792	2.43	1,134,164	2.45
Mentally Retarded	918,655	1.83	849,890	1.75	780,829	1.71
Learning Disabled	1,154,430	2.3	1,455,135	3.01	1,745,865	3.82

Source: Adapted from W.C. Healey, B.L. Ackerman, C.R. Chapell, K.L. Perrin, and J. Stormer, *The Prevalence of Communicative Disorders: A Review of the Literature* (Final Report). Rockville, Md.: American Speech-Language-Hearing Association, 1981; and U.S. Department of Education, *National Enrollment Statistics, 1982–83.*

3.28% in 1982–83). In addition, while in 1969 only 120,000 learning disabled children were reported to be enrolled in the public schools (Kirk & Gallagher, 1983), the increase to 1,745,865 in 1982–83 is phenomenal over a 14-year period. It now appears to be the largest enrollment of any category of exceptional children. It is possible that some children previously classified as mentally retarded and speech impaired are now being classified as learning disabled.

Alarmed by this phenomenal increase in enrollment, in 1978 Congress introduced a resolution that not more than 2% of the school population could be classifed as learning disabled. This so-called "cap" was removed in 1979, but efforts to reinstate it persist. In a questionnaire study of teachers' perception of learning disabled children enrolled in their classes, DeLoach, Earl, Brown, Poplin, and Warner (1981) reported that approximately 30% of the students in learning disability classes were not considered learning disabled. This conclusion has been supported by many others, who find that a disproportionate number of non-learning disabled children are assigned to classes for learning disabilities.

Summary

- Learning disabilities is an educational term that encompasses a heterogeneous group of disorders not included in the traditional categories of exceptionality such as deafness, blindness, and so forth. The term became popular when several parent groups organized into the Association for Children with Learning Disabilities (ACLD) in 1963.

- Programs for learning disabled children were organized to serve children who were having difficulty in learning to talk, to read, to write, or to calculate but who were not sensorially handicapped or mentally retarded or otherwise served in programs for handicapped children.

- In 1968 the federal government defined *learning disabilities* as a disorder in psychological process that "manifests itself in imperfect ability to listen, think, speak, read, write, spell, or do mathematical calculations." This definition was included in P.L. 94-142 (89 Stat. 794) in 1975. Most states accepted or slightly modified this definition.

- Learning disabilities can be classifed under two general categories: (1) developmental learning disabilities of basic psychological functions of attention, memory, perception, thinking, and oral language, and (2) academic disabilities of reading, handwriting, written expression including spelling, and arithmetic.

- The three criteria used to identify children with learning disabilities include (1) a discrepancy criterion, (2) an exclusion criterion, and (3) a special education criterion.

- Not all educationally retarded children are learning disabled, since educational retardation can result from mental retardation, lack of school opportunity, cultural and economic disadvantage resulting in lack of motivation, serious emotional problems, or sensory handicaps.

- Prevalence figures for learning disabled students tend to include educationally retarded children. The best estimate for the prevalence of learning disabilities is from 1 to 3% of school children.

Thought questions

1. Have you known a learning disabled child or adult? Describe his or her characteristics and problems.

2. What would you consider to be the major factors which appear in all definitions? How do the definitions differ?

3. Which definition can help you determine whether or not a child is learning disabled?

4. Can children be deaf or blind or mentally retarded and still be learning disabled? If your answer is yes, explain the characteristics of those children.

5. Why is oral language listed under developmental learning disabilities instead of under academic disabilities?

6. In your experience, have you known a preschool child with a developmental learning disability? Describe.

7. What do you think would be a discrepancy in developmental disabilities?

8. If a child of 10 or 12 is equally retarded in spelling, reading, writing, arithmetic, and language, what would you suspect is the problem or problems? Try to suggest both extrinsic and intrinsic problems.

9. How would you differentiate between educational retardation and learning disabilities?

10. Can you explain why the enrollment in learning disability services now exceeds enrollment in other services for handicapped children?

2

Historical perspective

The field of learning disabilities is relatively new, but the disorders of human behavior and the basic concepts upon which the field is based are not new. They have existed under one name or another for several centuries. Perhaps the best way to understand this new and exciting field of study is to examine the original ideas and thinking of the early contributors to the study of disorders of language and reading in the 18th, 19th, and early 20th centuries.

The discipline now called *learning disabilities* had its beginning in the early contributions of neurologists who studied the loss of language in adults who had suffered brain damage. They were followed by neuropsychologists and ophthalmologists who were concerned about children's inability to develop language or to read or spell. These developments required objective diagnoses by psychologists and psychoeducators who devised tests to assess learning capacity. The identification of adults and children with learning problems through tests and observations led psychologists and educators to develop remedial procedures. These programs required legislation to establish school programs for children who were not learning language, or reading, or spelling, or arithmetic. This chapter will describe these programs, from the early contributions to the present extensive services for learning disabled children and adults.

Early contributions of neurology to the study of aphasia

As in all areas dealing with handicapped people, the profession that first became interested in disorders of learning was medicine—more specifically, neurology. When difficulties in reading, writing, speaking, or doing mathematical calculations resulted from brain injuries in adults, neurologists were asked to diagnose and treat those conditions. Thus evolved the medical terminology denoting the loss of a function as a result of an acquired brain injury. The word *aphasia,* for example, was used with adults who had lost the ability to express themselves through speech. Similarly, *alexia* referred to the loss of the ability to read; *agraphia,* the loss of the ability to write; and *acalculia,* the loss of the ability to calculate. These disorders were all conceived of as resulting from insults or trauma to the brain, including head injury during war and brain damage resulting from an accident, a brain hemorrhage, or a disease affecting the brain.

In 1802 *Francis Joseph Gall* pointed out the relationship of brain injuries to disorders of language (aphasia) (Head, 1926). This Austrian neurologist studied adult patients who had lost the ability to communicate orally because of brain injuries. He attempted to localize certain operations such as memory, personality, mathematics, speech, and intelligence in specific parts of the brain. Although his brain theories were accepted by his colleagues, his discipline of phrenology, which purported to determine and predict personality, intelligence, and other behaviors by studying the bumps on the head, was not as readily accepted.

Later, in 1860, a Frenchman, *Pierre Paul Broca,* accepted Gall's localization of brain functions involved in aphasic disorders (Penfield & Roberts, 1959). He accumulated data from post-mortem studies of the brains of 15 former patients who had lost the ability to speak as a result of head injury. His studies lead him to postulate (1) that the left side of the brain functioned differently from the right side and (2) that disorders of speech and language were due to injuries and damage to the third frontal convolution of the brain. This area is still referred to as *Broca's area.* (See figure 2.1.)

In 1872, at the age of 26, *Carl Wernicke* (1908) published a classic monograph on aphasia, *Der Aphasische Symtomencomplex.* In this monograph he localized an area of the brain in the left temporal lobe which he stated dealt with verbal comprehension, the understanding of sounds, and the association of sounds to written language and writing. This area is known as *Wernicke's area.* While Broca's area deals with the production of speech, Wernicke's area deals with the comprehension of speech. Both these areas are shown in figure 2.1.

John Hughlings Jackson (1915) pointed out that there were different kinds of aphasia, including the loss of the ability to speak, the loss of the ability to write, and the loss of the ability to read. He felt that these disorders were disorders of symbolic thinking. His theories of brain function were based on his personal studies of brain-damaged adults and epileptics. His writings and his studies influenced many neurologists later in the 20th century (Taylor, 1958).

Early 20th century neuropsychological contributions

Henry Head (1926), an English neurologist who was greatly influenced by the works of Hughlings Jackson, is considered the most noteworthy authority on aphasia. Following World War I, Head had the opportunity to study soldiers who had suffered head injuries and had lost the ability to understand language or to speak. His clinical observations and insights led him to postulate that damage to different areas of the brain produces different disorders. For example, Head claimed that syntactic disorders (disorders of grammar and word order) are caused by lesions on the upper convolutions of the temporal lobe, while lesions in the supermarginal gyrus cause disorders of understanding of symbolic significance and intentions. Head found that lesions in the posterior portion of the angular gyrus destroyed the power to remember names and other expressions. He concluded that individuals who have had brain hemorrhage and are unable to remember names of objects have defects in the neighborhood of the angular gyrus.

In addition to the studies of aphasia, or language disorders with adults, many neuorologists referred to reading and writing disorders as well. *James*

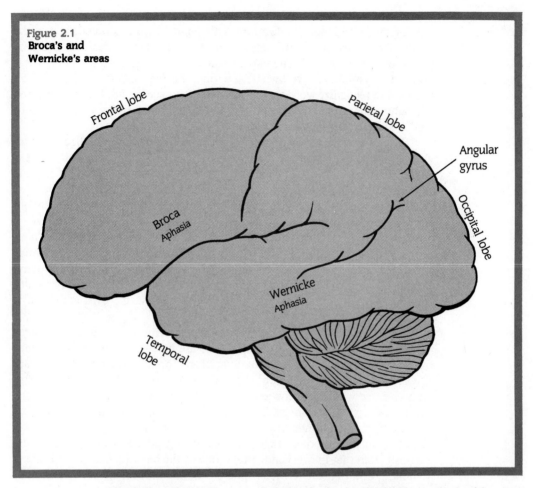

Figure 2.1
**Broca's and
Wernicke's areas**

Hinshelwood (1917), an ophthalmologist in England, worked with many school children who were having difficulty learning to read. Teachers reasoned that if a child reads with his eyes and has difficulty learning to read, there must be something wrong with his eyes. These teachers consequently referred children to Hinshelwood for a visual examination. He found that very few of the children referred to him as reading failures had visual defects and concluded that the cause of their reading failure was not a visual problem.

While Hinshelwood was pondering this problem, he received a 58-year-old patient who had had a brain concussion. This man had read very well prior to the brain insult but lost the ability to read following the accident. Hinshelwood found that, though the man was unable to read, his visual acuity was intact. Hinshelwood used the word *alexia* to describe this condition, meaning that the man had lost the ability to read after it had been acquired. He found that this man was unable to recognize previously known words and phrases and had lost the ability to learn a word as a whole. Hinshelwood hypothesized that this problem was due to the destruction of areas in the visual cortex controlling visualization. This condition, he contended, was the result of a disturbance in the central process rather than a defect in the peripheral process of vision. The patient was able to write sentences from dictation but was unable to read what he wrote. Hinshelwood attempted to teach this man to recognize words as wholes but was unsuccessful. He then resorted to teaching the patient to respond to isolated letters and thereby taught him to read a little by the spelling method.

Several years later the patient contracted pneumonia and died. By previous agreement Hinshelwood was able to obtain the brain and study the extent of cortical damage. He found a lesion in the angular gyrus of the left cerebral hemisphere. As a result of this and similar cases, Hinshelwood postulated that the reading center was in the angular gyrus of the left hemisphere and that lesions in that area would produce alexia, or what he called "word blindness." He further postulated that children who have difficulty learning to read probably had an injury or an underdevelopment of the left angular gyrus. He differentiated between adults who lost the ability to read as having "acquired word blindness" and children who were unable to or had difficulty learning to read as having "congenital word blindness." This condition is also referred to as *dyslexia*.

The United States has produced several contributors to the field of neuropsychology and learning disabilities who are noteworthy and whose names frequently appear in the literature. One of the foremost of these was *Samuel T. Orton,* a professor of neurology at the University of Iowa. Orton (1928) did not agree with Hinshelwood's localization of a reading disability in the left angular gyrus, but instead believed that reading difficulties were due to "a lack of cerebral dominance." He believed that the lack of cerebral dominance produces stuttering in children and also produces reading disabilities. He postulated that in every individual, one of the hemispheres of the brain is dominant, and that the left hemisphere is dominant in right-handed individuals. When only one side of the brain is dominant, a person has less difficulty learning to read and less tendency to reverse letters and words. When neither hemisphere is dominant over the other, the child tends to stutter and reverse letters and words and thereby has difficulty learning to read. Orton called this condition *strephosymbolia,* meaning twisted symbols.

Orton's theories stimulated a great deal of controversy among people specializing in language and reading disorders. Among Orton's associates and followers were Lee Edward Travis, Wendell Johnson, and others who specialized in the treatment of stuttering. Today Orton's name is perpetuated in an organization called "The Orton Dyslexia Society."

Many neurologists, neurosurgeons, and neuropsychologists have attempted to unravel the mysteries of the brain and the abnormal behavior manifestations that result from brain lesions and cerebral dysfunctions. Even today our knowledge of language and reading disabilities is inferred primarily from clinical cases rather than from experimental studies. At McGill University in Montreal, Canada, for example, Penfield and Roberts (1959) studied adult patients suffering from brain tumors. Through electrical stimulation of different parts of the brain, they were able to elicit recall of past sensations and memories. Their studies threw new light on the speech mechanism and on language. Similarly the great Russian neuropsychologist, Aleksander Romanovich Luria (1966), through clinical studies of brain-damaged adults, was able to formulate theories of brain functions and the behavioral systems associated with brain dysfunction. Halstead (1947) and Reitan and Davidson (1974), working with adult aphasia cases, developed neuropsychological tests that could identify brain injuries in adults and children.

Thus the history of learning disabilities finds its heritage in the neuropsychological studies of adult patients who lost the ability to speak, read, write, or calculate after suffering brain damage. These theories were extended to children who failed to develop normal language or reading abilities.

Many educators today allege that the terms *aphasia, alexia, agraphia,* and *acalculia* are inappropriate to use with children who have never acquired language or reading or writing, since these terms originally referred to a *loss* of the abilities once acquired. These terms, however, are still used by medical professionals to denote the lack of development of these skills.

The assessment of learning disabilities

While neurologists, neuropsychologists, and ophthalmologists were doing early work on the results of brain damage, psychologists were concentrating on the assessment of behavior. A majority of the theoretical approaches, tests, and remedial principles used with learning disabled children was taken from the wealth of knowledge generated from the fields of psychology and remedial education. A helpful way of studying the history of the field of learning disabilities is to study the development of the concept of intelligence and efforts to assess intellectual functioning and cognitive abilities. If we are to understand specific learning *disabilities,* then we must first become familiar with specific learning *abilities.* This section will briefly review some of the contributions of psychologists who have played a significant part in the development and understanding of cognitive abilities and the learning process.

The Stanford-Binet Intelligence Scale

In 1905, a French psychologist, *Alfred Binet* (1911), was commissioned by the French government to identify children in the public schools who did not have sufficient intelligence to profit from the usual instructional program. It was believed at that time that teachers' judgment of children's abilities was faulty and biased and that parents and others could not depend solely on teachers' judgments. What was needed was a set of objective tests to measure the intelligence of children on a comparable basis. Consequently, Binet and a medical colleague, *Dr. Theophile Simon,* developed a graded series of tests ranging from simple to complex to provide a measure of general intellectual level. This French test became popular in the United States when *Louis Terman* (Terman & Merrill, 1937), standardized the test on American children in 1916 and entitled it the *Stanford Revision of the Binet-Simon Intelligence Scale* (commonly called the *Stanford-Binet*).

Bifactor theory of intelligence

The idea of intelligence as a single factor or entity was challenged by an English psychologist, *Charles Spearman* (1927), who concluded that there are two factors operating in intelligence: (1) the general intelligence factor, which is an overall factor, and (2) the specific intelligence factor, which is specific to a particular ability. This bifactor theory maintains that all intellectual activities share a common single factor called a general factor or *g*. In addition, there are numerous specific factors or *s*'s, each being specific to a single activity or mental operation. This concept of specific abilities directed attention toward the idea that intelligence is made up of many different abilities.

Primary mental abilities

In the 1930s, *Lewis L. Thurstone* concluded from a series of research studies that intelligence does not consist primarily of a single general factor, but instead is made up of a number of specific abilities. Thurstone's seven factors of intelligence, which he called *primary mental abilities,* are (1) memory, (2) word fluency, (3) reasoning, (4) space visualization, (5) perceptual speed, (6) verbal comprehension, and (7) numerical ability. These abilities were determined from a statistical factor analysis of a large number of psychological tests.

Following his extensive factor analysis studies of the nature of intelligence, Thurstone and his wife Gwen proceeded to develop tests to measure the primary mental abilities in adolescents and adults. Following this development, *Gwen Thurstone* (Thurstone & Thurstone, 1965) organized the much-used *Primary Mental Abilities Test* (PMA), which measures seven primary mental abilities of preschool and primary-aged school children.

Wechsler Intelligence Scales

The *Wechsler Intelligence Scales for Children–Revised* (Wechsler, 1974) consists of tests for a nonverbal or performance IQ and tests for a verbal IQ. When combined, these tests provide a full-scale IQ. This test is widely used with learning disabled children today to point out discrepancies between verbal and nonverbal abilities, as well as to give an estimate of the combined learning potential of a child.

Illinois Test of Psycholinguistic Abilities

Samuel A. Kirk, James J. McCarthy, and *Winifred D. Kirk* (1968) developed the *Illinois Test of Psycholinguistic Abilities,* a diagnostic test designed to assess psycholinguistic abilities believed to be necessary for the understanding and use of spoken language. The battery of subtests is designed to test the linguistic functions of visual and auditory reception, visual and auditory association, and verbal and motor expression, as well as visual and auditory memory and visual and auditory closure. The results of this test yield a profile of the child's specific psycholinguistic abilities and disabilities. (See figure 1.3, page 12). The ITPA sparked the development of a number of remedial programs to improve language, perceptual, and other developmental abilities. Chief among these are the *Peabody Language Development Kits* by Dunn, Smith et al. (1967, 1968, 1969, 1982); the *MWM Program of Language Development* by Minskoff, Wiseman, and Minskoff (1972); the *GOAL Language Development Kits* by Karnes (1972); and the *Damron Reading Language Kit* (1978).

Developmental Tests of Visual Perception

Frostig, Maslow, LeFever, and *Whittlesey* (1964), working at the Marianne Frostig Center of Educational Therapy in Los Angeles, were the first to develop a test of visual perception designed to assess five visual-perceptual abilities: (1) eye-hand coordination, (2) figure-ground, (3) perceptual constancy, (4) position in space, and (5) spatial relations.

Frostig and *Horne* (1964) also developed a remedial program designed to improve the five visual-perceptual abilities. The program at the Frostig Center used the Frostig test along with other diagnostic tests to formulate remedial programs.

Diagnostic reading tests

Marion Monroe, a colleague of Samuel T. Orton, concentrated her efforts on constructing and standardizing a diagnostic reading test for children reading below the fourth-grade level. This test used oral reading, word recognition, word discrimination, and silent reading to determine the level of reading and analyze the errors a child makes in reading. The errors analyzed were repetitions, reversals, letter and word omissions and additions, substitutions, and other errors. Monroe's hypothesis was that remediating the specific reading errors would improve the level of reading. Her book, *Children Who Cannot Read* (1932), was one of the first attempts to systematically diagnose reading errors in children.

Shortly after the publication of the Monroe test, other diagnostic tests were developed. *Donald Durrell* developed a widely used test entitled the *Durrell Analysis of Reading Difficulty* (1937, 1955). This test assesses oral and silent reading and listening comprehension, word recognition and word analysis, learning rate, spelling, phonics, and handwriting.

Another contributor in the 1930s was *Arthur Gates,* who developed a series of diagnostic tests for reading, including tests of phonics and learning style. The test has since been revised by Gates and McKillop (1962). In 1972 *George Spache* developed the *Diagnostic Reading Scales* to assess skills in oral reading, silent reading, and auditory comprehension. This test also includes tests of phonic skills.

In addition to these psychometric and diagnostic instruments, many other tests were developed to assess separate abilities such as auditory discrimination, visual discrimination, and memory. Many similar diagnostic tests for spelling, arithmetic, and language also have been developed.

Remedial education

Interest in remediating handicaps in children has been growing for several centuries. This section will review briefly the early attempts by Europeans to remediate cognitive deficits in children as well as early American contributions to remedial education.

Early European influences

In the early 19th century, remedial education in France was stimulated by *Jean-Marc Gaspar Itard,* a French physician who tried to train a wild boy found in the forest of Aveyron in 1799. This 11-year-old child behaved like a young savage, used no language, and moved about on all fours. Itard believed that through educational training the psychologically crippling effects of the child's extreme deprivation might be overcome. He attempted to interest the child in social life, awaken nervous sensibility, extend the range of ideas by giving him new needs, develop speech through imitation and necessity, and apply the developed mental processes to solve his physical needs. Itard's work is an early example of sensory education. He believed that education and knowledge are acquired through the senses, and therefore the senses should be developed in order to improve the mind. Itard tried to improve auditory and visual discrimination, memory, and generalization to help the child attend to increasingly complex relevant cues.

Although Itard's success with the wild child was limited, his work raised an important question which still influences modern-day instructional practices: Is it possible to train the mind by developing the senses through sensory training? Many of Itard's perceptual training activities are currently used in reading readiness activities with normal children as well as with handicapped children with learning problems (Itard, trans. 1932 by Humphrey & Humphrey).

Edouard Seguin (1866), a physician and a student of Itard's, developed an educational approach to sensorimotor disorders based on a physiological and neurological hypothesis. Seguin attempted to remediate deficiencies, in the peripheral and central nervous system, that he believed "locked" children's learning processes. Basic motor skills and mobility were taught first while tactile functions were trained through activities such as seizing, holding, letting go, and handling objects. Other mental abilities including perception, attention, color appreciation, awareness of distance, and form and spatial perception were taught. Listening, reading, writing, and speech were taught through imitation techniques, aided by the sense of touch and the use of flashcards and concrete objects.

Seguin was one of the first people to try to ameliorate disabilities in the perceptual-motor processes. Although his physiological method was directed toward mentally retarded children, many aspects of his theory and methods are used today with normal preschool children as well as learning disabled children.

Maria Montessori (1912), a pediatrician, began her work in a psychiatric clinic in Rome where she worked with insane and mentally retarded patients. Her experiences and the studies of Seguin and Itard convinced her that the problem of mental deficiency was pedagogical rather than medical. In 1907 Montessori opened a school in Rome where she educated young normal children of working mothers. It was during this time that she organized her work experience with mentally disturbed, mentally retarded, and normal children into the Maria Montessori method. This method is based on the concept of "auto-education" or self-teaching. The teacher's role is to organize activities and materials so that children can teach themselves, while the teacher supervises their activities. Sensory education and language are taught through didactic materials consisting of 26 different items. These materials are used to educate visual abilities, such as discrimination of color, shape, size; hearing abilities; sensitivity to temperature; touch discrimination; and weight discrimination. Montessori's method has attracted world-wide interest in the education of preschool children. Her methods are still in use today with some handicapped and normal children.

A giant in the area of measurement and remedial education is the well-known French psychologist, Alfred Binet. He is known as the father of the mental testing movement, but he could also be known as the father of special education for mentally retarded children. After constructing and standardizing the *Binet-Simon Scale of Intelligence* in 1905, he turned his attention to the education of intelligence. He subsequently organized classes for mentally retarded students in Paris with the specific aim of educating intelligence. He described his efforts in a chapter entitled "The Education of Intelligence" in his book *Modern Ideas About Children* (1911). In this chapter Binet stated, "after the evil, the remedy; after exposing mental defects of all kinds, let us pass on to their treatment." He also stated, "I regret that I have found a prejudice against the educability of intelligence" (trans. in Kirk & Lord, 1974, p. 200).

Binet proceeded to organize a curriculum for mentally retarded children which he called "mental orthopedics." In this curriculum he attempted to train attention, speed of motor response, motor skills, verbal expression, memory, discrimination, and other functions. He stressed the active role of the students and advocated what we now call the *discovery method* in teaching these children.

The brief accounts of the works of Itard, Seguin, Montessori, and Binet illustrate physicians' and psychologists' early interest in remedial education of cognitive functions. Although these individuals were trained in medicine and psychology, their major contributions were in diagnosis and remedial education.

American
contribu-
tions to
remedial
education

In the United States a series of procedures for remedial education were developed for different kinds of learning disabled children. These procedures can be classified as (1) remedial education for perceptual-motor disorders, (2) remedial education for reading disabilities, and (3) remedial education for language disordered children. Many of these methods are eclectic and use a combination of techniques.

*Remedial
education for
perceptual-
motor
disorders*

In 1937 *Alfred Strauss* migrated to the United States from Germany and began to work with so-called "brain-injured" children. He was a psychoneurologist who had worked in Germany with Kurt Goldstein, a noted authority on the effects of brain injury on language disorders. Strauss' early work in Germany was in child neuropsychiatry, where he encountered brain-injured adults and children who had difficulties in learning. His original work in the United States was with mentally retarded children at the Wayne County Training School in Michigan. He concluded that there are two kinds of mental retardation. One type he called *endogenous,* a result of familial or inherited characteristics, and the second type he labelled *exogenous,* meaning that something happened to the brain before, during, or after birth. He called these children *brain-injured* or *brain-crippled.* His years of work with these children resulted in a book coauthored with *Laura Lehtinen* entitled *Psychopathology and Education of the Brain-Injured Child* (1947). Many parents who had been unable to obtain services for their children in the public schools were stimulated by this book. Consequently, the parents began to organize classes on their own and to obtain professional services for their children through these classes.

Strauss gave the initial impetus to the field of learning disabilities, not because he used that term, but because of his emphasis on the learning problems of brain-injured children. When parents organized classes for children who were having difficulty in learning, they called their groups "classes for brain-injured children." Others thought that the term *brain-injured* was not accurate because many of their children were not so diagnosed by the neurologists. Subsequently, these classes were given various names, including classes for aphasoid children, classes for dyslexic children, and classes for perceptually handicapped children.

William Cruickshank worked with Strauss at the Wayne County Training School. Since then he has continued and extended Strauss' work with cerebral palsied and other brain-injured children under the area of psychoneurology. His contributions have been compiled in two recent volumes of selected papers (Cruickshank, 1981a).

Newell C. Kephart, a collaborator with Strauss, believed that sensorimotor abilities are basic to visual perceptual abilities and that perceptual-motor development is the basis of all learning. Kephart developed the *Purdue Perceptual Survey Rating Scale* (Roach & Kephart, 1966), together with remedial activities for assessing and remediating perceptual-motor disabilities.

These are described in his book *The Slow Learner in the Classroom* (1971). Kephart emphasized the importance of identifying the point at which a breakdown in the developmental hierarchy has occurred. When the point of breakdown has been identified, the necessary learning must be stimulated to help the child develop further.

The approaches taken by Seguin and Kephart are quite similar. Both are concerned with ameliorating disabilities in the perceptual-motor processes. Both approaches are based in part on neurological and psychological hypotheses. Both stress the importance of differential diagnosis and the principles of child development. Some of the training activities and equipment, such as the trampoline, are similar.

Frostig and Horne (1964), referred to earlier as authors of the *Developmental Test of Visual Perception,* also developed a remedial program designed to improve visual perceptual abilities, which they believe are fundamental to academic success. Their training program also develops gross and fine muscle coordination, ocular-motor coordination, body image, and other readiness skills necessary for the visual-motor tasks required in word recognition, reading, writing, spelling, and other school tasks.

Other professionals developed specialized procedures for one or more of the perceptual-motor handicaps. *Gerald Getman* (1965), an optometrist, developed a program for training visual perception, based on a developmental sequence of visual growth patterns during the first 5 years of life. The major hypothesis of Getman's theory and methods is that educational success depends on visual adequacy.

Raymond Barsch collaborated with both Strauss and Getman and shared their views on the importance of the perceptual-motor aspects of learning. Barsch (1967) developed a "movigenics" curriculum designed to improve muscular strength, dynamic balance, body awareness, spatial awareness, tactual dynamics, kinesthesis, auditory dynamics, visual dynamics, bilaterality, rhythm, flexibility, and motor planning. These training activities were organized for children who exhibited delays in motor or visual-perceptual development or both.

Remedial methods for reading disabilities

In the early 1920s psychologist *Grace Fernald* was struggling with the problem of why some children with average or above average intelligence are unable to learn to read or to spell. By trying different approaches, Fernald and Keller (1921) succeeded in teaching five nonreaders to read by writing words and phrases from memory. She called their system "The Kinesthetic Method" since the child used touch and muscle movement while learning words and sentences. In 1943 Fernald published a book reviewing the success with children taught by the method. This procedure has stood the test of time; it has been used in various forms since 1921. The Fernald Clinic at the University of California continues to emphasize this method with the addition of other approaches.

Marion Monroe (1932), who was described earlier as one who developed the first truly diagnostic reading tests, also developed a remedial program to eliminate errors discovered in children with reading disabilities. Her remedial work was continued by two of her students who studied with her at the Institute for Juvenile Research in Chicago. Their work resulted in a highly programmed phonetic procedure entitled "The Remedial Reading Drills" (Hegge, Kirk, & Kirk, 1936). These phonetic exercises are still being widely used for severely disabled nonreaders.

At about the same time, *Anna Gillingham* and *Bessie Stillman* worked with Orton to develop teaching methods for children with language problems. The Gillingham and Stillman (1936, 1973) method, though primarily phonic, uses a visual, auditory, kinesthetic-tactile (VAKT) approach to the development of reading skills. Children are taught the parts of words (i.e., sounds of the phonograms and how to write the phonograms). The children see, say, and trace the phonogram and then write it in the air. Drill cards with key words and pictures are used. When several sounds have been learned, they are combined into phonetically correct words. The children are then given stories to read that are composed of the words in their sight vocabulary. Little emphasis is placed on comprehension during the early stages of training. This method has been successful with many severe cases.

Remedial education for oral language disorders

Helmer Myklebust's early work was with deaf children. He became interested in the relationship between deafness and the development of oral language. The results of his clinical work and research led Myklebust (1954) to the study of aphasia and other auditory disorders in children. His work contributed to differential diagnosis for disorders caused by deafness, mental retardation, sensory aphasia, receptive aphasia, and word deafness. Myklebust believed that neurological dysfunction is the basis of learning disabilities. He used the term *psychoneurological learning disabilities*. Johnson and Myklebust described the behavioral symptoms of various kinds of learning disabilities and extended their diagnostic procedures to remedial principles and practices for remediation. Their book *Learning Disabilities: Educational Principles and Practices* (1967) was one of the first comprehensive books in the field of learning disabilities.

M.A. McGinnis (1963) developed the association method for remediating childhood aphasia at the Central Institute for the Deaf in St. Louis. McGinnis was a teacher of deaf children who also worked with aphasic adults. She noticed a similarity between aphasic adults and some children who were referred to the school for the deaf because of their delay in language and speech development. Those children were not deaf; they were found to have relatively normal hearing and intelligence. They did not show signs of severe emotional disturbance, yet they did not talk or understand language. McGinnis recognized two general types of language-delayed children: (1) expressive aphasics (those who could understand others' speech but could not talk themselves) and (2) receptive aphasics (those who could speak but did not seem to understand others' speech). To develop both auditory reception and verbal expression, McGinnis began with an elemental approach to communication by first using a phonic method of teaching sounds, then using the learned sounds to form words, and then matching the words with pictures to derive meaning. Once the child has learned to understand some words auditorily and to express them verbally, he or she begins to add vocabulary from incidental learning.

Numerous other language remedial methods have been developed and will be discussed in greater detail in chapter 9, "Oral Language Disorders."

Development of programs in public schools

This section will describe briefly why and how the field of learning disabilities became a part of the public school system. It will cover early neglect of the problem, the parent movement, and state and federal legislation.

The early neglect of the problem

Reading instruction has always been a function of the public schools. Schools have basically stressed developmental reading, i.e., the natural step-by-step unfolding of the reading process as taught to all children. When a child would fall by the wayside, the teacher would give the child additional assistance. A small number of disabled readers who had severe problems learning to read were often referred to reading clinics if they were available.

Earlier, the field of speech rehabilitation advocated assigning speech clinicians to the schools to help children with speech and hearing problems. In the 1940s and 1950s speech clinicians concentrated their efforts on the treatment of stuttering, cerebral palsy speech, cleft palate, vocal disorders, hearing disorders, and especially articulation problems. A survey made by the American Speech and Hearing Association (1961) showed that 75% of the speech clinicians' time was spent in the kindergarten, first, and second grades, and that 80% of these children displayed functional articulation disorders. Language disorders in children were rarely treated by speech clinicians. Cases of aphasia, primarily in adults, were treated in hospitals and special clinics. Children with delayed language or with oral language disorders were often referred to classes for mentally retarded students. This referral was usually made because of their language handicap, which caused them to get low scores on intelligence tests.

The field of learning disabilities seems to have emerged for two major reasons. First, many parents refused to accept the diagnosis of mental retardation for their children. Their children performed normally or above average on too many tasks for their parents to accept the label of "mental retardation." Second, the public schools did not provide needed services or programs for children with severe oral language or reading problems, unless the children qualified as handicapped in the areas of mental retardation, emotional disturbance, sensory impairment, social or emotional handicap, orthopedic handicap, or speech disorder. The neglect of children who appeared to be normal, but who had specific kinds of learning problems for which there were no services, stimulated parent groups to take political action.

The parent movement

Because of the scarcity of programs for children with learning problems not caused by a known handicapping condition, frustrated parents banded together to organize services for their children. This movement expanded in the 1950s, and by 1960 many classes had been organized in churches, storefronts, and other private buildings. Like other parent groups, after they had organized their own private services, these parents proceeded to ask their local schools and state legislators to help support programs for their children, who needed special services for their development.

In 1963 members of many of these parent organizations met in Chicago to discuss the national problem of brain-injured children and to establish a national organization. They invited professional speakers to discuss the problems the parents encountered in organizing programs for their children. In one address, Kirk (1963) stated that names and labels are sometimes detrimental and that the term *brain-injured* has little educational significance. These parents were advised that if they were interested in educational services for their children they should use a term relating to teaching or learning. Kirk stated that, for want of a better term, he had recently used the term *learning disability* in his text *Educating Exceptional Children* (1962) to describe this diverse group of handicapped children.

At the business meeting the parents discussed various terms and finally decided on the name "Association for Children with Learning Disabilities" (ACLD). The name and category "learning disabilities" struck a receptive cord throughout the country. Learning disabilities, as a separate category of exceptionality, was born. It became a part of local, state, and federal legislation dealing with the support of services for these children.

State and local legislation

Following the organization of the Association for Children with Learning Disabilities, state and local education agencies began to take notice of the new category. It was easier for them to pass legislation for one group (learning disabilities) than for many separate programs such as reading disabilities, arithmetic disabilities, and oral language disorders.

In 1963 President Kennedy introduced a bill in Congress, P.L. 88-164, to expand programs for handicapped children, but the bill did not include the terms *learning disabilities* or *brain-injured children*. It included provisions for research and for the training of personnel for the "mentally retarded, hard-of-hearing, deaf, speech impaired, visually handicapped, crippled or other health impaired children who by reason thereof require special education and related services." It was under the caption of "crippled or other health impaired children'' that the federal government began to support the training of personnel and research in learning disabilities. In 1964, four universities were awarded grants to train personnel in learning disabilities. This federal program expanded gradually, and in 1968 the National Advisory Committee on Handicapped Children (1968) defined learning disabilities (see chapter 1) and recommended to Congress an extension of the program. This recommendation resulted in the *Specific Learning Disabilities Act of 1969* (P.L. 91-230), which provided a separate appropriation for children with learning disabilities.

As a result of P.L. 91-230, state governments began legislating provisions for some services for the learning disabled. Currently, all states have programs for learning disabled children and adults (Gillespie, Miller, & Fielder, 1975).

In 1975, P.L. 94-142 was enacted into law. The definition of *learning disabilities* formulated by the National Advisory Committee on Handicapped Children (1968) was included in the new law, and the category learning disability was also included in the definition of handicapped children. The *Federal Register* (1977c) published the regulations under which these programs were to operate.

Today learning disabilities is one of the largest programs for exceptional children in the public schools, and because of its heterogeneous membership, one of the most controversial.

Summary

- The history of learning disabilities finds its heritage in neurology, ophthalmology, psychology, and remedial education.

- The early workers in the field studied adult patients who had lost the ability to speak, read, write, or calculate after a head injury resulting from war, accident, or brain hemorrhage.

- Children's inability to develop language, reading, writing, spelling, or arithmetic caused neuropsychologists to infer that children with language and academic disabilities must have an underdevelopment of the areas of the brain dealing with these functions.

- Assessment of learning abilities stimulated the development of (1) general intelligence tests, (2) tests of primary mental abilities, (3) diagnostic tests of psycholinguistic and perceptual functions, and (4) diagnostic reading and arithmetic tests.

- Diagnostic testing led to remedial education. Stimulated by the early work of Itard, Seguin, Montessori, and Binet, remedial educators in the United States developed remedial methods and materials for children with reading, language, and perceptual-motor problems.

- The programs for learning disabilities did not become a part of school systems until after parents' groups organized classes and then asked state and local systems to offer services for their children.

- By 1969 the *Learning Disabilities Act* (P.L. 91-230) had been passed by the federal Congress, and most states began providing services for learning disabled children.

- P.L. 94-142, passed by Congress in 1975, included learning disabilities in the definition of handicapped children and made it mandatory that all schools provide services for all learning disabled children.

Thought questions

1. How can you account for the progression of theories and services from neurology to psychology to education?

2. What are the pros and cons of labelling children as *brain-injured,* or as *aphasic, dyslexic,* and so on?

3. What are the differences between an adult who has lost the ability to speak and a school-aged child who has not developed speech and language?

4. Of the tests with which you are familiar, which ones are used primarily for classification and which ones are used for diagnosis for the purpose of formulating remediation?

5. How has the development of standardized tests influenced the development of diagnostic and remedial programs for learning disabled children?

6. Do you think that the inclusion of the work of Itard, Seguin, Strauss, and others who worked with mentally retarded children is appropriate in a book on learning disabilities? Why?

7. How do the remedial methods developed by American contributors differ from the traditional methods used in the regular schools?

8. What do you think the role of parents of learning disabled children should be—political pressure groups, advisors to teachers, or assistants in the teaching process? Discuss.

9. If the federal government had not intervened in passing legislation supporting teacher preparation and research, what would learning disability programs be today?

10. Do you think it is worthwhile to study the historical background of any movement? Why?

3
Causes and contributing factors

One of the first questions asked by a parent of a learning disabled child is, "Why? Why is my child learning disabled?" To that question professionals must usually give rather general answers. In the past many tried to answer the question hypothetically by saying, "The child has brain damage." If that statement could not be proven through neurological examinations, an alternate explanation of "minimal brain dysfunction (MBD)" was often given. To the professionals, the lack of normal development suggested the possibility of a brain dysfunction. This, of course, is circular reasoning; that is, the child has dyslexia (inability to read) as a result of minimal brain dysfunction and the evidence for the brain dysfunction is the child's inability to learn to read.

This chapter will discuss some of what we do know about the causes and contributing factors to learning disabilities. The chapter will deal with (1) some basic facts relating to the brain and neuropsychology, (2) etiologies or causes of learning disabilities, (3) contributing factors, and (4) interrelationship of causes and contributing factors.

The brain and neuropsychology

The brain is the control center of the body. It receives incoming messages along receptive (afferent) nerves from eyes, ears, skin, muscles, and internal organs. It sends messages by way of outgoing (efferent) nerves to all parts of the body. The brain interprets, integrates, and makes decisions. It stores information. It controls speech, initiates movement, and affects the functioning of many body systems such as the vascular system, digestive system, muscular system, and lymph system. The brain and all its interconnections compose the central nervous system.

Damage to the brain has many and varied results. In children, brain damage, as indicated by Strauss and Lehtinen (1947), may occur before, during, or after birth and may result in a variety of handicapping conditions: cerebral palsy, mental retardation, learning disabilities, and many other physical and mental abnormalities.

Some functions of the brain

The brain has two hemispheres, known as the left brain and the right brain. The left hemisphere principally controls the right side of the body, while the right hemisphere principally controls the left side of the body. Right-handed individuals usually show a dominance of the left hemisphere for motor and speech functions. Damage to the motor cortex of the left hemisphere results in motor incoordination or paralysis of some parts of the right side, while an injury to the right motor area of the right hemisphere may result in paralysis or motor incoordination of some parts of the left side. Vision is represented in both hemispheres since the optic chiasma crosses and has representation in both hemispheres.

Most people are right-handed and therefore have left hemispheric dominance for motor activities and for language and speech. In general the right hemisphere is dominant for nonverbal behavior such as sensing spatial relations, music, and so forth, while the left hemisphere is dominant for verbal behavior.

The two hemispheres of the brain, or the two brains, have been the subject of much research. They are separate and have different functions, but at the same time are related through the corpus callosum, an area in the brain connecting the two hemispheres. Research has shown that when we train the left hemisphere, we can test the right hemisphere and find that it also has learned. But when the corpus callosum is cut in animals, training the left or right hemisphere does not result in arousing activity or learning in the opposite hemisphere. These split brain experiments have increased our knowledge of the functions of the two hemispheres.

In an article on cognitive processes and the brain, Wittrock (1978) reviews the studies on the right and left hemispheres of the brain. He states that in general the "left cortical hemisphere (in about 98% of right-handers and in about ⅔ of the left-handers) specializes somewhat in a propositional, analytic-sequential, time-oriented serial organization well adapted to learning and remembering verbal information" (p. 65). He cites experiments demonstrating that the left hemisphere is involved in verbal processing, while the right hemisphere deals with auditory tasks involving melodies and nonmeaningful human sounds, visual-spatial tasks, and other nonverbal activities. In general this is true for right-handed persons and for most left-handed persons. Wittrock hypothesizes from his review of the literature that it may be possible in the future to match some instructional methods with children who are left-brained and apply other instructional methods to right-brained children. At present, however, our knowledge does not permit us to make definitive recommendations.

Figure 3.1 shows a simplified drawing of the cortex of the brain and possible behavior functions that could be disturbed by an insult to certain areas of the brain resulting from accident, disease, birth trauma, or prenatal conditions. A further explanation of figure 3.1 may be in order since the terms used occur frequently in the neuropsychological literature dealing with learning disabilities.

The *cerebellum,* located at the lower end of the brain stem, integrates the smooth coordination of muscular activity. Damage to the cerebellum can result in general motor clumsiness. This clumsiness may in turn interfere with "manual dexterity, perceiving imbedded figures, writing, and other fine muscle performance" (Gaddes, 1980, p. 42). Quiros and Schrager (1978) present evidence that the cerebellum controls the proprioceptive function (deep sensitivity) and the vestibular (balance) functions of the inner ear. According to

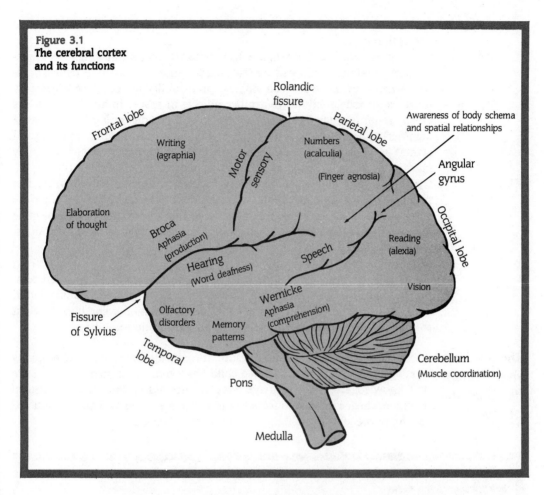

Figure 3.1
The cerebral cortex and its functions

Rolandic fissure

Frontal lobe

Parietal lobe

Awareness of body schema and spatial relationships

Writing (agraphia)

Motor

sensory

Numbers (acalculia)

(Finger agnosia)

Angular gyrus

Elaboration of thought

Broca Aphasia (production)

Occipital lobe

Speech

Reading (alexia)

Hearing (Word deafness)

Wernicke Aphasia (comprehension)

Vision

Fissure of Sylvius

Olfactory disorders

Memory patterns

Temporal lobe

Cerebellum (Muscle coordination)

Pons

Medulla

these scientists, a dysfunction of the cerebellum may result in problems of equilibrium, motor control, body image, laterality, and sometimes in reversal errors in reading and speech.

The *occipital lobes* or *visual cortex* deal primarily with vision. Each eye has representation in both left and right hemispheres. Figure 3.2 illustrates the relationship of the eyes to the visual cortex. Sensations from the outside (right) half of the right eye lead to the right geniculate body, which in turn radiates to the right visual cortex. The sensations from the inner (right) half of the left eye are also registered in the right geniculate body and in the right visual cortex. A lesion in the right visual cortex results in blindness in the inside or nasal half of the left eye and in the outside or temporal half of the right eye and results in partial blindness in both the left and right visual fields. From the visual cortex, nerve pathways lead to the higher centers in the parietal lobes, where the visual sensations acquire meaning. Lesions in the visual cortex and the association areas in the parietal lobe sometimes result in visual perception deficiencies.

The *parietal lobes* (see figure 3.1) appear to deal with tactile (touch) recognition. Lesions in this area are reported to cause inability to recognize numbers when they are traced on fingers, poor ability to recognize objects by touch, and poor ability to remember objects in space. In addition, Gaddes (1980) reported that *ideational apraxia* (e.g., demonstrating how to use a hammer) or *ideomotor apraxia* (e.g., involving problems with mimicking and acting) are affected by brain lesions. In small children these conditions may interfere with such actions as dressing or undressing.

The *frontal lobe* is reported to be involved in intellectual activities. The frontal lobe makes connections with the opposite hemisphere through the corpus callosum. Luria (1966) hypothesized that the frontal lobes determine the individual's capacity for abstract thinking, planning, and carrying out intentions.

The *temporal lobe* deals primarily with hearing. Nerve pathways from each ear go to both the right and left hemispheres. Lesions in the left temporal lobe cause disturbances in understanding language and recalling verbal material. Like the occipital cortex in vision, a sensation going into the right ear arouses sensations in both the right and left temporal lobes.

The relationship of brain functions to behavior

There are some educators who question the educational value of determining whether or not a learning disabled child has a brain dysfunction. They state that knowledge of brain damage does not necessarily alter the educational treatment; hence the search for a brain injury is a waste of time if conducted for the purpose of prescribing an educational program.

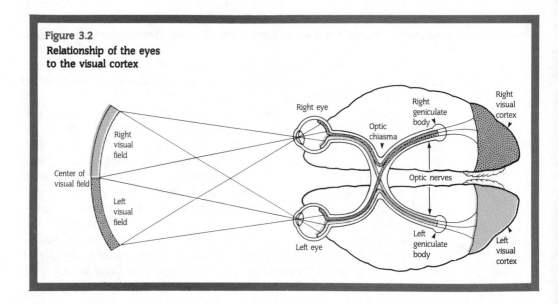

Figure 3.2
Relationship of the eyes to the visual cortex

The relationship between minimal brain dysfunction and learning disabilities is obscure. Research in this area is difficult since we cannot experiment with children's brains, and the research on animals does not deal with language, speech, or reading. We have only clinical evidence that some children and some adults with brain injuries show disturbances of memory, language, and reading. As Denckla (1978) states, the term "minimal brain dysfunction (MBD) is now in its midteens and viewed anthropomorphically it is indeed experiencing the turmoil and controversy appropriate to adolescence" (p. 223). Some are opposed to the concept of minimal brain dysfunction (MBD), stating that the term is not a diagnosis of the child's problem but may be an escape or an avoidance of making an accurate behavioral diagnosis. Some object to the inference of minimal brain dysfunction on the basis of a child's lack of achievement.

Over and above these controversies about the relationship of brain function to behavior, to learning, and to education, however, are some fundamental concepts that should be considered.

First, it is obvious that without a brain there is no behavior. Second, with adult clinical cases, as indicated in chapter 2, there is considerable evidence that disturbances of neurological structure affect psychological functions. Third, the three disciplines of neuroscience, psychology, and education are related, but there are gaps in knowledge of the specific relationships between education and psychology and between psychology and neuroscience. Speculation attempts to fill in the gaps while interdisciplinary researchers attempt to decrease the gap empirically. When science progresses sufficiently, we will think of educating a child on the basis of his or her psychological behavior, which may have been determined in part by the neurological make-up of that child.

The interest in the relationship of the brain functions to learning disabilities tends to wax and wane from one decade to another. As described in chapter 2, an effort to understand the relationship between neurology and behavior was dominant in the 19th century and the first half of the 20th century. During the 1950s and 1960s neuropsychological interest in learning disabilities was deemphasized for two major reasons. The first was a reaction against the simplistic diagnosis of learning disabilities as being the result of brain injury. Many psychologists and educators informed parents that their child was brain-damaged in an effort to explain the child's difficulties. Upon examination, neurologists were unable to find a brain dysfunction in many of these children. Nor did psychological testing clearly establish the diagnosis of brain injury. Furthermore, many children with known brain damage such as cerebral palsy were not necessarily learning disabled. A second reason for decreasing interest in neuropsychology was the revival of behaviorism. Behaviorists rightly stressed the point that education deals primarily with symptoms of behavior, not causes, and that psychology is not physiology.

In the 1970s and 1980s there has come a renewed interest in the neuropsychology of learning disabilities. Increased numbers of articles, monographs, and books support the relationship between learning disabilities and neurological conditions. Among these supporters is Cruickshank, who has stated, "neurological dysfunction leads to perceptual processing deficits which, in turn, result in a variety and complexity of learning disabilities" (in Gaddes, 1980, p. vi).

Gaddes' (1980) book on learning disabilities reviews the relationship of the brain to learning disabilities and explains the neuropsychological relationship to learning disabilities. His point of view may be illustrated by his statement that:

> Neuropsychology is a well established science with a large body of experimentally verified knowledge. These data are essential to the understanding and treatment of both the brain-damaged child and the learning-disabled child with a perceptual, cognitive, or motor deficit. Underachievers with normally functional nervous systems can usually be treated by purely behavioral or motivational means. (p. 15)

In other words, purely behavioral treatment is suitable for the normal (neurologically intact) child who is not achieving, but the underachieving child with developmental learning disabilities requires more intensive study and differential treatment.

The increased interest of educators in the contribution of the neurosciences to learning and to difficulties in learning is shown by the publication of the *Seventy-Seventh Yearbook of the National Society for the Study of Education* (Chall & Mirsky, 1978). This book, entitled *Education and the Brain*, marks the first time the National Society for the Study of Education has covered this field. This indicates that educators and psychologists are seeking information from neuroscientists in their efforts to improve the education of children, and especially of children with learning disabilities.

Etiology (causes)

The history of learning disability discussed in chapter 2 deals primarily with brain injuries in adults which result in disorders of language or reading. As explained earlier, these causes in adults have been translated and extended to children, where it is assumed that something has affected the brain, which has in turn affected the behavior. Because all thinking, perceptual, and other cognitive processes emanate from the brain, we would not be able to read, write, spell, or calculate without a brain.

Prevention of learning disabilities depends on adequate scientific answers to the causes of cerebral dysfunction. Scientists have been searching for the causes of cerebral dysfunction in (1) acquired brain damage, (2) brain dysfunction resulting from genetics, (3) biochemical abnormalities, and (4) lack of proper nutrition or other environmental factors affecting the normal development of the brain.

Acquired brain damage

The most common etiological factor hypothesized as a cause of a learning disability is brain damage or minimal brain dysfunction (MBD) acquired before, during, or after birth. Dysfunctions of the brain can have prenatal, perinatal, or postnatal origins.

Prenatal causes (occurring before birth), other than genetic, include the mother's nutritional deficiencies during pregnancy (Cravioto & DeLicardie, 1975) and diseases of the mother that affect the embryo. Rubella (German measles), for example, during the first trimester of pregnancy is apt to cause any of a variety of abnormalities. Maldevelopment of the nervous system may occur from many causes, including alcohol abuse and the use of drugs during pregnancy (Martin, 1980).

Perinatal causes refer to those conditions that affect the child during or about the time of birth. These include anoxia (lack of oxygen during birth), birth injuries from medical instruments, and prematurity (Rie & Rie, 1980).

Postnatal causes (occurring after birth) include accidents leading to brain concussions and childhood diseases, such as encephalitis, meningitis, and even measles and scarlet fever, that can affect the brain and other parts of the nervous system (Strauss & Lehtinen, 1947).

Genetics

There have been several studies concerning the inheritability of reading, writing, and language disabilities. Some studies have been made on families with many members with reading or language problems. Hallgren (1950) conducted an extensive family study. He studied 276 people with dyslexia (reading disabilities) and their families in Sweden and found that the prevalence of reading, writing, and spelling disabilities in the relatives provided sufficient evidence that such conditions run in families and are apparently subject to the laws of inheritance.

Hermann (1959) studied one dozen pairs of identical twins, none of whom had learned to read. He contrasted that group of identical twins with 33 pairs of fraternal twins of which at least one in every pair did not read. Only ⅓ of the fraternal twins showed both children to be dyslexic, as compared to all of the identical twins. He stated that this evidence supports the hypothesis that reading, spelling, and writing disabilities are inherited.

Critchley (1970) reviewed the studies of the inheritance of word blindness. He concluded that dyslexia tends to run in families. Bannatyne (1971), after reviewing studies of language, reading, and spelling disabilities, also concluded that there is adequate evidence for a genetic basis of dyslexia.

Decker and DeFries (1980) and DeFries and Decker (1981) conducted an extensive family study on reading disabilities at the Institute of Behavioral Genetics at the University of Colorado. They administered an extensive battery of psychometric and reading tests to 125 reading disabled children, their parents, and their siblings, and to 125 matched control families. Reading disabled children obtained significantly lower scores than control children not only on reading tests but also on two cognitive ability tests (spatial reasoning and symbol-processing speed). DeFries and Decker (1981) concluded that their "data conclusively demonstrate the familial nature of reading disability" but they also cautioned that the "evidence is necessary, but not sufficient, for demonstrating genetic influence" (p. 23).

DeFries and Decker (1982) also report that Smith (1978) has tentative evidence that a relationship has been found between a marker on chromosome 15 and a dominantly inherited form of reading disability. The child represented in figure 1.2 may be such a case. This language disordered child did have a chromosomal translocation. It is necessary to question the genetic nature of such a chromosomal aberration and its relation to learning disabilities.

The fact that there is some evidence for the inheritance of learning disabilities does not mean that these children cannot profit from instruction. It does mean that it is more difficult for these children to learn by ordinary methods of instruction than it is for children who do not have such an inherited predisposition. In other words, more enterprise in teaching, more systematic instruction, and more effort on the part of the child are needed to compensate for the inherited disability.

Biochemical factors

Many children with learning disabilities do not have known neurological problems or any history of genetic aberration or environmental deprivation. It has been hypothesized that some cases of learning disabilities may be caused by some unknown biochemical imbalance, similar to that which has been found to cause phenylketonuria, which is one cause of mental retardation. This hypothesis has led to the use of drugs with hyperactive children. The use of drugs, diet, and megavitamin treatment is discussed in chapter 5 under "Attention."

The study of the relationship of learning disabilities to the use of drugs, diet, and vitamins is still in its infancy, and final conclusions must await more scientific studies to determine the value and dangers inherent in such theories and treatments (Kornetsky, 1975).

Environmental deprivation and nutrition

There have been many studies on the effects of inadequate early environmental stimulation and on the effects of severe malnutrition at an early age. Many authorities believe that malnutrition or lack of early sensory and psychological stimulation can operate on a child in such a way as to make it difficult for him or her to learn.

Cravioto and DeLicardie (1975) reviewed research and conducted research of their own on environmental and nutritional factors and concluded:

> It is apparent that children who survive a severe episode of malnutrition of sufficient duration early in life are handicapped in learning some of the more fundamental academic skills and are therefore less able to profit from the cumulative knowledge available to the human species in general and to their socioeconomic group in particular. (p. 96)

In a summary of research on the topic of nutritional deficiency, Martin (1980) concluded that there is evidence that early malnutrition in children, especially during the first year of life, is apt to retard physical growth and especially growth of the central nervous system. In addition to nutritional deficiencies, some have claimed that allergies in children affect learning ability (Rapp, 1979).

The relationship of etiology to education

In general, whether or not there is evidence of brain damage, lack of cerebral development, genetic deficit, early environmental and nutritional deprivation, or a metabolic imbalance, the task of the teacher is about the same. His or her duty is to remediate the behavioral deficit. Educators must recognize that though biological factors (brain dysfunction) may retard the ability to learn, part of the disability may be due to lack of training and the inability of the school to adapt instruction to a child's unique needs.

During the growing stages, a child with a biological defect will find it uncomfortable to perform certain functions and will tend to avoid activities in those areas. A child with a brain dysfunction may find it uncomfortable to talk, and hence avoid talking. He or she may find it difficult to perform motor acts and thus avoid completing routine tasks. Parents can contribute to the disability by praising and showing off their children on activities they can do well and avoiding requesting them to perform in areas in which they perform poorly. Teachers also allow children to follow their own interests and avoid activities in which they are uncomfortable. If a child can read but cannot calculate, he or she will avoid arithmetic. As the child grows, without practice, the use of the defective function may not develop. As a result of lack of practice, the behavioral deficit area will be intensified. Later the child will show wide discrepancies between abilities and achievements. When remediation is introduced for the behavioral deficit area, the goal is to build the skills that were not learned earlier. The philosophy of remediation assumes that the deficits are in part behaviorally caused and can be ameliorated through adequate teaching procedures.

It is possible that education may do more than just fill in the inability to perform resulting from disuse. As mentioned earlier, in 1978 the National Society for the Study of Education published *Education and the Brain*. A few quotations from the summary of the book by the editors, Chall and Mirsky (1978), may be enlightening:

> In essence the neuroscientists writing in this volume are saying to educators that education is central for optimal brain development. (p. 371)

> ...Over and over again the evidence indicates that practice and stimulation at the right time will foster learning, particularly among those with brain injuries. (p. 372)

...For educators who fear that physical brain dysfunction or defects are permanent and irreversible, the evidence presented in this volume is reassuring. (p. 372)

...The earlier years are emphasized with the implication that as far as stimulation is concerned, "the earlier the better." (p. 373)

These statements reemphasize what has been stated before. When our knowledge increases, when we are able to fill the gaps between the biological basis of behavior (neuroscience) and the study of human behavior (psychology) and what we do with children (education), we will have entered the era of "neuro-psychological-education."

Contributing factors of learning disabilities

Contributing factors of a disability refers to factors that, through research, are frequently associated or correlated with the disability. If, for example, poor attention is frequently found with a reading disability, attentional disorders are considered to be contributing factors of reading disabilities. If confused spatial orientation is found in children diagnosed as having arithmetic disabilities, spatial orientation could be considered a contributing factor of an arithmetic disability. If language understanding is related to poor progress in reading, spelling, or arithmetic, the language understanding is a contributing factor of the disability.

Thus the contributing factors of a learning disability are physical and developmental incapacities occurring more often among learning disabled children than among children in the normal population. Contributing factors, sometimes referred to as *correlates,* are in most instances amenable to improvement through training, while basic causes are less treatable. In this sense a contributing factor differs from a cause in that its existence does not assure that a disability will follow.

The physical correlates of poor vision, poor audition, confused spatial orientation, mixed laterality, and so forth, are factors which can interfere with learning, but are not necessarily a cause of learning disabilities. For example, one child may have marked difficulties with an eye-muscle imbalance of one eye that tends to interfere with the perception of words when the child uses both eyes in reading. In this situation he may become markedly retarded in reading. But another child with the same visual defect may suppress the image of one eye and learn to read well with the other eye alone.

Another contributing factor could be a sound-blending disability, which could contribute to poor reading when a phonic method is used. Using a phonic method requires the ability to recognize words by integrating a series of sounds into a word. Poor sound blending should not be considered a *cause* of poor reading, since deaf children learn to read and do not have auditory sound-blending ability. It could, however, be considered a contributing factor, especially when the child is being taught by a phonic method.

The search for contributing factors or correlates of a learning disability is a search for related factors, physical or psychological. Much research has attempted to uncover the contributing factors of learning disabilities, particularly in reading. Some of these factors and their relation to learning disabilities will be discussed in the chapters on reading, writing, spelling, and arithmetic, and in the last chapter, which deals with the research literature in this area.

Interrelationships of causes and contributing factors

In studying a child with a learning disability, the examiner attempts to diagnose both the errors made and the strategies used by the child to read, write, spell, or calculate. The examiner also looks at related behaviors that might be associated with the problem. The analysis of contributing factors sometimes leads to the possible or hypothetical cause. These relationships are illustrated in the following case study.

William remained a nonreader after 4 years of school. A number of teachers tried various approaches to teaching him with little success. The question was, Why had William failed to read while other children in the class learned to read with ease? Was he born with a disability (genetic)? Was there a biochemical cause? Was he brain-damaged? To say he has minimal brain dysfunction (MBD) raises the question of the cause of the brain dysfunction.

On a variety of reading tests William scored at the lower first-grade level, while on nonverbal tasks he performed at age level. The examiners found that William was disoriented in space, exhibited marked reversal errors in writing, and showed poor visual memory. The medical history was negative except for a note that the labor before his birth was difficult and prolonged.

The physical disabilities found in William were visual problems, laterality confusion, poor posture, poor equilibrium, and clumsiness in motor movements. The cause of William's spatial disorientation, poor balance, reversals, and perceptual-motor problems was unknown. We can, however, guess at the etiology if we accept Quiros and Schrager's (1978) findings that damage to the cerebellum before, during, or after birth can result in disorders of equilibrium, disorientation, and perceptual-motor problems. We could hypothesize from the behavior and the birth history that (1) the child's problem was caused by damage to the cerebellum during the birth process, which (2) resulted in the physical correlates of problems of laterality, posture, and equilibrium, which in turn (3) resulted in space disorientation, marked reversal tendencies, and visual memory problems, which in turn (4) inhibited or interfered with William's achievement in reading. However, these etiological factors (assuming dysfunction of the cerebellum) are not treated by psychologists or educators. Their task is to help ameliorate the abnormal behavior by training William or by adjusting the environment.

Table 3.1 shows some causes and contributing factors that are frequently associated with academic disabilities. The etiological factors of brain damage, biochemical aberrations, genetics, nutritional or environmental deprivation, and childhood diseases may partially explain delays in development—physically, psychologically, academically, and socially. According to some advocates, many aberrations of behavior are caused by a deficiency in the biological organism. Proponents of this view hold that the defect in the biological organism results in physical defects of eyes, ears, and body motion, which in turn contribute to psychological developmental problems, which in turn lead to academic disabilities. Discovery of the basic causes by the medical scientists could lead to procedures for prevention.

The physical correlates described in table 3.1, defects in vision, audition, laterality, and so forth, are not all the result of brain damage, genetics, or other causes, but may occur for other reasons. Unlike *causes,* these difficulties can be treated by physicians and educators. Visual problems in most instances can be corrected by eye specialists and aided by vision training. Hearing defects can be improved with hearing aids and auditory training. Laterality and motor incoordination can be ameliorated by physical and occupational therapy. As indicated earlier, if the physical or developmental contributing factors can be trained or ameliorated, they should be considered contributing factors and not causes of developmental and academic disabilities.

Deficient developmental or psychological contributing factors can be ameliorated with proper instruction and an adequate environment. Some physical disabilities are sometimes associated with the developmental learning disabilities. One child who was handicapped as a result of rubella in the

---

Table 3.1
Some causes and contributing factors of learning disabilities

Causes (etiology)	Contributing factors	
	Physical disabilities	Developmental learning disabilities
genetics	vision	attention
brain damage	hearing	memory
biochemical abnormalities	laterality	perception
nutritional deficiencies	body image	thinking
severe environmental deprivation affecting the brain	hyperkinesis	language
childhood diseases	orientation in space	etc.
etc.	motor control	
	vestibular imbalance	
	etc.	

mother during pregnancy had a marked visual defect including acuity problems and nystagmus. This resulted in a deficit in speed of perception. In 4 months of intensive training on a tachistoscope, the child's speed of perception for pictures increased from 10 to 15 seconds to 1/25 of a second. The nystagmus was not improved, but the child's speed of perception and visual perception in general were markedly improved as a result of the training. In addition, developmental disabilities are sometimes related to each other, and a developmental delay in one can result in a developmental delay in another. Language development, for example, is sometimes related to defects in memory, attention, and other abilities.

It has been alleged that these causes and contributing factors affect academic, social, and occupational adjustment. Academic disabilities of reading, writing, spelling, and arithmetic are acquired at the school-age level. The diagnosis and remediation of these subjects will be discussed in greater detail in the chapters in Part 3.

Social and occupational adjustment is associated in some cases with difficulties in academic achievement. It has been known for some time that delinquent children are educationally retarded. This does not mean that the learning disability is a cause of delinquency, since delinquency may affect educational progress. It may mean, however, that one disability could affect the other.

Summary

- The field of learning disabilities today is an outgrowth of the contributions of neurologists and especially Strauss' early work with children who had conceptual, perceptual, hyperkinetic, and linguistic disorders. He ascribed these behavioral manifestations to brain injuries before, during, or after birth.

- Neuroscientists have for centuries attempted to study the relationship of parts of the brain to behavior. Although localization of function is not a point-to-point correspondence, there is some evidence that the frontal lobe deals with elaboration of thought, while the visual or occipital cortex deals with vision. The parietal and temporal lobes also demonstrate some functions, while the cerebellum has responsibility for balance, equilibrium, and related functions.

- Split brain experiments have revealed different functions for the left and right cerebral hemispheres. The left hemisphere in most people specializes in verbal processing, while the right hemisphere deals with auditory tasks such as melody, visual-spatial tasks, and nonverbal activities.

- Neuropsychology attempts to study the relation of brain functions to behavior and to learning disabilities. The gaps in knowledge between neurology and psychology and between psychology and education are becoming smaller as scientists in neurology, psychology, and education study the relationships. The hope is that scientists will decrease the gap so that eventually we will have a discipline of neuro-psychological-education.

- The discovery of causes of learning disabilities is important for prevention. With the present state of knowledge, except in rare instances, the determination of a basic cause—genetics, brain dysfunction, biochemical abnormalities, and nutritional deficiencies—is difficult to establish.

- Contributing factors of learning disabilities refer to physical and psychological (developmental) defects or disabilities that affect learning.

- A contributing factor in most instances is amenable to training, while basic causes are not generally altered by educational intervention.

Thought questions

1. What would you expect the behavior of a child would be if he or she had a large tumor removed from the left visual cortex?

2. If a child had a concussion that damaged the left temporal lobe, what would you expect the child's learning disability to be?

3. If a brain operation removed the right hemisphere of an individual, what disabilities would result?

4. Of the causes of a learning disability listed in the text, which one is most common? Give your reasons for your selection.

5. Is repetitive practice on a deficit area designed to remediate the disability, to alter brain function, or both? Discuss your point of view.

6. What is your criticism, positive or negative, of the notion presented in this text that contributing factors must be discovered if adequate remedial procedures are desired?

7. What are the possible relationships between physical contributing factors and developmental learning disabilities, and between developmental learning disabilities and academic learning disabilities?

4
*Educational diagnostic and
remedial procedures*

Any child who is having difficulty learning should have an instructional program designed to meet his or her individual needs. This is particularly true for children with specific learning disabilities. The *diagnostic-remedial process* refers to the methods used to determine the difficulties children are having in learning and to provide direction for planning remedial programs.

This chapter will (1) discuss the stages of diagnosis for academic and developmental learning disabilities, (2) present three approaches to remediation, and (3) review some of the basic principles underlying the technology of teaching.

Assessing or diagnosing a child suspected of having a learning disability requires the determination of discrepancies in development as well as disparities between potential and academic achievement. The diagnosis of preschool children requires a diagnosis of their developmental learning disabilities, while a diagnosis of school-aged children requires an assessment of academic achievement as well as a diagnosis of developmental learning disabilities.

The diagnosis of preschool children

The early identification of infants and preschool children with developmental problems is very important for their normal growth and development. Identification of the preschool population makes it possible to provide help to those who have problems and to take preventive measures to avoid potential problems from developing in the future.

The diagnosis of preschool children is the last step of a three-stage process (Lerner, Mardell-Czudnowski, & Goldenberg, 1981). The first stage is locating preschool children with problems. This is a community problem and requires increasing public awareness through radio, television, press releases, flyers, telephone surveys, and agency referrals.

The second stage is screening the preschool children to identify those who might have a problem and are considered potential high-risk. Screening programs usually provide a cursory examination of sensory, motor, social, emotional, conceptual, and language abilities.

Children who are identified as having possible problems during screening go into the third stage, namely an individual diagnosis. The purpose of this diagnosis is to determine whether or not there is a problem of sufficient severity to require early remediation or preventive measures. The comprehensive diagnosis of a preschool child suspected of having a problem may include an in-depth assessment in many areas, such as motor, neurological, psychological, sensory, speech, language, and social or emotional development. Emphasis is placed on the child's level of attainment on the developmental hierarchy. Data are obtained through parent interviews, examinations with standardized tests, criterion-referenced tests, and the use of observational checklists.

Developmental learning disabilities may be found in three major broad areas: language development, cognitive development, and visual-motor skill development. Preschool children with learning disabilities may show discrepancies in development *among* these three areas. For example, a child may be delayed in language development and yet be developing normally in the cognitive and visual-motor performance areas. A child may also have a discrepancy *within* one of these three areas. A child with delayed language development, for example, may understand much of what is said, yet have difficulty expressing himself or herself through oral language. In the cognitive areas a child may have difficulty remembering what is heard, yet have an excellent visual memory for what is seen. One of the major indications of a developmental learning disability is a discrepancy either among or within the language, cognitive, and visual-motor performance areas. The most common problems in preschool children are discussed below.

Language development

The most common learning disability noted in preschool children is a language disability. Generally the child is referred because he or she is not talking or is progressing at a slower rate than did his or her siblings or because the child does not respond adequately to directions or verbal statements. These disabilities have been divided into (1) auditory-receptive disabilities, (2) thinking or organizational disabilities, and (3) verbal-expressive disabilities. The child described in figure 1.2 is a child with an auditory-verbal disability, since his auditory-verbal disabilities are 3 or more years below his visual-motor performance.

Auditory-receptive disabilities

In adults, auditory-receptive disabilities are called receptive aphasia or sensory aphasia. In the case of a child, these terms refer to one who does not understand or who only partially understands language. Many children in this category are thought to have impaired hearing, but upon examination are found to have normal hearing; yet they are unable to understand verbal language.

Auditory-thinking or organizational disabilities

These disabilities have sometimes been referred to as problems in inner language (Myklebust, 1954), symbolic aphasia, central aphasia, or simply association disability. These disabilities refer to the inability to relate what is heard to past experience or the inability to conceptualize or generalize.

Verbal-expressive disabilities

Verbal-expressive disabilities have been referred to as expressive or motor aphasia. With young children, this condition is not a loss, but the inability to acquire verbal expressive ability. Such a child does not talk at the age of 2 or 3 or is delayed in learning to talk. Some prefer to label this disability delayed speech, childhood aphasia, or oral language disability.

Cognitive disabilities

The intellectual development of young children involves attention and discrimination, memory, sensory integration, concept formation, and problem solving. Cognitive development provides the foundations prerequisite to thinking, learning, and academic performance. The development of cognitive abilities may be observed as children begin to adapt to people and the environment around them.

Attention and discrimination

Some children have great difficulty attending to the relevant stimuli that are important for learning a particular task or skill. Other children have difficulty discriminating among what they see, hear, or touch. When a child does not show interest in or single out the details of what is seen or heard, his or her ability to analyze the surrounding environment is affected and the ability to learn is impaired. A child who does not attend to spoken language or who does not differentiate between words will be delayed in the understanding and use of spoken language.

Memory

Another common disability that may be noted in preschool children is an inability to store and retrieve experiences. By age 2, for example, a child should be looking for missing toys, recalling yesterday's events, and identifying many pictures. Preschool children should show a very rapid increase in the number of spoken words they understand and use in their own speech. Preschool children who have difficulty remembering what they see or hear will have difficulty learning the names of colors, numbers, objects, events, and motor skills.

Multiple sensory integration

As the nervous system develops, certain senses and combinations of senses are relied upon more heavily than others at different developmental stages. There seems to be a gradual development of integration between the sensory systems (Birch & Lefford, 1963). There are children, however, in whom intersensory development is impaired. For example, a child may function normally when receiving information through a single system or modality, such as listening to the teacher say "cat" or looking at the printed word *CAT*. This same child, however, may be unable to hear the teacher say "cat" and look at the word *CAT* and receive both the auditory and visual stimuli simultaneously. Such children have difficulty receiving information through two or more sensory modalities at the same time. Because many learning tasks require the use of vision, hearing, touch, and movement, children with integrative disabilities will find it difficult to learn under rapid simultaneous presentations.

Concept formation

Disabilities may be found in the area of conceptualization. To organize their experiences and to order and simplify the world around them, children begin to group things and events. This requires the ability to identify common factors among unlike objects and to develop concepts. For example, an apple, a banana, and an orange are not alike except they all have something in common that classifies them as "fruit." A chair, a table, and a bed are not alike, yet they are classified as "furniture." Children begin developing concepts with respect to things they can see, hear, or touch, and then proceed to develop more abstract concepts such as "good" or "bad." Some children have disabilities in generalizing and conceptualizing and consequently have difficulty thinking and learning.

Problem solving

Children usually begin solving problems at an early age. For example, a 2-year-old may push a chair to some location and climb onto the chair to reach a desired object. By age 4 or 5 children are asking numerous questions, moving from one thing to another, and solving simple problems. Their minds are curious and lively and, when confronted by an obstacle, they will try to overcome the problem. The desire and ability to engage in problem solving depends upon the normal development of the other cognitive skills (Gagné, 1967). Children who, for whatever reason, do not respond to problem situations as something to be overcome will develop an attitude of helplessness and give up whenever faced by an obstacle. Preschool children who do not develop problem-solving skills may have difficulty as learners.

Visual-motor disabilities

Children who fall behind in their visual-motor development and motor coordination will exhibit problems at an early age. These problems will be seen in the child's failure to achieve the developmental tasks all children must attain. When these children enter school, their visual-motor disabilities may cause problems in reading, writing, and spelling tasks where visual-motor coordination and spatial organization abilities are required.

Children who have delayed development fall behind in acquiring control of both gross and fine motor movements. Later, the problem may be observed in failure to learn self-help skills such as dressing, undressing, eating, and manipulating toys and materials.

Developmental disabilities in the visual-motor area can be identified through observation and by comparing children's performance with developmental norms for normal children.

Fine motor coordination

One of the earliest indications of a developmental disability is delayed development in eye-hand coordination. Infants first begin developing fine motor control when they begin tracking with their eyes, reaching for objects on sight, grasping with tilted hand and thumb, and transferring objects from one hand to another. Later they develop finger-thumb opposition while grasping and can release objects voluntarily. Gradually, fine motor activities such as turning the pages of a book page by page, stringing beads, using a spoon, drawing, and using play materials are mastered. Delayed development in these kinds of tasks may indicate a possible visual-motor problem.

Gross motor performance skills

It is not uncommon for children to have disabilities in the coordination of their large muscles. Tasks such as crawling, creeping, rising to a standing position by holding on to furniture, standing unassisted, walking, running, jumping, skipping, climbing up and down stairs, catching or thowing a ball, and playing games require coordinated movement. Children with deficits in coordinating the large musculature of the body may have difficulty mastering these tasks.

The diagnosis of academic disabilities

At the school-aged level, many children are referred by teachers and parents because they are failing in basic school subjects: reading, writing, spelling, and arithmetic. To diagnose such a child it is necessary to follow some systematic plan of assessment, which will identify the child's abilities and disabilities and lead to an appropriate remedial program.

A six-stage plan for systematically identifying, evaluating, and planning remediation for students with academic disabilities is outlined in figure 4.1.

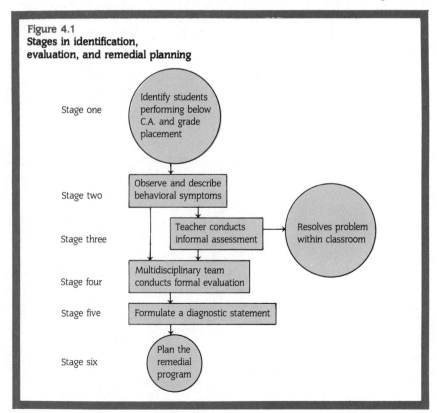

Figure 4.1
Stages in identification, evaluation, and remedial planning

Stage one — Identify students performing below C.A. and grade placement

Stage two — Observe and describe behavioral symptoms

Stage three — Teacher conducts informal assessment → Resolves problem within classroom

Stage four — Multidisciplinary team conducts formal evaluation

Stage five — Formulate a diagnostic statement

Stage six — Plan the remedial program

Identifi-cation

The first stage of the diagnostic process may occur either at home or at school when it is determined that a child is performing well below the achievement level of his or her peers. Roswell, an 8-year-old boy in the third grade, for example, was experiencing great difficulty reading and was not achieving academically at his age and grade placement level. Both the teacher and his parents were quite concerned about his lack of progress.

Observation and description of behavior

The second stage of the process is to observe and describe the child's behavior in terms of what he can or cannot do. It is necessary to go beyond the child's reading grade level and describe exactly how the child reads. What kinds of errors does he or she make? Are they reversals, substitutions, omissions, or distortions of words or letters? What kinds of word attack skills are used? How fast does he read? Does he lose his place? What words confuse him? This kind of information can be obtained by observing the child read or by administering criterion-referenced or diagnostic reading tests.

For example, though Roswell could tell the sounds of the different letters in isolation, he sounded only the first letter or two of a word. It was also noted that he had difficulty learning to write his name and was unable to reproduce short words from memory easily. He guessed at many words from context or from interpreting the pictures in the book. He knew a few sight words but often confused similar words such as *that* and *what, the* and *ten, see* and *she.*

Informal assessment

The third stage is to conduct an informal evaluation to determine if there might be obvious extrinsic or intrinsic factors contributing to the child's problem. In Roswell's case, there were no observable extrinsic problems. The child came from a very concerned family who supported the school. There were no cultural disadvantages, no bilingual problems, and Roswell had the advantage of being educated in a good school. Roswell seemed intellectually normal during conversation in class as well as in his performance on the playground. He had no apparent physical problems in vision, hearing, or motor performance skills, and was emotionally comparable to his peers. The boy was cooperative and tried to read but seemed to experience great difficulty in acquiring a sight vocabulary and in decoding words. He did not seem to remember what he had studied the previous day.

Whenever possible the teacher attempted to resolve the problem within the regular classroom. In Roswell's case the teacher made every effort to improve his sight vocabulary and to teach phonic skills in a small group and in individual tutoring sessions. When the teacher was unable to help Roswell, he was referred for an individual diagnostic evaluation by a multidisciplinary team. There may be instances when a child's behavioral symptoms are so severe that the teacher refers the child directly to the multidisciplinary team without conducting an informal assessment.

The multi-disciplinary diagnosis

The fourth step of the process is for a multidisciplinary team to conduct an individual evaluation to determine the nature of the problem. The multidisciplinary team may determine that a child has a specific learning disability if:

(1) The child is not achieving commensurate with his or her chronological age and ability levels when provided with appropriate learning experiences.

(2) The child has a severe discrepancy between achievement and intellectual ability in such areas as oral expression, listening comprehension, written expression, basic reading skill, reading comprehension, mathematics, calculation, or mathematics reasoning.

The team may *not* identify a child as having a specific learning disability if the severe discrepancy between ability and achievement is primarily the result of a visual or motor handicap, mental retardation, emotional disturbance, or environmental, cultural, or economic disadvantage.

The multidisciplinary team that examined Roswell found that this 8-year-old third grader (1) tested at the lower end of the first grade in reading, (2) did not have visual, auditory, or other physical problems which could explain his retardation, (3) obtained an IQ of 104 on a standardized intelligence test, and (4) obtained a second-grade score on an arithmetic computation test. He was able to understand and answer questions when read a story in a fourth-grade book, indicating that his listening comprehension was normal. On the basis of the discrepancy between his reading achievement and his ability as estimated by his normal language and intelligence, he was considered to be learning disabled in the area of reading. Roswell's retardation in reading was not the result of a sensory handicap, low intelligence, emotional disturbance, or lack of the opportunity to learn.

Although the boy could tell the sounds of the different letters in isolation, he sounded only the first letter or two of a word. It was also noted that he had difficulty learning to write his name and found it difficult to reproduce short words from memory. He guessed at many words from context or from interpreting the pictures in the book.

In the search for factors that might contribute to the reading difficulty, the psychoeducational diagnostician administered tests that might reveal some developmental correlates. The tests did show marked intraindividual differences among Roswell's perceptual abilities and in some of his mental operations. For example, though functioning at or above his chronological age on most of the tests, this boy was very deficient in visual sequential memory (the ability to remember a sequence of figures or letters), auditory closure, and auditory synthesis (sound blending). These are developmental learning disabilities sometimes associated (together or in isolation) with poor reading.

Formulating
a diagnostic
statement

The fifth stage is to formulate a diagnostic statement that might explain the child's inability to learn. The diagnostic statement is formulated by analyzing the results of the diagnosis and identifying the relationships among the symptoms and correlates that seem to be inhibiting the child's progress in learning to read, write, or spell.

For Roswell two working hypotheses evolved from the information at hand. The first inference was that he had not learned the skill of sound blending because he did not sound more than the first letter or two of a word, though he knew the sounds of all the letters in isolation. That conjecture was verified by his low score on a sound-blending test. This disability would explain why he had so little success in trying to use phonics in decoding unknown words. The second inference came from Roswell's low score on the visual sequential memory test coupled with the fact that the boy had learned very few sight words and showed confusion and uncertainty on many of the ones he thought he knew.

The diagnostic statement was that Roswell's inability to remember a sequence of letters made it difficult for him to identify sight words because he had poor memory of what the complete word was supposed to look like. The hypothesis was supported by his difficulty in learning to write his name and to reproduce short words from memory. The two handicaps—difficulty in using a phonic approach to identify words and the inability to use a sight-word approach—left this boy with no usable techniques for decoding the printed page.

Planning a
remedial
program

The sixth stage of the process is to develop a remedial program based on the diagnostic hypothesis. According to P.L. 94-142, an Individualized Education Program (IEP) must include a statement of (1) the child's present level of performance, (2) annual goals and short-term objectives, (3) specific special education and related services to be provided, (4) dates for the initiation and duration of services, and (5) evaluation procedures and criteria for achieving objectives.

In Roswell's case, recommendations were given for improving visual sequential memory in reading. Recommendations included the use of a kinesthetic method in learning new words and thereby training visualization ability and visual sequential memory in the task of reading. Likewise, specific suggestions were made for developing sound-blending ability. The remedial program began by teaching the boy words and phrases by the kinesthetic method (to develop visualization ability) and then introducing exercises in sound blending and phonics. Through these approaches Roswell learned to read.

Three approaches to remediation

A great number of commercial remedial materials and remedial procedures are available. The decision to select one remedial approach over another depends upon the philosophy of the teacher. Because there are several differing philosophies of remedial procedures, controversy surrounds the treatment of children with learning disabilities. These philosophies will be described under three broad educational strategies: (1) task training, in which the emphasis is on the sequencing and simplification of the task to be learned; (2) ability or process training, in which the focus is on the remediation of a specific developmental learning disability; and (3) task-process training, in which the first two approaches are combined and integrated into one remedial program.

Task training

Task training is the direct training of specific skills necessary to perform a given task. One of the fundamental strategies that teachers have always used with children who are having difficulty learning reading, writing, or arithmetic in school is to (1) state their objective, (2) break the task down into its component subskills or smaller and simpler units, (3) determine which subskills the child can or cannot perform, and (4) begin teaching the subskills that have not yet been learned in sequential order. *Task analysis,* as this procedure is called, allows the child to master elements of the task and then synthesize the elements or components into the complex level required by the total task.

In academic subjects such as reading, mathematics, or writing, the task analysis strategy would be to simplify complex tasks so that the components can be mastered independently. The task is reduced to a point where the child can respond comfortably and then move step by step into more complex behavior. The teacher, for example, can break up the complex task of reading a paragraph into learning a sentence, learning separate words in a sentence, learning syllables or phonic elements in a word, and then building up the skills to the point of eventually reading the word, sentence, and paragraph.

The task training approach does not assume any special developmental learning problem in the child or any ability deficit within or intrinsic to the child other than lack of experience with the task itself. This point of view is supported by the applied behavior analysts. They advocate (1) finding out what the child can do and cannot do in a particular skill, (2) determining whether or not the child has the behaviors needed to succeed in the task, (3) defining the goals in observable terms, and (4) organizing a systematic remedial program using reinforcement techniques. The applied behavior analysts do not infer processes or abilities that underlie difficulties but rely solely on the child's interactional history and the current behavior and environmental situation. They believe that their approach, which is task-oriented and observable, is the most parsimonious approach; some believe it is the only approach needed in any type of learning disability (Ysseldyke & Salvia, 1974).

Process or ability training

In the second major remedial approach, the teacher or remedial specialist identifies a particular disability in the development of an individual child that, if not corrected, might continue to inhibit the learning process. The teaching emphasis focuses on remedial attempts to ameliorate the particular disability that seems to be blocking progress. There has been some confusion and controversy about the "process training" approach, because the term means different things to different people.

To some, process training refers to the improvement of underlying mental abilities or operations with the expectation that the trained process will transfer to other skills at a later date. Some educators have taken this approach to an extreme that has resulted in heated controversies. For example, it was found that poor readers had many eye fixations per line whereas good readers had fewer fixations per line. The process of eye fixation was then isolated for training, based on the assumption that if the eye could be trained to fixate three or four times on a line the children would become fast readers. Books were constructed that had five dots on the page, and the students were asked to fixate on the dots across the page. The next section had four dots on each line and the third section in the book had three dots. This procedure (training of saccadic eye movements) was introduced into the schools to improve speed of reading. The purpose of this method was to help poor readers who had six or seven eye fixations on one line of print reduce the number of eye fixations per line to only three or four. The training of saccadic eye movements to increase speed of reading did not work, and the method was discontinued.

It was found that increasing speed of reading could best be accomplished by using direct strategies in the reading task itself. Many speed reading systems currently taught use various approaches to increase reading speed. These include mechanical devices or other procedures that urge the child to exert greater effort to read faster.

Process training or the training of developmental learning abilities is part of the preschool curriculum. No one objects to teaching preschool and kindergarten children to look, listen, compare and contrast, understand what they hear, speak, generalize, memorize, pay attention, or solve problems. Many people would consider these readiness skills to be learned and would not view them in terms of psychological processing functions. The activities forming the curriculum in most kindergartens and preschools are viewed as prerequisite skills to later learning. The diagnostic-remedial teacher takes into account the process demands of each of these skills and attempts to improve the process within the teaching of that prerequisite skill.

For example, if a child needs to learn form discrimination to solve block puzzles, the diagnostic-remedial teacher will emphasize the systematic teaching of form discrimination on the block puzzle task. The purpose is to improve form discrimination *on the task being taught.*

If a child has a problem in visual discrimination, it is more practical to teach visual discrimination of letters and words than discrimination of circles and squares.

One example of the controversy which has arisen over process training is in the area of psycholinguistic training. Hammill and Larsen (1974a) reviewed

38 studies on psycholinguistic training and concluded that "the idea that psycholinguistic constructs...can be trained by existing techniques remains non-validated" (p. 1). Lund, Foster, and McCall-Perez (1978) examined the same studies and questioned the conclusions of Hammill and Larsen. They pointed out that a substantial number of the studies did produce positive results. In a reply, Hammill and Larsen (1978a) stated that the "overwhelming consensus of research studies...is that it remains essentially unvalidated" (p. 412).

Kavale (1981a) applied a statistical technique called *metaanalysis* to the 38 studies reviewed by Hammill and Larsen and concluded that the research reviews underestimated the positive effects of intervention and that the data demonstrate the effectiveness of psycholinguistic training.

The controversies on the effects or values of training processes may be a matter of semantics. Note the following conversation between a process trainer and one opposed to process training.

> *Process Trainer*—Tell me, if a child isn't talking would you try to teach him to talk?
> *Opposition*—Yes, but I do not call "talking" a process.
> *Process Trainer*—But Osgood had three processes in his learning model, decoding or understanding verbal language, association, and encoding of verbal or motor expression. Therefore, in Osgood's concept of process, verbal expression or encoding is a process.
> *Opposition*—But I don't label it a process.

The conversation just cited reminds us of the story given by the philosopher William James. He said that he went to a picnic and found the picnickers in a heated theoretical argument. They said, "There is a squirrel on the tree and a man circling the tree. The question is, Is the man going 'round' the squirrel?" One half of the persons said that he was and the other half said he was not, since the squirrel always moved to the opposite side of the tree as the man went around it. They asked James to settle the dispute. His reply was, "The answer depends on what you mean by 'round.' If by 'round' you mean going from in front of the squirrel to the side, to the back, and then to the front, the man was not going 'round' the squirrel. But if you mean going from the North to the East to the South to the West and back to the North, then the man was going 'round' the squirrel."

James ended his essay by saying that most controversies can be settled if we define and agree on the definition of the crucial terms. Similarly, many of the controversies in the field of learning disabilities could be solved if we could agree on the meaning of crucial words and concepts.

Mann (1979) has summarized and discussed the controversies surrounding process training and has provided a historical perspective on cognitive processes and their training. A few quotations to highlight the key points of the controversy may be instructive.

We have seen that process training is, in fact, one of the oldest forms of education and that, despite periodic discontinuances in this practice, it is continued unabated into our own day. Its philosophies and precepts must certainly have had a powerful appeal and conviction to survive so many centuries, fashions, opinions, and attacks—and they continue to do so. For let the behaviorists insist, as they will, that all we should do is devote our attention to the here and now of inputs and responses, all of us (including the behaviorists), cling to the belief that there is something within us that is more than gristle and bone, more than attention and response. To the process trainer, it is the mind and its powers, i.e., abilities, capacities, faculties—processes. (p. 537)

In concluding his analysis of process and process training, Mann stated:

There is no form without content, as Aristotle said; no process of learning external to the substance of learning. We can most certainly help children to perceive better, to carry out motor functions better, to remember better, and so on. But we will not be doing so through the remediation of any particular type of ability—except in the metaphorical sense. (p. 542)

We agree that training processes in isolation in most instances is not as effective as training the processes in the tasks themselves.

The task-process training approach

Every time a teacher asks a child to do a particular task, specific demands are made on the child. The task analysis approach focuses on the subskills involved. Process trainers focus their efforts on improving mental operations. The task-process training approach integrates key concepts from both approaches.

In the task-process approach, psychological processes or operations are *not* viewed as discrete mental abilities that can be trained in isolation. Processes are viewed as a series of learned mental operations, behaviors, or conditioned responses with respect to a particular task. A known series of mental operations or behaviors on a task is concrete and therefore measurable and susceptible to modification through training (Chalfant & King, 1976).

Instead of teaching visual discrimination of abstract meaningless symbols, the teacher who uses the task-process approach will train visual discrimination of letters and words. The task-process approach integrates remediation of the process dysfunction with the task to be learned. Educators who practice this approach are often called "diagnostic-prescriptive" or "diagnostic-remedial" teachers.

The task-process approach may be described as having three stages. First, an assessment is made of a child's abilities and disabilities (child analysis). Second, an analysis is made of those tasks in which the child is failing to determine the sequence of behavioral and cognitive skills required by the task itself (task analysis). Third, the results of both the child analysis and the task analysis are compared and instructional methods and materials are designed on a highly individualized basis.

An example in reading illustrates the task-process approach to remediation. Tom, who had attended school regularly up to the age of 9, was referred because he was unable to learn to read in spite of his tested IQ of 120. Analysis of the child's information-processing abilities showed a deficit in visual memory. He was unable to reproduce in writing and from memory words presented to him visually. He demonstrated the deficit in visual memory both on norm-referenced tests and on criterion-referenced tests. The procedure for task-process remediation in this case called for a program that would develop visual memory with the words and phrases to be taught. This procedure of training the ability of visual memory on the task itself is task-process training. The Fernald (1943) kinesthetic method is a system of training memory for words, not in the abstract—as is done in ability training of memory for digits or objects alone, but directly with the words and phrases needed by the child in learning to read. The Fernald method is a task-process approach since it trains visual memory for words and phrases.

Raschke and Young (1976a, 1976b) support the task-process training approach. They compared the behavior analysis model with a diagnostic-prescriptive process model. They proposed what they call a "dialectic-teaching" approach, which they assert can integrate the two approaches into one system. Essentially, the model calls for the teacher to assess the abilities and disabilities of the children, perform a task analysis of the skills to be learned, and prescribe remediation in the functions and skills to be developed. This dialectic system, they maintain, "permits the teacher to assess, program, instruct, and evaluate the child's psycholinguistic characteristics in the same system as his skill competency and consequential variables" (1976b, p. 245).

An attempt has been made to briefly present three different strategies of remediation for children with learning disabilities; namely, the task training approach, the process training approach, and the task-process training approach. Each of the remedial approaches is adequate in different situations and with different children. Each is valuable when used in the appropriate setting. Direct task training is sufficient for minor academic problems in children, especially for those who have no developmental learning disability. Their retardation in reading or arithmetic may be due to lack of motivation, poor instruction, lack of school attendance, and so forth. The process remediation approach is suitable in training the ability for its own sake, especially at the preschool level. The task-process approach may be necessary for the severe cases involving a multiple deficit, a specific developmental disability, and an academic disability.

Dogmatic allegiance to one approach or another is not warranted. Each teacher needs to apply or match the method best suited for the child and his or her needs at a particular stage in that child's development. From a practical point of view it may be advisable to try the direct task teaching approach first, and if it is not obtaining satisfactory results, discard it for the task-process approach.

The technology of remedial teaching

Whether a person is using task training, process training for its own sake, or a task-process training approach, it is necessary to apply the known principles of learning and the technology of teaching. Some of the basic principles in the technology of teaching children are presented in this section.

One of the most important aspects of remediation is the thought given to deciding what to teach and how to teach it. This section presents 10 general principles for planning remedial instruction.

Discover the special needs of the child

The first task in remedial planning is to assess the child in such a way that his or her specific needs are clearly identified. This assessment should identify any factor that might interfere with the child's development or performance in school and accurately reflect the child's aptitude and achievement level. The child's special physical, intellectual, social, emotional, and educational needs are the basis for planning. It is important to discover what a child can or cannot do as a basis for planning what to teach and how to teach it.

Develop annual goals and short-term objectives

The second step is to decide *what* should be the focus of the instructional program. Annual goals should be written that describe what the child should be able to do by the end of the year following instruction—for example, attain third-grade reading ability or be able to add and subtract numbers up to 20.

Short-term objectives should be written to include the behavior to be achieved, the condition under which the behavior is to occur, and the criteria for achieving success. Precision in stating instructional objectives can be increased by writing (1) the objective in terms of what the child must do to be successful (response), (2) the conditions for presenting the task (stimulus), and (3) the standards for success (measurement). Clarity in stating objectives reduces the probability of presenting tasks that are too complex or vague, which in turn reduces the probability of errors.

Analyze tasks to be taught

Children learn by performing increasingly complex tasks. Each skill or task to be taught should be broken down into its component subtasks. This will give the teacher a more thorough understanding of the steps a child must master and will provide direction for beginning instruction at the appropriate level. Task analysis is useful in observing children performing tasks and identifying the subtask level where performance breaks down.

The purpose of task analysis is to simplify the task to insure success. This is accomplished by altering the stimulus demands, focusing on a small part of the task, using minimal change from one stimulus to the other, and repeating materials. These are achieved when a child responds to each stimulus without error or failure.

Begin instruction at the child's level

Instruction should begin with the child at the point at which the child can respond comfortably. Simple tasks are presented first and gradually increased to more complex tasks. Success on a sequence of simple tasks will reinforce the child and contribute to the desire to master more complex tasks. Instructional programs should therefore always introduce concepts and skills at the child's level of performance and understanding, or entry behavior level.

Identifying entry behavior is probably the most valuable of all the strategies for preventing errors or inappropriate responses. An analysis of almost any task will reveal that it is made up of a sequence of subtasks and that specific abilities and skills are required to perform each subtask. Before trying to teach a child a new task, the teacher should determine if the child has the prerequisite abilities and skills to perform each subtask successfully. If the child is deficient in these prerequisite behaviors and is unable to perform one or more of the subtasks, he or she will fail to perform the task properly. The number of inappropriate responses can be reduced by presenting children with tasks for which they have the necessary entry behavior.

Decide how to teach

There are three major decisions which should be considered in deciding *how* to teach a child (Chalfant & Foster, 1974).

Select the channel for responding

Before instruction begins, decide exactly what the child must do in response to your teaching efforts. Two kinds of responses can be made. The first is a motor response where the children point, manipulate objects, or nod their heads "yes" or "no." The second kind of response is vocalization, where the children might produce some kind of sound or utterance or use spoken language as a means of responding.

Modify tasks to adapt to children's cognitive problems

Each time a teacher asks a child to do something, a demand is made on the child's abilities to attend, analyze, remember, integrate, and think through a correct response. When children have cognitive difficulties, it is important to modify the nature of oral and visual presentations, alter the nature of the child's response, or select a less demanding task at a lower level. There are six questions with respect to cognitive problems to consider in modifying tasks:

(1) What kinds of attending behaviors are required?

(2) What kinds of discriminations must the child make?

(3) To what extent must the child use recall to reproduce something or use recognition to identify something he or she has seen, heard, or felt before?

(4) How much input is a child able to receive and integrate in a given period of time?

(5) What prerequisite concepts are necessary for successfully completing a task?

(6) What kinds of problem-solving skills are required to do the task?

Select procedures for presenting information to the child

Six considerations in selecting the most appropriate method for presenting information to children are:

(1) The kind of stimuli to be used—visual, auditory, tactile

(2) The intensity of the presentation—loudness, brightness, and so forth

(3) The number of things to be presented

(4) The rate of presentation or the amount of time each item is presented

(5) The number of times each item is presented and

(6) Whether several items should be presented one at a time or simultaneously.

Select appropriate rewards for the child

It is necessary, especially at the beginning of instruction, to reinforce the child for appropriate responses. Generally the reinforcement should occur immediately after the response. For example, when a child responds adequately, the instructor might reinforce with praise, such as "good." Only appropriate responses should be reinforced.

There are many kinds of rewards. The most effective reinforcers are intrinsic; that is, where the child derives pleasure and satisfaction from successful performance itself. The second kind is extrinsic; that is, where the child is rewarded with some tangible object such as a token or candy or money or with verbal praise after each successful response. A reward with tangible objects may be necessary during initial lessons, but the ultimate objective is to bring the child to the point where intrinsic rewards become dominant. Rewards have to be adjusted to the child since one reward may be effective with some children at certain stages of development, but not effective with other children or at other stages of development.

Provide for errorless lessons

Lessons should be programmed so that the child makes no or few errors in responding. Carefully selected materials, workbooks, texts, and worksheets should be within the child's ability to respond without error or with minimal errors. If a child makes errors the materials or lessons may be too difficult or may not be presented with minimal change from one step to another; or the child may be fatigued or not have tolerance for continuous work. In any case, the teacher should not proceed if errors are made, but instead should perform a task analysis of the lessons and materials to discover the basic reasons for the errors.

Provide for overlearning of materials

Overlearning aids retention. Many times children only partially learn the materials presented to them. The next day, upon testing, they are found to have forgotten some responses previously learned. Overlearning tends to aid maintenance (retention of materials learned) and is essential if the child is to progress systematically.

Provide for feedback

Learning is enhanced when the teacher provides feedback (informs the student of the accuracy of the response). Feedback can be provided in a number of ways. The most common is for the teacher to repeat what the child says or does and tell him or her it was correct. A child generally wants to know if a response is accepted and whether or not it was correct. For example, a teacher could tell a child what the target word is—*dog*. The teacher then asks the child, "What is the word?" The child responds "dog." In this instance, learning is enhanced if the teacher then confirms the response by saying, "dog, good" (praise).

Measure the child's progress

One of the most important procedures in remedial education is to measure the extent to which a pupil is progressing under the instructional procedures being used. Measuring student progress requires the teacher to decide what to measure, how to measure it, and when the measurement will be conducted. A data collection schedule should be devised for collecting data. The child should assume responsibility for measuring his or her own performance whenever possible. Self-evaluation requires the child to be aware of the criteria for success.

Summary

- Diagnosis of preschool learning disabled children requires an assessment of language development, cognitive development, and visual-motor development.

- The diagnosis of language development includes an assessment of auditory receptive abilities, auditory thinking abilities, and verbal expressive abilities.

- The diagnosis of cognitive abilities requires an assessment of attention and discrimination, memory, multiple sensory integration, concept formation, and problem solving.

- The diagnosis of visual-motor abilities includes fine motor coordination and gross motor performance.

- The diagnosis of academic disabilities involves determining the specific problem, analyzing the behavior symptoms, identifying physical and psychological correlates, evolving a diagnostic hypothesis, and organizing an appropriate remedial program.

- Three general remedial programs have been identified: task training, process training, and task-process training.

- Task training is suitable for minor problems; process training for teaching a process for its own sake; and process-task training for the multiple handicaps of developmental and academic learning disabilities.

- Ten basic principles of teaching based on learning principles were summarized.

1. At what age can a preschool child's developmental learning disabilities be reasonably diagnosed?

2. How is it possible for a child to develop normally in one area of development (language, cognitive, visual-motor skill) and yet be delayed in other areas of development?

3. What kinds of training should regular classroom teachers receive to diagnose academic learning disabilities in the classroom?

4. What kind of diagnostic and remedial skills should be represented by an effective multidisciplinary team?

5. Describe one learning problem for which task training is most appropriate. Describe one for which process training is most appropriate, and one for which task-process training is advisable.

6. Is it possible to improve underlying mental abilities or operations with process training? Might some process areas be more easily remediated than others? Which ones?

7. Teaching has been called more an art than a science. How can educators better improve the technology of teaching?

8. Of the 10 principles of learning described in the chapter, which three do you think are the most important? Why?

part 2

developmental learning disabilities

5
Attentional disabilities

One of the most frequent comments about children who are not doing well in school is that they do not pay attention. This observation is usually made when children fail to concentrate on an assigned task, do not orient their head and eyes toward the teacher when instructions are being given, or fail to follow directions. Conversely, sustained work on a task, orientation of head and eyes, alert facial expression, carrying out directions, and successful performance are usually considered indications of attending behavior. It is important to remember that attention is a cognitive operation and cannot be observed directly. Teachers can only observe a child's performance and make inferences as to whether or not the child is attending. That is the reason behavior analysts refer to attention as "attending behavior."

Most teachers can recall children who have failed to progress in school because of a deficiency in attention. In some cases, deficiencies in attending behavior may be slight, which may or may not create learning problems. When children present severe deficiencies in attention, however, the impact on learning can be devastating. The following case study is an example.

A case study

Six-year-old Suzy was having a very difficult time in school. In class Suzy did not stay on task more than a minute or two. She did not follow directions, had difficulty beginning tasks, and after 6 months had not mastered even the basic skills taught during the first weeks of school. Because of Suzy's lack of concentration and apparent inability to learn, the teacher referred her for a psychological examination.

The psychometrist who examined Suzy obtained an intelligence quotient of 57 on the *Revised Stanford-Binet Scale*. This suggested that Suzy was mentally retarded, but all who knew Suzy agreed that she was not mentally retarded. She had learned many things that the other children at her age level had not mastered. She was socially perceptive and understood many advanced concepts that were reflected in her vocabulary and oral language. She also had adequate motor skills, having learned to ride a bicycle at an early age. An attempt at a reexamination showed that this child's distractibility made it impossible to obtain an adequate measure of her intelligence since she could not be expected to answer questions to which she was not attending. It was hypothesized that her inability to succeed in basic first-grade tasks was undoubtedly due to this same attentional disability. Her behavior in class, as in the testing situation, was characterized by restlessness, distractibility, excessive motor activity, and difficulty in inhibiting her impulse behavior.

As a consequence, Suzy did not learn to read in the first grade. At the end of the year her problem was discussed with the parents and two alternate plans were proposed: (1) the parents could employ a remedial teacher for the summer or (2) she could repeat the first grade. The parents chose to employ a remedial teacher who worked with Suzy 1 hour a day 3 days a week.

A remedial program was developed to help Suzy overcome her attentional disability. Suzy received individual tutoring 1 hour a day in her home during the summer months. The tutor organized reading lessons that could be accomplished in short periods, gave reinforcement for correct responses, and in general used sound instructional procedures (which will be detailed at the end of this chapter). At first the tutor was able to hold Suzy's attention for only a few minutes at a time. Gradually, the tutor increased the length of the periods of focusing attention on the reading task.

The next school year the second-grade classroom teacher applied similar techniques whenever possible. By the end of the school year, Suzy was functioning up to grade level in both reading and arithmetic. With increased maturity she succeeded with minimal help in the second grade and beyond. The help and training this girl received in the primary grades helped propel her later into a successful life as an effective teacher.

The purpose of this chapter is to help teachers improve their understanding of how to cope with problems of student inattention. The chapter will discuss (1) definitions of attention, (2) classification of attentional deficits, (3) attentional demands of learning tasks, (4) guidelines for assessing problems of attention, (5) writing of remedial objectives, and (6) methods for improving attentional behavior.

Definitions of attentional deficits

Attention is difficult to define since it is not directly observable. In common usage few people would ask for a precise definition since it is assumed that everyone knows what attention is. Because so many stimuli bombard children in a classroom, it is impossible for an observer to know which of the many stimuli are receiving the child's attention. It is important, therefore, to observe and note distinctive attending behaviors. Berlyne (1970) suggested that the term *selective attention* be used to describe the capacity to intentionally select specific stimuli on which to focus one's attention.

Ross (1977) also uses the term *selective attention* and states that the research on attention and learning disabilities strongly suggests that a learning disability represents "a developmental lag in the ability to sustain selective attention" (p. 186). Reid and Hresko (1981) think of attention as the capacity to focus awareness upon either external or internal stimuli. On the other hand, Zeaman and House (1963) describe attention from a behavioral point of view, stating that attention is generally limited to only one or a few stimuli at one time and that children learn to attend to or disregard stimuli when reinforced.

There seems to be an area of agreement between cognitive and behaviorist psychologists, who propose that attention is a selective process of focusing on the relevant stimuli in a situation. This is a useful concept for educators, since sustained selective attention is necessary for the mastery of academic tasks.

For our purposes, we shall define *attention* as the process of selectively bringing relevant stimuli into focus.

Classification of attentional deficits

In addition to defining what we mean by *attention,* we can describe different kinds of deficiencies in the process of attending. In 1947, Strauss and Lehtinen described the attentional disabilities of brain-injured children as: (1) hyperactivity, characterized by excessive motor movements; (2) distractibility, in terms of focusing on irrelevant stimuli and having difficulty sustaining attention; (3) disinhibition, or the tendency to respond to internal as well as external distractions; and (4) perseveration, or repeating behaviors when they are no longer appropriate.

Psychiatric classification
The Diagnostic and Statistical Manual of Mental Disorders, 3rd Edition, of the American Psychiatric Association (1980) lists two subtypes of the attention deficit disorder: (1) attention deficit with hyperactivity and (2) attention deficit without hyperactivity.

Attention deficit disorder with hyperactivity
The essential features are signs of inappropriate inattention, impulsivity, and hyperactivity.

    A. Inattention: At least three of the following:
       (1) Often fails to finish things he or she starts.
       (2) Often doesn't seem to listen.
       (3) Easily distracted.
       (4) Has difficulty concentrating on school work or other tasks requiring sustained attention.
       (5) Has difficulty sticking to a play activity.
    B. Impulsivity. At least three of the following:
       (1) Often acts before thinking.
       (2) Shifts excessively from one activity to another.
       (3) Has difficulty organizing work (this not being due to cognitive impairment).
       (4) Needs a lot of supervision.
       (5) Frequently calls out in class.
       (6) Has difficulty awaiting turns in games or group situations.

C. Hyperactivity. At least two of the following:
   (1) Runs about or climbs on things.
   (2) Has difficulty sitting still or fidgets excessively.
   (3) Has difficulty staying seated.
   (4) Moves about excessively during sleep.
   (5) Is always "on the go" or acts as if "driven by a motor."
D. Onset before age of seven.
E. Duration of at least six months.
F. Not due to Schizophrenia, Affective Disorder, or Severe or Profound Mental Retardation. (p. 41)

Attention deficit without hyperactivity

The behaviors of children with attention deficit disorders without hyperactivity are similar to those with hyperactivity except that they are not hyperactive and the associated features and impairment are generally milder.

Psycho-educational classification

Some children appear to be uncontrolled and driven by internal stimuli (hyperactive), while others appear not to be driven at all (hypoactive). These conditions may be due to neurological, biochemical, or emotional conditions. Conditions such as hyperactivity and its opposite, hypoactivity, are considered attentional deficits and tend to interfere with the selective attention required for school achievement. Some of the more common kinds of attentional deficits will be discussed.

Hyperactivity is considered an attentional deficit and a contributing factor to learning disabilities. This means that hyperactivity and learning disabilities sometimes occur in the same child. Not all hyperactive children are learning disabled, and not all learning disabled children are hyperactive.

There seem to be three major components of hyperactivity. The motor component, in which a child is on the go all the time, is prominent between birth and age 5. The cognitive component is exhibited during the elementary school years. The children appear unable to stick to a task or maintain orientation on a task long enough to accomplish the lesson. The social component tends to peak during adolescence.

Wender and Wender (1978) describe a hyperactive child as follows:

> He is incessantly in motion, driven like a motor, constantly fidgeting, drumming his fingers, shuffling his feet. He does not stay at an activity long. He pulls all his toys off the shelf, plays with each for a moment and discards it. ...He cannot color for long. He cannot be read to without quickly losing interest....At school his teacher relates that the child is fidgety, disruptive, unable to sit still in his seat....Sometimes the hyperactive child is as overtalkative as he is overactive, talking as ceaselessly as he moves. (p. 6)

Hypoactivity is another manifestation of an attentional deficit; it is the opposite of hyperactivity. In these conditions children withdraw from their environment. Their behavior is characterized by lack of response to the stimuli of the environment. In extreme cases these children may be autistic. In minor cases they may be daydreaming and may not complete the tasks assigned to them or rarely participate in discussions with other children. In these instances the child may be attending to some internal stimulus which to the child is very relevant. It is the teacher's task to direct the child's attention to the relevant stimuli and bring those stimuli into focus. This form of attentional deficit is often related to fixation of attention, as described below.

Fixation of attention is another characteristic of some learning disabled children. These children may become fixated or overly attentive to stimuli that are no longer relevant to the task at hand or that are insignificant (Bangs, 1968). Ross (1976) refers to attending to one aspect of the stimulus as *overexclusive attention.* Young children may attend to a single feature of a stimulus to the relative exclusion of all other features and stimuli. Some brain-injured children tend to overfixate or perseverate on specific stimuli (Strauss & Lehtinen, 1974).

Distractibility is a label attached to some children who are unable to maintain sustained attention to a task. The child, in these instances, responds to other stimuli in the environment and is unable to select the relevant stimuli or maintain on-task behavior to complete the task. Strauss and Lehtinen (1947) decided to isolate these children in cubicles so that they would not become distracted by irrelevant stimuli in the environment. They suggested in some instances that the teacher dress in drab clothing and not wear earrings or other jewelry that would distract the children from the task at hand. These suggestions were made to dilute the strength of extraneous stimuli in the environment so that the distractibility will decrease.

Impulsivity or disinhibition is another form of attentional deficit in children that tends to interfere with selective attention, with school achievement, and with interpersonal relations. In these cases the children seem to be driven to give fleeting responses to any and every external or internal distraction, thus diverting their attention from the task to be accomplished.

Attentional demands of learning tasks

Each time a teacher presents a child with a task to be accomplished, the nature of the task and the setting determine the demands made on the child (Krupski, 1981). Most tasks require children to perceive auditory, visual, or haptic stimuli; to cognitively process information and think about the task; and to respond verbally or motorically. In school, children must meet the many demands placed on them by the tasks of reading, writing, spelling, arithmetic, motor performance skills, social behavior, and concept learning.

There is one task demand that is basic to all learning tasks, and that is *attention.* If children are to learn, they must attend to and focus on the relevant requirements of a learning task. This section will describe four common attentional demands that school tasks make on the learner: (1) stimulus selection, (2) duration of attending behavior, (3) attending to serial presentation, and (4) attentional shifts.

Stimulus selection

One of the key demands in learning a new task is to focus on relevant stimuli and screen out irrelevant stimuli (Berlyne, 1970). Many learning disabled children are more likely to be distracted by the irrelevant features of a task than are normal children. There are three kinds of task demands with respect to stimulus selection: intrasensory selection, intersensory selection, and multiple-sensory selection.

Intrasensory stimulus selection refers to the act of screening out irrelevant stimuli and focusing on the relevant stimuli when the child receives competing stimuli through the same channel. For example, a child must learn to focus on what the teacher is saying and screen out irrelevant and distracting sounds such as coughing, chairs being moved, papers rustling, and other students whispering and talking. The same kind of intrasensory demand may be made in the visual channel. For example, a child must learn to concentrate on silent reading at his or her desk and to ignore the movements of classmates as well as the Christmas decorations in the classroom. Johnson and Myklebust (1967) have pointed out that children who have difficulty filtering out extraneous stimuli are generally labelled *distractible*.

Intersensory selection refers to the act of selecting from among competing sensory information received through two or more sensory channels at the same time (Senf, 1972). For example, a student may be listening to the sixth-grade teacher explain how to develop an outline for a science report (auditory stimulus) and at the same time must disregard the sight of children filing past the open door in their Halloween costumes (visual stimulus). Many learning disabled children have problems attending to the information received through a single sensory modality when competitive stimuli from other channels disrupt their attention. This creates an intersensory selection problem (Chalfant & Scheffelin, 1969), and again the child is labelled as being *distractible*.

Multiple-sensory selection refers to the ability of a child to focus selective attention on two or more stimuli received through different sensory channels at the same time. For example, when a teacher is explaining the procedures for subtracting numbers of two or more digits on the chalkboard, the child must listen to the explanation as well as watch the teacher demonstrate the procedure on the chalkboard. This kind of multiple-sensory integration task is particularly difficult because attention must be directed simultaneously to both visual and auditory stimuli (Senf, 1972).

Duration of attending behavior

To accomplish a particular task, the child must sustain attention for a given period of time (Bryan & Bryan, 1975). This duration of attention necessary to master a task depends on three factors: (1) the difficulty of the task, (2) the condition of the child, and (3) the ability of the teacher to adapt instruction to the level and interest of the child.

It is obvious to anyone that when a child or an adult is faced with a learning task that is too difficult for him or her, the person will tend to withdraw attention from that task. Unless the content to be learned is within the student's immediate grasp, the student's attention will begin to wander. For example, when reading materials are very difficult to understand or are uninteresting, a child's attention will tend to wander to something more pleasant or acceptable. When a child fails to respond to instruction, it is a clue that the child may be withdrawing attention because it is too uncomfortable to keep trying.

The child's physical condition during the instructional period also tends to affect the ability to focus on the task and to sustain attention for the time required to learn. A child who has a marked eye muscle imbalance may focus binocularly on reading materials for a while. When the eyes become strained, the eye muscles tend to relax and blur the visual impression. Soon the child will stop reading. Attention is difficult to sustain if the child's condition interferes with proper reception of learning materials.

Difficulty in learning becomes greater if the teacher does not adapt instruction to the child's level and rate of learning. With a learning disabled child, this is very important. If a child does not respond adequately to the task or the materials, it is a clue to the teacher that the materials or the procedures are not programmed adequately to help the child give errorless responses. Whether this is due to the procedure or the materials or to some condition within the child, the problem must be resolved if the child is to respond to instruction appropriately.

Remedial instruction for maintaining the necessary duration of attention can be adjusted by controlling the difficulty of the task or adapting the teaching procedure to the condition of the child.

Attentional shifts

The world is a very busy place, and so are most classrooms. The things we see, hear, touch, and taste make constant demands on our attention. To fully appreciate all that is occurring, children must shift their attention from one point of focus to another.

Learning tasks also require children to shift their attention from one task requirement to another. Visual tasks require visual-spatial shifts in attention. In reading, for example, a child's attention must shift from image to image, word to word, paragraph to paragraph, and page to page. Verbal tasks often require conceptual shifts. For example, in a group discussion a sixth grade student still may be thinking about the previous class discussion of Magellan's voyage rather than attending to the current discussion of the natural resources of Hawaii. Attentional shifts are important in learning motor tasks as well. In handwriting, for instance, visual and motor attention is required to motorically shift from one letter to another.

Learning disabled children often have difficulty shifting from one stimulus to another (Dykman, Ackerman, Clements, & Peters, 1971). Strauss and Lehtinen (1947) refer to the inability to shift attention as *perseveration,* in which the child perseverates or continues to do the same thing over and over again without shifting to an appropriate response following a new stimulus. When a child learns the sound of "at" in *c/at, s/at, m/at* and is presented with new words such as *cap, sap, map,* the child may respond *c-at-p, s-at-p, m-at-p.* This is a perseverative response.

Attending to serial presentation

Many learning tasks are taught in a step-by-step method of serial presentation, i.e., presenting the child with tasks that are arranged sequentially. Some learning disabled children have difficulty in attending to serial presentations. There may be several explanations for this problem. The child may focus on the first stimulus and fail to attend to the remaining stimuli. The child may grasp the first part of a direction, but fail to hear the last part of the instruction (Tarver, Hallahan, Kauffman, & Ball, 1976). Children who have memory problems may only remember or respond to the last thing they heard or saw. Children with limited attention spans often have difficulty with serial directions. A learning disabled child may have difficulty paying attention and remembering directions such as "work the first five problems on page 73 and problems 17, 18, and 19 on page 74." Serial presentations require selective attention and memory.

Guidelines for assessing problems of attention

To develop a remedial program for children who have attentional deficits, the teacher must carefully observe the attentional problems and identify those factors which may be contributing to the problem. This will provide the information necessary to select specific attentional objectives to be taught. Five steps for assessing attentional problems and selecting remedial objectives will be discussed.

Step one— Describe attending behaviors of concern

The first step in assessing attending behavior is to obtain a precise and detailed description of the behaviors of concern. For example,

(1) Exactly what does the child do that indicates lack of attention?
(2) How often does this lack of attention occur?
(3) What kinds of attentional demands are required for the learning tasks being presented?

Step two— Identify situational and environmental factors

The second step is to identify the precise conditions under which inattentive behavior occurs.

(1) What conditions existed prior to, during, and after the inattentive behavior?
(2) Does the inattentive behavior occur during specific situations or specific time periods?

(3) Are there situations when attentive behavior is present? What are the characteristics of those situations?

(4) Is the inattentive behavior related to all learning tasks, or is it task-specific?

(5) What demands do the tasks make on the child? Are the tasks too complex? Not sufficiently challenging? Does the task require serial or simultaneous attentional operations?

(6) Does the child attend when the task is made easier or more difficult?

Step three— Identify possible instructional factors

In some cases there may be things a teacher does during instruction that either increase or decrease attending behavior. There are several questions that a teacher might ask about his or her performance with respect to attention.

(1) Why do I believe the problem is attentional?

(2) Are my expectations of the child realistic and appropriate?

(3) Did the child understand he or she was to attend and respond?

(4) Were my instructions explicit?

(5) Was my choice of vocabulary appropriate?

(6) Was the rate of presentation of auditory and visual information appropriate?

(7) Were tasks broken down into manageable steps?

(8) Was too much presented at once?

Step four— Identify possible physical, emotional, and experiential factors

Educational histories, health records, psychological reports, and so forth can be used to determine whether or not there is something contributing to the child's failure to respond. Physical factors should be ruled out or treated by a physician.

(1) Does the child have normal vision and hearing?

(2) Does the child have a health problem? Is medication involved?

(3) Is the child functioning in the normal intellectual range?

(4) Have previous experiences equipped the child for the task at hand?

(5) Have previous experiences developed fear or rejection of certain types of tasks?

(6) Does the child's emotional state interfere with performance on the task at hand?

Step five— Select attentional objectives

In selecting an attentional objective, it is helpful to choose a specific situation where attending is a problem and attempt to improve attentional performance in that situation. For example, a teacher might select a particular class period, such as arithmetic, where a series of directions is given to the group. The initial efforts to improve a child's attending behavior to oral directions would be made during this class period, at which time the child would be given a cue for attentional behavior. There are three considerations in writing an instructional objective.

(1) Select the desired behavior the child must perform (e.g., to listen to the teacher when seatwork assignments are made orally).

(2) Select the condition under which the child must perform (e.g., in arithmetic class).

(3) Select the standard for having achieved the objective (e.g., turn to the correct page and work the assigned problems four out of five times).

The entire objective would be written as follows:

> To listen to the teacher when seatwork assignments are made orally in arithmetic class, turn to the correct page, and complete the assigned problems four out of five times.

Improving attending behavior

Attending behavior, like other developmental skills, cannot be improved in the abstract. All instructional procedures to improve attention must be developed in relation to a specific task. We do not train attention. We train attention to something.

Many years ago Alfred Binet (1911) organized classes for mentally retarded children. Since a part of Binet's definition of intelligence included attention, he attempted to ameliorate the attention deficits of mentally retarded students. His system in class was to play the game of statues, which consisted of asking the children to assume a physical posture and maintain it as long as possible. The child who could maintain the physical posture the longest was the winner. This procedure may help the child to maintain a physical posture, but there may not be any transfer of "attention" to other tasks. In other words, "attention" is not a unitary ability that can be trained and generalized to all situations. It is necessary to train attending behavior in a specific activity, such as attention to reading, or to spelling, or to movement as in dancing, or to similar learning tasks, whether or not it transfers to other activities.

When the attentional behaviors to be taught have been selected, the teacher must find instructional techniques and strategies for increasing motivation and attending behavior on specific learning tasks.

This section will present instructional strategies and techniques that may help improve the learning disabled child's selective attention.

Work on selective attention to relevant stimuli

Learning disabled children often have problems focusing on the relevant stimuli of a learning task. In learning to read, for example, a child may focus on the length of a word or its configuration rather than on the sequence of letters. Learning disabled children may be distracted by and attend to unessential features of a learning task. There are several strategies that can be used to help children select relevant stimuli.

Tell the child which stimuli are important	Through task analysis, the teacher should determine which stimuli are important and inform the child prior to presenting the content (Zeaman & House, 1963). The child should be cued. For example, left-to-right direction is important in discriminating *was* from *saw*. Learning disabled children must be cued to look at letter sequence and shape in order to read these words correctly. Sometimes a simple cue will be sufficient, such as "Remember!—Begin here and read across" while indicating the left-hand side of the page (or line) and direction with the finger.
Reduce the number and complexity of stimuli	When a large number of competitive stimuli are presented, children often have difficulty selecting the relvant stimuli from the irrelevant stimuli. If the teacher reduces the number of stimuli per presentation, the total number of stimuli will be reduced (Dykman et al., 1971). Some learning disabled children, for example, can work one or two arithmetic addition problems on a page; but when confronted with a page of different kinds of problems, the complexity of the task may result in complete failure. In a case like this, the teacher should reduce the number and variety of arithmetic problems to make the task less difficult.
Increase the intensity of relevant stimuli	Sudden noises, movement, and color are stimuli that can be used to attract a child's attention visually. For example, if a learning disabled child is having difficulty recognizing and reading short vowels, the teacher may color short vowels red to draw attention to them. In time, color coding can be faded from the task entirely.
Use novelty	An effective strategy for directing children's attention is novelty, surprise, or humor (Scott, 1966). The introduction of something new, different, or unusual in a learning situation will often attract a child's attention (Lewis, 1975). For example, novelty presents children with stimuli that are easily detected and with which they have not experienced failure. An abacus, counter, or pocket-sized digital computer used in lieu of an arithmetic workbook are examples of novelty.
Employ touch and movement	Attention can be increased by using the senses of touch and perception of movement. Touch helps isolate the relevant stimuli and increases the probability of focusing on the relevant stimulus dimensions. The Fernald (1943) system of teaching reading is a good example of how the sense of touch and movement can help children attend to visual stimuli by tracing the contours of the letters while saying the letter name and sound.
Present material in common sets	Information can be presented in sets that share common dimensions (Scott, 1966). Word families in reading, the different kinds of leaves, and methods of transportation are examples of learning content in sets. Using sets enables the child to learn to attend to specific stimuli because there is a mental set for these related concepts. For example, by presenting common sets in remedial

reading, the learning disabled child's attention can be focused on the relevant stimuli in the set (e.g., long vowels).

Using meaning and prior experience

Sensory cues in and of themselves may not be sufficiently strong devices to prompt attention. Meaning and prior experience are important in stimulus selection (Grey & Wedderburn, 1960; Treisman, 1964). Prior experience and the expectations of the situation can be very useful in attending to and analyzing incoming information. For example, in teaching a learning disabled adolescent to improve reading comprehension in a literature class, it may be helpful to relate the reading content to his or her own experience and emotions. This may help the student relate to the characters in the story, their feelings, motivations, and goals. This kind of identification may increase interest in and attention to the literature assignment.

Increase duration of attention

Some learning disabled children are able to select and attend to the relevant stimuli, but the duration of the attending behavior is quite limited (Douglas, 1972; Ross, 1976). The following techniques can be used to help children increase the duration of their attending behavior.

Explain exactly what must be accomplished

It is helpful to structure the scope of work that needs to be done to accomplish the task. It is also helpful to break down the tasks into their subtasks. When children know exactly what is expected of them and understand what constitutes each phase of the work, they are better able to judge the relation of each subtask to the completion of the task as a whole. This procedure is particularly useful with children who have difficulty maintaining attention over a period of time.

Use a timer

Allow children with attentional disabilities to set their own time estimates on work periods. A timer can be used and reinforcement given when each child works the agreed amount of time.

Gradually increase time on task

The children should be encouraged and reinforced to increase the amount of time spent on one task. Initially the duration of time required to perform a task should be commensurate with the child's span of attention. Then the amount of time on the task should be increased gradually. For example, a teacher may want to give a child a series of short assignments and then gradually increase the length of each assignment. In time, the child can be given an assignment requiring extended attending behavior. It is important to give children a feeling of accomplishment and success by increasing the time gradually and having them maintain a record of improvement. Daily graphing of the amount of time on task may serve as an incentive for children to increase the duration of attention.

Manipulate the frequency of work breaks

A learning disabled child who is distractible and has difficulty attending to assignments can be given frequent work breaks. This provides legitimate time for not attending and helps the child to differentiate attending from nonattending situations. In time the duration and frequency of work breaks can be reduced and the child encouraged to establish his or her own work-rate schedule.

Reinforce increases in duration of attentiveness

It is often possible to increase attending behavior by reinforcing increased duration of attending behavior on specific tasks. The teacher can graph the time the child is able to attend—60 seconds, 75 seconds, and so forth. Later, the child can observe and record his or her own duration of attending behavior.

Increase flexibility of controlled attentional shifts

Learning often requires sequential attentional shifts from one task to the next (Bangs, 1968). Attentional shifts may involve moving the focus of the eyes, the hand, or the body from one point in space to another. Attentional shifts might involve changes in time, thinking about now, before, and after. For example, if a teacher is speaking to the class and then draws attention to a problem on the blackboard, the children must shift their attention from the teacher to the blackboard and from auditory to visual stimuli. If the teacher talks and works the problem on the board at the same time, the task is compounded for the children because attention must be divided between the auditory and visual channels. Some learning disabled children cannot process information from more than one channel at a time. Other learning disabled children need multiple inputs to increase their attention.

Make demands on one channel at a time

Attention is limited to only one or at most a few of the many possible stimulus dimensions available (Zeaman & House, 1963). For this reason, it may be helpful to make demands on one sensory channel at a time. For example, when a teacher is talking, demands are being made on the child's auditory channel. If the teacher wants the child to attend to what is said, the teacher should refrain from using any visual aides that would make a simultaneous demand on the visual channel. When the teacher has finished speaking, the child's attention then can be shifted to the visual aids.

Allow time for attentional shifts

Many children with attentional disabilities need additional time to shift from one stimulus to the next. Teachers can help children make attentional shifts by drawing their attention to the next stimulus and then giving them time to make the shift. Time is not only necessary for shifting from one sensory channel to another, but from one concept to the next. Children can be reinforced or rewarded for making quick attentional shifts.

Reduce time for attentional shifts

The time period allowed for making attentional shifts can be reduced gradually. This will help children learn to increase the speed and flexibility of shifting their attention from one important stimulus or point to the next.

Improve serial attention	Often a task involves a sequence of operations that must be executed in a specific order. This requires a variety of attentional demands; e.g., attention to the requirements of order, attention to the specific sequence, and attention to the function of each operation. The following suggestions may help in developing serial attention.
Increase the number of items	Attention to various components of a serial learning task can be improved by initially presenting a short series and gradually increasing the number of serial items (Parrill-Burnstein, 1981).
Chunking	Grouping the components of a serial task is useful in organizing the units to which attention should be given (Pick, Christy, & Frankel, 1972). For example, the alphabet can be chunked or grouped into units of three letters for ease of learning (e.g., *a b c—d e f—g h i*—etc.).
Rehearsal	Items which are stored in either the short-term or long-term memory are more apt to be recognized, recalled, and attended to as important and relevant. Rehearsal, or the practice of repeating the response to be remembered, is helpful in storing and attending to specific stimuli. For example, a child is more apt to attend and respond to the serial steps of a task such as computing a subtraction problem if the steps have been rehearsed and practiced until the sequence is remembered.

Additional strategies for improving attention

The aim of individualized instruction is to increase the child's attention span and to show the child that he or she is capable of learning. In due time the program can be gradually transferred to the classroom situation where familiarity with the materials learned in an individual situation can lead to success in a group situation. There are several techniques that may be used to enhance attending behavior. A few are discussed below.

Teach the child in an individual situation	For severely learning disabled children who have problems in attention, it is helpful to teach the child in an individual situation whenever possible. Resource teachers or itinerant teachers often remove children from the classroom setting and tutor them in a room isolated from the distractions of the classroom. In such a situation the environment can be controlled and attention sustained more easily.

Keep lessons within the child's discriminative capacity

In programming lessons, be sure the steps are minimal and changes are introduced only as fast as the child can respond correctly. Many years ago, Pavlov (1928), the Russian psychologist, pointed out that as soon as he taxed the discriminative capacity of an animal or child, the animal or child developed distractibility and ceased to respond to the stimulus. In his first experiment, Pavlov conditioned a dog to salivate when shown a circle. This was accomplished by presenting the dog with meat powder at the same time he was shown the circle. Through this procedure the dog learned to salivate to the circle without the meat powder. Pavlov then presented the dog alternatively with a circle, then a straight line. The dog salivated to the circle and did not salivate to a straight line. The line was changed to an oval, then to a rounder oval, until the oval was close to the shape of a circle. When the dog could not discriminate between a circle and an oval, the dog began to tear at his harness and salivate to *all* stimuli in the laboratory.

Pavlov's second experiment was conducted with an 11-year-old boy. He was conditioned (taught) to respond to a metronome beat of 140 per second and not to respond to a metronome beat of 90 per second. The 90 beats per second were increased to 100 and presented alternately with the 140 beats per second. The boy responded accurately until the 90 metronome beat was increased to 120 beats per second. At this point, according to Pavlov, the boy's discriminative capacity was taxed and he reacted negatively and became highly distractible in the laboratory.

Promote success

If children are repeatedly given difficult tasks which they cannot perform, they will cease to attend to the stimuli in that task situation. Repeated frustration develops expectations of failure, which in turn result in poor attending behavior (Scott, 1966). Failure sets can be avoided by presenting tasks with which the child has some success and by interspersing relatively easy tasks with more difficult tasks. If a child is failing in arithmetic, he should be given easier problems within his ability range. Remedial education should be organized so that the child will respond successfully to all presentations. This can be arranged by carefully programming instruction and incorporating the principle of minimal change. This will help maintain the child's attention to the task.

Reinforce attention to relevant stimuli

In a situation where learning disabled children must choose between two sets of information, such as computing an arithmetic problem or listening to the whispering of two classmates, they will select the stimulus which is most reinforcing (Zeaman & House, 1963). Children who have a history of failure on a task often have been conditioned to disregard the relevant stimuli. If the teacher wants children to attend to a particular stimulus, it is essential that the responses to this stimulus be made reinforcing (Hewett, 1964). This can be done by reinforcing appropriate responses with verbal praise, games, stars, and markers, and creating feelings of success.

One method of reducing attention to irrelevant stimuli is to ignore the inappropriate behavior. Because the child's response is ignored, reinforcement is withheld, and the incorrect response should soon become extinct. Under ideal circumstances, it is expected that the child would be motivated toward performing the desired response to obtain the reinforcement contingencies. There are many situations when it is best to ignore inappropriate responses. These include situations when a child has a history of having gained attention by misbehavior, when a child has experienced repeated failures, and when it is necessary to avoid delay and move the child or the group more rapidly.

Teach self-monitoring techniques

A useful strategy in improving attention is to teach children to monitor their own attending behavior on specific tasks (Kneedler & Hallahan, 1981). This can be done by (1) the child and the teacher deciding what kind of attending behavior is to be developed; (2) teaching the child to monitor and record when he or she is or is not paying attention on a specific task; and (3) agreeing on a reinforcement that can be used to reward attending behaviors (Broden, Hall, & Mitts, 1971; Glynn & Thomas, 1974). Hallahan, Lloyd, Kosiewicz, Kauffman, and Graves (1979) used a tape recorder that randomly produced tones that served as signals for a child to monitor his attending behavior. For example, when the child heard a tone he would ask himself, "Was I paying attention?" He would then record "yes" or "no" on a monitoring form. Later the child monitored his attention without the tape and used self-praise as a reinforcer. There are four necessary components for self-control: self-assessment; self-recording; self-determination of reinforcement; and self-administration of reinforcement (Glynn, Thomas, & Shee, 1973). The self-monitoring technique satisfies all of these components for self-control. Alley and Deshler (1979), after experimenting with monitoring procedures with learning disabled students, also pointed out the benefit which students obtain from monitoring their own work.

Medication

Medication is sometimes used to treat children who exhibit marked hyperactivity. The medical treatments are usually amphetamines, under the name of Dexedrine, and methylphenidate, under the trade name of Ritalin.

Therapy with stimulant drugs appears to decrease the incidence of many of the negative characteristics of hyperactivity. The most obvious effect is a reduction in the excessive amount of motor activity (Barkley, 1976, 1977). Because stimulant drugs are generally associated with excitation, the calming effect on hyperactive children is paradoxical.

In reviewing the research on the effects of stimulant drugs on attention and cognitive deficits, Gadow (1981) cites studies that found stimulant drugs produced a more normal behavioral response and improved performance on tasks that required reaction time, sustained attention, paired associate learning with certain stimuli, perceptual-motor ability, activity level, interpersonal relationships, and impulsivity. Gadow (1981) points out it is unrealistic to expect medication alone to alter the course of school failure significantly. Studies are needed which compare the efficacy of stimulant medication, special education, and a combination of medication and special education, with academic achievement as the dependent measure.

In examining the use of stimulant drugs, Adelman and Compas (1977) reviewed the extensive literature on stimulus drugs and stated:

> Our review of research on treatment efficacy has emphasized that it remains unproven that children taking stimulant drugs manifest important changes over the long term (and for many not even over the short term) in their learning and behavior at school and at home. (p. 409)

Adelman and Compas also concluded that stimulant drugs sometimes have a short-term effect in decreasing hyperactivity but that the results are not maintained. In addition, they conclude that we are not yet sure of the long-term detrimental effects of these drugs.

Unfortunately, drugs have all too frequently been prescribed and used without proper consideration of the viewpoints and information from the school system, the parents, and the child (Sprague & Sleator, 1973). A combination of psychostimulant medication and behavior therapy may be more effective in the short term than either treatment alone for hyperactive children in school settings (Pelham, Schnedler, Bologna, & Contreras, 1980).

Diet

Another treatment was proposed by Feingold (1975), who claims that hyperactivity in children is caused by diets including artificial colorings, flavorings, and some preservatives that are used in processed foods. The diet recommended by Feingold for hyperactive children is called a "food-additive free diet."

Holborow, Elkins, and Berry (1981) gave the Feingold diet to 244 children age 5 to 12 in Australia and compared this group to 37 similar children who did not receive the diet. The results showed decreased hyperactivity for the experimental group, as rated by the teachers. However, few studies have been conducted on the diet. The degree of success claimed for the diet, the effects of the diet on the family constellation, and the consistency of results remain controversial (Adler, 1978). The effects of nutrition on the behavior of hyperactive children require additional study before it should be regarded as an effective form of treatment for hyperactive behavior.

Summary

- Attention or attending behavior is considered a basic prerequisite to achievement in school. In this book *attention* refers to an individual's capacity to selectively narrow and focus on relevant stimuli.

- Deficits in attention include inattention, hyperactivity, hypoactivity, fixation of attention or perseveration, distractibility, and impulsivity or disinhibition.

- Common attentional demands in learning tasks include stimulus selection (intrasensory, intersensory, and multiple-sensory), duration of attention, attentional shifts, and attending to serial presentations.

- Assessment of attentional problems includes a detailed description of the inattentive behavior, a description of the situational factors contributing to inattention, a determination of possible instructional factors contributing to inattention, and identification of possible contributing emotional or experiential factors.

- Strategies for improving attending behavior are discussed, as well as teaching strategies that can aid in helping the child select relevant stimuli, increase duration of attending behavior, appropriately shift attention from one stimulus to another, and attend to serial presentation.

Thought questions

1. What are the major components in the definitions of attention?

2. The text has discussed five kinds of attentional deficits. Can you describe other kinds?

3. How do you differentiate between children who have attentional deficits and children who are bored or unmotivated?

4. What attentional demands are made on a child who is asked to copy a sentence from the blackboard?

5. How would you instruct a parent to assess attentional problems at home?

6. Is it possible to train attention as an "ability" that can be generalized to all tasks?

7. In remediating attentional deficits would you use task training, process training, or task-process training? Explain your rationale.

8. What is your opinion about the use of drugs to enhance attention? Are they beneficial or detrimental? Explain.

6

Memory disabilities

Memory is an essential part of the learning process. To acquire new facts, skills, and ideas, the results of specific learning experiences must be retained and accumulated. Memory allows children to capitalize on past experiences, profit from present experiences, and prepare for new experiences. A memory disorder can retard learning and cause difficulty during early childhood, the school-aged years, and adulthood (Alley & Deshler, 1979; Piaget & Inhelder, 1973; Talland & Waugh, 1969).

A young preschool boy, for example, may have difficulty visually recognizing places, faces, and things he has seen before; learning the names of people, places, and objects in his immediate environment; or remembering a sequence of self-help skills in dressing or undressing, such as putting on a sock before a shoe. The child may have difficulty remembering finger plays, nursery rhymes, or where he left a certain toy.

At school the demands on memory are sharply increased, which may result in learning difficulties. Roger, for example, had difficulty remembering what things looked like (visual memory) or what they were called (auditory memory) and consequently had difficulty recognizing and naming printed words. Although Roger was placed in a sixth-grade classroom, he had achieved only a low second-grade level in reading. Mary had difficulty remembering what she heard (auditory memory). She also had problems learning to count, saying the alphabet, spelling, and learning arithmetic facts by rote.

Memory has been studied by philosophers and psychologists for centuries. The search has been for those factors that assist us in remembering or cause us to forget. The purposes of this chapter are to (1) define memory, (2) classify the different kinds of memory disabilities, (3) propose guidelines for assessing memory performance, and (4) offer suggestions for the remediation of memory disabilities.

Definitions

It is not surprising that *memory* has been defined many different ways, depending upon the purposes of those in search of a definition. Some view memory as a unitary ability. Bower and Hilgard (1981) describe *memory* as "the faculty of retaining and recalling past experiences, or the ability to remember" (p. 2). Richter (1966) defines *memory* as the capacity of an organism to behave in a way which is modified by previous experience.

A second approach considers memory not as a single unitary ability, but as a sequence of cognitive activities. Myklebust (1964) refers to *memory* as the ability to associate, retain, and recall experience. Similarly, Hunter (1957) defines *memory* as the activity of remembering, with the word *memory* referring to a vast number of related activities or processes. Hulse, Egeth, and Deese (1980) describe the memory process as consisting of three operations: (1) the classification of information, (2) the ability to store and keep information in memory for future use, and (3) the ability to retrieve or recognize and recall the classified and stored information. There are other cognitive definitions of *memory* that emphasize the processes involved in organizing, storing, and retrieving information (Chalfant & Flathouse, 1971; Johnson & Myklebust, 1967; Lerner, 1981). All refer to the organism's proclivity to recognize or reproduce past experience.

Memory disabilities and learning disabled children

The ability to learn is highly associated with memory. The effects of a learning experience must be retained in order for experience to be cumulative and for learning to occur. The impact of a memory difficulty may present many different symptoms, depending upon the nature and severity of the memory difficulty and the task being learned. If a child is having difficulty recognizing or recalling auditory, visual, or haptic information, performance will be affected on any task that makes demands on the processing area or areas which are involved.

The study of memory in learning disabled children has not provided us with a comprehensive view of the problem. We do have general conceptual theories relating to organization, storage, and retrieval of information. One useful approach to understanding the memory problems in learning disabled children focuses on deficiencies in the strategies needed to actively participate in the learning process (Torgesen, 1977a). Difficulty in performance on memory tasks is viewed as a deficiency in strategies rather than as an ability deficit (Hagen, 1971; Torgesen, 1977b). This point of view characterizes the learning disabled child as one who lacks the intent to learn, has not acquired the necessary skills needed to succeed in the learning process, and may not know how to apply the skills he or she has already learned (Bower, 1972; Brown, 1978). When a learning disabled child is faced with a problem, therefore, the end result is inactivity.

Classification

Psychological literature makes reference to many kinds of memory, including long-term memory, short-term memory, visual memory, auditory memory, haptic memory, rote memory, and semantic memory (memory for the meaning of words). This section discusses approaches to memory from several viewpoints. We will begin with an overview of the different kinds of memory classifications used by educators and psychologists.

Short- and long-term memory

Some learning disabled children have difficulty remembering what they have seen or heard after an interval of only a few seconds, minutes, or hours (Atkinson & Shiffrin, 1971). This is a problem with short-term memory. Long-term memory usually refers to the retrieval of information after 24 hours. Children may have adequate short-term memory but have difficulty retrieving information at a much later time. A common example is sight vocabulary in reading. The child has seen the printed word, studied it, and been able to read the word aloud. The next day, however, he or she is unable to recall the name of the printed word.

Recognition and recall memory

Recognition memory refers to the identification of something present that has been studied or experienced previously. A multiple choice question is a good example of a recognition memory task. Four possible answers to a question are presented, and the child must recognize which answer is the correct one. Learning disabled children recognize fewer items previously seen than children who are not learning disabled (Torgesen & Goldman, 1977).

In contrast, recall memory is more difficult; children must reproduce a previously experienced stimulus in its absence. Fill-in-the-blank tests are recall tasks. Oral or written spelling requires recall memory. The child who has studied the word *house* must be able to retrieve the word and reproduce it in writing. Torgesen (1977a) found that children with reading and spelling disabilities experienced difficulty in applying efficient strategies to facilitate recall.

Auditory, visual, and motor memory

Memory may be viewed from the standpoint of the hearing, seeing, and motor systems.

Auditory memory is important for the development of receptive and expressive oral language. For example, children with an auditory memory disability may have difficulty identifying noises and sounds they have heard before; attaching meaning to words or number names; learning labels of objects, actions, mathematic facts, and concepts; following directions; and developing conceptual understanding. Problems in expressive oral language related to a deficit in auditory memory are sometimes observed in children who overrely upon gestures, pantomime, and sound effects to communicate.

In reading, children may fail to associate the sounds of vowels and consonants with the written symbols. In oral spelling, auditory memory is important for learning proper sound sequences. Memorizing math facts in addition, subtraction, multiplication, and division; learning numeral names; and counting by rote all rely upon auditory memory (Talland & Waugh, 1969).

Visual memory is important in learning to recognize and recall printed alphabet letters, numerals, and sight vocabulary, as well as in developing spelling and written language skills. It is important for visual matching tasks and copying figures, computing arithmetic problems, and learning to use equipment and games.

Motor memory involves the storage, retention, and reproduction of movement patterns or sequences. Visual imagery may be involved in helping children remember the overall pattern series of motor acts. Motor memory makes it possible to organize the body to perform a series of movements smoothly and quickly, with one movement merging into the next. The sense of touch and the deep kinesthetic sensation are always parts of the sensory background for every movement pattern. If a child has problems in motor memory, he may have difficulty learning skills such as dressing, undressing, tying shoes, dancing, writing, throwing a ball, or using equipment (Luria, 1966).

Meaningful and rote memory

Meaningful memory refers to the process of understanding and retaining information by relating it to what the learner already knows. For example, a child might remember a new reading word such as *forefather* by relating the new word to two known words, *before* and *father*—the father who came before. In contrast, a child using rote memory would treat the new word as a piece of discrete and isolated information without establishing any relationships or meaning. He may verbally memorize the *f-o-r-e-f-a-t-h-e-r* alphabet letters in sequence. In learning content material, meaningful memory is superior to rote memory because new material is anchored to existing conceptual systems. However, in certain rote activities, such as spelling or learning number combinations, rote memory is important.

Guidelines for assessing memory performance

There are many different factors that can influence the storage and retrieval of information. A thorough assessment should consider each factor to determine whether or not it is related to the child's memory problem. Assessment should include the following steps.

Identify and describe those tasks in which memory seems to be a problem

The first step in assessment is to identify and describe those tasks in which the child seems to have difficulty remembering the appropriate response. Is the child's memory problem related to a specific task or does it seem to be present in nearly all tasks? For example, Roger had difficulty remembering sight words, but experienced no difficulty remembering his arithmetic facts. When the tasks in which memory is a problem have been identified, it is helpful to analyze the characteristics of those tasks. There are six task characteristics to consider.

(1) What are the conditions under which on-task memory problems occur? The child's memory problems may be related to environmental condi-

tions such as noise, excitement, emotional upset, interpersonal problems, or other distractions.

(2) Are the amount and complexity of the content to be learned factors in forgetting? Some children may be able to learn and remember a small and noncomplex piece of information, but fail when confronted with a large amount of complex information. This can be observed in children who can remember short sentences but fail to recall longer, more complex sentences.

(3) Is the task content meaningful to the child? Remembering is more likely to occur when the material is meaningful and the child can relate it to prior experiences.

(4) Does the task make demands on a particular channel—auditory, visual, or haptic systems? In many cases, a memory problem is more pronounced on tasks that make demands on one of the sensory systems. Mary, for example, had difficulty on tasks which required remembering what she had heard. In contrast, Mary could remember materials that she had seen or written.

(5) To what extent does the task require deliberate effort to organize and rehearse information to be remembered?

(6) What kind of response does the task require? Does the task require a recall or recognition response? An immediate or delayed response? A motor or vocal response? Some learning disabled children may have greater difficulty with one kind of task response than with others.

Teachers who analyze those tasks where memory problems are observed are often able to predict other memory tasks on which the child may or may not perform successfully.

Determine if instructional factors are affecting memory

There are some things teachers might unwittingly do during instruction which could contribute to children's failure on memory tasks. Memory problems may result from the teacher's failure to establish the expectation to remember or to emphasize the importance of retention to the child. If the teacher does not obtain the child's attention or gives instructions that are not clear or understood or are beyond the child's memory span, the child may have memory problems on the task. The rate of presentation, the number of times information is presented, and the amount of time taken for each presentation are factors that might contribute to the child's memory problems.

Assess physical, social-emotional, and other factors

Poor performance on tasks requiring memory can result from physical problems such as poor health or low auditory and visual acuity. Social and emotional problems and severe attentional deficits can also impair memory performance. These kinds of factors should be assessed to determine if they might be contributing to the child's memory problem.

It is helpful to discover what kinds of learning strategies children use on memory tasks. This may be done by identifying tasks which a child is having difficulty learning and then selecting one or two of those tasks that require memory for mastery. While teaching the child, carefully observe the kinds of strategies the child employs to organize, form associations, rehearse, retrieve; and monitor memory performance.

(1) What organizational strategies does the child employ for selecting and storing relevant information? For example, in memorizing a poem, does the child read the poem as a whole over and over again until it is memorized, or does the child memorize the first two lines, then the next two lines, then repeat all four lines, and then learn the next two lines, and so forth?

(2) How does the child rehearse or practice for memory responses? Learning disabled children often lack a specific time or place for rehearsal and fail to allocate sufficient time for practice. Because the amount of practice necessary to learn a new response varies from child to child, it is helpful to determine how many repetitions it takes to learn a new sight word or a new spelling word and compare it to the repetitions the child uses in rehearsal. This may be determined by studying the child's rehearsal procedure and measuring its effectiveness.

(3) What strategies does the child use in retrieving information? Many learning disabled children do not have a strategy for "trying to remember." Assessment should attempt to determine what the child does to remember. Does the child try to visualize, use verbal means as a cue, or review sequences of action? Another critical factor in assessment is the amount of time spent in retrieval activity before becoming discouraged. In some instances, children may be able to "remember" by trying to reactivate the state of mind that existed when the information to be remembered was experienced or to recall the place where the fact to be remembered was learned. This kind of reflection often triggers associations that facilitate recall.

(4) Does the child monitor his or her performance on memory tasks? Many learning disabled children do not attempt to self-monitor or verify the correctness of their responses to memory tasks. Assessment should attempt to determine if the child is aware of, certain, or doubtful about responses on a memory task. Self-monitoring on memory tasks is an important factor in actually improving performance in recognition and recall tasks. Children who do not monitor their performance never know when their responses are right or wrong, and therefore find no need to improve their performance (Alley & Deshler, 1979).

(5) Does the child forget memory materials because he or she only partially learns the materials? This occurs in what is known as *retroactive* and *proactive inhibition*. Retroactive inhibition refers to the fact that later learning interferes with earlier learning. When a child learns to read 10 words in the morning and later learns 10 new words in the afternoon, the learning of the new 10 words might interfere with the recall of the 10 words learned in the

morning. Overlearning instead of partial learning of the 10 words learned in the morning will tend to counteract the effects of retroactive inhibition.

Proactive inhibition is the opposite of retroactive inhibition. The child who learns 10 words in the morning will have more difficulty learning 10 words in the afternoon than a child who has not learned 10 words in the morning. In this case the earlier learning interferes with the later learning. That is one of the reasons we might teach reading in the morning and arithmetic in the afternoon.

Remedial suggestions

Learning is an active process. When the material to be learned is familiar to the child, and the child is very interested, learning may seem to occur almost spontaneously. A large quantity of material which is unfamiliar or of little interest to the child will not be learned easily.

This section presents suggestions which the teacher can use to help the child remember what has been learned or experienced. Figure 6.1 presents six stages for the teacher to consider when planning remediation.

Strategy I— Select content and write memory objectives

Study the information to be memorized and decide what parts of the content are familiar to the child and what parts are new and need to be memorized. Help the child select content that is meaningful and somewhat familiar and progress gradually to content that is unfamiliar.

The next step is to write an objective for those tasks to be memorized. For example, if a child does not remember the number names for written numerals, an objective may be written for that task as follows:

> The student will be able to recall and say the number names *one* to *ten* by looking at the corresponding numerals in random sequence with 100% accuracy for 5 consecutive days.

An analysis of this objective indicates that the child must recall the corresponding name for each numeral. The academic task includes recall memory as an important part of the instructional objective. The child must look at random numbers from 1 to 10 and then recall and say the appropriate number-name. Having made the memory component of the objective explicit, the teacher can then proceed to develop the instructional plan accordingly.

Strategy II— Set the expectation to remember

Children should understand exactly what is expected of them during instruction. If a child is to respond appropriately to memory tasks that make recognition or recall demands, the child should have the intent and expectation to remember (Torgesen, 1977a). Understanding task expectations is important if a child is to actively employ strategies for remembering. If a second-grade boy is going to learn to multiply, he must have the intent and motivation to

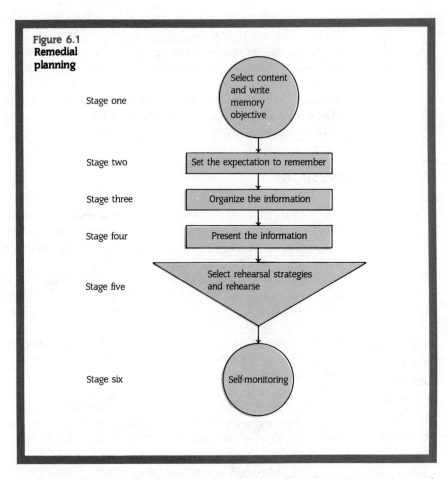

Figure 6.1
Remedial planning

Stage one — Select content and write memory objective

Stage two — Set the expectation to remember

Stage three — Organize the information

Stage four — Present the information

Stage five — Select rehearsal strategies and rehearse

Stage six — Self-monitoring

remember the multiplication facts. The teacher, therefore, must make an effort to prepare the child to remember by helping him understand the expectation of the learning task and creating the motivation to remember.

Strategy III—Organize information to be remembered

A third strategy for helping children remember is to organize the information to be remembered. This may be done by grouping the information into smaller subsets for more efficient remembering, establishing relationships and associations, or developing an overall structure or framework to help the child remember. Six organizational strategies are presented here.

(1) *Organize information in temporal and spatial frameworks.* To remember events, it is necessary to organize the facts in some logical framework. In a history class, for example, a student can use a map to help organize the historical events of the Western movement in the United States spatially, while a list of dates can help organize the same events temporally.

(2) *Chunking* refers to the technique of grouping information into optimal sized subunits or conceptual categories for efficient remembering (Johnson, 1969). For example, a child may learn the four southwestern states by grouping them together. The first letters of the states—Colorado, Arizona, New Mexico, and Texas—form the word *CANT*.

(3) *Rhymes*. Information to be remembered can be grouped through rhyming (e.g., ''Thirty days hath September, April, June, and November. All the rest have thirty-one, except February alone, which has twenty-eight days clear and twenty-nine in each leap year.)

(4) *The link system* is most helpful in remembering lists of items, events, or activities by linking one to another to form a memory chain. For example, it is possible to remember a 14-item grocery list by making links between items. The first link is the salad, which requires lettuce, cucumbers, radishes, and tomatoes. The second link is the dressing, which requires vinegar and oil. The third link is the rolls, butter, and jelly. The fourth link is the main course, consisting of pork chops, potatoes, and green beans. The fifth link is the sugar needed for the tea. In this example the links of the memory chain consisted of the five parts of the meal, beginning with the salad and concluding with the beverage. It is obviously easier to remember five subgroups than to remember a random list of 14 items.

(5) In *the loci system,* the child is taught to form a series of mental images of familiar locations in a logical order. For example, in doing errands such as picking up the laundry, going to the bank, going to the store, and going to the post office, you can plan how to do the errands by visualizing yourself going from one place to another. This kind of visual sequencing is useful in remembering each location to be visited. The loci system requires associations between that which is to be remembered and a particular geographical location.

(6) *Coding*. The child may also use coding as an aid in remembering. For example, ''Mary's violet eyes make John stay up nights painting'' is a mnemonic device for remembering the nine planets and their respective distances from the sun (Mercury, Venus, Earth, Mars, Jupiter, Saturn, Uranus, Neptune, Pluto). If children can remember the sentence, the first letter of each word will help them remember the number and names of the planets in order from the sun.

Strategy IV—Present the information to be remembered	The learning environment and the manner in which the teacher presents information to be remembered are critical factors for remembering. The time of day for scheduling memory activities is important because memory activities require active attention and concentration. Adequate rest is important for maximum concentration. Also, distractions in the classroom should be held to a minimum during school activities in which children are given information to be remembered.

It is useful to find the most appropriate rate and duration of presentation for each child. Also, it is necessary to determine the average number of presentations that must be made for the child to recognize or recall that which is being taught. Information should be presented through the most intact modality. For example, if a child has a visual-perception problem, information to be remembered might be presented through the more intact auditory and haptic channels first. Later the visual images might be developed in association with the stronger channel.

One of the most important points to remember in presenting material is to obtain the child's attention. To recognize or recall material accurately, the child must attend to or focus on the relevant stimuli. There are several strategies that can be used to focus a child's attention on a memory task.

(1) Make the information to be remembered meaningful to the child.

(2) Relate the information to the child's previous experiences.

(3) Use context as a clue for remembering.

(4) Use multiple stimuli to stengthen association.

(5) Use novelty, rhythm and rhyming cues, spatial cues, mnemonic devices, and temporal cues to strengthen associations.

(6) Group information by color, form, and conceptual category.

Strategy V—Select rehearsal strategies

Rehearsal refers to the repetition of information by the child after content has been taught or the practice of a skill after it has been learned. Torgesen and Goldman (1977) studied normal and learning disabled children on labelling tasks and rehearsal and found that learning disabled children labelled and rehearsed less frequently than children who achieved normally.

Flavell (1971) has pointed out that it is necessary to *deliberately* rehearse in order to increase performance in storing and retrieving information. Young children are less knowledgeable about their own thought processes than older children (Piaget & Inhelder, 1973), and this often results in the lack of spontaneous rehearsal (Flavell, 1970). Similarly, learning disabled children often lack awareness of rehearsal strategies with the possible exception of rote repetition and often do not employ deliberate rehearsal strategies (Bauer, 1977).

Learning disabled children who lack rehearsal strategies must be taught to rehearse information to be remembered. There are several considerations in establishing a rehearsal plan for a child.

(1) It is helpful for both the teacher and the child to *deliberately* establish the time and place for the rehearsal activity either at home or at school.

(2) Teach the child to use the most appropriate rehearsal technique (Flavell & Wellman, 1977). This might be an auditory-vocal rehearsal procedure, a visual-motor procedure, or some combination of both. Visual aids in the form of pictures, lists, diagrams, and illustrations can be very helpful in re-

hearsing. Writing material in their own words may be a helpful strategy for some children. During rehearsal children should be reminded to use reauditorization and revisualization strategies by trying to hear or see the images to be remembered (Johnson & Myklebust, 1967).

(3) Rehearsal should be scheduled as distributed or spaced practice. The amount of time for practice should be broken by periods of nonpractice. This helps avoid fatigue and loss of attention and results in greater efficiency in learning and remembering.

(4) Restrict the amount of information to be rehearsed at one time.

(5) Provide sufficient time to rehearse the information or skill to be remembered.

Strategy VI—Self-monitoring

When children have rehearsed the material to be memorized, they should be taught to monitor their performance on both recognition and recall tasks. The teacher can begin by monitoring the children's performance on memory tasks, but eventually the children should monitor their own performance.

Self-monitoring is related to what Flavell and Wellman (1977) have christened *metamemory,* "the individual's knowledge of and awareness of memory or of anything pertinent to information storage and retrieval....a person has metamemory if he knows that some things are easier for him to remember than others" (p. 4). Metamemory training can be helpful in teaching children to identify the characteristics of memory tasks that are easy or difficult for them to remember. Children should be taught which memory strategies help them remember best. By stepping back and consciously studying his or her memory performance, a child can decide to use strategies for improving memory performance.

A child's confidence can be strengthened through memory monitoring. When given a difficult memory task, the child should be encouraged to respond and taught to estimate a level of confidence about the response. This involves comparing the feelings of "knowing" and "not knowing" with responses that are correct and incorrect. In this way, the child's self-confidence in what can be remembered accurately may be increased.

Summary

- Memory is an essential part of the learning process. Many learning disabled children have some kind of memory problem.

- There are several approaches to the study of memory. One group considers memory as a unitary faculty, while another group considers memory as a complex information-processing system. In general, memory refers to the organism's proclivity to recognize or reproduce past experience.

- Many learning disabled children are deficient in learning the strategies for remembering rather than in ability.

- The educational-psychological classifications of memory include short-and long-term memory; recognition and recall memory; auditory, visual, and motor memory; and meaningful and rote memory.

- Four steps for assessing memory disorders were presented: (1) identify and describe those tasks in which memory seems a problem, (2) determine if instructional factors are affecting memory performance, (3) assess physical, social-emotional, and intellectual factors, and (4) study the learning strategies used on memory tasks.

- A six-stage model for remedial planning includes (1) selecting content and writing memory objectives; (2) setting up the expectation to remember; (3) organizing the information to be remembered; (4) presenting the information to be remembered; (5) selecting rehearsal strategies; and (6) self-monitoring.

Thought questions

1. Why is it difficult to define a process like memory?
2. From your knowledge of memory how would you classify memory activities? What kind of tasks would you classify as rote memory? Short-term memory? Long-term memory? Motor memory?
3. Of the different types of memory disabilities described, which kinds relate more closely to reading? To language? To arithmetic?
4. Find a child whom you suspect has a memory problem and apply the guidelines for assessing his or her memory performance. Do these guidelines assist in assessing the major deficiencies?
5. Who should formulate the objectives to be learned, the student or the teacher? Explain.
6. What techniques can be employed to help the children understand what end products are expected of them?
7. What rehearsal activities did you use in the last lesson you had in any course?
8. Do programmed learning or self-study guides allow for monitoring?
9. Can the ability of "memory" be improved by training?
10. What techniques would you use in memorizing a part in a stage play?

7
Perceptual disabilities

One of the developmental learning disabilities listed in chapter 1 and in figure 1.1 was perceptual disabilities. This type of disability covers a wide variety of visual, auditory, and tactile mental operations that will be discussed in this chapter. Although the field of perception has been studied for many years, the disturbances of perception in children are not well understood because of their relationship and overlap with memory, attention, thinking, and language. We will attempt to delineate and describe some of the more common disturbances of perception.

A case example

An example of a perceptual-motor disability is found in Frances, an 8-year-old child. She was diagnosed by neurologists as having diffused brain damage, with major disabilities in the integrative functions of the nervous system. Behaviorally Frances was highly verbal but appeared to be defective in motor expression and in visual-perceptive abilities. Her parents reported that she talked a great deal but was very inadequate in motor abilities. Frances seldom touched, felt, explored, or manipulated objects with her hands. She had trouble learning to button her coat, tying her shoes, and manipulating toys or other objects. Despite her parents' special efforts to teach her, Frances was unable to master everyday visual-motor activities.

Psychometric tests showed a girl of borderline intelligence with verbal ability significantly higher than visual-motor abilities. On tests of auditory comprehension and oral expression, she scored at the average ranges of 7 and 8 years. On tests of visual comprehension and motor expression, she scored at the 3- and 4-year levels. There was a discrepancy of more than 3 years between her higher auditory comprehension and verbal performance and her lower visual-motor perceptual performance. An example of her performance was demonstrated when she was given two boxes of raisins and asked to determine which box had the most raisins. Frances would shake the boxes at her ear and try to discriminate on the basis of sound rather than by weight. In addition, she could not discriminate left from right, was disoriented in space, and had a distorted body image.

Remedial activities for this child were directed toward attending to and discriminating visual, tactile, and kinesthetic cues. Frances was blindfolded and given tactile and kinesthetic tasks that required her to discriminate on the basis of touch and movement. Visual cues were reinforced by having Frances copy patterns and designs, by placing blocks or drawing forms and squares, and by attending to angles and directional changes. Later Frances was asked to follow spatial directions such as "Place the block in the upper left-hand corner [the lower right-hand corner, etc.]" Practice was given in three-dimensional space by building boxes with six sides, putting lids on jars, using scissors, folding paper, combing hair, and playing catch with a ball.

The teacher focused remediation on Frances' visual-motor perceptual skills over a period of 7 months. This resulted in marked improvement. The significant improvement was noted at home as rated by her mother, in school as reported by the teacher, and by performance on psychometric tests. An example from the *Binet* pre- and posttest items is shown in figure 7.1. Note that the posttest results after 7 months showed marked improvement in directional and spatial orientation. Achieving success in everyday activities and games which required visual-spatial ability seemed to result in an increase in Frances' self-esteem.

Perceptual-motor theories

Much of the early emphasis in the field of learning disabilities was on perceptual-motor activities. *Perception* refers to the psychological operation of deriving meaning from sensation. Perception organizes, structures, and interprets auditory, visual, and haptic stimuli. Children who have a perceptual disability usually have difficulty interpreting and obtaining meaning from their environment (Schiff, 1980). Since the term *motor* refers to the movement of the body, a disability in motor development may cause difficulty in learning tasks that require fine motor skills, eye-hand coordination, and balance (Cratty, 1967, 1969). These problems may be purely motor and affect the use and control of the muscles, or they may be caused by poor coordination of perceptual and motor functions.

The terms *perceptual-motor* and *sensorimotor* are often used because so many tasks require the combined input of sensation and the output of motor activity (Forgus & Melamed, 1976). It is, furthermore, difficult to deal with perception or motor activity in isolation.

There are many kinds of perceptual activities. First, we pay attention to the stimulus. We then localize the direction from whence it comes, then we separate this particular stimulus from background stimuli, and then discriminate the stimulus from other stimuli. We tend to sequence stimuli; we tend to classify them and relate them to past experience. When there is a breakdown or inadequate functioning of any of these activities, we consider the inadequate response a perceptual disability.

The interest in perceptual-motor disabilities was initiated in the United States by Strauss and Lehtinen's (1947) work with brain-injured children. They described these children as having perceptual handicaps, which in turn contributed to educational underachievement. The original field of learning disabilities was called the "education of brain-injured children." Since it was

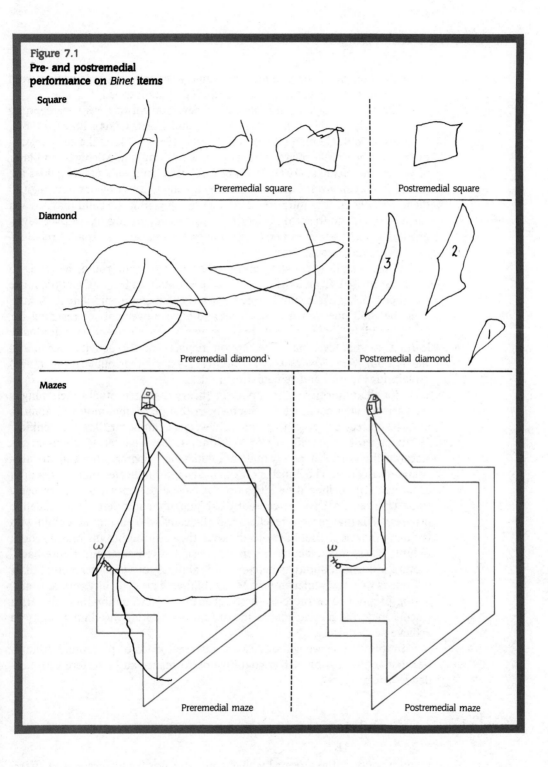

Figure 7.1
Pre- and postremedial performance on *Binet* items

Square

Preremedial square   Postremedial square

Diamond

Preremedial diamond   Postremedial diamond

Mazes

Preremedial maze   Postremedial maze

difficult to diagnose the brain injury in many children, the area was referred to by some as "education of the perceptually handicapped."

The work of Strauss stimulated the development of several perceptual-motor theories by theorists such as Frostig and Horne (1964), Barsch (1967), Delacato (1966), Getman (1965), and Cratty (1967). Among the early contributors was Newell Kephart, who worked with Strauss in Michigan and later in Wisconsin. Kephart (1971, 1975) believed that children's first activities are motor. They gain awareness of objects by touching or hitting or bumping into them. Only later does purposeful contact develop. But the child may "reach for the moon," so to speak, because the perceptual process has not yet developed. The child achieves perceptual understanding such as spatial relationships through repeated experiences.

When a child is crawling and sees a ball across the room, he tends to reach for the ball from a distance. Unable to obtain it, he crawls a little more and then reaches again, until he can reach the ball and manipulate it. A little later the child does not use such trial-and-error movements of reaching for the ball until he gets close to it. In other words, space perception is gradually learned so that eventually perception replaces motor activity. Kephart's classic book *The Slow Learning Child* (1971) and other publications (1975) explain his theories and remedial methods.

Not all authorities subscribe to the theory that perceptual functioning is the basis for later cognitive development or that perceptual-motor disabilities must be corrected before academic achievement can occur (Arter & Jenkins, 1977; Larsen & Hammill, 1975; Vellutino, 1979). Chapter 16 discusses the research literature on perceptual disabilities and their relationship to academic disabilities. The conclusion of this chapter indicates that all reading, arithmetic, or spelling disabilities do not have a perceptual basis; however, some children do have perceptual disabilities that interfere with academic progress. For that reason, teachers and clinicians who encounter a child who is failing in school should try to discover the contributing factors to school failure. These may include attention, visual discrimination, figure-background distortion, auditory-perceptual disabilities, or visual-perceptual disabilities, as well as visual memory, Many children have difficulty with a combination of any two or more of these correlates. By evaluating these factors a teacher may find a contributing factor that is inhibiting the child's ability to achieve academically.

In this chapter we will discuss the different kinds of perceptual disabilities that could possibly affect cognitive performance and interfere with academic achievement.

Discrimination disabilities

Discrimination is the process by which one perceives the likenesses and differences among related stimuli. The recognition of differences among things seen, such as letters or sequential arrangements, among phonemic differences in words, or among shapes gives meaning to activities. In learning to understand and use oral language, to read, to write, to compute arithmetic problems, to spell, or to develop motor skills, children must be able to discern the differences between what they see, hear, touch, taste, and feel. Children who are able to perceive the differences between stimuli (e.g., *was* and *saw*) are better able to learn to make different responses to different stimuli.

Disabilities in discrimination can be categorized in six major classifications: (1) discrimination of what we see, (2) discrimination of what we hear, (3) discrimination of what we touch, (4) discrimination of what we feel through movement, (5) discrimination disabilities which involve both touch and movement (haptic), and (6) figure-background discrimination. This section will describe how deficiencies in these areas can affect learning in the classroom.

Visual discrimination disabilities

Children with a visual discrimination disability may have normal visual acuity but have difficulty discerning the difference between two or more visual stimuli such as *a* and *b* or *was* and *saw*. When children fail to discriminate characteristics such as shape, size, distance, depth perception, and other appropriate details, they may have problems learning to recognize and use printed letters, numbers, and words in reading and arithmetic (Barrett, 1965). Copying, drawing, and handwriting may be affected by the child's inability to detect differences in visual stimuli.

Auditory discrimination disabilities

In some cases, a child has normal hearing acuity but has difficulty detecting the differences or similarities between pitch, loudness, rhythm, melody, rate, or duration of sound (Chalfant & Scheffelin, 1969). Auditory discrimination is necessary for learning the phonemic structure of oral language. Failure to discriminate between similar consonants or vowels or between syllables or words causes difficulty in learning to understand oral language as well as in expressing yourself. Childen with problems in auditory discrimination often have difficulty learning by phonic approaches to reading or spelling.

Tactile discrimination disabilities

The sense of touch provides information about the environment. Children who have a disability in the sense of touch will have difficulty performing tasks which require sensitivity to touch—using a knife, fork, and spoon; buttoning; writing; picking up or carrying small objects; or performing any task which requires the coordinated use of the fingers. Touch discrimination is important in learning to avoid such things as fire, sharp objects, insect bites, scratches, and cuts (Geldard, 1953). Children who are insensitive to pain do not learn avoidance behaviors and usually suffer more injuries than do other children (Sternbach, 1963, 1968). A blind child who has a tactile discrimination deficit will have difficulty learning to read Braille.

Kinesthetic discrimination disabilities

Bodily movement provides information about the body itself, such as the dynamic movement patterns of the trunk, arms, legs, fingers, lower jaw, and tongue; static positions of limbs; and sensitivity to the direction of linear and rotary movement of the skull, limbs, and entire body. Movement also provides information about the location of objects in the environment in relation to the body itself. Muscular efforts such as pushing, pulling, lifting, and lowering objects give information about the weight of objects and the relationship of the body to gravitational pull.

Disorders in kinesthetic discrimination interfere with sensory feedback from the body, resulting in difficulty in learning movement patterns and assuming static postures with the body and in general motor control. Without kinesthetic discrimination, children have problems mastering basic developmental skills, such as crawling, walking, and eating, and self-care skills, such as dressing, undressing, and using a toothbrush. Kinesthetic discrimination is also important in learning more advanced and complex skills such as handwriting, dancing, riding a bicycle, and other sports activities.

Haptic discrimination disabilities

Haptic discrimination refers to the simultaneous input of touch and movement perceptions, which provide more information about the environment and bodily movement and their relationships than either system used alone (Sternbach, 1968). Children with simultaneous touch and movement disabilities will experience great difficulty in performing fine motor tasks such as writing, manipulating tools and equipment, and learning motor performance skills.

Figure-background discrimination disabilities

There are cases in which children have difficulty focusing on or selecting relevant visual, auditory, or haptic stimuli (the figure) in the presence of competing stimuli (the background). For example, a child with a visual figure-background problem might have difficulty differentiating an object from the background in which it is embedded. Similarly, a child with an auditory figure-background disability might have difficulty listening to the teacher's instructions (the figure) while hearing students shout on the playground or classroom noises (the background). These kinds of problems are associated with selective attention and perceptual speed. Wepman (1975) has elaborated on the figure-background problem and claims that children who do not focus on the relevant stimuli and ignore the background stimuli have difficulties learning. Figure-background relationships may be observed in the reversible figure in figure 7.2, where two faces or a vase can be perceived.

Closure disabilities

Closure refers to the recognition of a whole when one or more parts of the whole are missing. For example, if a child with a closure disability were

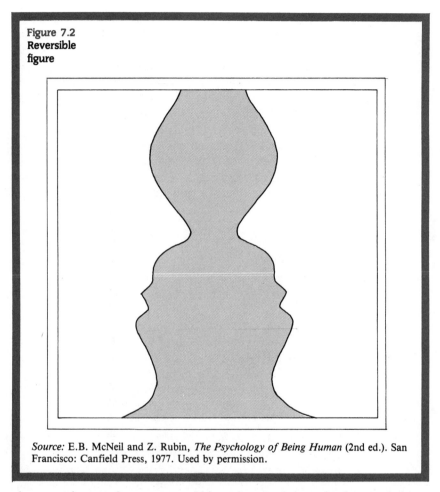

Figure 7.2
Reversible
figure

Source: E.B. McNeil and Z. Rubin, *The Psychology of Being Human* (2nd ed.). San Francisco: Canfield Press, 1977. Used by permission.

shown a picture of a cat or a rabbit and part of the animal was missing, a child with a closure problem would have difficulty recognizing the animal. This is a visual closure disability. Similarly, a child with an auditory closure disability would have difficulty recognizing a spoken word if he heard only part of the word (e.g., "telepho__"). Someone listening to a speaker with a foreign accept must use closure in order to understand what is said. The listeners must infer the words from the sounds which are recognizable. They must recognize the distortion and eliminate irrelevant sounds and fill in (mentally) the missing parts.

A reader does not perceive every letter in every word or every word in every sentence. Most readers recognize words by filling in or closing on the missing parts (e.g., "air__ane"). Only a part of a word or a sentence is necessary to close on the remainder. The linguistic background of the reader is used to help fill in the missing parts.

Sound blending is another closure phenomenon that requires the synthesis or integration of isolated sounds into a word. A child who hears three isolated sounds *k-a-t* must close and blend the sounds together to form the word *cat*. Children who have a disability in sound blending may know the sounds for the printed letters and yet have difficulty decoding words because they cannot synthesize the sounds into a word. Sound blending will be discussed further in chapter 10 on reading. Lip reading or speech reading depends upon the child's ability to comprehend the whole from the presentation of the part. A speech reader reads the lips, facial gestures, and other movements, each of which represents only a part of the communication message. In one experiment, Sharp (1972) found that children who are superior in speech reading scored higher on visual closure tests than children who were poor speech readers.

Visual-motor disabilities

Children who have difficulty coordinating their motor movements with what they see have failed to develop what Kephart (1975) calls the "perceptual-motor match." The child has problems in making a complicated series of matches between the position of his or her eyes and hand in contacting or manipulating objects. Breakdowns may occur at three key points in the development of visual-motor coordination.

First, a child may fail to develop an internal awareness of the left and right sides of the body and their differences (laterality). This may be observed when a child is not able to use each side of the body independently. Both sides of the body may perform the same act at the same time, or one side may perform small abortive movements. In observing a child who is writing on the blackboard with his right hand, for example, you may see the left hand and arm performing fragmentary and uncoordinated movements at the same time. It seems as if a small portion of the motor activity of the right hand and arm has spilled over to the left hand and arm. In other cases, a child may be completely one-sided with one side leading while the other side is inactive or dragged along.

Second, failure to develop left-right awareness within the body will prevent the child from perceiving left-right directional characteristics such as the difference between *b* and *d*. This is sometimes the case in children who have not learned to distinguish between the left and right sides. This is called a *directionality deficit*.

Third, some children have a breakdown in visual-motor coordination when the child's development is arrested at the stage where the hand leads the eye. During early development, directional information from the kinesthetic pattern in the hand is transferred to the kinesthetic pattern in the eye. When visual-motor matching is perfected, the eyes are used as a projective device to determine distance and direction in space beyond the reach of the hand. At this stage the eyes lead the hand.

Breakdowns in directionality can be seen when children either hesitate or are reluctant to move their hand across the midline of the body to perform a motor act. These children usually have difficulty controlling motor movements of their hand and fingers when their hand crosses the body midline.

Problems in visual-motor coordination may be observed in (1) paper-pencil activities such as writing, copying, staying on a line, reversing letters and numbers, and determining where to start, stop, and change direction; (2) throwing; (3) catching; (4) cutting; (5) manipulating toys or tools; and (6) learning any new eye-hand coordination task.

When a child has difficulty integrating information being transmitted through two or more modalities such as relating the word name *k-a-t* (auditory) with the printed word *cat* (visual), the child has an intersensory problem.

Perceptual speed disabilities

Perceptual speed refers to the length of time required to respond to a stimulus. Children with a disability in perceptual speed may have difficulty responding quickly to auditory or visual stimuli. For example, some children require a great deal of time to look at printed words, numbers, figures, or pictures, and indicate the names of what they see. Other children may take an inordinate amount of time to respond to a comment, direction, or command. Children with slow perceptual speed seem to require excessive time to analyze auditory or visual input and to mobilize and execute an appropriate response. This kind of disability can slow the rate of learning in reading, writing, or arithmetic. The game of finding all the birds in a tree, found in some children's books, is an example of speed of perception. One child will be able to find 15 birds in 1 minute, while another child will find only 8 birds in the same amount of time.

Sequencing disabilities

Sequencing is related to memory of the order of events and things. Some children do not attend to the sequence of what they hear, see, or do. For example, children who do not attend to word order in sentences may not grasp the meaning of what is said or learn to express themselves properly. When these children are given a command with three things to do, they may not do them in sequence (de Villiers & de Villiers, 1973). This could present problems in following directions. Other children may have difficulty attending to visual-spatial sequences. This could cause problems in learning arithmetic operations, writing, motor performance skills, and using tools and equipment.

Perceptual modality

Perceptual modality preference refers to the visual, auditory, or haptic style of learning used most effectively by a child. Although most children can learn through any or all modalities, there are a few children who have modality deficits and definitely learn more readily through a particular modality. One girl, for example, had difficulty recognizing her classmates until they spoke, even though her vision was normal. She was an auditory learner. Another child was unable to learn words presented visually, but learned these words when spelled letter by letter. This child was also an auditory learner.

There has been considerable research on modality preference and teaching methods. Tarver and Dawson (1978) and Kampwirth and Bates (1980) have summarized the group research results on modality preference and methods of teaching. They concluded that the evidence that children have modality preferences in learning is questionable. As we will discuss in chapter 16, this conclusion may be adequate for the large proportion of children, but does not include children with severe modality deficits. We know that the deaf have a visual and haptic modality preference in learning, and the blind have an auditory and haptic preference. We also find children who are not blind or deaf but who have great difficulty in learning visually or auditorily or haptically. These are the children who require remediation.

Perseveration

Strauss and Lehtinen (1947) pointed out that some brain-injured children tend to perseverate by continuing an activity after it is no longer needed. In these cases the children repeat what they have said or done and are unable to modify or stop their inappropriate activity. We can note such perseveration in a child who has learned to spell the word *four* and then continues to spell the word *forty* as *fourty*. Perseveration is like an after-image; the child is in a rut and has difficulty moving out of a learned mode of response to a new mode of response.

Remediation of perceptual-motor disabilities

Remedial procedures for perceptual-motor disabilities have been developed by occupational therapists, physical therapists, recreational therapists, and by the perceptual-motor theorists, Kephart, Barsch, Getman, Frostig, and others. Remediation depends upon the age of the child and upon the kind and degree of faulty perception found on tests and inferred from behavior.

Occupational therapists, generally dealing with physically handicapped children, have developed teaching procedures to ameliorate deficiencies in eye-hand coordination, in fine motor skills, and in activities requiring perceptual-motor skills. The physical therapists, also working with physically handicapped individuals, use many perceptual-motor activities. The recreational therapist and the physical education teacher also help correct perceptual-motor deficits. Many of these activities have been incorporated in training programs by Kephart (1971) and others, and include such activities as:

(1) Walking on boards to teach the child directionality, posture, and balance

(2) Using balance boards to help the child pinpoint the center of gravity and establish right and left balance

(3) Jumping on trampolines to help establish body image, bodily coordination, and dynamic balance

(4) Doing rhythm exercises to coordinate bodily rhythm with tactile, visual, and auditory rhythm. Kinesthetic rhythms, according to Kephart, must be integrated with tactile and auditory rhythms. This gives the child a concept of rhythm in the total organism.

A task-process approach consists of four basic steps. First, conduct a task analysis to determine the subskills necessary to learn the task. Second, test the child's performance on subskills of the task to determine what he or she can do and cannot do. Third, determine the perceptual-motor process necessary to accomplish the task. Finally, write instructional objectives and select remedial procedures that integrate task-process objectives and procedures with the task.

An example of task-process remediation

To illustrate the task-process training, we will present a case involving difficulty in manuscript handwriting. Dick is 7 years, 2 months old and is attending the second grade. He is having difficulty learning to write. Dick's teacher followed the four basic steps to develop the remedial plan.

Task analysis

The first step in the task-process remediation is to break down the subskills required in the task of manuscript writing. Five subtasks were identified: (1) holding a pencil; (2) scribbling, (3) tracing, (4) copying geometric forms, and (5) copying alphabet letters, words, and numbers.

Child analysis

The second step is to test the child on the five subskills to find out what he can do and what he cannot do. In this case, Dick had difficulty on all tasks except holding the pencil.

Process analysis

The third step is to determine whether or not the child has any perceptual-motor disabilities that might be interfering with learning how to write or with any of the subskills that are closely related to writing. In Dick's case, perceptual-motor disabilities were found in (1) visually discriminating between geometric forms, letters, and numbers of similar shapes; (2) sequencing forms, letters, and numbers from memory; (3) spatial orientation; (4) left-to-right tracking and scanning; and (5) fine visual-motor coordination.

Write remedial objectives and procedures

The fourth step is to prepare the procedures and remedial objectives. To teach Dick manuscript handwriting, the task-process approach was used to remediate the perceptual-motor disabilities within the context of handwriting. This requires activities structured to make demands on the perceptual-motor abilities that are inherent in the task. Five objectives were established for helping Dick learn to write. These objectives and the remedial activities for each are as follows.

(1) *To visually discriminate between geometric forms, alphabet letter, and numbers.* Dick must be taught that all letters and numbers must be written and read in only one way. Reversals (*d* for *b*) and rotations (*w* for *m*) are unacceptable. Forms, letters, and numbers should be traced with the fingers on sandpaper or other textured surfaces if necessary. Tracing adds kinesthetic and tactile cues to the visual cues for each form or symbol. Particular emphasis should be given to the starting point, directional changes, and ending point of each letter. Letters with similar beginning strokes should be grouped and taught together. Letters differing widely in height and shape should be taught first. In time the child should be asked to visually distinguish between letters, forms, and numbers of similar shapes. Throughout, the remedial training drill should emphasize the major characteristics distinguishing one letter, number, or form from another. Tactile and kinesthetic materials should be discarded as soon as the child begins to distinguish letters visually. Letters on flash cards should be used for drill as soon as possible.

(2) *To use appropriate spatial relationship in writing letters and words.* Developing appreciation of spacial relationships usually begins during discrimination training. Children should be given practice in comparing, matching, and grouping letters and words of varying sizes. Similarly, practice should be given in matching the amount of space between words or between letters in words. When the child can visually distinguish appropriate letter sizes and spacing, training should be given in writing letters and words which are properly formed and spaced. Touchpoints on the paper can be used to help establish proper letter height. Uniformly spaced slant lines can be used to provide guidance for properly spacing and slanting letter and space formation (*/cat/*). The number of slant lines can be gradually reduced until they are no longer necessary. When the child is writing without slant lines, he can compare the letter size and spacing of his writing to a model.

(3) *To recall and arrange sequences of letters and numbers using appropriate size and spacing.* Handwriting should become an automatic sequential skill. When the child has learned to distinguish one symbol from another and is able to write using appropriate letter size and spacing between letters and words, practice should be given in studying and reproducing sequences of

written symbols. This can be accomplished by presenting the child with chips that have letters or numbers on them for study, preferably short words like *on, no, saw, was, put, top, pot,* and so forth. The child is then asked to re-arrange the chips from memory to recreate the pattern sequence. The amount of time given to studying the patterns should be reduced and the pattern or sequence gradually made more complex. This kind of exercise should increase the child's perceptual speed in identifying sequence, size, and spatial cues in patterns.

(4) *To develop an automatic left-to-right tracking and scanning pattern.* Reading and writing English require the eyes to move smoothly from left to right. One training strategy is to use the Michigan Primary Symbol tracking system for left-right progression, a tachistoscope, or a controlled reader machine. In reading, the left index finger can be used as a place holder while the right index finger serves as a guide. Cues for left-to-right writing can be used. The teacher places a green dot where the word begins and a red dot where the word ends. Practice in tracking can also be given by having the child's eyes follow a pen light moving from left to right or reading a sentence in unison with the teacher as the teacher's finger guides the child's eyes across a sequence of letters, words, or sentences written on a blackboard or chart.

(5) *To increase eye-hand coordination.* Instruction for improving eye-hand coordination for writing can begin by providing training on activities such as buttoning, tying laces, finger painting, bead stringing, cutting, and molding clay. Tracing patterns with a pencil, connecting dots with a continuous line, and drawing with a stylus or crayons also give practice in manipulating writing instruments. Emphasis should be placed on smooth rhythmic movements in making vertical, horizontal, diagonal, or curved lines, and the child should have exercises that provide opportunity for practice. The speed of writing should be increased gradually until the child has achieved automatic motor patterns in writing.

Summary

• The early emphasis on perceptual disturbances in brain-injured children was initiated by Strauss and Lehtinen in 1947. They alleged that brain dysfunctions in children results in numerous perceptual disturbances, which in turn affects the child's behavior and ability to learn academically.

• This chapter described some of the more common kinds of perceptual disabilities. These include (1) discrimination disabilities (visual, auditory, tactile, kinesthetic, haptic, and figure-background); (2) closure difficulties (auditory, visual, and sound-blending); (3) visual-motor disabilities (laterality, directionality, left-right awareness, visual-motor coordination); (4) perceptual speed problems (visual, auditory); (5) sequencing disabilities; (6) difficulties with perceptual modality; and (7) perseveration.

• Perceptual-motor disabilities have been remediated by physical and occupational therapists, by recreation workers, and by a group of psychoeducational specialists who have incorporated many physical visual-motor activities into training programs.

- The task-process approach to perceptual-motor remediation includes four stages: (1) task analysis, (2) child analysis, (3) process analysis, and (4) writing remedial objectives and procedures.

- The application of the process-task remedial procedures has been illustrated by the case of a boy with a severe handwriting disability.

Thought questions

1. What are the basic arguments of those who emphasize the importance or lack of importance of perceptual-motor disabilities in cognitive development and academic achievement?

2. How do disabilities in discrimination, figure-background discrimination, closure, visual-motor coordination, spatial orientation, perceptual speed, and sequencing affect learning in different academic subjects?

3. How does the task-process approach to remediating perceptual-motor disabilities differ from a task approach?

4. How does one conduct a task-process analysis for purposes of instructional planning?

5. What contributions have the perceptual-motor theorists made to the whole field of learning disabilities? Is the perceptual hypothesis useful?

6. How many ways can you define *perception? Perceptual-motor?*

7. What activities do you find in a kindergarten or preschool that purport to develop perceptual-motor abilities?

8. Are all perceptual-motor disabilities related to cerebral dysfunction?

8
Thinking disabilities

Although practically everyone would agree that an important goal of education is to teach children to "think," there are a number of reasons why educators have not put a major emphasis on improving thinking among children with learning problems. First, the movement in education toward accountability and writing behavioral objectives has increased the focus on learning academic skills. Second, and more significant, thinking is a very complex process that involves many kinds of mental operations that are not fully understood. People casually use the word "think" to refer to a wide variety of cognitive operations. For example,

- What do you *think* is wrong?
- What time do you *think* we should go?
- I will have to *think* about that.
- He doesn't *think* straight.
- Which one do you *think* is better?
- He is *thinking* about how he can improve his performance.

Thinking involves judgment, comparison, calculation, inquiry, reasoning, evaluation, critical thinking, problem solving, and decision making. All of these components of the thinking process are difficult to define or describe. All of them require the ability to organize concepts and pieces of knowledge and relate them to each other in the process of reaching a goal or achieving a new level of understanding. It is important to be able to relate one concept to another and to organize and reorganize concepts to achieve more complex and abstract levels of meaning.

One reason it is difficult to define and pinpoint the activities involved in thinking is that thinking itself cannot be observed. For example, if you were to have watched Edison while he was trying to invent the light bulb, it would have been possible to observe what he did physically, but it would not have been possible to observe how he thought. Similarly, no one knows the mental operations Einstein used to arrive at the theory of relativity. Research that investigates thinking can only study the end product or the result of thinking. Thinking occurs within the individual, and evidence of thinking can only be inferred by others. Even the subjective evaluation by the individual can be misleading. The steps in reasoning, problem solving, and planning often occur in a flash without recognition of discrete or interrelated steps, making analysis difficult.

A number of behaviors manifested by learning disabled children suggest that they do not use effective thought processes. Chief among these are impulsiveness, overdependence upon the teacher, inability to concentrate, rigidity and inflexibility, dogmatic assertive behavior, extreme lack of confidence, missing the meaning, resistance to trying to think, difficulty in sustaining attention, and poor organization and categorization (Chalfant & Scheffelin, 1969; Havertape & Kass, 1978; Raths, Wassermann, Jonas, & Rothstein, 1967; Stone, 1981). These behaviors often indicate difficulty in forming concepts, seeing relationships, or reasoning and solving problems. Feuerstein (1979) has pointed out the relationship between thinking and other kinds of behavior.

We suggest that children should be taught and given the opportunity to apply effective thinking operations within the context of specific learning tasks or problem situations. There are many routine classroom activities in which effective thinking habits can be developed. In this chapter, we will discuss two major components of thinking: concept formation and problem solving. We will also provide practical guidelines for assessment and remediation.

Concept formation disabilities

During the first 5 years of life, infants and preschool children encounter sights, sounds, objects, situations, ideas, and daily phenomena that are new and unknown to them. Learning to identify and relate these to each other is one of the first stages of learning to think, i.e., to form verifiable concepts of things around them. During the school-aged years a systematized and formal approach is added to provide new knowledge, ideas, and skills. In order to give meaning and structure to the many experiences encountered, the individual must impose some sense of order or organization. This is necessary in concept formation, which involves recognizing relationships among experiences and classifying objects, events, ideas, and situations in terms of their various attributes.

Unfortunately, many learning disabled children have difficulty developing concepts from their own experiences (Johnson & Myklebust, 1967; Lerner, 1981; Pysh & Chalfant, 1980). The model presented in figure 8.1 describes six stages in thinking that occur during the formation of a new concept. This section will describe the kinds of thinking that occur at each stage, identify the kinds of difficulty many learning disabled students have at each stage, and present a focus of remediation for each problem. We will now look at the six stages presented in figure 8.1 in more depth.

Attend to characteristics of things experienced

The first stage of concept formation is to be aware of various attributes or features that characterize objects, situations, events, or ideas (Mulford, 1977; Smith, Shoben & Rips, 1974). Learning disabled children who have difficulty in selectively attending to what they see, hear, touch, or taste may experience problems in developing concepts at either a concrete level or at a more ab-

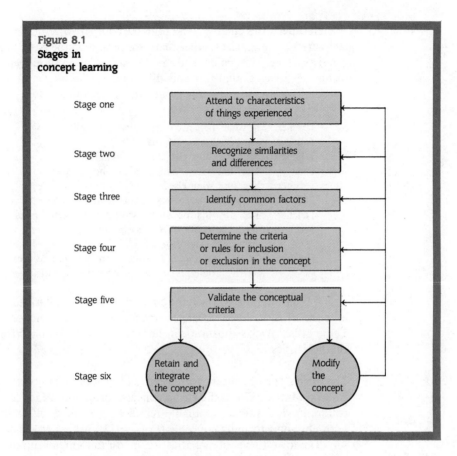

Figure 8.1
Stages in concept learning

Stage one — Attend to characteristics of things experienced

Stage two — Recognize similarities and differences

Stage three — Identify common factors

Stage four — Determine the criteria or rules for inclusion or exclusion in the concept

Stage five — Validate the conceptual criteria

Stage six — Retain and integrate the concept / Modify the concept

stract level. Chapter 5 on attentional disabilities discusses the problems of attention and suggests principles for remediation.

Recognize similarities and differences

The second stage of concept learning is to compare the characteristics of objects, events, situations, or ideas in order to identify similarities and differences (Chalfant & Scheffelin, 1969; Gagné, 1970).

A case in point is Ted, a 10-year-old fifth grader of above average intelligence, who failed to identify the major similarities and differences while comparing objects, situations, and ideas. Ted usually identified only obvious, tangible characteristics. Ted would say, "A car and a train are alike because they both have wheels," where a more mature response would involve use or function such as "transportation" or "they carry people." He said, "A pen and a pencil are alike because they are long and thin" instead of "You can write with them." Although Ted's responses were partially correct, they were the kind of responses that a younger child would give. The answers did not reflect the more definitive similarities between the objects.

In other cases children tend to make comparisons on the basis of a single characteristic (e.g., size) rather than comparing on the basis of multiple characteristics (e.g., size, color, and shape). Remediation should emphasize recognizing as many similarities and differences as possible. A point could be awarded for every characteristic noted. For example:

Teacher:	In what ways are a train and a car alike?
Ted:	They both have wheels.
Teacher:	All right, how else are they alike?
Ted:	They are both made of metal and glass.
Teacher:	Yes, and what else?
Ted:	They move and carry people from one place to another.
Teacher:	Yes, now tell me all the ways that a car and a train are alike.
Ted:	Well, they both have *wheels,* are made of *metal* and *glass*, and *move* and *carry people.*
Teacher:	Good! You named five ways that a train and a car are alike. You get five points. Now tell me how they are different.

It is also helpful to teach the child to organize similarities and differences in terms of size, shape, color, composition, texture, function, and so forth. These areas of classification can help the child focus on different kinds of characteristics.

Identify the common factors within a group of items

The third stage of concept formation is to group objects on the basis of some common factor. This is the key to concept formation. Many learning disabled children who are conceptually handicapped have difficulty organizing, grouping, and forming concepts (Boll, 1972; Strauss & Kephart, 1955).

The lowest level of classification is to randomly group objects in a trial-and-error grouping by irrelevant associations. Beyond trial-and-error grouping, Wallach and Kogan (1965) discuss three higher levels of groupings: the concrete level, the functional level, and the abstract level. Learning disabled children who function at the concrete level tend to group objects on the basis of concrete associations or physical bonds (Strauss & Lehtinen, 1947). A typical concrete grouping would be made on the basis of color, size, shape, or texture. A higher level of classification is to group according to use or function, such as to eat, to wear, to play with, or to ride. The highest level of conceptualization is to recognize abstract factors which cannot be seen. Children with brain damage or oral language disabilities typically have difficulty learning abstract verbal concepts such as "freedom," "pronoun," "nation," "state," or "environment" (Goldstein, 1948; Reeves, 1972).

Before training a child to classify, the teacher should determine if the child is functioning at the random, concrete, functional, or abstract level by observing the basis for classification or grouping. There are five guidelines which might be considered in helping children improve their grouping or classification ability.

(1) Help the child raise the level of classification by pointing out some meaningful basis for grouping. For example, a stamp and a baggage ticket are both made of paper; but more important, they both are used to carry something (a letter or baggage) from one place to another.

(2) Teach the child to identify as many characteristics of objects as possible, rather than focusing on a single characteristic. David, a learning disabled fourth-grader, had developed misconceptions about the concepts "alive" and "dead" because he attended to and identified only a single attribute—movement. Anything that moved was alive, and anything that did not move was dead. Using the attribute of movement, David classified trees, bushes, clouds, and newspapers blown by the wind as being alive because they were moving. In contrast, rocks, houses, tables, a sleeping cat, and a chair were "dead" because they did not move. Such a child needs help to find multiple characteristics that unite similar objects.

(3) Teach the child the names of the categories into which objects must be classified as well as the names of the specific items that make up the category (e.g., fruits include apples, oranges, bananas, grapes, and so forth). Later, ask the child to find the appropriate category into which objects can be placed. It is also helpful to teach children the vocabulary of the language of comparison, such as *alike, the same, different,* and *almost.* This helps in describing relationships for purposes of classification.

(4) Demonstrate sets and subsets to the child. For example, take animals, birds, and fish, and show that pets are all animals but not all animals are pets; trout are fish, but not all fish are trout; robins are birds, but not all birds are robins. Then show that among animals there are families of cats and families of dogs.

(5) Always begin at the child's level of understanding and progress to a more complex level. If the child classifies a pencil, a piece of chalk, and a pen as long, for example, help the child identify more complex characteristics such as composition (e.g., one is made of wood, one of chalk, one of plastic) and function (e.g., all three make marks for writing or drawing).

Determine the criteria or rules for inclusion or exclusion in the concept

The fourth step in concept formation is to be able to state the criteria, principle, or rule for inclusion or exclusion in a conceptual category (Ausubel, 1958). A child who can state why an object belongs in a particular category has a greater probability of applying the concept appropriately. If a child uses a criterion, principle, or rule that is incorrect or partially correct, the child's behavior may appear to be unusual or even bizarre.

An example of difficulty in stating an accurate principle, rule, or criterion for developing a concept is demonstrated in the case of Alice, a learning disabled fifth-grader. All of a sudden Alice would not comb her hair and she frequently refused to turn the lights or radio on or off or take a bath. Her parents were concerned over this behavior. The teacher thought Alice might be emotionally disturbed. Later it was learned that her science class had studied a unit on electricity. The class had made a small generator which created a mild shock, and the teacher used a comb and tissue paper to show how combing your hair also generated electricity. After these demonstrations, the teacher stressed the danger of electricity. She told the class not to touch electrical appliances such as light switches, radios, and televisions during severe electrical storms and to avoid going swimming during electrical storms. Alice developed a partial concept, i.e., "Electricity is dangerous and can kill you." If a little hair combing could generate a little electricity, a lot of combing might generate a fatal charge. If there was a storm, clouds in the sky, or if it looked like rain, Alice avoided touching all electrical appliances. She had developed an inadequate principle about the concept of electricity and acted upon it.

Language facilitates conceptual learning (Ausubel, 1963; Sigel, 1975). Children with language disorders who state invalid criteria for inclusion in a concept may overgeneralize (Clark, 1974), as Alice did in trying to understand electricity. Learning disabled children with oral language disabilities may have difficulty formulating rationales, criteria, principles, or rules for categorical inclusion or exclusion. Remedial efforts at this stage should be directed toward the improvement of receptive, integrative, and expressive language skills. These skills are discussed in chapter 9, "Oral Language Disabilities."

Validate the concept, criteria, or rules

The fifth stage of concept formation is to apply the rules or criteria to other objects, situations, events, or ideas to determine if the criteria are valid. This hypothesis-testing step is particularly important for learning disabled children because of their tendency to form misconceptions due to lack of complete information or background experience, failure to interpret the information properly, and lack of cognitive sophistication in discriminating and making comparisons, recognizing relationships, and forming abstractions (Alley & Deshler, 1979; Maker, 1981).

The need to teach reasoning skills and hypothesizing skills in learning disabled children has been discussed by Fraenkel (1973) and Stone (1981). Learning disabled children who form misconceptions must be taught how to validate conceptual criteria. In classifying animals and fish in a science class, Dennis, a learning disabled fifth-grader, hypothesized the rule that "Fish live in the water and mammals live on the land." Dennis then mistakenly classified whales as fishes. In this kind of situation, the child must be taught to determine whether the criteria or rules devised for a newly formed concept are valid or not. For example, a teacher might teach validation skills as follows.

Teacher: Dennis, you said that a whale is a fish and not a mammal. Let's see if your rule for identifying fishes from mammals is correct. Begin by stating your rule.

Dennis: OK! Fish live in the water and mammals live on land.

Teacher: All right, now tell me what we've learned about fish.

Dennis:	Fish live in the water.
Teacher:	And what else?
Dennis:	Well, they have scales and fins.
Teacher:	How do they breathe and reproduce?
Dennis:	Their gills breathe air dissolved in water and they lay eggs.
Teacher:	All right. Now tell me about whales.
Dennis:	Well, whales live in the water too.
Teacher:	Yes, but do they have scales?
Dennis:	No, whales don't have scales, but they sort of have fins or flippers like fish.
Teacher:	And how do whales breathe and reproduce?
Dennis:	Oh! Whales have to come up for air in order to breathe, and they have babies like cows and horses.
Teacher:	And what are cows and horses?
Dennis:	Mammals. Then whales are mammals.
Teacher:	That's right, Dennis. Now go and read about birds and bats and then tell me if a bat is a bird or a mammal and why.

This kind of hypothesis-questioning process provides the child practice and a system for applying conceptual rules to objects or situations to determine if the criteria for inclusion or exclusion are valid or not (Levine, 1975). Children with language disorders usually have difficulty testing hypotheses as efficiently as normal children. These children need language training to help them reason and solve problems during hypothesis testing.

Retain and integrate the concept

As an extention of the process of concept formation, organized thinking requires the ability to relate the concepts already acquired and use them in developing broader and more complex concepts; in reasoning, planning, evaluating experiences; and in critical thinking. Each piece of knowledge gained from one experience makes subsequent experiences more interesting.

During the learning process, children must continually relate one thing to another. The organizing process which links what is seen, heard, or felt at a concrete level and which connects information and ideas at a more abstract level is basic to cognitive development. Some learning disabled children have trouble with this operation.

If you ask a child "Do wingless birds fly?" it is necessary for the child to understand and integrate the concepts of "bird," "fly," and "wingless." A 6-year-old child probably understands the concept of "bird" and the concept of "fly." To understand "wingless," the child must recognize that there is a category of birds, such as the kiwi and the ostrich, without functional wings. When this is understood, the child has a better chance of answering the question correctly by integrating the three concepts.

Well-developed thinking requires this facility of seeing a concept in relation to many other concepts as well as a broad base of knowledge and content. Isolated concepts are not sufficient. To complete an analogy such as "An eagle is large; a sparrow is _____," one must search for an attribute of a sparrow that would be not only *true* but also *parallel* to the attribute of the eagle's largeness.

Children who do not integrate their past experiences with present or future experiences may do foolish things because they do not see similar situations in juxtaposition. They have difficulty generalizing. A child with this deficit, when asked to talk about a picture of people doing something, is apt to label tangible things in the picture rather than tell a story about it. In the *Revised Stanford-Binet Test of Intelligence,* response to pictures is given credit at age 3½ for spontaneous enumeration of at least three items in the picture, but to receive credit at age 6 the child must bring the elements of the picture together either by describing or integrating.

Consider a picture of two boys, one running away and one lying motionless on the ground beneath a tree that has a rope hanging from a branch. A very young child might respond, "A boy, a boy," or "A boy lying down, he's hurt." Unless the child interprets the picture by saying that a boy fell from a hanging rope and became unconscious and another boy is running for help, the child has not integrated the elements of the picture.

The hypothesis-testing approach to concept formation as outlined above is applicable here. By this approach teachers can prepare the environment and ask leading questions, but basically the children must construct their own hypotheses as to the concepts developed. The discovery method of teaching allows the student to form generalizations from multiple examples of a specific concept and develop the implications for expanding knowledge.

In discussing how to remediate deficits in this area, Kirk and Kirk (1971) hypothesize the need to hold two or more concepts in juxtaposition and identify increasingly complex relationships. In particular, they emphasize helping the child learn to classify and categorize objects and ideas by identifying similarities and differences and to note many kinds of relationships such as opposites, part-whole relationships, cause-effect relationships, time-space relationships, and number relationships.

Modify the concept

If the criteria or rules for including or excluding objects, situations, or ideas in a concept are validated in stage five, then the concept is retained in stage six. If, on the other hand, the criteria or rules tested in stage five do not prove valid, the child must try to modify the rule for the concept. A learning disabled child who does not attempt to modify concepts that are known to be only partially correct or inaccurate will continue to function inappropriately whenever the concept is involved in a task, as did Alice in her behavior toward electrical appliances.

Remediation should stress helping the child to take concepts that have not been validated in stage five and systematically move through the concept learning stages in order to form the appropriate concept. This would include (1) attending to the characteristics of things encountered, (2) recognizing similarities and differences, (3) identifying the common factor(s), (4) determining the criteria for inclusion and exclusion in the concept, (5) validating the concept, and (6) either retaining or once again trying to modify the concept. In many cases, the child's problem may be found in one or two stages. The teacher can focus remedial efforts at those stages where the problems are found.

Problem solving

An important part of growing up is learning to cope with difficult situations, overcoming obstacles, answering perplexing questions, and finding solutions to the everyday problems of living. Unfortunately, many learning disabled students often (1) fail to see problem situations develop, (2) do not identify a problem with themselves, (3) lack the attitudes, mental abilities, or problem-solving techniques to cope with the problem, or (4) fail to use organized and systematic strategies for problem solving (Maker, 1981; Parrill-Burnstein, 1981; Pysh & Chalfant, 1980).

It is important, therefore, that learning disabled students be aided in developing strategies for problem solving that will enable them to respond more adequately to everyday problems and enrich their lives with the discovery of unique ideas and new insights.

Approaches to problem solving have been described in many ways, including trial-and-error behavior, impulsive behavior, reflective behavior, creative inspiration or insightful behavior, original thinking, direct and logical thinking, and inductive and deductive thinking. Although scholars have differed in describing problem solving, there seems to be general agreement about the dynamics involved (Dewey, 1933; Kingsley & Garry, 1957; Osburn, 1963; Wallas, 1926).

Of course, there is usually no single way to solve problems. Figure 8.2 is a model that portrays six major phases in the problem-solving process. A breakdown at any one of these stages could interfere with effective problem solving. This section will present guidelines for assessing student performance at each stage of the problem-solving process as well as suggestions for remediation.

Recognizing that a problem exists

The first stage in the problem-solving process is to recognize that a problem exists (Bruner, 1973). A problem may be said to exist when a situation is encountered for which the student has no ready response. The lack of a response creates feelings of discomfort or disequilibrium which motivate the student to find a solution (Dewey, 1938; Shulman, 1965).

Many learning disabled students lack awareness of existing problems in their daily life and fail to recognize the threat of potential problems. These students typically express surprise when they discover that they do, in fact,

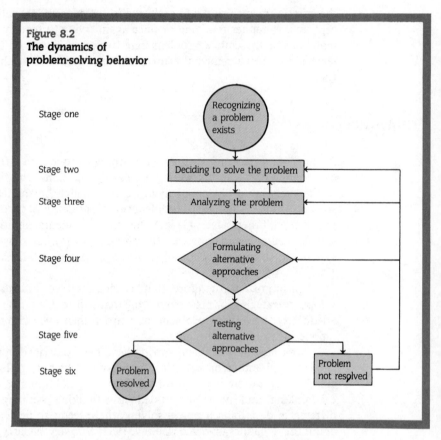

Figure 8.2
The dynamics of problem-solving behavior

Stage one — Recognizing a problem exists

Stage two — Deciding to solve the problem

Stage three — Analyzing the problem

Stage four — Formulating alternative approaches

Stage five — Testing alternative approaches

Stage six — Problem resolved / Problem not resolved

have a problem. By the time the student is aware of the difficulty, it is often too late to do anything about it.

For example, on October 1st a learning disabled student was asked to prepare a paper for history class due on November 1st. The student began work on the paper on October 29th and was surprised when she received a failing grade. A teenager wandered away from his scout troup on a hike in the mountains. He knew he had become separated from his group but felt he could find his way back easily. After 20 minutes of walking, he became somewhat concerned; after 30 minutes he knew he was lost and finally recognized he had a problem.

Why do these kinds of problems occur? Are learning disabled students simply forgetful? Do they fail to attend to what is going on around them? Are they easily distracted? Do they fail to recognize a discrepancy between existing circumstances and what should be? Or are they unfamiliar with cause-effect relationships?

A child's difficulty in recognizing that a problem exists can be assessed by selecting a particular problem situation which has arisen and observing how the child responds to it. Situations can be selected from almost anywhere, such as problems in academic areas, interpersonal relationships, planning, or the manipulation of physical tools or playground equipment. Study the problem situation and try to determine the extent to which a student becomes aware of the problem. It may be helpful to talk with the student to determine why he or she did not recognize the problem situation. Students must be taught to recognize potential problems as they emerge.

For example, Gil was a learning disabled ninth-grader who had failed four out of five courses during the fall semester. His teacher used four steps in helping Gil to recognize when he had potential problems developing in his schoolwork.

First, the teacher helped Gil to recognize the desired state of affairs. Gil should maintain his study schedule for each course, complete each reading and writing assignment daily, and maintain grades at C level or above on daily work.

Second, a chart was developed to help Gil record the number of study sessions not kept, the number of assignments not read or written, and any grades below C. This chart helped Gil recognize when he was beginning to develop a problem.

Third, the teacher and Gil developed criteria to help him determine when he was beginning to get into difficulty. Missing more than two study sessions per week, not completing more than one assignment per week, and receiving more than one D grade were all danger signals.

Fourth, the teacher helped Gil recognize when outside help was needed. Gil was expected to ask his teacher for help if he failed to maintain his performance up to criteria for two weeks in succession.

Learning disabled students often need this kind of structure and assistance in learning to recognize problems. In time, the teacher should provide less structure and the student should assume more responsibility for recognizing emerging problems.

Deciding to solve the problem

The second stage of the problem-solving model in figure 8.2 is to decide whether or not to solve the problem. The problem must create enough dissatisfaction and dissonance to be perceived as a problem (Shulman, 1965), and the student must feel the need and have the emotional investment to seek a solution (Alley & Deshler, 1979).

Many learning disabled students are reluctant to engage in problem solving if they believe they will not be successful. Research conducted by Dweck and Licht (1980) identified two subgroups among normal children. The first group were mastery oriented children who expected to succeed. They actively pursued solution-relevant strategies and emphasized the positive. In contrast, a second group was characterized by learned helplessness. These children believed either that they did not have the ability or that the environmental situation which caused the failure was unalterable. Children who were characterized by learned helplessness tended to discount any former successes, dwelled on the negative, and did not persist on tasks. Obviously, learning disabled children with a learned helplessness syndrome would be reluctant to engage in problem solving and probably would not persist very long if they did.

There are four different strategies a teacher can use to encourage learning disabled students to decide to engage in problem solving.

(1) Create a felt need. When a learning disabled student is reluctant to engage in problem solving, there may be no felt need or motivation for resolving the problem. The teacher should try to create the felt need by helping the student recognize the consequences of the problem to himself or to others. It is important to clarify cause-effect relationships (Johnson & Myklebust, 1967).

(2) Teach the student to consider his or her own strengths for coping with a problem situation (Feldhusen & Treffinger, 1977). Some learning disabled students do not accurately estimate the degree of problem difficulty or their competence and skill in the situation. An example is when one non-swimmer jumps into the water to save another nonswimmer. It is very important, therefore, to determine how a student analyzes the given problem situation as well as his or her strengths or weaknesses in trying to cope with that situation. Learning disabled students who have developed an attitude of learned helplessness need assistance in forming more realistic perceptions about their abilities and their personal control over success or failure (Dweck & Licht, 1980). This can be accomplished by using stories, movies, and situations to point out how everyone has strengths and weaknesses. Although Franklin Delano Roosevelt could not walk or run, he became president of the United States. Through repeated situations and examples, students should learn to accurately understand their strengths and weaknesses and relate them to different problem situations.

(3) Teach the child to cope with failure. There are several important attitudes that need to be fostered in the classroom to encourage learning disabled students to engage in problem solving. Chief among these is acceptance of failure. Students should be able to fail without censure and learn that failure is a normal part of the learning process. Follow-up tasks should be given so they will learn that they can profit from former failure and be successful.

(4) Reinforce problem-solving attempts. Children should be reinforced for trying to engage in problem-solving behavior. Children need to develop the attitude that it is better to try and fail than not to try at all. The process of problem solving should be presented as a positive activity that can be fun. In the beginning, the problem-solving process should be highlighted and more strongly reinforced. This may be more effective than solving the problem.

Analyzing the problem The third stage of problem solving is to analyze the problem. The thinking processes involved in problem analysis are very complex and include careful observation and collection of information, organization of information, and interpretation. Bruner (1973), Fraenkel (1973), and Piaget (1969) describe in detail the complexities of the thinking processes involved in problem solving.

For our purposes, there are three major considerations in helping learning disabled students analyze problem situations. First, students must be taught to describe problem situations objectively and as accurately as possible. This can be done by taking everyday problem situations which arise at home, on the playground, or in the classroom and helping them describe the problems as clearly as possible. Students who are unable to describe problem situations because of a language disability may need language remediation as well (Borys & Spitz, 1979).

The second consideration is to identify the reasons or circumstances that may be contributing to the problem. This includes identifying cause-effect relationships that have led to the problem in the past as well as current cause-effect relationships, and ignoring variables that are not related to the problem. This can be done through individual and group discussions.

The third consideration is to teach students to accurately estimate the degree of problem difficulty. The perceived difficulty of a problem is often based on an individual's emotional reaction to the problem rather than an objective estimate of the problem situation. The boy scout who suddenly realizes he is lost in the mountains, for example, might panic and begin running randomly in hopes of seeing a familiar landmark or fellow scout. A nonemotional analysis of the situation, however, would create a more accurate estimate. Since the boy had only been by himself for about 30 or 40 minutes, he probably was not separated by more than a mile from his scout troup. Teachers can help students create more accurate estimates of problem difficulty by teaching them to describe the problem situation thoroughly and to control their own subjective feelings. Estimating problem difficulty also involves evaluating one's own strengths and weaknesses in relation to the skills necessary to solve the problem. After having thoroughly analyzed the problem, individuals sometimes decide that they are not capable of solving the problem. They may return to stage two and decide not to try to resolve the problem.

A thorough analysis of several similar problems often helps the child develop a set for analyzing that kind of problem (Parrill-Burnstein, 1981). A valid analysis of a problem situation is the basis for formulating more realistic approaches to the problems encountered (Patton & Griffen, 1973).

Formulating alternative approaches

The fourth stage of problem solving is to formulate alternative solutions for solving problems. Kagan (1966) describes two kinds of responses to a problem: impulsivity and reflection. When a learning disabled student is confronted by a problem that produces anxiety or frustration, the child might respond very quickly and without thinking (Cunningham & Barkley, 1978). Learning disabled students often behave impulsively and choose the first alternative that seems to be correct (Hallahan, Kauffman, & Ball, 1973). When a student is overreflective and perceives a problem to be more complex than it really is, barriers are created that prevent the formulation of alternative solutions.

In studying problem-solving behavior in learning disabled students, Havertape and Kass (1978) found that 40% of the students' responses consisted of random or impulsive answers without consideration or reference to the factors involved in the problem. Impulsivity, therefore, interferes with the analysis of the problem situation. In contrast, a reflective student would consider the situation more carefully before acting (Haskins & McKinney, 1976).

For purposes of assessment, a teacher should try to determine if the student generates many imaginative solutions or just a single solution, combines two or more solutions, searches for relationships and principles underlying a problem rather than relying on trial and error, or generalizes experiences and previously learned principles to new situations.

Guidelines for remediation for helping learning disabled students improve their performance in formulating alternative solutions include:

(1) Provide the student with as many experiences as possible in the problem area. The more experiences a child has, the greater the likelihood that he or she will be able to apply these experiences to new problems (Bruner, 1973).

(2) Teach cause-effect relationships. Students who are older and have acquired knowledge about cause-effect relationships begin to generalize from one situation to another and develop a more systematic, hypothesis-oriented approach to problem solving (Ausubel, 1958).

(3) Give the student the time and opportunity to try to solve the problem. There are occasions when a student suddenly seems to discover the solution to a problem. This unexpected emergence of a solution has been called *insight* (Kohler, 1925). Insightful solutions generally follow a period of random search and manipulation. The student may be vaguely aware of the parameters of the problem and the logical operations involved. When insight comes, what usually happens is that the student discovers a system of relationships that underlie the problem.

(4) Provide training and practice to teach learning disabled students to go beyond the information given and form generalizations, principles, or rules from the similarities and differences noted during their analysis of the problem situation (Bruner, 1973).

(5) Provide students with a systematic approach for applying experiences, concepts, principles, and rules to different kinds of problem situations and for generating alternative solutions (Alley & Deshler, 1979).

(6) Teach learning disabled students to use the brainstorm technique for formulating surprising and imaginative ideas (Davis, 1973). Brainstorming is a form of "forced" creativity used to prod imagination. The goal of brainstorming is to produce as many ideas as possible. Osburn (1963) lists four ground rules for using the brainstorm process.

- *First,* all criticism is ruled out. All ideas are listed without judgment or negative comments. Even criticism of one's own ideas can interfere with flexible, freewheeling thinking. Judgment of ideas must be deferred.
- *Second,* freewheeling ideas are welcomed. Students should be urged to view ideas from novel perspectives and try to think of unusual solutions.
- *Third,* quantity is wanted. The larger the number of ideas listed, the greater the probability of generating potentially valuable ideas or combinations of ideas.
- *Fourth,* combination and improvement of ideas is sought. An effort is made to modify ideas or to join two or more previously unrelated ideas together (Ausubel, 1958).

Brainstorming techniques often used with gifted students can be taught individually or in a group to learning disabled students. The activity is fun because of the humor which accompanies creative and unique ideas (Davis, 1973; Patton & Griffen, 1973).

(7) A list of questions can also stimulate idea combinations (Osburn, 1963). For example, students could be given a question that could guide their thinking in generating creative ideas. What else is like this? How can I change it? What could be added or increased? What could be subtracted or decreased? What could be used instead? How could things be rearranged? Can it be reversed? What can be combined? Can the form be changed?

(8) Teach learning disabled students to look for direct analogies or remote problem parallels from their experience that might be applied to the new problem (Gordon, 1961). For example, a boy from New York City taking a winter hike in the mountains was looking for a place to get warm. In the city he went into stores for warmth in the winter. In the summer he could go into air-conditioned stores to get away from the hot sidewalks and pavements. He remembered how the concrete sidewalks and pavements retained and radiated heat, so he began looking for a rock face with a southern exposure to the sun for warmth.

Testing alternative approaches

The fifth step in solving a problem is to test the alternative approaches that have been formulated (Fraenkel, 1973). Parrill-Burnstein (1981) found that learning disabled children tested hypotheses less frequently than normal children and that their responses were not always consistent with feedback. They did not retain or repeat the response when feedback was correct, eliminate or change their response when feedback was negative, or select a new hypothesis for testing after a previous hypothesis was tested.

A teacher may assess how children test hypotheses by observing how the child tests the effectiveness of the alternative solutions. This can be done by discovering if the child has criteria for evaluation, studying the child's persistence in finding a solution, and determining if the child's problem-solving behavior is motivated from without (extrinsic) or from within (intrinsic).

By observing a child attempting to solve a particular problem in the classroom or on the playground, it is often possible to identify which stage or stages of the model (figure 8.2) may be interfering with the child's problem-solving performance. This information can be used to provide focus and direction for remedial planning.

First, the child should be taught to select potentially promising solutions by comparing the attributes of the solutions with the attributes of the problem situation and judging the practicality of each potential solution. Children must learn to search for the reasons why a solution might work as well as for the reasons why it might not work.

Second, practice should be given in testing hypotheses or writing potential solutions to problems.

Third, the development and use of criteria should be emphasized for evaluating the effectiveness of potential solutions. Criteria can be applied to concrete physical problems, then applied to academic problems, and eventually to more abstract interpersonal problems.

Fourth, when a potential solution is not successful in resolving a particular problem, the child should be taught how to modify the "solution" in view of the results or to select another solution for study.

Fifth, reflection and persistence during the testing stage should be reinforced by the teacher. In time, the actual solving of the problem should provide sufficient reinforcement to maintain the desired problem-solving behavior.

Problem resolution

The sixth stage of the model in figure 8.2 deals with the solution or lack of solution to the problem. If resolved, the problem-solving behavior is no longer needed. If the alternative solution did not resolve the problem, the learning disabled student must persist and continue his or her problem-solving efforts. The student may select a second alternative solution for testing and decide to reanalyze the problem and begin the problem-solving process from stage two on. It is at this point where the learning disability teacher must interfere and assist the child in moving successfully through the remaining problem solving stages.

A life situation

Caroline, age 17, and her younger brother, Stan, age 14, were driving to school. The car passed over a bump and the engine faltered and then again began to run normally.

*Stage 1—
Recognizing a
problem exists*

Stan said, "What's wrong?" "Nothing," said Caroline. A few moments later the car bounced over a series of rough places and the engine sputtered and then stopped. Caroline steered the car to the edge of the road and parked. She tried to start the car again. Although the engine turned over, the car did not start. Caroline and Stan knew they had a problem.

Stage 2— *Deciding to* *solve the* *problem*	Stan said, "What are we going to do? We'll be late." "We've got to fix it," Caroline replied.
Stage 3— *Analyzing the* *problem*	Stan asked Caroline what she thought was wrong. "I'm not sure," said Caroline. "The starter works, but the engine doesn't start. We have half a tank of gas. The lights work so it isn't the battery. Maybe there is something stopping the gas from getting into the carburetor or maybe we have a loose wire somewhere."
Stage 4— *Formulating* *alternative* *approaches*	Stan wanted to call their father or walk to the nearest garage for help. Caroline, who had taken a course in car maintenance in high school, wanted to see if she could locate the problem and try to fix it. Stan was skeptical.
Stage 5— *Testing* *alternative* *approaches*	Caroline got out of the car, opened the hood, and looked at the engine. She found the battery cables were in place and the fan belt was tight. The gas hose did not have a hole in it, and Caroline could see no gas leaking to the pavement. She hoped it wasn't the fuel pump, because that would require a mechanic to fix it. A large wire from the distributor was fastened securely. However, Caroline found that a third wire between the ignition and the coil was broken. "I think I've found it," said Caroline. She peeled the covering of the wire back, wrapped it around the outlet on the coil, and tightened it. Caroline got into the car and turned the key.
Stage 6— *Problem* *resolved or* *not resolved*	The ignition worked, the car started, and Caroline and Stan drove to school. The problem had been resolved.
A classroom problem	Rick, a learning disabled boy, and Joe, his friend, were given 10 word problems in arithmetic to complete before the end of class. This kind of problem-solving situation calls upon children to apply skills that they have previously learned.
Stage 1— *Recognizing a* *problem exists*	Both boys realized they had a problem. All the problems had to be completed within 30 minutes.
Stage 2— *Deciding to* *solve the* *problem*	Joe quickly read the 10 word problems and knew that he would be able to complete the assignment easily. Rick, however, knew that he wasn't going to do very well. Arithmetic was hard for him and he believed he was really "dumb" with numbers. Nevertheless, Rick knew he should try to work the

problems and get as many right as he could. A grade of D was better than a grade of F.

Stage 3—
Analyzing the
problem

Joe and Rick both read the first problem and tried to determine if the problem required addition, subtraction, multiplication, division, or some combination of these operations.

Stage 4—
Formulating
alternative
approaches

Joe quickly decided what the correct operations should be and decided to work the word problem by translating the word problem into number algorithms. Although Rick knew how to add, subtract, multiply, and divide, he was unable to analyze the correct operations in the new context of the word problems. Rick considered peeking at Joe's paper, asking the teacher for help, or trying to work the problem using popsicle sticks and counting.

Stage 5—
Testing
alternative
approaches

Joe worked the problem as follows.

$$
\begin{array}{ll}
\quad 35 \text{ apples} & \quad 23 \text{ apples} \\
\underline{-12 \text{ apples}} & \underline{\times .10\text{ ¢}} \\
\quad 23 \text{ apples} & \$2.30
\end{array}
$$

Rick counted 35 sticks, removed 12, and counted the remainder, which was 23 sticks. He then wrote 23 in a column 10 times and added. His answer was $230. Rick forgot that the number 230 represented cents and not dollars. The system of counting was very inefficient and required a great deal of time.

Stage 6—
Problem
solved or not
resolved

In Joe's case the word problem was resolved correctly. Unfortunately, Rick did not resolve the problem correctly. The teacher sat down beside him and showed him how to analyze word problems into number algorithms. Because Rick could do mechanical arithmetic computation, he needed help in learning how to analyze word problems (stage 3).

Summary

- Thinking involves a large number of cognitive operations including judgment, comparison, calculation, inquiry, reasoning, evaluation, critical thinking, concept formation, problem solving, and decision making.

- Learning disabled children manifest behaviors of impulsiveness, overdependence upon the teacher, inability to concentrate, rigidity and inflexibility, missing the meanings, and so forth.

- It is difficult to define *thinking* since it cannot be observed except by observing the end product, such as logical verbal behavior. Only two major areas, concept formation and problem solving, are discussed in this chapter.

- A disability in concept formation is a problem which interferes with the process of identifying ideas from particular instances. Six kinds of concept formation problems were discussed: (1) attention to characteristics of things experienced; (2) recognizing similarities and differences; (3) identifying common factor(s); (4) determining criteria, principles, or rules for inclusion or exclusion in the category; (5) validating the concept; and (6) either retaining and integrating or modifying the concept.

- Problem solving refers to the activities a child uses in coping with a problem situation for which he has no previously learned response. A model describing the dynamic steps to problem solving was presented. It consists of six stages: (1) recognizing a problem exists; (2) deciding to solve the problem; (3) analyzing the problem; (4) formulating alternative approaches; (5) testing alternative approaches to the problem; and (6) either resolving the problem or continuing problem-solving behavior.

- Guidelines for assessing thinking disabilities in concept formation and problem solving were presented for teachers' use in the classroom. The first step is to select a specific task in which the student is having difficulty. The second step is to observe the child in the situation, study how the child attempts to cope with the problem, and identify where the points of breakdown might be occurring within the thinking process under study.

Thought
questions

1. Watson, a behavioral psychologist, once said thinking is subvocal behavior; that is why we talk to ourselves subvocally. Do you "think" we can think without words?

2. What kind of thinking processes occur when preschool children sort blocks into shapes, colors, or sizes or recognize that a hammer goes with a nail?

3. What school activities assist the child in recognizing similarities and differences?

4. How can a teacher move a child from a concrete level to an abstract level of classification?

5. Modern math uses a discovery method of teaching. Children are asked to formulate a rule or generalization on the basis of a series of experiences. Give an example.

6. Give an example of hypothesis testing.

7. What thinking process is necessary to answer the following analogy? "Father is a man; mother is a _____."

8. If someone is usually rude to you, what steps do you take to solve this problem in terms of the six stages in the text?

9. Billy, age 12, is unpopular with his classmates, yet he wants to be liked. How can he analyze the problem and arrive at alternative solutions?

10. There is an apple sale. Mother gave Betty a dollar and told her to go to the store and buy apples for 5¢ apiece. She has the problem of figuring out how many apples she can buy. Trace the stages she must go through to arrive at a solution.

9

Oral language disabilities

One of the most important skills children must master is communicating—to understand what others are saying and to express their ideas verbally. Oral language is an arbitrary code people use to represent ideas in words and sentences and to communicate with each other. It is through communication —verbal and nonverbal—that we represent objects, events, and relationships to each other.

How children acquire the language of their culture and the factors or conditions that interfere with language acquisition are questions that have puzzled researchers for many years. What we do know is that the development of language is partly correlated with cognitive development. Children who have problems in thinking systematically, who lack selective attention, or who have difficulty in remembering or discriminating may be delayed in acquiring the ability to understand language or to express their ideas verbally.

Theorists have postulated different explanations for the development of language. Lenneberg (1967) and Chomsky (1965) believe in the nativist position that language develops naturally, like walking. They believe that a child is born with the proclivity for language in the same way that he or she has the native capacity and inclination to learn to walk. They hold that the child is biologically predisposed to learn language and that as the child matures language will be acquired just as walking and running are acquired. It follows that difficulties and delays in learning language may result from some biological abnormality that interferes with the ability to learn to talk.

Behaviorists, such as Skinner (1957), allege that language is verbal behavior and as such is developed through environmental influences just as other behavior is. The child learns to talk by imitation and reinforcement. While the child is a very young infant, there is no understandable verbal behavior. But through babbling, imitation, and selective reinforcement, the child learns to understand and use language. Parents and siblings are the reinforcing agents who respond positively when the child utters sounds that resemble words.

Other authorities, as reported by Bloom and Lahey (1978), believe that language is developed through the complementary interaction of the child's cognitive capacities and environmental experiences. As children mature neurologically, they mature perceptually and cognitively and simultaneously develop language, internal language as well as spoken language. This approach does not deny the nativistic position that children have the innate capacity to learn language, nor does it deny the influence of reinforcement theory. But as Bloom and Lahey (1978) state,

Neither the position of biological or innate determinism, nor the position of environmental determinism could be entirely correct. Both factors come together in the child's interaction with the context, and the child matures as an active seeker after new information. (p. 284)

The purpose of this chapter is to present a brief overview of oral language development, the kinds of oral language disorders that can occur, methods for diagnosing these disorders, and approaches to remedial instruction.

Language development

One of the fascinating aspects of normal child development is how children learn to understand and use the language code of the culture to which they are exposed in their everyday experiences. This learning involves the response to sounds heard as well as the child's own vocalizations. Between the second and third months of life, infants usually begin to turn their heads to the source of voices, bells, rattles, and so forth, in order to localize the sounds they hear.

Learning the language code is facilitated by the normal development of speech, which begins with the birth cry and progresses through a series of developmental stages. These stages may vary somewhat from person to person but in normal development are basically similar. Most children go through five stages in speech development.

Stages of language development

The first stage is what Berry and Eisenson (1956) call *reflexive vocalization,* during which crying and expelling air reflexively from the lungs produces sounds as the air moves over the vocal folds. Later hunger, pain, heat, thirst, skin irritation, and external and internal pressure cause different muscle-pattern sets and result in different cries.

Babbling is the second stage of speech development. This appears at about 6 or 7 weeks of age as the infant gurgles and coos and produces a number and variety of sounds at random. Although there is no predetermined order of appearance of the various sounds during the babbling stage, vowel sounds are likely to be produced before consonants. Babbling is almost a reflexive activity in which the child is internally stimulated by the exploratory sensations of the lips, tongue, and palate. Hearing is not essential for babbling to appear, and congenitally deaf children do progress through the babbling stage. They later lose these vocalizations because they receive little feedback from hearing their own voices.

The third stage of development is *lalling,* or the repetition of sounds or sound combinations the child has heard or made (e.g., *ba-ba-ba*). The child is reinforced by hearing his or her own voice and by feeling the physical sensations of the oral activity. Self-imitation prepares the hearing child to imitate others. Deaf children may repeat some sounds or sound combinations, but this is due only to tactile and kinesthetic stimulation.

The fourth stage of speech development is *echolalia,* in which the child begins to imitate sounds others make. This appears at about 9 or 10 months of age. Although there may be little or no comprehension of the sounds, the child continues to develop a repertoire of sounds heard in the language environment.

The fifth stage, *true speech,* begins at about 12 to 18 months of age, when the child begins to intentionally use sound patterns and words and anticipates a response to what he or she is uttering. This is the beginning of true speech and the development of the language code representing objects, actions, events, relationships, and ideas. By the time children reach the age of 2 years, they have developed a substantial vocabulary and are expressing themselves in short sentences of two or three words. From then on language develops rapidly, so that by the age of 5 years, when children enter kindergarten, they have developed language that is essentially complete in form and structure and are able to use sentences with hypothetical and conditional clauses.

Linguistic contributions

Modern linguists have analyzed language into structural components that remedial specialists must understand to analyze the problems of the children with language disorders. These analytical components include phonology, morphology, syntax, semantics, and pragmatics.

Phonology refers to the study of phonemes, which form words. Phonemes are the smallest units of the sound patterns of a language, including the consonants and vowels with distinctive characteristics. The sounds of the consonants and vowels that make up words are the phonemes of a language. There are some phonemes that are present in certain languages but not in others. To develop a language, a child must learn not only the differences between sounds but also the rules that determine certain sequences of phonemes that form meaningful words. Authorities agree that children learn phonology from the words that they hear and from the words they say. They do not initially learn words by learning each phoneme separately and then putting them together to make words.

Morphology refers to the study of morphemes, the smallest units of language that have meaning. Morphemes may include one or more phonemes that convey meaning, as in prefixes, suffixes, tenses, and plurals. "Root" words are also morphemes. A child may not have heard *runned* but he can dash into the house and say, "Mama, Mama, Mary runned across the street." In this instance, using the morpheme *-ed,* the child is telling the mother that the action occurred in the past.

Syntax is that part of language that involves word order, inflections, and other morphological changes of words to express meaning and the relationship of words in a sentence. The meaning of a sentence is affected by how the words are strung together. Two sentences using the same words do not have the same meaning. "Father called John," for example, does not mean the same as "John called Father." In addition, the sequence of words that could mean the same is sometimes determined by use rather than by rule. Although "the small black box" is the traditional way of connecting these words, the same meaning could be conveyed with a different order, "the black small box."

Semantics refers to the meaning of utterances, words, and sentences that express ideas and events. Semantics is related to the thinking process, concept formation, and meaning to be conveyed. As the child develops, the number of concepts used increases and sentences and expressions become longer and more complex.

Pragmatics refers to the use of language in such a way as to affect the listener's beliefs, attitudes, and behavior (Lucas, 1980). It is the social aspect of language, the way language changes with the situation. Thus even young children may use different expressions when speaking with peers than when talking to the teacher in class.

The content, form, and use of language

Current concepts in the study of language lean heavily on the work of Lois Bloom and Margaret Lahey, who have tried to describe normal language development in order to understand language disorders in children. Bloom and Lahey (1978) describe language in terms of content, form, and use.

The *content* of language refers to the topics that are discussed (encoded), such as reference to a table, to an action like running, or to some relationship such as the hat on a head. Thus language content is meaning or semantics, i.e., a representation of what a child knows about the world of objects, events, and relationships.

The *form* of language refers to the units of sound and serves as a means of connecting sounds or signs with meaning by way of sentence structure, parts of speech, word endings, and other aspects of syntax. Phonology, morphology, and syntax all bear upon form.

The *use* or function of language is determined by the social and cognitive behavior of the speaker in difference contexts. Asking a question is linguistically different from telling a story or making a command. The goals of the speaker and the context of the situation determine the use to which language is put.

Using content, form, and use as the components of language gives us a schema for describing the children's utterances, but it must be remembered that it is the integration of these three components that determines language competence or knowledge of linguistic rules. Children learn these rules by induction as they integrate content, form, and use in the language they hear. During the process of communication, children learn about language. Language is defined by Bloom and Lahey as "knowledge of a code for representing ideas about the world through a conventional system of arbitrary signals for communication" (p. 23).

Disabilities in oral language

Difficulties in language development in children are found in problems in phonology, morphology, syntax, semantics, and pragmatics, as well as in content, form, and use. Language disorders also may be classified as disorders of (1) receptive oral language, (2) integrative or inner language, (3) expressive oral language, and (4) all three (receptive, integrative, and expressive). These traditional categories of language disorders are the disorders found in adult aphasia associated with brain injuries (as reported in chapter 2).

Receptive language disabilities

Children with receptive language disorders can hear the speech of others but do not understand or comprehend the meaning of what is said. This condition has been referred to as *receptive aphasia, sensory aphasia, word deafness,* and *auditory verbal agnosia* (Goldstein, 1948; McGinnis, 1963; Myklebust, 1954; Orton, 1937; Schuell, 1953). The major characteristic of a receptive oral language disability is inability to receive and interpret spoken language. The major symptoms are failure to associate the spoken word with objects, actions, qualities, feelings, experiences, or ideas. Because the child does not comprehend what is heard, he or she has little or no meaningful language available for expression. These children may exhibit a wide range of symptoms depending on the severity of the disability. They may be inattentive to sound, fail to discriminate between words or groups of words, lack consistency in responding to spoken language, have difficulty in following instructions or commands, have difficulty learning the meaning of certain parts of speech such as prepositions and adjectives, and have difficulty learning multiple meanings for the same word.

A child of 5 was brought to a speech clinic because he was not talking. Earlier his parents had believed that he did not respond to oral speech because he was deaf. However, an examination by an audiologist had indicated that he could hear. His problem was the inability to understand language, to receive it, and to derive meaning from what he heard. He responded to gestures and motor commands and tended to respond motorically. "Come here" obtained no response, but a motion of the hand beckoning him to come obtained an immediate response. He had developed a motor communication system because he was unable to receive and interpret oral language. Because he was unable to understand language, he did not learn to talk. A psychological examination on a nonverbal performance test showed his intelligence to be average. He was a child with a receptive oral language disability.

Integrative language disabilities

Language development involves two types of integrative language behavior. The first type has been called *inner language* (Myklebust, 1954), *inner speech* (Vygotsky, 1962), *central language* (Richardson, 1968), and *preoperational speech* (Piaget, 1959). These terms describe the beginning of language, when infants and children think without words. The first integrative language occurs when young children begin to organize and integrate their daily experiences in meaningful ways. Inner language may be deduced when children begin to use objects appropriately, group objects in meaningful ways, arrive at logical conclusions in their play or daily activities, and project themselves meaningfully into imaginary situations. All of these behaviors indicate that a child is behaving symbolically—without spoken words. These kinds of inner language behaviors represent visual-experiential associations.

The second type of integrative language involves words as symbols. After children learn the characteristic meaning of spoken words through receptive language stimulation, they begin to use language to communicate with themselves. This talking to oneself is of major importance in thinking, drawing meaningful relationships from what is heard, categorizing objects verbally, using similes and metaphors, organizing information, forming generalizations, and understanding analogies, puns, proverbs, parables, jokes, or absurdities (Kirk & Kirk, 1971).

The term *integrative language* disability refers to difficulty in behaving symbolically. It is characterized by an inability to understand associations, such as analogies like "Father is a man; Mother is a _____." An integrative language disability is one of the most pervasive kinds of language disorders. Children with auditory oral integrative disabilities understand language, but have difficulty in associating what they hear with related past experiences. When shown a glass and asked to name it, they will respond "glass." But when asked, "What do we do with a glass?" or "What happens if we drop it?" they are unable to respond. When asked to relate objects visually, such as showing them a shoe, sock, ball, and bat, and asking them "What goes with a shoe?" they will point to the sock. But if asked verbally "What goes with a shoe?" they seem unable to respond "sock." They have difficulty integrating what they hear with past experiences.

Many children identified as having oral language disorders appear to have as their greatest language deficit an integrative language disorder. This has been revealed by an experiment by Luick, Kirk, Agranowitz, and Busby (1982). They analyzed the language responses of 237 children assigned to classes for severe oral language disorders (aphasia) in California and found that 97% of them had major deficiencies in auditory association and the use of syntax. These 237 children had been declared eligible for enrollment in classes for oral language disorders by a multidisciplinary team (medical, psychological, and speech-language pathologists) according to the California code and were given the *Illinois Test of Psycholinguistic Abilities* (ITPA). The ITPA profile for the mean scaled scores for the 237 children is presented in figure 9.1. The 10 tests of the ITPA used for the profile consist of 5 tests using the visual-motor channel and 5 tests using the auditory-vocal channel. As shown in figure 9.1, the children's auditory reception is lower than visual

Figure 9.1
ITPA profile of 237 children in
classes for oral language disorders

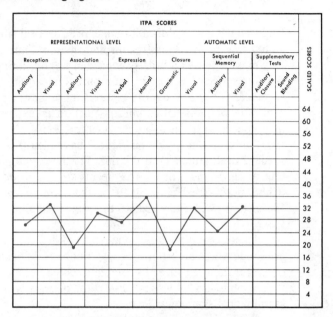

Source: A. Luick, S. Kirk, A. Agranowitz, and R. Busby, "Profiles of Children with Severe Oral Language Disorders," *Journal of Speech and Hearing Disorders,* 1982, *47,* 88-92. Reprinted with permission.

reception, and auditory association, the lowest test score, is significantly lower than visual association. Similarly, verbal expression is lower than motor expression; and grammatic closure, the lowest, is lower than visual closure. Thus auditory association (an integrative function), which is tested with an analogies test (a dog has hair; a fish has _____), is the most deficient; while grammatic closure (another integrative test), tested by orally presented items requiring grammatic closure (here is a dog; here are two _____; this dog likes to bark; here he is _____), is also deficient. The profile shows that the auditory receptive function as tested is slightly lower than visual reception and that verbal expression is slightly lower than motor expression. The two auditory integrative tests are markedly lower than the two visual integrative tests. The authors concluded that children assigned to classes for oral language disorders in California show their greatest deficiency in the association or integrative process. Because 97% of the children showed major deficiencies in the integrative process, the authors concluded that the remedial emphasis on listening (receptive) processes and expressive processes is not sufficient. Major attention should be given to "practice in recognizing and thinking about such concepts as opposites, cause and effect, time and space relationships, number and space, part to whole, tool and user, and product, sequential order, etc." (Luick et al., 1982, p. 92).

Expressive language disabilities

Children who have a disability in expressive oral language are deficient in the ability to express themselves through speech. During their early development they may be mute and rarely engage in jargon, imitative speech, or echolalia. A common symptom is the intermittent capability to use words, phrases, or sentences. They can identify pictures on request. Emotionally, they often appear quiet and amenable, but may lack facial expression. In some cases, they may appear to be lethargic (Myklebust, 1954).

Johnson and Myklebust (1967) have identified two distinct types of expressive oral language disabilities. The first type presents difficulty in selecting or retrieving words. This seems to be a problem in *auditory memory* (Chalfant & Scheffelin, 1969) or *reauditorization* (Johnson & Myklebust, 1967). Retrieving the words to be spoken is an important part of the expressive process.

The second type shows symptoms of defective syntax. These children can use single words and short phrases, but have difficulty organizing their words or expressing their ideas in complete sentences. Their speech is characterized by the omission of words, distortion of words, incorrect verb tenses, and grammatical syntactical errors.

Billy, who was 7 years old, was referred for diagnosis because of his difficulty expressing himself in school. The results of the *Wechsler Intelligence Scale for Children* (WISC) yielded a score within the normal range. A discrepancy of 12 points existed between Billy's verbal score of 86 and his performance score of 98.

Talking with Billy concerning his experiences at his recent birthday party and listening to him tell about pictures or about a story read to him revealed that he spoke with telegraphic speech, using one to three words at a time (e.g., "me want," "put cake over"). His sentences were primitive, and he had not developed fluent use of syntax. In contrast to his difficulty expressing himself orally, he had no problems understanding what he heard. The results of the assessment revealed a 7-year-old boy within the normal intellectual range whose receptive understanding of speech was at age level. In contrast, his use of expressive language was limited to single words or two- to three-word sentences typical of 3-year-old children. There seemed to be a 4-year discrepancy between his adequate receptive language and his low expressive language. The fact that Billy understood what he heard made it possible to focus remediation on acquiring verbal fluency by increasing vocabulary and on developing his ability to retrieve and use words more adequately.

Mixed receptive, integrative, and expressive disabilities

The most common type of oral language disability is the mixed receptive-integrative-expressive disability. The child shows symptoms of all three disabilities to varying degrees. These children are characterized by deficiencies in understanding what is said to them, integrating and manipulating symbols, and expressing themselves orally. Differentiation between receptive, integrative, and expressive disabilities is complicated even further because of the cause-effect relationships between these functions.

If a child has a problem in reception, he or she will necessarily be handicapped in integration and expression. But a child can have normal receptive abilities but be defective in semantic or integrative capabilities. In these cases, expression is also affected.

Figure 9.1 shows that, though the children assigned to classes for severe oral language handicaps had as their major deficiency an integrative (central) disorder, they also were deficient in receptive and expressive language. Their total auditory, integrative, and expressive functions were lower in all cases than their visual-receptive, visual-associative (integrative) and motor-expressive functions. These oral language disordered children could be considered children with mixed receptive, integrative, and expressive disabilities with a major disability in the integrative process.

The diagnosis of oral language disabilities

The development of oral language requires an intact peripheral sensory system, an intact central nervous system, adequate mental capabilities, emotional stability, and exposure to the language of the culture (Bloom & Lahey, 1978). A disorder in any one of these areas can result in an oral language disability. A comprehensive diagnosis in each of these areas would require the services of a multidisciplinary team, consisting of a speech-language pathologist, a neurologist, a psychologist, a social worker, and a psychiatrist. This section, however, will present guidelines that teachers may use during the initial language assessment of children who present symptoms of oral language disability.

First, it is important to determine whether a discrepancy exists between potential and language achievement. To determine this discrepancy, a psychoeducational examiner tests the child on verbal tests as well as on performance or nonverbal tests. A teacher, however, can estimate a child's potential by observing how the child handles nonverbal tasks like other children of the same age. How does the child solve social problems? Is the child's play in games like that of other children of the same age? Can the child solve visual puzzles like other children of the same age? If the child appears to have nonverbal abilities like those of other children but has marked problems in listening or speaking, the child can be considered to have a significant discrepancy between nonverbal behavior and verbal behavior.

The group of children in figure 9.1 illustrates this discrepancy. The children were relatively normal on visual- and motor-expressive tests, but significantly deficient in auditory verbal tests. They represented a group of children assigned to classes for oral language disorders. Children assigned to classes for the mentally retarded tend to be low in both nonverbal and verbal behavior. They do not represent a disparity between potential and achievement.

The second stage is to determine or describe the areas of language disability. Does the child have a receptive disability, an integrative disability, an expressive disability, or all three? These can be examined with formal tests, but teachers can make initial evaluations and observations for children with severe oral language disorders.

A common procedure for informally testing a child's language is to place before the child four familiar objects, such as a ball, a comb, a pencil, and a piece of paper.

(1) If the child is unable to name the objects when asked, you can conclude that the child may have an *expressive disability*. There are cases in which children may not be able to express themselves, but are able to understand what is said to them. These children have developed receptive language but have a disability in expressive language.

(2) If the child is unable to point to the ball, comb, pencil, or piece of paper when asked, you can conclude that there is a *receptive disability*. Children who have difficulty understanding language usually have accompanying problems in expressing themselves as well as problems in integrating oral language.

(3) As indicated earlier, *integrative disabilities* occur at the nonverbal level as well as the verbal level. Children can have receptive language and expressive language and also have an integrative disability, as illustrated in figure 9.1. In these instances children show a disorder in integration by having difficulty understanding verbal relationships, analogies, puns, jokes, generalizations, and so forth.

(4) In some cases, these procedures may reveal that a child has oral language disorders in all three areas—expressive, integrative, and receptive language.

These informal procedures may not be necessary if the teacher has had experience with the child and knows what he or she can and cannot do. For minor language problems the teacher can ask such questions as:

- Does the child attend and listen in class? (reception)
- How well does the child follow simple directions? Complex directions? (reception)

• How well does the child express his or her ideas as compared to classmates? (expressive)

• Does the child have problems in syntax or have difficulty in sequencing and word order? (integrative)

• Has the child developed concepts in harmony with his or her age? (integrative)

In addition to determining levels and discrepancies between reception, integration, and expression, the teacher can observe the child's problems in the use of phonemes, morphemes, syntax, and semantics. Content, form, and use can also be observed. With this in mind, a teacher can tell the child a story, discussing it with the child and observing the child's problems in understanding and expressing language. This will be discussed further under remediation.

The third stage is to assess physical, environmental, or psychological correlates. To assess physical and developmental learning disabilities (correlates) that may be associated with delay or disorder in language, the teacher should follow these guidelines.

(1) *Determine if a hearing loss exists.* Because the sense of hearing is the primary channel for learning to understand spoken language, any disorder in the auditory processing of sound stimuli can interfere with the normal development of spoken language. A teacher may informally evaluate hearing by noting when the child misunderstands directions or lessons. By standing the child with his or her back turned to the teacher at a distance of 20 feet and whispering words or numbers, the teacher can note whether the child might have a hearing loss and needs professional evaluation.

(2) *Determine whether the child is attending to sound.* Children who hear but do not attend to speech sounds, words, phrases, and sentences will experience difficulty and delay in establishing an auditory language system. Attention to sound is a prerequisite behavior for learning to understand what others are saying and for using speech for self-expression. Failure to attend to sound could be the result of hearing impairment, emotional problems, or organic disorders in the temporal lobe of the left cerebral hemisphere.

(3) *Determine if the child has difficulties in auditory discrimination.* To understand the oral language code, children must distinguish between different sounds, words, phrases, and sentences. If children are unable to hear the differences or similarities in initial, medial, or final sounds of words, consonant blends, or vowels, they will have difficulty acquiring receptive spoken language as well as expressive language.

Sound discrimination may be assessed by presenting pairs of sounds and asking the child whether they are "the same" or "different." The child can respond by nodding yes or no, saying "yes" or "no," saying "same" or "different," or repeating sound sequences. The child should first be asked to repeat isolated sounds such as /s/, then dissimilar sounds, such as /m/ and /k/, and finally sounds which are similar, such as /t/ and /k/.

(4) *Determine whether or not the child has an auditory memory deficit.* Many children with oral language disorders are deficient in auditory memory. These children have difficulty in recalling or repeating sequences of auditory information in serial order (Masland & Case, 1968; Menyuk, 1964; Stark, Poppen, & May, 1967). The ability to imitate and comprehend sentences varies directly with the length of digit span recall (Graham, 1968). The memory span of these children is typically short, often consisting of only three or four words. These children usually have trouble following a series of commands, reciting poems, counting, learning the names of new words, sequencing, and repeating what they hear (de Hirsch, 1967; Stark et al., 1967). Disorders in auditory memory also cause problems in developing a grammatical language structure and appropriate sentence patterns. Testing for auditory memory includes the repetition of digits, words, phrases, and sentences.

(5) *Determine if the child can form word-object associations.* Children learn the language code by establishing associations or correspondences between spoken words or sound units and objects, actions, experiences, and ideas. The child establishes a representational equivalent between the spoken word and whatever it represents. The word comes to represent the original stimulus, and the child will react to the word as if the word itself were the original stimulus and not just a symbol (Ausubel, 1963). The sensory integration between that which is heard and that which is experienced is basic to learning meaningful receptive language and then using it for self-expression. Teachers can observe this process of learning or test the child by presenting unfamiliar objects and verbal labels to determine if the child can learn these associations.

(6) *Determine if the child is having difficulties in thinking (problem solving, concept formation, and association).* When children begin to establish correspondence between words and the things around them and begin to develop classes of objects and events, they must test their hypothesis of what a word means in different situations. For example, the word *water* can refer to the ocean, rain, water in a glass, water lying on the ground in a puddle, and so forth. Similarly, in developing concepts, children must apply a criterion for membership to objects before they can be placed in a particular class. For example, a boat may be classified as a means of transportation, because it carries people from one place to another, as do horses, airplanes, and automobiles. In learning correct grammatical constructions, children must experiment to learn which word form is appropriate (e.g., "I losted my mitten"). To evaluate concept formation, association, and problem solving, the teacher creates situations to test whether the child (a) is aware of differences in the use of words, class membership, or grammatical constructions; (b) is concerned about appropriate meanings and use; (c) is able to generate hypotheses about what is or is not correct; and (d) can test these hypotheses.

The fourth stage is to establish a diagnostic hypothesis. To do this it is necessary to analyze the symptoms of inadequate speech and the contributing factors. Mary was found to have fair receptive ability and fair association ability, but her expressive abilities were deficient. Mary either did not talk or talked very inadequately. The analysis of the contributing factors showed that Mary had very poor auditory memory and inadequate selective attention. The diagnostic hypothesis was that Mary did not learn to talk because she had inadequate auditory memory and could not imitate speech. This condition was complicated by distractibility and lack of selective attention.

A child with a profile similar to the group profile in figure 9.1 has an oral language disorder or lags in language development. The contributing factors in these cases of oral language disorders are thinking disorders. Poor concept formation, inadequate integrative abilities, and poor problem solving contribute to the retardation of the child's general language development.

The last stage in the diagnostic process is to organize a remedial program. Remedial systems have been developed to ameliorate deficits or delays in language as well as the developmental learning disabilities that may have contributed to those delays. These remedial or intervention methods must be directed toward the deficits found in the diagnosis. General remedial suggestions are discussed in the next section.

Principles for remediating oral language disabilities

There are many approaches to teaching children who have problems understanding or using oral language. Most of these instructional programs, however, might be described as "developmental" programs in that the content taught follows the normal developmental hierarchy of language skills (Bloom & Lahey, 1978; Lee & Rubin, 1979; Wiig & Semel, 1980). Language instruction programs are based on seven major principles.

(1) The content to be taught is established by assessing the child's oral language performance or utterances.

(2) Instructional objectives are based on the developmental hierarchy of language skills.

(3) Children should be taught to understand or comprehend the meaning of words, phrases, or sentences (semantics).

(4) Children should be taught to acquire the grammatical code (syntax).

(5) Children should be taught to produce appropriate speech sounds (phonology).

(6) Children should be taught to cluster sounds into meaningful units or words, word items, prefixes, and suffixes (morphology).

(7) Children should be provided with experiences that will allow them to interact with the environment and use the language code both receptively and expressively (pragmatics).

Remedial programs that have been developed for oral language problems also include these seven instructional principles. Remedial programs for learning disabled children, however, include two additional principles.

(8) A child's specific learning abilities and disabilities should be considered in selecting the most effective method(s) to teach the child.
(9) Improvement in specific cognitive abilities should be part of the instructional program and should take place *during* the language training (task-process training).

In summary, remedial programs for children with specific learning disabilities must go beyond the usual developmental approach to oral language problems and consider the impact of the developmental learning disabilities on learning oral language. The teacher should attempt to remediate the developmental learning disability *during* the language training period.

General remedial approaches

Receptive oral language instruction

The major goal of receptive oral language instruction is to teach the child to respond appropriately to what he or she hears. This requires the child to associate the meanings of spoken words with objects, actions, qualities, feelings, and ideas. As the child develops a receptive oral language vocabulary, he or she should be taught to understand more complex phrases, sentences, and directions. Later, the child can be taught to respond to more complex grammatical structures. As a child becomes more familiar with the fundamental grammatical structures, the speed and accuracy of processing verbal information increases through variation and repetition. The child's attention can then be directed toward the content of the vocal message. In time, decoding receptive language becomes more automatic.

Integrative oral language instruction

One of the most important remedial objectives is to develop integrative or symbolic language in children. This can be done by placing the child in a play situation or providing experiences where the child must interact with the world around him or her. Children must be taught to attend; discriminate; remember what they see, hear, and do; organize and classify objects; and discern the relationship of one object or action to another. At this preverbal stage of training, modelling and imitation can be used to teach integrative skills. Children need experiences and play at a concrete level in order to begin drawing relationships and ordering the world around them. The materials and procedures described in the section on remedial systems elaborate on methods for developing thinking skills, association, grammatic closure, concept formation, and problem solving.

Expressive oral language instruction

In all language activities, whether receptive or integrative, the child should be encouraged to express his or her ideas verbally. Many children with severe oral language disabilities rely on manual gestures to express their ideas. Manual responses can be used and extended to develop vocal responses. The most effective association is by *doing* and *saying* at the same time. Instruction in listening and integration should always be accompanied by attempts at vocal response, even though the response is only an approximation. In all cases, appropriate responses should be immediately reinforced.

Remedial systems for oral language disorders

A number of remedial language systems have been developed for use with children who have oral language disorders. Remedial programs are based upon developmental approaches to language instruction (Swisher & Matkin, 1983), on the application of behavior modification principles (Gray & Ryan, 1973), or on cognitive information-processing models (Dunn, Smith et al., 1967, 1982; Johnson & Myklebust, 1967; McGinnis, 1963; Minskoff, Wiseman, & Minskoff, 1975). The developers of remedial language systems had worked in the areas of speech pathology, deaf education, aphasia, mental retardation, and early childhood education. Some of these systems are described briefly.

Swisher-Matkin system: A developmental approach

This approach facilitates language acquisition in both group and individual settings (Swisher & Matkin, 1983). It is currently used with children who have the following characteristics: (1) 2½ to 5 years of age; (2) normal hearing; (3) nonverbal intelligence within one standard deviation of chronological age; and (4) expressive and/or receptive language skills at least one standard deviation below that expected for the child's nonverbal intelligence level.

Language assessment

The language objectives are individually determined by assessing each child's oral language performance. Samples of spontaneous language are recorded in three different contexts: with parent or guardian, with a younger child, and with the clinician. These utterances are analyzed according to a procedure adapted from Bloom and Lahey (1978), which includes an evaluation of the semantics, syntax, and pragmatics of each utterance.

*Language
objectives*

Language objectives are sequenced according to the normal developmental hierarchy of expressive language skills. When the number of utterances in a given category exceeds four and the inclusion of all expected words in an utterance approximates 90%, that category is not considered for language objectives. Language objectives are selected from three or four of the categories at the lowest developmental level which do not meet the preceding criteria. Each language objective specifies the words to be spoken by the child; the words to be spoken by the clinician; the meaning of the words, e.g., rejection for "no" or denial for "no"; and the function of the child's utterance, e.g., to respond to a question or to self-initiate.

*Instructional
method*

The speech-language pathologist's role is to maintain the child at a level of 80% correct over a set of 20 communication exchanges pertinent to one language objective and to simulate normal child-adult language interaction. The child is encouraged to both respond to and initiate expressive language. Initiation is encouraged through the use of a communication partner who assumes the role of the child in the communication exchange when that aid is considered useful. It is considered critical that the child has something of interest to talk about and someone with whom to communicate who not only encourages language expression but also "scaffolds" the child to the next higher developmental level.

**The
Monterey
method: A
behavior
modifica-
tion system**

In this system, operant conditioning has been used with programmed materials for teaching language to nonverbal children (Gray & Ryan, 1973). The Monterey system teaches basic grammatical forms step-by-step. There are six variables for helping the child proceed through the extensive sequence of tasks for each grammatical form taught: (1) the stimulus provided, (2) the response required from the child, (3) the kinds of reinforcement given, (4) the reinforcement schedule, (5) the criteria for proceeding to each next step, and (6) the model that lets the child know what response is expected. The sequence of tasks begins with pictures, followed by stories, and finally conversation without pictures. The assumption made in this system is that the child will learn new grammatical forms and rules through his or her own experiences after he or she has developed a minilanguage of the forms that are taught.

The Monterey system is highly structured and formalized. The methods of presentation are standardized and allow for no variations. The token reinforcement schedule is gradually eliminated, but social reinforcement is always provided for appropriate responses. The child repeatedly hears and uses the critical grammatical forms because of the formal structure of the system. The vocabulary is determined for each child by the teacher, who must acquire story content and picture content that reflect the vocabulary.

This system is individualized. The point of entry to the program is determined by the child's performance on a criterion-referenced test. This program seems to be useful with children of age 15 months and over who have expressive oral language problems in form and syntax. It does not deal with semantics or the selective use of language.

The Monterey system has several advantages. It minimizes preparation time and provides an ordered developmental sequence, with a good procedure for point of entry into the program. It can be used by groups and can be administered by paraprofessionals. A weakness of this system is the lack of stress on meaningful language and the training of integrative or symbolic language.

The Johnson-Myklebust system

Johnson and Myklebust (1967) developed remedial methods for children with language disorders related to psychoneurological learning disabilities. Their approach is directed toward both receptive and expressive language. The methods grew out of Myklebust's earlier work with deaf and aphasic children.

When a child has a generalized deficiency in auditory learning, the remedial effort should be directed toward receptive language, i.e., to improve input and comprehension. This can be accomplished by training the child to be aware of and listen to sounds and words and respond to auditory stimulation and sound sequences.

In facilitating expressive language disorders, remedial efforts may be directed toward any one of three types of disorders: reauditorization, auditory-motor integration, and syntax.

Reauditorization is the ability to recall, to hear again internally, what has been heard—words, sounds, and melody. Exercises and games are prescribed to facilitate the recall of words. Sentence completion, pictures, experiences, naming objects, and visual, kinesthetic, and tactile cues are used to develop inner language, categorization, and associations.

Disorders in auditory-motor integration are characterized by difficulty imitating words even though the words are understood. This is apraxia (the inability to perform movements voluntarily). Johnson and Myklebust use the articulatory movements, phonemes, and words the child can produce as a basis for teaching new words. Visual clues such as watching the lips and touching or guiding the tongue and lips are used to develop speech.

Deficiencies in syntax or structure of language are remediated through meaningful experiences, play activities, and pictures. The child is taught simple noun-verb associations followed by increasingly more complex grammatic structures.

The McGinnis association method

McGinnis (1963) developed an association method for remediating children with aphasia at the Central Institute for the Deaf in St. Louis. McGinnis observed that aphasic children with relatively normal hearing and intelligence had delayed language and speech development similar to that of deaf children.

The first stage of the McGinnis method develops both auditory reception and verbal expression by teaching sounds, synthesizing sounds into words, and matching words with pictures for meaning. The second stage in the instructional hierarchy is to use phrases and sentences that have verbs and prepositions. The third stage develops more complex language.

Programs partly based on the ITPA model

The *Illinois Test of Psycholinguistic Abilities* (ITPA) has 12 subtests that attempt to assess both visual and auditory receptive, integrative, and expressive functions as well as visual and auditory sequential memory and visual and auditory closure. On the basis of the information-processing model from which the tests were generated, there has evolved a series of remedial methods. Karnes (1975) has explained the ITPA communication model as follows.

> A much oversimplified description of the ITPA model might go like this. Pretend that a person is a computer. A computer is a machine which receives information (INPUT) which may be stored (MEMORY) for later use or processed in some way (ORGANIZATION). Ultimately, the product of processing is expressed in some way, such as a tape or paper print-out (OUTPUT). People, to continue the analogy, receive information through their senses (RECEPTION). Sometimes this information is merely stored or remembered (MEMORY), but at other times partial information may be in some way completed for better understanding (CLOSURE) or several bits of information may be organized into a new and different whole (ASSOCIATION). Finally, expression is either verbal or gestural or both (VERBAL or MANUAL EXPRESSION). (p.2)

The Karnes programmed materials for developing language in young children

These materials are an outgrowth of Karnes' research on preschool mentally retarded and disadvantaged children at the University of Illinois over a period of 20 years. The research has been reported by Karnes, Zehrbach, and Teska (1974), who showed the efficacy of these programs through a follow-up to the third grade.

Karnes developed a series of kits that attempt to develop the functions in the model of the ITPA, including auditory reception, auditory association or integration, and verbal expression. The activities in the kits are varied and adapted to children of various ages. For example, the *Karnes Early Language Activities* (1975) were developed and tried with parents and teachers of children aged 18 months to 3 years. This program of graduated lessons in auditory reception, visual reception, etc., is used by parents when playing with their children, as well as by teachers of children of that age level. The kit *Learning Language at Home* (Karnes, 1977) was designed for parents for use with their children ages 18 months to 5 years. A more advanced series of materials has also been published under the title *GOAL: Language Development* (Karnes, 1972). These materials are for children aged 3 to 6, and children 6 years old and older.

The Peabody Language Development Kits	Developed by Dunn, Smith, and their colleagues (1967), these kits were initiated as a result of a doctoral dissertation by James Smith (1962), who designed language lessons for mentally retarded children and found that there was temporary improvement following a series of such lessons. The *Peabody* kits were the first instructional materials developed following the original clinical model of the ITPA. Since then the kits have been revised and enlarged by American Guidance Service (Dunn, Smith, et al., 1982). They are designed for children between the ages of 2 and 8. Emphasis in the lessons is on oral language. They are designed to develop the psycholinguistic processes of reception, association, and expression. Using pictures, tapes, puppets, and other instructional aids, the kits include a variety of exercises, games, and lessons. The directions for the teacher are explicit. Through these directions the teacher can follow a systematic approach to the development of oral language.
The MWM program for developing language abilities	The Minskoff, Wiseman, and Minskoff (1975) program for developing language abilities is also based on the model of the ITPA. It includes two levels: Level I for ages 5 to 7 and Level II for ages 7 to 10. Each level contains tasks in auditory and visual reception, auditory and visual association, verbal and manual expression, auditory and visual memory, grammatic and visual closure, and auditory closure and sound blending. Special games and exercises are programmed and prepared for use in individual and group settings.

The program gives specific instructions for using materials as well as their theoretical background. For example, auditory reception is broken down into subareas such as receptive vocabulary, understanding inflectional patterns, understanding lengthy meaningful materials, auditory reception of speech sounds, and auditory word analysis skills. Each of these is explained in the manual. In short, the system explains *what to teach* and *how to teach*. In addition, a program for teaching 43 language skills has been developed by Esther Minskoff (1979) under the title *Teaching Essential Language Skills* (TELS). It is programmed to provide a systematic approach to instruction in vocabulary and syntax for preschool and primary-aged language handicapped children.

Remediation of oral language disabilities: A synthesis	Many books and articles have been written about the natural development of language in children and about the deviations and delays in language development which have been referred to as *language disorders*. Teachers who wish to remediate language disordered children are confronted with many alternative methods and solutions. It becomes the task of the remedial teacher to select the procedure that is most appropriate for a particular child. In so doing, the teacher must individualize instruction and invent a remedial procedure, or modify a method to fit the needs of a particular child.

The perspective toward remediation advocated in this book is to use knowledge of normal language development with the remedial procedures that have been developed for children with language disorders. It is not sufficient to teach the normal course of language development, since the children have experienced this approach and have failed to develop. It is not sufficient to focus totally on linguistic training. It is not sufficient to remediate specific language skills in isolation. Nor is it sufficient to expect a child with a language disorder to gradually "grow out of it" without adequate help. Remedial efforts need to encompass certain aspects of each of these areas in an integrated or systematic plan.

In planning a remedial program, it is important that language learning take place in a social setting that incorporates social awareness, linguistic functions, and thinking abilities. The language a person uses depends partly on the existing social situation.

The role of social perception as a component of a language disorder cannot be underestimated. Children who understand a minimum of oral language or who cannot express themselves accurately often develop social perception problems which, in turn, exaggerate the oral language problem (Wiig & Semel, 1980).

Language disabled children who fail to interpret affect and attitude through facial expressions, gestures, and touches may not acquire social rules for situations such as relating to others, winning or losing, or asserting oneself appropriately. Children who respond inappropriately in a social setting are rejected and ridiculed. The end result is either withdrawal, aggression, or hostile behavior. The child's perception of himself is diminished.

A child who feels socially inadequate probably will be reluctant to enter into oral communication situations. Since oral language communication occurs in a social setting, it is important that remedial plans consider the child's social behavior.

You should recall from chapter 1, figure 1.1, that the primary developmental abilities are attention, memory, and perception and that these primary abilities are prerequisites to the secondary ability of thinking, which in turn is a prerequisite to language development. We know that to learn language a child must have developed the ability to attend, to remember, to perceive, to develop concepts, and to solve problems. In children who have not developed language or who are delayed in developing language, it may be necessary to teach attention, memory, perception, concept formation, and problem solving in the process of understanding and expressing language. Remediation consists of an integrative method utilizing all functions in the process of teaching language.

Teaching integratively means that in remediation it is necessary to integrate reception of language with past experience and with expression. These are best developed in the context of experience. This is the task-process approach in contrast to teaching an isolated skill.

In one experiment, Soroky (1979) divided children with oral language disorders into three groups. She assigned one group to a self-contained class taught by a speech-language pathologist. The second group was placed in the regular grades but was assigned to a speech-language pathologist as a consultant to the regular teacher. The third group was assigned to the regular elementary grades without extra help. The group assigned to the self-contained class made the most progress. Children in the second group, which had only partial help but remained in the regular grades, made some progress but not as great as those assigned to the self-contained class, and the group assigned to the regular grades made the least progress. The explanation for these results could be that the self-contained class integrated the language instruction with reading, arithmetic, and other school subjects and consequently obtained better results.

Summary

- Oral language is an arbitrary code whereby ideas are represented through words and sentences and communicated from one person to another.

- Theories of language acquisition range from a nativistic viewpoint that children are born with the proclivity to learn the language of their culture to an environmental viewpoint to an interaction viewpoint that says that language is acquired through an interaction of the biological organism with the environment.

- The stages of language development include reflexive vocalization, babbling, lalling, echolalia, and true speech and language.

- To master oral language, children must learn to understand and use the meaning component of language (semantics), the synthesis of speech sounds (phonology), changes in words to make meaning (morphology), proper word order to carry meaning (syntax), a variety of forms of language in different situations (function and use—pragmatics), and content, form, and use.

- Language disorders are classified into receptive, integrative, expressive, and mixed oral language disorders.

- In assessing a child's oral language disability there are five major areas to consider: (1) discrepancy between language achievement and potential; (2) symptoms of inadequate language; (3) the physical, psychological, and environmental correlates of language disorders, (4) the diagnostic hypothesis; and (5) the remedial program.

- Remedial programs for oral language disabilities usually follow the developmental hierarchy of language skills. Remedial instruction is usually directed toward specific receptive, integrative, or expressive oral language disorders or combinations of those.

- Remedial systems for language disabilities have been developed by a large number of authors using linguistic, behavioral, and cognitive information-processing models. They use procedures from normal language development adapted to the special disability of the child.

1. Three areas were discussed with respect to language development: (a) stages of language development, (b) linguistic contributions, and (c) content, form, and use. How do the nativist and behaviorist theories relate to these three areas?

2. What is the cause-effect relationship between receptive, integrative, and expressive language disabilities? Which disabilities might occur in combination? In isolation?

3. What kinds of nonverbal tasks can a teacher use to informally assess the potential of a language disordered child?

4. Why is it important to determine which physical, environmental, or psychological correlates are contributing to a language disorder? How many reasons can you list?

5. How does knowledge of the contributing factors (correlates) to an oral language disability influence how you plan for or teach a child?

6. What are the strengths and weaknesses of individual remedial systems?

7. What criteria should be used in selecting which remedial system to use for a specific child with a language disability?

8. What is the relationship between thinking disorders and language disorders? Give two examples.

part 3
academic learning disabilities

10

Reading disabilities

Reading is the one subject that permeates the whole school program. Children usually begin reading in the first grade, if not sooner, and continue to depend on reading throughout their school careers.

Failure in learning to read is probably the most common problem found in learning disabled children. A study made by Kirk and Elkins (1975), which surveyed federal demonstration projects on learning disabilities, showed that 60 to 70% of the children in these programs were there because of a reading disability.

Kinds of reading instruction

We can describe reading instruction at three different levels: (1) developmental reading, (2) corrective reading, and (3) remedial reading.

(1) *Developmental reading* includes systems of teaching reading that provide a sequential development of reading skills as a group program. These systems usually expect children to learn at a specified pace. Most children are subjected to developmental reading programs of one kind or another, and most children learn to read under these developmental or traditional methods. For the majority of children, therefore, exposure to these reading activities allows them to develop sufficient reading skills.

(2) *Corrective reading* refers to the methods used to correct bad habits in reading or gaps in knowledge acquired during the course of a developmental reading program. A child may need help in word recognition skills, in understanding vocabulary, in phonics, in reading faster, or in other areas in the interpretation of the printed page. The instructional procedures used for corrective reading were referred to in chapter 4 as "task training," that is, the direct teaching or correction of errors in reading so that the child can progress at a relatively normal rate.

(3) *Remedial reading* refers to the procedures used with children whose reading skills are still not developed after exposure to developmental reading and to corrective reading. These children, sometimes called *dyslexic*, probably have a developmental learning disability (attention, memory, perception, thinking, or language disorder) that has interfered with normal progress in reading. They require remediation of the developmental learning disability in conjunction with the task of reading.

The large majority of children beginning in first grade (probably 85 to 90% of them) make progress in reading in the usual way under developmental reading programs. Of the 10 to 15% who have difficulties in progressing normally, most can be helped with corrective reading procedures using task training and direct teaching methods. Of this group, 1% or at the most 2% will have an intrinsic developmental learning disability that could interfere with progress in learning by developmental reading methods. These children require special training that would correct or ameliorate the developmental learning disability in conjunction with the training of reading itself. As indicated earlier, this procedure is called the *task-process training method.*

Developmental stages in learning to read

Learning to read follows the same developmental stages as growth in general does. We can identify three stages in the process of human development—(1) *mass action,* (2) *differentiation,* and (3) *integration.*

These three stages occur in biological development and in most learning situations. In trying to swim for the first time, for instance, you move about in a generalized fashion, making many random and unselective movements. In this first stage of learning, the whole body is acting as a unit (mass action). Later, in the second stage, you learn or are taught to differentiate certain muscles and select certain movements, perhaps developing each movement separately. You may practice proper breathing; you may practice kicking; you may practice arm movements or trunk movements. In this second stage of the learning process, you learn to distinguish one part of the activity from other parts (differentiation). But you must go on from there to the third stage. You will never become a good swimmer until you can coordinate these different movements into one smooth operation. The various parts must work together and become automatic. All parts of the activity must become coordinated into a smoothly operating total activity (integration). Let us examine these three stages as we find them in reading.

Stage 1— Mass action or reading wholes

The common experience method of teaching reading requires children to tell a story in their own words, such as:

We went to the zoo.
We saw an elephant.
It was big.

The teacher then writes the story on the board and asks the child to read it. In this case the child remembers the story and, looking at the words, sees only vague blocks and gaps between words. He or she has a generalized view of the whole and does not recognize words or letters. This is comparable to the mass action of the swimmer. As the child reads similar sentences and stories, he must identify configurations and words in the paragraph in order to distinguish one paragraph from another. The child cannot differentiate the zoo story above from the fire station story below until he or she can distinguish between the word *zoo* and the words *fire station.*

We went to the fire station.
We saw an engine.
It was red.

When the child begins to discriminate one paragraph from another by recognizing different words or letters, he or she is going into the second stage—differentiation, or learning details.

Stage 2— Learning details (differentiation)

To learn to read effectively, a child must go into a second stage of the reading process, differentiation or learning details of sentences and words. Many children learn to discriminate paragraphs or words without systematic instruction. They learn to differentiate *dog* from *beautiful* by the configuration, but may have difficulty differentiating *dog* from *boy* until they have learned the difference between *d* and *b* and between *g* and *y*. This discrimination can be made visually without learning the names or the sounds of letters. By learning to identify a few words or letter sounds, by using context clues, and by sometimes guessing, children can differentiate and progress normally. If, on the other hand, they have difficulty noting details, they may have trouble achieving in reading. Without help, these children do not progress to the third stage, reading without awareness of detail.

Stage 3— Reading without awareness of detail (integration)

The ultimate purpose of reading is to understand the thought units of the printed page without being aware of the letters and words. This is accomplished by a process known as *cue reduction,* similar to the process used in learning to drive a car or to swim automatically. The perception of words becomes automatic, and you read the printed page without being conscious or aware of the words and letters as you were during the stage of learning details.

A reading disability results when a child is blocked at one of the stages. If a child is unable to learn to remember thought units and is unable to repeat, mostly from memory, the story of the zoo or fire station, the child will not be able to move from Stage 1 to Stage 2. If the child begins to read a paragraph from memory and has difficulty differentiating words and letters, the child is stunted at the second or decoding stage of differentiation. This kind of child will need intensive instruction in decoding. If the child has learned to differentiate the letters or sounds but reads word by word and pays little attention to the meaning, that child needs instruction in integration. One child learned to decode words phonetically and was able to score at the seventh-grade level on several oral reading tests. But on tests of comprehension he was able to score only at the fourth-grade level. He needed remediation in integration, or comprehension of the printed page, and not in decoding.

The remedial methods reported later in this chapter are different, not because one is wrong and the other right, but because each may apply to a child who needs help in Stage 1, Stage 2, or Stage 3. One boy was able to memorize stories in a primer by looking at the pictures on the page and reading the short paragraph on that page, without knowing a word or a letter. The teacher could show the child the picture, cover the paragraph, and the child would "read" it. A phonic method was used to teach him to decode words. Later his reading was slow and laborious, word by word. The remedial method was then changed from Stage 2 (phonics) to Stage 3 (integration and comprehension). At this stage, use of phonics was discouraged and meaning was emphasized. Errors in reading were now disregarded to help the child integrate perceptual with cognitive functions. This case illustrates the need to move from Stage 1, reading wholes, to Stage 2, differentiation or decoding, to Stage 3, integration or reading without awareness of details.

The purpose and nature of assessment

All teachers use informal methods of diagnosing their students whether or not they call their procedures *evaluation, assessment,* or *diagnosis.* They observe the child's response to reading materials and determine at what grade level the child reads, how well or how poorly he or she reads at that grade level, and what errors the child makes in reading. The teacher observes the child's rate of reading, comprehension, and the manner in which he or she decodes words. Based on these observations the teacher adjusts the reading program accordingly.

In any elementary classroom, there is a wide range of reading abilities. In a typical fourth grade a teacher will find that approximately 70% of the children will be reading at the fourth-grade level. Some of the children will be reading at the fifth- and sixth-grade levels, and a few may be reading beyond the sixth-grade level. There also may be a few children reading at the first-grade or beginning second-grade level, and possibly one who cannot read at all. It is these children who will require a more systematic and thorough diagnosis.

There are two kinds of assessment procedures available: (1) a formal diagnosis that uses standardized tests to evaluate a child's potential for reading and reading achievement and (2) a systematic informal procedure that does not use standardized tests but instead examines a child's reading level and errors with the books, papers, and materials that are used in the class for instruction. Informal assessment is initially used by most teachers. When it fails to diagnose the problem, the teacher refers the child for formal testing and evaluation. This section will deal only with a systematic approach to informal assessment that can be used without formal tests.

There are many ways to evaluate reading behavior informally. These include teacher-made tests, observation of the student's behavior, diagnostic teaching, and other special methods. Questions have been raised about the validity of informal examination by teachers. In one report on the few studies that have been made, Farr (1969) stated that the informal assessments were often reliable and valid. There are several advantages of informal assessment over formal assessment. First, a larger and more varied sample of reading behavior can be taken. Second, the samples can be taken over a period of time, and a variety of samples can be used. Informal assessment requires less time and is less expensive. Finally, it can be used during an instructional period.

Informal methods of assessment use common procedures and materials. They help the teacher assess the student's performance in various learning situations. They also help the teacher note errors and style of learning, the student's interest, and the student's attitude toward reading.

Parameters of informal assessment

In making an informal assessment, the teacher first identifies a child in a classroom who is reading markedly below grade level. The teacher then observes the child's errors and style of reading. Third, the teacher tries to determine whether the child has the potential to learn to read at the appropriate grade level. Next the teacher determines the degree of disparity between the child's potential and level of reading. Then the teacher tries to identify factors contributing to the child's reading underachievement, and finally the teacher synthesizes the information acquired and plans a program of remediation.

An example of a second-grade teacher's approach to informal assessment is the case of Jason. After school began in September, Ms. Jones noted that Jason was not participating in the reading lesson and was not paying attention to his workbook assignment. When Ms. Jones found time, she asked Jason to come to her desk and read the first page in the second-grade basal text used in the class. He was unable to read the first page except to recall a few isolated words. Ms. Jones then selected a few words from the text and asked Jason to read them in isolation. Jason spelled the first letter of each word and then guessed at it erroneously. Ms. Jones noted that he had no systematic method of decoding. She asked herself, How did Jason finish the first grade and get placed in my second-grade class without learning to read? Does he have the potential to learn to read? Has Jason developed sufficient language to learn to read? What contributing factors inhibit his reading achievement? What can I do to teach him to read?

Ms. Spencer, a teacher of a fourth grade, noted that Jessica, age 10 years, was not reading her assignments and seemed to lag behind the class except in arithmetic, where she was doing average work. Ms. Spencer asked Jessica to read a fourth-grade level reader. Jessica was unable to read the book. Ms. Spencer then tried her on the third-grade book, then on a second-grade book, and finally on a first-grade reader. Jessica was able to read the first-grade book with some adequacy, but she stumbled over the words in the second-grade book. Ms. Spencer estimated Jessica's reading level at the beginning second-grade level. Ms. Spencer then presented words in isolation from each of these basal readers and found that Jessica had difficulty decoding words out of context. Ms. Spencer then wondered whether Jessica's language understanding was a contributing factor for her reading underachievement. She read passages from each of the basal readers to Jessica to test her listening comprehension. Jessica understood the passages in the fourth-grade book, and even in a fifth-grade basal reader. Ms. Spencer then asked questions including:

(1) What is this child's potential for reading?

(2) At what level does she understand these paragraphs when read to her?

(3) At what level does the child read words in isolation?

(4) At what level does the child recognize words in a group of words (word discrimination)?

(5) At what level does the child read silently with comprehension?

(6) What kinds of errors does the child make in paragraph reading and in word reading?

(7) What contributing factors have inhibited the child's progress in reading?

(8) What remedial method should I use to improve the child's reading behavior?

The following section will describe a systematic informal procedure that will attempt to answer questions (like those raised by Ms. Spencer) that can be asked by a teacher, an educational diagnostician, or a learning disability teacher.

Informally estimating reading potential

The sequence of procedures used to informally assess children with reading disabilities often varies from child to child. The entry point during assessment depends upon the kinds and amount of information the teacher already has. If the child seems to be functioning at a low intellectual level overall, the teacher should probably begin informal assessment by estimating reading potential. On the other hand, if the child seems to be functioning at a fairly high intellectual level, the teacher's initial entry point in assessment might be estimating reading level and describing reading behavior.

Recall that one of the diagnostic stages for learning disabilities (chapter 4) is the determination of a discrepancy between potential for reading and actual reading achievement. In an informal examination of a child, a teacher must estimate the child's potential for learning to read without using formal intelligence tests and other indices of potential. All teachers observe the behavior of their students and form impressions of the general level of intelligence. If Ms. Spencer's Jessica performs well in arithmetic computation, in discussion groups, or in predicting the outcome of stories; understands riddles; or has knowledge of many scientific facts, one would suspect a high potential ability in general. If, on the other hand, Jessica is generally unresponsive and slow to understand directions and is doing poorly in other school subjects, especially arithmetic, then poor reading ability would not be surprising. Some of the most pertinent factors to consider in estimating potential for reading include (1) chronological age, (2) listening comprehension, (3) arithmetic computation achievement, and (4) mental maturity.

**Chrono-
logical age**

Initially, we estimate at what grade level the child should be reading based on chronological age. A rough estimate of grade expectancy according to chronological age is the actual age minus 5.5. A child of 11½ years of age would be expected to read at the sixth-grade level (11.5 − 5.5 = 6.0), for example. Jessica, who was 10 years old, would be expected to read at the fourth-grade level (10.0 − 5.5. = 4.5). The child with a reading disability, however, is significantly retarded in reading below his or her chronological age reading-grade-expectancy.

**Listening
comprehen-
sion**

Reading skill depends upon facility in language. It is therefore necessary to estimate the child's grade level in listening comprehension. Although there are some published tests of language development, a teacher can estimate a child's level of listening comprehension fairly well by reading graded books aloud to him or her in order to find out the level at which the child understands what has been read. For example, for a 10-year-old child who is supposed to be in the fourth grade, a teacher may read from a graded series of books and ask the child questions about each passage read. It is advisable to read a book one grade below the child's chronological age expectancy, then another book at his CA level, and finally a book above the CA expectancy. Because Jessica was 10 years of age, Ms. Spencer read her paragraphs from fourth-, fifth-, and sixth-grade readers. Her language age was estimated to be at the fifth-grade level since she was able to understand the content of the fifth-grade book that was read to her.

**Arithmetic
computa-
tion**

Computation skill is another factor to observe. Some children with specific reading disabilities learn arithmetic computation more readily than reading. If they do not, the problem may be more complex than a reading disability. It could be the result of emotional disturbance, mental retardation, or a severe attention deficit, any of which may retard achievement in all school subjects. If the teacher has not given the child an arithmetic computation test, he or she may estimate the grade level of the child through the following interview procedures.

(1) Ask the child to give answers to practical questions requiring knowledge of number combinations between 1 and 10. If the child is able to answer questions in addition adequately, you can assume that his or her arithmetic computation skills are at least at the first-grade level.

(2) Give the child some oral questions involving subtraction of numbers between 1 and 10. If the child is able to subtract, it could be estimated that he or she is at the grade two level in arithmetic.

(3) Give the child some multiplication questions involving 2's, 3's, and possibly 4's. If the child is able to solve problems such as 2×3, 3×5, and 4×2, you can estimate that the child's arithmetic computation level is at about the third-grade level.

(4) Give the child simple division questions involving numbers between 1 and 10. If the child is able to do these, it could be estimated that he or she is at about the fourth-grade level in arithmetic computation.

(5) The teacher can proceed this way through fractions and decimals and can thus estimate from this informal interview the child's approximate arithmetic grade level.

Mental maturity

A fourth and important criterion for estimating potential is mental ability. Mental age is sometimes considered the best single criterion for predicting reading ability. A teacher can judge, within limits, the child's mental ability by asking information questions to determine how alert the child is. If a 10-year-old boy understands a sixth-grade book when it is read to him, or if a girl is able to compute arithmetic at near her age level, you can assume the child's mental maturity to be average. Listening comprehension and arithmetic computation plus general information expected from the child's chronological age are good indexes for judging mental age or mental maturity.

Putting it together

In Jessica's case, the teacher listed the following informal estimates of Jessica's potential for reading:

- Estimate of expectancy based on CA—fourth grade
- Estimate of expectancy based on listening comprehension—fifth grade
- Estimate of expectancy based on arithmetic computation—third grade
- Estimate of expectancy based on mental maturity—fourth grade.

Thus the potential as estimated is roughly fourth grade. The next question Ms. Spencer raised is, What is Jessica's reading level?

Informally estimating reading behavior

This section includes three procedures for informally estimating reading behavior: (1) estimating the reading level, (2) determining the errors in reading behavior, and (3) constructing a reading inventory.

Estimating reading level

There are a number of factors to consider in informally evaluating a child's reading level. The first is to assess the grade level at which the child reads. In this assessment the teacher tries to estimate whether the child is reading at the primer level, the third-grade level, or the eighth-grade level. Another factor is the degree of accuracy with which the child reads. It has been suggested by Betts (1946) and later by Johnson and Kress (1965) that there are three accuracy levels: the independent level, the instructional level, and the frustration level.

The *independent level* refers to the ability to read a passage without help and with about 100% accuracy. The *instructional level* refers to the ability to read without some help with about 75% accuracy. The *frustration level* refers to the level of reading when the reader reads with considerable difficulty with about 50% accuracy.

A teacher can use different kinds of reading in estimating the reading level, including oral reading, silent reading, word reading, and word discrimination.

The *oral reading level* is obtained by having a child read paragraphs from several graded readers. The teacher asks the child to read a short passage orally from each of the books selected. If a child reads a second-grade reader fluently, the teacher asks him or her to read a passage from a third-grade book, then a passage from a fourth-grade book, and on until the child reads a passage with difficulty. The child's oral reading level then would be the level at which he or she reads with about 75% accuracy (at the instructional level).

The *silent reading level* is obtained by having the child read passages silently from the graded readers at his or her instructional level and then asking questions to determine comprehension. The child's instructional level for silent reading can thus be estimated. Sometimes silent reading is higher than oral reading, or vice versa.

The *word reading level* can be obtained by testing the child in reading words in isolation from graded readers. Some graded readers have a vocabulary list at the end. In this case the teacher can estimate the child's word reading or word recall in reading words out of context.

The *word discrimination level* can be obtained by presenting six words from the vocabulary list and saying, "One of these words is _____; point to _____." Sometimes the child can only read one or two of the words, but is able to recognize twice as many words.

In the case of Jessica, the teacher made the following estimates of reading levels:

- Oral reading of paragraphs—first grade
- Silent reading—second grade
- Word reading—first grade
- Word discrimination—second grade.

It is obvious from the study of potential and reading level that Jessica had the capacity or potential for reading at the beginning fourth-grade level but was actually reading at only the first- or second-grade level. There is a disparity of at least 2 years between reading potential and achievement. This answers the major question in the diagnostic process; that is, there is a significant disparity of 2 years between capacity or potential and reading achievement.

The degree of discrepancy between potential and reading achievement will change as a child grows older. A child whose potential is fourth grade but who reads at the second-grade level has a discrepancy of 2 years. If the rate of progress remains the same, with the child learning one-half grade each year, the child will be reading at the third-grade level in the sixth grade and at the fourth-grade level in the eighth grade. Thus the deficiency of 2 years in the fourth grade will be similar to 3 years in the sixth grade and 4 years in the eighth grade.

Determining errors in reading behavior

Discovering the errors of poor reading requires observation of the child's reading habits. As the child is being examined in oral reading, silent reading, word reading, and word discrimination, the teacher can observe the child's reading style and any difficulties encountered. These observations can also be made during daily reading lessons.

If a child does not respond to a word, but just looks at it, that is an indication that the child has not developed any method of decoding words. This means that remediation should include a procedure to teach decoding skills.

The child may attempt to sound a word or spell it and still not decode it properly. Some learning disabled children do not learn words as wholes, so they resort to a piecemeal method of decoding. These trial-and-error methods sometimes mean that the child has not been taught phonics adequately or has not been taught to decode words by sounds or syllables.

Many developmental reading programs teach children to sound the first letter of a word and guess at the rest of the word from the context. The child may not go beyond this attempt at phonics and hence may be unable to decode words adequately.

The child may appear not to be able to use context clues in reading. Such a child is concentrating on the decoding process and is not paying attention to the meaning of phrases and sentences.

Some children make the following errors in reading.

(1) *Omissions.* Children tend to omit words in reading or sometimes omit parts of words read. If the text is "Mike saw a dog," and the child reads "Mike saw dog," the child is omitting the word *a.*

(2) *Insertions.* Sometimes a child inserts a word in the text that does not exist. He reads "The man saw a big fat bear" when the text did not include *big fat.*

(3) *Substitutions.* In this case the child substitutes one word for another. "Sally is a good kitten" could be read "Sally had a good kitten."

(4) *Repetitions.* Some children repeat words and sentences, especially when they encounter a word they do not know. "See the blue automobile" might be read "See the blue [stalls on "automobile" and repeats]...see the blue...see the blue...."

(5) *Omission or addition of sounds.* The child omits sounds or adds sounds to a word he or she reads.

(6) *Reversal errors.* A child would tend to read *was* as *saw* or *on* as *no.*

(7) *Fast and inaccurate reading.* Some children rush over reading materials, making many errors, especially omissions of words they cannot read.

(8) *Slow word-by-word reading.* Some children read slowly, word by word. This may be a habit developed because of concentration on decoding.

(9) *Lack of comprehension.* Some children decode words but pay little attention to the meaning of the text.

Constructing a reading inventory

There are on the market a number of informal reading inventories (IRI). Many publishers of basal reading series will supply teachers with an IRI based on their reading materials. In the absence of adequate reading inventories, the teacher can develop his or her own reading inventory from materials in class. These could include informal inventories for oral paragraph reading, word reading, word discrimination, and silent reading.

Oral reading

Oral reading can be observed by having a child read a graded text at either the instructional level or the frustration level. While the child reads, the teacher notes the kinds of errors the child is making, together with the other questions raised in the preceding section. Does he read fast or slowly? Does he have a method of word recognition? Does he use context clues? What kinds of errors does the child make in reading these graded paragraphs?

An efficient system of developing an informal oral reading inventory is to select a paragraph or two from each of several graded readers from the primer level to grade five or six. The test will then contain a graded series of paragraphs. Several such tests can be provided so that the teacher can test a child without having to search for and find graded readers every time. In testing a child, it is best to have two sheets, one for the child and one for the teacher to use in recording errors as the child reads.

The teacher can develop his or her own system, such as writing error responses over words and underlining repetitions.

saw him   s sh
The bear was seen running up the mountain side.

Word recognition

Some children use context clues to decode words. It is therefore necessary to see how a child reads words out of context. The list of words the teacher can use should be taken from the graded readers used in the class. The last page of many readers contains a list of words used in the book. These words can be used to test the child on word recognition. It is sometimes economical for a teacher to select a graded set of words from the readers used in testing. In this way the teacher can note (1) the child's level of reading (reads most of the words from a first-grade reader, but stumbles over many words from a second-grade reader); (2) the errors the child makes in reading words; and (3) the style of word attack, i.e., tries phonics, spells the words, reads some words from sight but does not try to decode words not recognized immediately, and so forth.

As with oral reading, the errors and comments can be noted on a scoring sheet prepared for that purpose.

Word discrimination

Some children are unable to recall words when they are presented to them but can recognize the same words when allowed to select them from among other words. A word discrimination test can be constructed from a list of words prepared by the teacher, as:

> *boy*
> *dog*
> *was*
> *no*
> *saw*
> *on*

If the child is able to read only one or two of these words, the teacher can say, "One of these words is 'dog'; look at the words on the page and point to 'dog'." Proceed in the same way with the other words. Sometimes children will be able to recognize five of the six words, though they could only read two of them in isolation. This diagnosis means that a child has partial knowledge of the words, which may differentiate him or her from another child who is unable to point to any of the words correctly.

In addition, the teacher can note what words were selected. That is, did the child select *saw* for *was, no* for *on, dog* for *boy,* or *boy* for *ball?* The child may be recognizing the first consonant and consequently recognizing the word. This type of test also gives clues to the child's mode of word recognition and style of decoding.

Silent reading

In this informal test, the teacher asks the child to silently read graded paragraphs similar to the oral reading paragraphs and then relate what he or she has read. The teacher also questions the child to determine whether or not the child understands the content of the passage. Children who can use context clues and who make inferences and closure can sometimes read silently at a higher grade level than they can read orally.

Finding contributing factors to reading disabilities

In addition to the observation of errors in reading and learning style, the teacher may wish to look into the developmental learning disabilities that might have inhibited the child's ability to learn to read. If no developmental learning disabilities (such as poor focus of attention, short-term memory, or poor concept formation) are found, then direct training and correction of errors are in order. If, on the other hand, a developmental learning disability is found, it is important for the teacher to organize a remedial program that would remediate the developmental learning disability in the task of reading.

The search for contributing factors of a reading disability is a search for factors that have inhibited the child's ability to learn under ordinary instruction. The following section will deal with some of the major physical and developmental psychological contributing factors or correlates that have been found to be related to reading disabilities in some children.

Physical contributing factors

Under physical contributing factors we find such conditions as visual defects, auditory defects, confused spatial orientation, mixed laterality, hyperkinesia, poor body image, undernourishment, and other conditions which under certain circumstances serve as an obstacle to learning academic subjects. As indicated in chapter 3, the relationship between contributing factors and causes is not clear, but we do know that some children who have these conditions have difficulty in learning to read.

Visual defects

The studies on the effect of visual defects on reading have been equivocal. Robinson (1946) compared children with visual defects and those without visual defects and did not arrive at any clear-cut conclusions. Some studies, for example, have concluded that near-sighted children read better than far-sighted children. Other studies conclude that severe eye muscle imbalances have a more detrimental effect on reading than does visual acuity. Still other studies indicate that visual defects in children have no direct relationship to failure in reading (Goldberg, Shiffman, & Bender, 1983). On the other hand, clinicians cite case studies of individual children as possible examples of reading failure resulting from a visual problem.

One reason for the lack of consistency in the results of research is the great flexibility of the human organism. One child with a muscle imbalance who tries to read with both eyes (binocular vision) may have difficulty learning. Another child with the same degree of eye-muscle imbalance may suppress one eye and learn to read with the other eye, thus avoiding confusion. Or the child may compensate by using a phonic method in learning how to read, thus avoiding total reliance on the visual stimulus of the printed word.

An example of a possible relationship between an eye muscle imbalance and a reading problem is found in the case of a child who exhibited marked reversal errors. He was 12 years old, had an IQ of 80, but was unable to adequately read a first-grade text after 5 years in school. In addition to reversal errors he could read the reversed reflection of words in a mirror (mirror reading) almost as well as without a mirror. He was right-handed, right eyed, and right-footed. An ophthalmological examination showed a marked convergence defect that caused both eyes to look straight ahead instead of converging inwards to focus on the printed word. His remediation consisted of pencil-to-nose exercises as recommended by an ophthalmologist and remedial reading for short periods at a time with a phonic system.

A possible explanation of the relationship between eye muscle imbalance and reversal errors may be illustrated in the following experiment. Look between the square and the dot and gradually bring the page to your eyes.

When you bring the paper close enough that you cannot converge further, the dot will go into the square. This is probably what happened to this boy. For example, *no* became *on* when he could not converge. His convergence problem may have contributed to his reversal errors. Another child with a similar convergence problem may suppress one eye and learn to read with the other eye without having reversal errors. That is why experiments do not obtain consistent results. Chapter 16 will discuss the discrepancy between group research results and clinical observation.

The major controversy surrounding the relationship of visual defects to reading is in training. Some believe that eye exercises will improve reading, while others deny the value of exercise for improving reading. The boy who received pencil-to-nose exercises also received individualized remedial reading instruction. The child's success could be ascribed to the remedial reading sessions, but the value of the pencil-to-nose exercises cannot be ascertained. In our view, any eye exercise should be accompanied by remedial reading instruction because reading materials presented properly would be the eye exercise needed (task-process approach).

Goldberg and colleagues (1983) state that it is necessary to correct visual defects with glasses or surgery because "a child with poor sight will have difficulty identifying details of the printed word" (p. 72). In general they state that reading is accomplished with the brain and not the eyes, since children can have eye deficits and still learn to read well.

Hearing defects

Like vision, research has not shown any clear-cut relationship between defective hearing (other than deafness or near-deafness) and reading failures. Some studies suggest that emphasis on phonics with hearing handicapped children results in more reading problems than does the sight method of teaching (Fendrick, 1935). Instructional procedures can be altered to correct the contributing factor or compensate for it. The major factors to seek in this area are auditory discrimination, auditory closure, and auditory sound blending. These are remediable with proper training.

Laterality and body image

Following Orton's (1928) work on strephosymbolia, hundreds of studies were conducted on handedness, eyedness, mixed laterality, and body image as related to reading and language. Those who have studied these investigations have concluded that the relationship between these factors and reading difficulties is not clear. At the same time, clinicians can point out cases of children who have been failing as a result of these kinds of problems.

Left-handed children tend to make more reversal errors than do right-handed children. Also, many children who change from left-handedness to right-handedness after infancy may have some problem in orientation and tend to reverse letters and words. There is some evidence that certain types of lateralities do result in mirror reading and mirror writing. If you ask a right-handed child to write with the left hand, that child may show tendencies for reversal with his or her left hand. This is discussed further in the chapter on handwriting (chapter 11).

Developmental psychological contributing factors

In chapter 3, figure 3.1 showed the physical and developmental learning disabilities that could be contributing factors to learning disabilities. This section will deal with some of the developmental learning disabilities that may be contributing factors to reading disabilities.

Language

It is obvious that if a child does not acquire language he or she will have difficulty in learning to interpret the printed page and to understand the language of mathematics. Some children understand language but are unable to talk; some are able to talk mechanically but have difficulty organizing their ideas; and some have difficulty in grammar. A language handicap should be remediated for its own sake, as indicated in the last chapter. A deficit in language, however, serves also as a contributing factor to a reading disability.

Attention

It is obvious that if a child is unable to concentrate on the printed page, he or she will have difficulty learning to read. Chapter 5 discussed this developmental learning disability in some detail.

Auditory functions

Many studies have been made on reading disabilities and auditory functions, including auditory figure-background problems, auditory closure including sound blending, auditory sequential memory, and auditory discrimination. Auditory sequential memory and reading disabilities have had considerable attention in the research literature. As in many other areas, the research has been contradictory. Hammill and Larsen (1974b), after reviewing selected studies, concluded that the relationship between auditory perceptual skills and reading was not sufficiently clear for practical purposes. Rugel (1974), Torgesen (1978, 1979), and Kavale (1981b) found a significant relationship between auditory sequential memory and learning disabilities, particularly in reading. In analyzing this problem further, Ring (1976) and Richie and Aten (1976) found that poor readers were inferior to good readers in both meaningful and nonmeaningful tasks because they were unable to use mnemonic or problem-solving strategies to aid their auditory sequential memory.

Children who have a disability in auditory sound blending (auditory synthesis) appear to have more difficulty in learning to read than those who do not have this disability. Even on this function, Elkins (1974) states that sound-blending disabilities are found more frequently among poor readers than among good readers at the first- and second-grade levels, but sound blending is not an important factor in children reading at the third-grade level and above. A review of the literature on sound blending (Harber, 1980) shows discrepancies in results which compared good readers and poor readers. The majority of studies, however, show that good readers in the first grade tend to have better sound-blending ability than do children who are poor readers. At the third- and fourth-grade level, sound blending is not important.

Some teachers instructing children in phonics teach the children the sound-symbol relationship and assume that the children will blend the sounds. This assumption is correct for most children. But if a child has a sound-blending disability, the response to a series of sounds will be of little value.

An auditory sound-blending test should be administered by a teacher who finds a child reading at the first- or second-grade level and having difficulty reading at his or her potential, especially in decoding words. To test the child, start with two-sound words like *sh-oe, m-e,* and sound them with 1-second breaks between each sound. If the child blends two sounds, present three sounds, *s-a-t, m-a-p,* and then four-sound words, *c-l-a-p.* If the child is able to blend three and four sounds presented at intervals of 1 second between sounds, conclude that the child does not have an auditory sound-blending disability. If the child has a sound-blending disability and is unable to learn by the visual method, the child may have difficulty decoding words. The child will then need auditory training in sound blending.

Visualization or visual memory

Visual memory, the ability to reproduce visual materials from memory, has long been associated with reading ability. Decades ago Hinshelwood (1917) stated that the visual memory center is in the left angular gyrus of the left hemisphere and that a lesion in this area produces word blindness. Studies by Kass (1966), Macione (1969), and others have shown that poor readers in the primary grades have poorer visual sequential memory than good readers of the same grade level (Harris & Sipay, 1975). But again, results of studies are not consistent.

To test visual memory for words informally, the teacher can use the following procedure. Write the word *horse* or any relatively nonphonic word like *rough* or *though* on the board or on paper. Ask the child what it is. If the child does not know the word, tell him, and have him say the word. Then remove the word and ask the child to reproduce the word from memory. A child with a visualization problem will have difficulty reproducing the word even after he sees it three or four times. On the other hand, a child who does not have a visualization problem is usually able to reproduce unknown words common for his age level from memory after one or two presentations. This is an informal method of testing visual memory. Children who have a visual memory problem should be trained in visualization in reading itself using the same procedure as was used in testing. The Fernald kinesthetic method (which will be described later) is a method of training visualization in the process of reading itself.

Closure

The term *closure* is used to indicate the response to familiar items from which a part has been omitted. Closure can be either visual or auditory. If a child has good visual closure, he or she will be able to give a reasonable response when part of a word or picture is omitted. Similarly, children who have good auditory closure will be able to complete a spoken word or a phrase from the presentation of a part. Poor auditory closure is common among poor readers. According to Elkins (1972), this problem is more prevalent in the third grade than in the first grade. Closure may also apply to a child's comprehension of meaning.

The "cloze" procedure can be used in diagnosing a child's ability to comprehend meaning. This is used when a child can decode words but has difficulty with comprehension. A cloze test could involve omitting every fifth or sixth word in the text, for example, and having the child fill it in as he or she reads. If the child is unable to fill in the missing words, he or she has difficulty in comprehension. In preparing cloze materials to test comprehension, the teacher should use a sequence of paragraphs from graded readers.

Harris and Sipay (1975) discuss many other correlates or contributing factors of reading. These include other aspects of visual and auditory perception, discrimination, sequencing, visual-motor performance, integration of modalities, and lateral dominance. Many of these will be discussed further under spelling and written expression.

Relationship of contributing factors to reading disability

Reading, writing, and spelling disabilities cannot be consistently explained by any one of the contributing factors or developmental learning disabilities alone. Chapter 16 discusses contradictory results from group studies. The studies have contradictory results because physical, environmental, and psychological characteristics of children with difficulties cannot be isolated from the method used in teaching them to read. Retardation in reading is generally related to many factors. A child with a visual-memory problem often compensates for this developmental learning disability by using a more auditory approach, such as a phonic approach to reading. Likewise, a child with auditory perception problems, such as in auditory discrimination or sound blending, can often compensate if his or her visual memory and linguistic abilities are intact. Deaf children do not have sound blending and auditory discrimination abilities, but compensate when their visual memory abilities are intact. More severe problems arise when a child has both auditory perceptual disabilities and visual memory problems. In this case the double handicap will inhibit the child's ability to learn to read.

Since we cannot ascribe reading disability to a developmental learning disability alone, how can we account for it? It is probably more scientific to state that a reading disability results from the lack of adaptation of a method of teaching to the characteristics of the child than to ascribe the difficulty to laterality, vision, hearing, visual memory, speed of perception, or other problems.

Children with difficulties in reading, writing, and spelling can often be remediated when a method is found that matches the child's abilities, ameliorates the deficit in the task of reading, or compensates for the particular deficit. It is the responsibility of the examiner to discover the contributing factors and to find or invent a remedial method that will ameliorate the disability or compensate for it.

Remedial methods for decoding

There are many remedial methods that can be adapted to each child's level of reading. Different variations of a phonic approach are used for nonreaders or readers who have not been able to decode words by the ordinary methods of instruction. A tracing or kinesthetic method has also been used with children who are nonreaders. For older children who have learned to decode words but have difficulty interpreting the printed page, the phonic or kinesthetic methods are not useful. These children require different methods of remediation to increase comprehension.

Remediation for children who are nonreaders or who are severely underachieving in the primary grades generally consists of a multisensory approach. The VAKT Approach to remedial reading is an attempt to use several sensory modalities in learning to read. VAKT refers to visual (V), auditory (A), kinesthetic (K), and tactile (T) senses. The use of all of the senses in one approach is thus called the *multisensory* approach. It assumes that the child needs to use all sensory avenues in the learning process, and that by so doing, learning will be reinforced and enhanced. In this approach, the child can be asked to *say* the word, which is auditory; *see* the word, which is visual; *trace* the word, which is kinesthetic; and, if he or she traces it with the finger, it could be *tactile.* Cautions against the indiscriminate use of multisensory techniques have been raised by a number of authors (Berry, 1969; Johnson & Myklebust, 1967). Some learners, it is said, are unable to process the stimuli of several modalities simultaneously. The indiscriminate use of all sensory fields should not, of course, be used as a substitute for careful diagnosis of a child's particular difficulties. It should *not* serve as a "cafeteria" approach, hoping that the needed approach will be supplied somehow among the choices. We will discuss some methods using the VAKT approach, since the multisensory approach to reading has been used in many remedial methods.

The Fernald method

In California in the 1920s, Grace B. Fernald and Helen B. Keller developed a kinesthetic method of teaching reading and spelling. The Fernald method has been continued at the University of California at Los Angeles in the reading clinic (Fernald, 1943). The method incorporates language experience and tracing techniques in a multisensory approach.

In the Fernald method, the childen dictate their own stories to be learned. Thus, the students select the vocabulary. In this method, the children say the word, see the written word, trace the word with the fingers, write the word from memory, see the word again, and read the word aloud for the teacher. In this method the word is taught as a whole, with no phonics. The method provides four stages in learning.

Stage I

The teacher writes the word on paper or on the board. The child traces the word. He or she traces it with finger contact and says each part of the word as it is traced. This is repeated until the child can write the word without looking at the copy. In other words, the child ultimately looks at the word, says the word, and then when it is erased or taken away, writes it from memory. Visual memory is trained in the process of reading words and phrases. The child then writes the word in a story taken from the child's experience. Finally, the story is typed and the child reads the story in print.

Stage II

This stage is reached when the child no longer needs to trace to learn new words. At this stage, students are able to learn the words themselves when they are written by the teacher. They continue to write the words from memory and to read the typed copy of what is written.

Stage III

At this stage pupils learn the printed word by first saying it to themselves and then writing it. A child now learns directly from the printed word. Many children eventually acquire the ability to glance over a word, say it once or twice to themselves, and then write it without a copy. In other words, they have developed their visual memory for words. At this point books are introduced.

Stage IV

At this stage the child is able to recognize new words from their similarity to words already learned. The child has now reached the stage of generalizing from known words to new words. The teacher supplies enough reading material so that the child can develop concepts that will help him or her recognize new words, develop a reading vocabulary, and understand the meaning of word groups when reading any new content.

The Fernald method has been used since 1920 with children and adults of normal intelligence who have had extreme difficulty in learning to read. Many have used the method with variations, such as the elimination of tracing in Stage I. Its use over the years has demonstrated its validity for some children.

The Gillingham method

Gillingham and Stillman (1973) also used a multisensory approach to reading, writing, and spelling by teaching units of sounds or letters of the alphabet. This method was developed in the 1930s as an instructional method for the kinds of children diagnosed by Orton as language disordered.

The method was originally called the *alphabet method*. The sounds represented by the letters of the alphabet are learned one at a time, using a multisensory approach. The learner sees the letter, hears the sounds it represents, traces it according to certain specified hand movements, and writes it. In this way, the visual, auditory, kinesthetic, and tactile modalities are used simultaneously.

The method is spelled out by the authors and follows a systematic procedure of learning the letters, learning the sounds, and blending the consonants and vowels together into a word. The words are then put into sentences and stories.

Gillingham and Stillman call their method an *association* method because it consists of three parts: (1) association of the visual symbol with the name of the letter, (2) association of the visual symbol with the sound of the letter, and (3) association of the feeling of the child's speech organs in producing the name or sound of letters as he hears himself say it. The method attempts to associate visual, auditory, and kinesthetic modalities.

Slingerland (1974) produced an adaptation of the Gillingham method called "A Multisensory Approach to Language Arts for Specific Language Disability Children." Slingerland's materials include a teachers' guide and a set of auxiliary teaching materials. The manual for these materials details the Gillingham approach for classroom use for primary grade teachers. Another variation of the Gillingham material is the *Recipe for Reading* by Traub and Bloom (1970).

Although the Gillingham method and the Slingerland adaptation have been criticized on several grounds (Dechant, 1982; Frostig, 1966; Wepman, 1960), the method has many advocates. Otto, McMenemy, and Smith (1973) state that the system has been successful when used with modifications.

The Hegge-Kirk-Kirk remedial reading drills

These exercises were developed for educable mentally retarded children at the Michigan Wayne County Training School (Kirk, 1936). This phonic reading system was systematically developed using the principles now known as *programmed instruction*. A description of the first drill may suffice to illustrate the system.

First, the sound of the short vowel *a* is taught along with the consonants. Each drill is divided into four sections with minimal changes for each. In the first section, only the initial consonant changes, i.e., *s-a-t, m-a-t, f-a-t*. In the second section, only the final consonant changes, i.e., *s-a-t, s-a-m, s-a-p*. In the third and fourth sections, the initial and final consonants both change.

This system has been used since 1936 without revision. The authors insist that this highly programmed phonic system is not a method of teaching all children to read, as advocated by Rudolph Flesch in *Why Johnny Can't Read* (1955). Kirk and Kirk (1956) state that they constructed the phonic drills for only those children who need a systematic step-by-step approach to develop independence in word attack.

The DISTAR system

The DISTAR Reading Program (Engelmann & Bruner, 1974) was designed to teach reading skills to children with below average communication ability. It was developed with preschool culturally different children. According to its author, the program enables virtually all children who have mental ages of 4 or above to learn to read (Engelmann & Carnine, 1982). The materials are intended for both slow and disabled readers.

The materials and methods use a behavioral approach to teaching reading and give specific directions for the teacher's wording and actions. The DISTAR program includes three types of tasks.

(1) Symbol-action games are used to teach skills such as left-to-right orientation and linear sequence.

(2) Blending tasks are used to teach children to decode words by sounding (say it slow) and to blend quickly (say it fast).

(3) Rhyming tasks are used to teach children to recognize the relationship between sounds and words.

The DISTAR system emphasizes code-breaking skills. Directions for teachers are quite specific. The teacher is directed to present the material in a specified structured, step-by-step program. Everything the teacher is to say and do is included in the manual, including tone of voice and hand movements.

Becker and Engelmann (1976) have reported an extensive follow-up study in 20 school districts of disadvantaged children who were taught with DISTAR. They presented evidence that the model is effective with low income and low IQ students.

Other remedial methods

There are many remedial methods or variations of those we have described that assist children who are blocked at the stage of differentiation. These include the Rebus Method (Woodcock & Clark, 1969), which substitutes pictures for words within a sentence; the Glass Analysis Method (Glass, 1973), which emphasizes developing perceptual conditioning for decoding letter clusters within a word; and Edmark (1972), which is a programmed method for teaching 150 relevant words, primarily for low IQ children.

Remedial methods for comprehension

The remedial methods described in the preceding section deal with procedures for reading disabled children in the primary grades who need to develop decoding skills. Those procedures are aimed at helping children differentiate and retrieve words and phrases. Once the child has learned to decode, the remedial procedures for word analysis are no longer necessary. The major problems then become speed of reading and comprehension and integration. Retarded readers who score above grade three usually need improvement in interpreting the printed page without being conscious of the individual symbols.

It is interesting to note that mentally retarded children are able to learn to decode words, but reach their limits in reading at the third- to fifth-grade level. The reason is that they are unable to comprehend the materials in reading much above the fourth-grade level. The same situation exists with deaf children. Studies on deaf children show that they too plateau at the fourth- or fifth-grade level (Kirk & Gallagher, 1983). In these situations the marked language handicap interferes with the child's further progress in reading. Some deaf children, however, are able to break the language barrier, read complex materials, and succeed in college. Their language develops through systematic and extensive reading.

Harris and Sipay (1975) have discussed in detail procedures for improving comprehension. Only a brief outline of their analysis will be given here.

(1) First, it is important for the reader to understand the vocabulary in the reading materials. It is not sufficient to decode a phrase in Spanish if one does not understand the vocabulary. Students should be taught to use the dictionary to look up words they do not understand and to study synonyms, antonyms, and word origins.

(2) The discussion of concept formation in chapter 8 of this book is important for comprehension in reading. It may be easy to understand the concepts of nouns, but it is much more difficult to understand the vocabulary of relationships.

(3) The reading skills that may be important for comprehension are:
  (a) Reading to note and recall detail
  (b) Reading for main ideas
  (c) Following a sequence of events or steps
  (d) Drawing inferences and reaching conclusions
  (e) Organizing ideas
  (f) Applying what is read to solving problems
  (g) Evaluating materials for bias, relevancy and consistency.

(4) The development of adequate comprehension in experiential background, preferably correlated with related reading materials. Integrating the school curriculum with systematic reading instruction or including a reading task in all lessons will tend to improve comprehension in reading.

Gibson and Levin (1975) state that reading is a cognitive process that begins at the perceptual level and ends at the conceptual level. They claim that reading is a language function. In reading the child abstracts the essential features of a passage, ignores irrelevant characteristics, and gradually filters the relevant abstractions. This is the integration stage of reading. Hook and Johnson (1978) conducted an experiment on reading strategies and found that reading disabled children had difficulty developing economy in their processing of reading materials and were not able to use language structure cues as well as the proficient reader'' (p. 75).

Many specific procedures have been developed to improve comprehension in reading. A sample of these are discussed below.

Motivation

The first task of a remedial teacher is to help the child establish a purpose for comprehension and a desire to improve in reading. A child who is 1 to 3 or 4 years below his or her classmates in reading is naturally discouraged and in many instances will withdraw from reading behavior. Some suggestions to use with such a child are:

(1) Present the child with a task for which he or she can succeed, and praise the child for the effort.

(2) Give the child a purpose for reading, such as asking questions, which will require concentration in reading.

(3) Organize materials in such a way that the child can note success, such as having the child graph progress in comprehending lessons if possible. Show the child progress is being made.

Vocabulary development

Understanding the meaning of words in a text is essential for comprehension. If the child has an oral language disorder, remediation should emphasize receptive and expressive language in relation to reading. Some suggestions for improving vocabulary are:

(1) Teach the child to use the dictionary to acquire new meaning of words in reading materials used.

(2) Give practice in using synonyms.

(3) Give the child the task of making his or her own dictionary and glossary of words that are difficult to understand.

(4) Give the child practice in classifying animals, plants, and so forth.

(5) Give the child practice in finding opposites.

(6) Teach the child about compound words, prefixes, and suffixes.

(7) Teach the child to understand multiple meanings of words in context, such as:

I pay for my *board* and room.

I nailed a *board* on the stairs.

Develop reading skills required for adequate comprehension

(1) Point out to the child that the main idea in a passage sometimes comes in the first sentence of a paragraph, but not always. Try to select the main part of the passage.

(2) Have the child read a short story or paragraph and give the story a title. This type of assignment is interesting and helps the child note the main idea.

(3) Have the child read part of the story and then guess at what will come next. He or she can verify the guess by reading the rest of the story or paragraph.

(4) Use questions over a passage that call for the child to note main ideas, recall detail, or anticipate sequences.

(5) Use the cloze procedure to improve reading comprehension. Select passages from books to be used for instruction. Retype the passage, deleting every 5th, 8th, or 10th word, with an underlined blank in place of the word. Instruct the child to read the passage and fill in the missing blanks. The cloze procedure is purported to improve comprehension by having the children select appropriate words to fill in the blanks.

(6) Work on study skills. Reading disabled children tend to have poor study skills. They generally have not learned to outline their work as they read; they do not ask themselves questions they want answered from their reading; they do not review or rehearse what they have read. It is the task of the remedial teacher to systematically instruct the child on study skills so that he or she can retain and retrieve the content of what has been read or studied.

(7) Teach listening skills. Berger (1978) and others reviewed by Stanovich (1982) have found evidence that children with poor comprehension displayed deficits in listening comprehension, especially in the upper elementary grades and beyond. Thus, it is necessary to teach listening comprehension. As Stanovich states,

> Comprehension deficits in poor readers have lead an increasing number of researchers to advise that comprehension strategies such as question asking, text structure identification, self-questioning, text-scanning, imagery, and comprehension monitoring should be explicitly taught....Experimental evidence has generally supported the conjecture that such training can partially reduce the reading performance deficits displayed by poor readers. (p. 552)

Improving rate of reading

Comprehension may be affected when a child spends too much time decoding words or reading word by word. Reading thought units as wholes enhances comprehension. Many systems have been developed to increase rate of reading and to enhance comprehension.

First, the neurological impress method is an approach to remedial instruction designed for students with severe reading disabilities (Heckelman, 1969; Langford, Slade, & Barnett, 1974). It is a system of concert reading in which the student and the instructor read together. The teacher uses a finger as a locator, pointing to each word as it is read. The finger follows the spoken word. The instructor varies his or her voice and speed, sometimes louder and faster than the student. The object is to cover as many pages of reading material as possible within the time available without causing fatigue. The idea underlying the procedure is that the auditory feedback from both the student and the teacher establishes the learning or imprinting process, increases speed of reading, and enhances comprehension.

Skimming is another method for increasing rate of reading. It is designed to enhance rapid reading and to obtain an overall but superficial impression of the contents. An example of skimming is to look over a list of cities to find out if yours is listed.

Free reading has been advocated as an effective method of increasing rate of reading as well as comprehension. If a child is motivated to read books that are relatively easy to read and have high interest level, that child automatically increases his or her speed of reading.

Flexibility refers to varying the rate of reading according to the difficulty of the material. Good readers vary their rate according to their purpose in reading and in relation to the difficulty of the materials. Children should be taught to skim some materials and read other materials more slowly to obtain full comprehension.

Summary

- Reading disability is the most common type of disability found in classes for learning disabled children; 60 to 70% of children enrolled in such classes are reading disabled.

- Learning to read follows the same pattern as any aspect of human growth: (1) mass action (reading wholes), (2) differentiation (awareness of details), (3) integration (deriving meaning from the printed page without being conscious of the symbols).

- Most children learn to read by developmental and corrective methods, but 1 to 2% require the remediation of a developmental learning disability in the task of teaching reading.

- In lieu of extensive testing, many experienced teachers can approximate more formal diagnostic decisions. This chapter outlined a diagnostic procedure by which a teacher using classroom materials can (1) estimate potential, (2) estimate reading level, (3) observe errors in reading, (4) examine possible relevant correlates or developmental disabilities, (5) evolve a hypothesis that gives cues to remediation, and (6) organize a remedial program.

- A system of developing a reading inventory is described. The teacher uses paragraphs from different graded readers and word lists from these readers. The teacher-made inventory will involve oral reading, word reading, word discrimination, and silent reading.

- Suggestions are made for informally delineating physical correlates that may lead to developmental psychological correlates. Suggestions are also made for detecting developmental learning disabilities that may be inhibiting the child's achievement.

- A reading disability cannot be the result of a physical or psychological correlate alone. It may be more accurate to state that a reading disability results from the lack of adaptation of a method of teaching to the characteristics of the child.

- Many of the remedial methods for nonreaders tend to use some form of multisensory approach, using visual, auditory, kinesthetic, and tactile stimuli (VAKT) simultaneously.

- The remedial methods of Fernald, Gillingham, and Hegge-Kirk-Kirk, the neurological impress method, the DISTAR system, and the cloze procedure have been discussed.

- Improving comprehension is the major problem with learning disabled children in the upper elementary grades and in secondary school.

- Comprehension in reading depends upon the cognitive, language, and experiential background of the child.

- Improvement requires training in vocabulary, listening, study skills, and reading skills of noting details, following sequences, drawing inferences, and organizing ideas.

- Techniques for improving rate of reading include the cloze procedure, neurological impress method, skimming, and free reading.

Thought questions

1. How can you apply the three developmental stages in reading to learning to swim?

2. Find a child in the lower elementary grades and, with a series of readers, practice diagnosing the child following the steps outlined in the text. Do you think you succeeded in assessing potential, level of reading, errors made, and possible contributing factors if the child is markedly retarded in reading?

3. From these basal readers, can you construct a reading inventory that will assess reading skill in oral reading, word reading, word discrimination, and silent reading?

4. What common errors did you find after examining a child informally? Can you outline the child's problem?

5. Which contributing factor do you think is most common with reading disabled children?

6. Why do you think a unitary factor like laterality or visual memory or auditory discrimination need not inhibit the child's ability to learn to read? When do these developmental disabilities affect reading? Under what conditions will they have no effect?

7. With what kind of a child would you use the Fernald method? The Gillingham method? The Hegge-Kirk-Kirk method?

8. What procedures would you use with a high school student who reads slowly and is unable to complete assignments?

9. What are the major factors to look for in teaching an adolescent who reads at the third-grade level?

11
Handwriting disabilities

Children begin to "write" at an early age by scribbling in imitation of their parents and older siblings. The availability of pencils and crayons in the home often leads children to use them on the walls or furniture, much to the consternation of their parents. At this stage, of course, the child does not know that adult writing uses symbols to convey meaning. Some preschool children begin to form letters, and some are taught to write their names at home. Formal training in writing, however, usually does not begin until the child enters kindergarten and first grade.

There are two styles of writing: manuscript (resembling print) and cursive. Manuscript writing is the preferred form for children in the first and second grades, while cursive writing is generally taught in the second or third grade. During the early part of the century, children began by being taught cursive writing, probably because this was the form used by adults. It was soon found that children could more easily learn to form the letters in print-script form. Schools made the shift because it was believed that manuscript writing (1) resembles print, thus aiding spelling and reading, (2) is easier to learn, (3) is more legible, (4) is preferred by children with motor handicaps, and (5) requires fewer movements to form the letters in a word.

The proponents of cursive writing claim that children need it if we expect them to read materials written in cursive style. It aids in the correction or avoidance of letter reversals since the sequence is continuous from one letter to another, it is faster, and it is easier to write.

In a review of handwriting research and practice, Graham and Miller (1980) state:

> There is considerable evidence, however, that manuscript is more legible than cursive writing, leads to greater gains in reading achievement, can be written as fast, and is easier to learn. The bulk of the evidence, then, tends to support the claims of manuscript style proponents. Nonetheless, the evidence is not conclusive and the relative effectiveness of the two styles has not been adequately demonstrated. (p. 3)

Handwriting is a prerequisite skill to spelling and to written expression. Thus a deficit in handwriting can become an obstacle to written expression. To progress in the latter, it is helpful if children first learn to write letters and words accurately and rapidly.

Contributing factors to handwriting disabilities

To learn to write, a child must be mentally mature enough and have desire and interest in learning how to write. In addition, the child should have developed eye-hand coordination, motor coordination, visual-spatial orientation, visual discrimination, visual memory, the ability to relate his or her body to the surrounding space (body image), the concept of writing from left to right, and a definite hand preference.

Difficulties in handwriting may be related to many factors. Hildreth (1936) surveyed difficulties in handwriting and delineated many sources of trouble. She grouped these difficulties into two broad groups. One grouping consisted of difficulties arising from inadequate environment and poor instruction. The possible compounding factors included forced instruction, group instead of individual instruction, practicing errors, lack of proper supervision, and transfer from one style to another. The other main grouping dealt with factors intrinsic to the child, such as disorders of motor control, disorders of visual and spatial perception, deficiencies in visual memory, left-handedness, and ambidexterity.

Working with cerebral palsied children, Harrison (1970) also found many factors that interfered with the development of handwriting in these brain-damaged children. Harrison noted that the problems differed from child to child and tended to be categorized into:

(1) Visual perception (recognition of objects or pictures) and visual discrimination

(2) Visuo-spatial relationships, including perceiving position in space and synthesizing parts into wholes

(3) Visual-motor ability, the ability to manipulate spatial relations

(4) Eye-hand coordination, i.e., to reproduce or draw what has been perceived.

Some of these contributing factors to handwriting disabilities are discussed below.

Disorders of motor control Learning to write requires the control of the body posture, head, arms, hands, and fingers. Any motor disorder that interferes with learning to perform the motor movements necessary to trace, copy, or write letters or words will disrupt the development of the smooth, continuous motor patterns necessary for automatic-sequential handwriting.

Myklebust (1965) refers to the partial inability to write as caused by a suspected brain dysfunction known as *dysgraphia*. The child is unable to remember the motor sequence for writing letters or words. The child knows the word he wishes to write. He knows what it sounds like, can say it, and can identify it when he sees it, yet he is not able to organize and produce the necessary motor movements in copying or writing the word from memory. Orton (1937) also described cases in which the loss of the ability to write was restricted to the motor function. In discussing *developmental agraphia,* Orton (1937) cited cases in which the speed of writing was rapid, but the quality of handwriting was extremely poor or illegible. Conversely, other cases were reported where children were capable of producing well-formed letters, but their handwriting was painstakingly slow and inefficient.

Goldstein (1948) referred to a motor dysfunction in handwriting as *primary agraphia,* which may take several forms. For example, the formation of letters may be disturbed. This problem is usually found equally in both hands. Copying is disturbed, and writing from dictation is no better than spontaneous writing. There is some difficulty in recognizing letters and in identifying the mistakes in inaccurately written letters. Children with this kind of problem, however, can usually write words for which they have developed good automatic motor movements. Another form of primary agraphia Goldstein (1948) described is a lack of impulse. The child may have difficulty beginning to write or completing a word. In these cases, copying or writing from dictation is usually better than spontaneous writing because spontaneity is not required.

Disorders of motor control may result from a disability in *motor output,* that is, in sending the appropriate signals to the body, arm, hand, and fingers to produce the necessary movement for writing. There is a condition called *apraxia,* in which children have difficulty performing purposeful, voluntary motor movements (Luria, 1966). A related condition is *ataxia,* in which a deficit in the central nervous system results in motor incoordination, poor balance, and jerky movements. These disorders interfere with the motor movements necessary for learning to write legibly.

Motor control may be disrupted by reduced *sensory input* through touch and movement. The lack of sensation in the fingers may result in difficulty learning to grasp and manipulate writing instruments. *Agnosia* is a condition in which the child does not perceive sensory information from the sense of touch (Luria, 1966). Gerstmann (1924) also found that finger agnosia tended to occur with difficulties in learning to write.

In an article on teaching beginning writing, Larsen (1970) emphasized the development of perceptual-motor behavior by special exercises using gross muscular movements in writing, including up, down, forward, diagonal, and left to right. Madison (1970) used finger painting to develop the kinesthetic and tactile senses in producing forms in pictures and letters.

Disorders of visual perception

Learning to write requires the child to visually differentiate between shapes, letters, words, numbers, and so forth. Telling the difference between a *d* and a *b,* for example, requires the child to identify the dominant feature of each, that is, direction. Some children require more time to discriminate than others do. Children who have difficulty visually discriminating letters and words also have difficulty reproducing or copying them accurately (Johnson & Myklebust, 1967).

Problems in perceiving visual-spatial relationships also have been correlated with writing disorders (Kephart, 1971). Disorders in visual-spatial relationships have been described as difficulty in left-right discrimination, avoidance of crossing the midline of the body with the hand, poor depth perception, reversals *(b/d)*, rotations *(p/d)*, and difficulty in perceiving one's own body in space (Kephart, 1971; Nielsen, 1962). Children with these kinds of problems typically have difficulty matching geometric shapes; maintaining a sense of direction; discriminating vertical from horizontal; copying shapes, letters, numbers, words; reading; telling time; using maps; and writing.

Disorders of visual memory

Children who fail to visually remember what letters or words look like tend to have difficulty in learning to write. Johnson and Myklebust (1967) say that revisualization is a correlate to handwriting disorders. Children with visual memory problems can speak, read, and copy, but cannot recall and reproduce letters or words from memory. The impact of memory on handwriting may be observed as the child attempts to form and sequence the letters to be remembered. In some instances children who cannot recognize a letter or a word visually can identify or recognize the letter or word through the sense of touch by tracing. This phenomenon, the inability to recognize objects despite normal vision, is referred to as *visual agnosia.*

Left-handedness

Hand preference in children does not become firmly established until the child is several years old. He or she then gradually develops right-handed preference (dextral), left-handed preference (sinistral), or no preference (ambidextrous). Approximately 90% of children are right-handed, 8 or 9% are left-handed, and 1 or 2% are ambidextrous.

Left-handedness in itself does not result in difficulties in writing. What causes the difficulties is the failure of instruction to provide a left-handed child with an early beginning in correct writing in a right-handed world.

Because this *is* a right-handed world, some parents become concerned when their 2- or 3-year-old child uses his or her left hand in manipulating objects, such as in eating with a spoon. One parent, sitting to the left of the child at the table, handed a spoon to her child, who used the nearest hand, the left, to grasp the spoon. The mother became concerned that the child would be left-handed. She was told to try sitting on the right side of the child and handing her the spoon from that side. The child then grasped the spoon with the right hand and used it in eating. This child was right-handed.

One of the questions raised by parents and teachers is, Should I try to change my left-handed child to use the right hand? Although little research is available, our clinical experience leads to the following advice.

(1) If the child is ambidextrous, that is, uses either hand in manipulating objects, it would be advisable to give the child practice in the use of the right hand. In school, the child should be encouraged to learn to write with the right hand.

(2) If the child is left-handed, it may be a disservice to the child to try to change the hand preference. Left-handed children who have been changed to write with their right hands tend to reverse letters and numbers in their attempt to write. If a young school-aged child learns to write 3 with his left hand, he may write a reversed 3 ($\mathcal{E}$) with his right hand. Ask a 6- or 7-year-old child to place a piece of chalk in each hand, blindfold the child, and ask the child to write the number 7 rapidly with the two hands. The child may write a reversed 7 (Γ) with the left hand and a nonreversed 7 with the right hand. A similar result may be obtained with the number 3.

(3) Learning to write from left to right with the right hand results in a tendency to write from right to left with the left hand. That is the reason why interfering with strong left-handedness may result in spatial disorientation, reversals, and related directional confusions.

(4) If a child is left-handed, he or she should be assured that left-handed people do everything right-handed people do but that there are some things they have to do differently. These include (1) seating the child at a desk with a left-hand arm instead of a right-hand arm; (2) seating the child in a position at a desk or table that provides the same freedom of movement that a right-handed child has; (3) positioning the child's hand on the paper the reverse of a right-hander.

In cursive writing the left-hander slants the paper to the left so that he or she will see what is written, similar to the right-hander who slants the paper to the right. In manuscript writing, both left- and right-handers place the paper squarely in front of them for best results. In discussing this problem, Otto, McMenemy, and Smith (1973) point out that right-handers pull the pen, while left-handers push the pen. They also note:

> Some left-handers will show up in the upper grades as remedial cases because they never received proper early instruction and have, therefore, developed an extreme back slant, a hooked writing position, or other faulty characteristics. (p. 355)

A cerebral-palsied boy who was more spastic in his right hand was asked by his teacher to write with the left hand because his pediatrician had diagnosed him as left-handed. He did have greater fine muscle coordination in the left hand than in the right hand, but in writing the child seemed to persist in reversing many letters and sequences in the words. The teacher tried several strategies to teach him to write without reversals but had little success. The consultant to the class requested that the child try to write with the right hand. The boy wrote words and sentences with the right hand with difficulty but without reversals. This example demonstrates that the hand that has the best coordination may not be the dominant hand for writing.

Assessing and diagnosing handwriting disabilities

Teachers usually begin the process of assessing and diagnosing difficulties in handwriting when they note that a child is unable to write or writes illegibly as compared to other children of the same age. There are handwriting scales available that can be used to assess handwriting and to note illegibility in writing. A list and description of these scales are found in Graham and Miller (1980). Of particular interest is one study by Otto, Askov, and Cooper (1967), who reported that experienced teachers are capable of making reliable judgments in assessing the handwriting legibility of children.

The assessment of handwriting, like other disabilities, is of little value unless it leads to remediation. The duty of teachers is to teach and remediate problems in children. Logically the individual who is responsible for remediation is the person who should make the assessment since the assessment should lead directly to remediation. In the assessment of writing in particular, most problems can be detected by experienced teachers, since writing is a visual-motor act, with a minimum of cognitive contributing factors such as concept formation or problem solving. A teacher can observe and assess the child's hand preference and fine motor coordination and the major errors made in attempts to write.

Although attending behavior, motivation, memory, and discrimination can be considered contributing factors, we will discuss two major factors in assessment: (1) the assessment of hand preference and laterality and (2) the assessment of errors in legibility.

Assessing hand preference and directionality

When a child is having difficulty in handwriting, is unable to write legibly, and is making reversal errors, the first assessment that should be made is the determination of hand preference and right-left discrimination. There are many tests of hand preference and a number of tests of right-left discrimination. These have been discussed in great detail by Benton (1959).

Hand preference

By observing a school-aged child, a teacher can determine the hand he or she uses in writing, batting, picking up materials, and so forth. It is only when a difficulty arises that a teacher wonders about the hand preference. The following observations can be made if a child is writing with the right hand but is uncoordinated and making reversals, or uses the right hand for some activities and the left hand for other activities.

(1) If the child can write her name, ask her to write it with the preferred hand. Then ask her to write her name with the other hand. Note the ease, speed, and legibility of each hand. Does the child write more freely and legibly with the right or left hand?

(2) If there is a question about hand preference, ask the child to make crosses on a piece of paper as fast as she can. Time her for 30, 45, or 60 seconds. Then ask the child to make crosses with the other hand for the same period of time. Repeat the process, twice with the right and twice with the left hand, alternatively. Count the crosses made in the time allotted. This test gives a good indication of hand preference.

(3) Test eye and foot preference. Eye preference can be determined by having a child look with both eyes through a small hole in a paper to see an object on the floor while the teacher covers the right and then the left eye. If the child loses the object when the left eye is covered, the child is using his left eye. Give this test two or three times to be sure the eye preference is consistent. Footedness is tested by having the child kick at an object on the floor or step up on a chair. A left-footed child will kick with the left foot or stand on a chair or stool with the left foot first. If the child is using his right hand but is left-eyed and left-footed, it is possible that the child's handedness was changed from left to right at an earlier age.

(4) From the history, determine if the child had a left-hand preference at an early age and had his or her hand changed.

Right-left discrimination

Another contributing factor that may relate to illegibility in writing is a confusion in right-left discrimination. The question here is whether or not the child recognizes left from right. To assess this function a teacher can say to the child, "Show me your left hand...your left ear...your right foot...your right eye...." The Benton (1959) tests of right-left discrimination include more complicated directions, such as "touch your right ear with your left hand."

Also, a picture of a man could be shown to the child, requesting him or her to point to the left hand, right arm, left ear, and so forth. Informal testing will give an indication of possible disorientation or directional confusion. There is some evidence (Benton, 1959) that directional confusion is correlated with problems in reading and writing.

Assessing illegibility

There are two methods that teachers use in observing children's difficulties in writing. The first informal procedure is to ask the child to copy a word or a sentence. In this test, the teacher writes words in lowercase letters and observes the number and frequency of illegible letters the child produces. If the child is more advanced in writing, the teacher can present a sentence that contains most of the lowercase letters and ask the child to copy it. Such a sentence is "The quick brown fox jumps over the lazy dog" (Otto, McMenemy, & Smith, 1973). These samples give the teacher an opportunity to analyze the child's error types. A second test, known as free writing, is sampling the handwriting of a child who is writing about a picture or an event.

Studies on the illegibility of handwriting have pointed out that illegibility is confined primarily to a few of the consonants and vowels. The most extensive study was made by Newland (1932), who examined the handwriting of 2,381 elementary school children, high school students, and adults. He found that over 50% of the illegible letters were in writing *e, n, d, t, r, i, a, h,* and *b.* The letter *e,* the most frequently used vowel in English, had the greatest frequency of illegibility, accounting for 15%. Later studies confirmed Newland's tabulation of error types.

An interesting analysis of errors in manuscript writing for first-grade children was conducted by Lewis and Lewis (1965). They found that (1) errors were most common in letter forms in which curves and vertical lines merge; they were less frequent in letter forms constructed of vertical lines or horizontal lines; (2) the errors made most frequently were with the letters *j, u, f, b, m, n, r;* (3) those with higher mental maturity scores made fewer errors than did those with lower mental maturity; and (4) left-handed children made more errors than did the right-handed children. The left-handed children exceeded the right-handed children in number of reversals, rotations, and inversions.

In addition to noting errors in the formation of letters, a teacher should look for the following 10 subskills.

(1) Position of body, head, arms, and paper
(2) Grasp of the pen or pencil
(3) Strokes
    (a) Vertical—up, down
    (b) Horizontal—left, right
    (c) Curved to the left and right
    (d) Slant of the lines—left, right
(4) Letter formation—size, shape
(5) Alignment
(6) Spacing—between letters, margins
(7) Quality of the line
    (a) Pressure—too heavy, too light
    (b) Firm and unwavering line
(8) Connecting lines
(9) Closing of letters
(10) Crossing.

Remediation of handwriting disabilities

Children with handwriting disabilities must achieve competency in (1) visual-motor subskills and (2) letter formation, both of which are necessary in learning to write.

Remediation for visual-motor subskills

Faas (1980) lists 97 tasks or subskills that must be achieved in learning to write. These fall into six skill groups, which can be summarized as follows:

(1) Prewriting skills
    (a) Grasping and manipulating the writing instrument and positioning paper
    (b) Producing strokes and lines
    (c) Drawing forms
    (d) Drawing strokes, lines, and forms using guidelines

(2) Manuscript and numeral writing skills
    (a) Producing uppercase forms of letters
    (b) Producing lowercase forms of letters
    (c) Copying numbers
    (d) Making words
    (e) Writing dictated lists of numbers
    (f) Leaving appropriate space between letters, words, and numbers
(3) Transition from manuscript to cursive writing
    (a) Learning to connect cursive letters
    (b) Learning to slant cursive letters
(4) Cursive writing skills: lowercase
(5) Cursive writing skills: uppercase
(6) Use of cursive handwriting skills
    (a) Writing words from a model
    (b) Writing dictated letters, words, and sentences.

It is necessary to remember that children with different kinds of learning disabilities will experience different kinds of problems in attempting to learn these skills, and that the selection of the most appropriate remedial procedure for each will depend upon the nature of the disability. Johnson and Myklebust (1967) discuss a number of special educational procedures designed for specific disabilities. A sample of remedial principles is outlined below.

Training motor patterns

When the visual guidance system is defective and appears to be unresponsive to remediation, a motor-kinesthetic approach to handwriting should be used. The purpose of the motor-kinesthetic approach is to train the motor patterns necessary to automatically produce letters and words without visual control (Orton, 1937).

Motor pattern habits can be trained by (1) guiding the child's hand according to letter form and gradually reducing guidance and increasing pupil independence; (2) tracing on a pane of glass under which patterns are placed; (3) writing the letter while the child watches so he or she can imitate the sequence of movement; and (4) combining the formation of movements with other movements (Goldstein, 1948). Similar procedures were used by Orton (1937) and Agranowitz and McKeown (1959), involving tracing activities, copying from a pattern, using templates, and providing practice in motor movements with the eyes closed or blindfolded. Only through repetition and practice can automatic-sequential motor patterns be developed. Repetition of the same or similar movements can be reinforced by teaching letters with similar movement patterns sequentially and in families (vertical, horizontal, ascending, descending, curved, sweeps, slants, circular, etc.).

Increasing cutaneous and kinesthetic feedback

Children who do not receive cutaneous input from the sense of touch or kinesthetic input from the ligaments, joints, and muscles usually have difficulty holding and manipulating writing instruments. A plastic grip may be placed on the pencil to enable the child to grasp the pencil more securely. These may be purchased commercially, or a piece of sponge or a clay mold can be placed about ¾ inch from the point of the pencil (Turnbull & Schulz, 1979). Using an oversized pencil or a plastic, clay, or sponge grip lets the child receive increased sensory feedback from the increased surface areas of the fingers in contact with the grip. It also provides a larger and more stable object to hold while writing.

Improving visual-spatial perception

Problems with visual-spatial perception may be alleviated by (1) changing hands for writing; (2) training automatic motor patterns; (3) using motor-kinesthetic approaches to improve sensory feedback; and (4) improving visual memory for letters and words. All of these methods may be brought to bear on visual-spatial disabilities.

Strauss and Lehtinen (1947) suggest that brain-injured children with visual-perceptual disturbances not be taught manuscript writing because they tend to space letters and words inappropriately, reverse letters, and have difficulty seeing the unified word form as a whole. Instead, Strauss and Lehtinen recommend that children with visual-perceptual disorders be taught cursive writing. Cursive writing has several advantages. Chief among these are (1) the letters of words are joined to form a whole, (2) spacing of letters is less of a problem, (3) the formation and joining of letters in cursive writing reduces the probability of making reversals; and (4) it is more useful and will save time by developing writing skills that will be expected in the later school years. Others recommend that cursive writing should not be taught until manuscript writing is developed (Wallace & Kauffman, 1978). This point of view reflects the position of the traditional developmental approach to classroom instruction in handwriting and does not consider the task demands of manuscript writing on learning disabled children with visual-perceptual handicaps.

Improving visual discrimination

Children with visual discrimination problems must be taught to identify likenesses and differences in shapes, sizes, letters, words, numbers, and so on. The signal qualities between stimuli upon which discriminations are made must be made obvious to the child. The child should have the opportunity to practice discriminative responses.

Improving visual memory for letters and words

Children who can revisualize letters are more apt to be able to write the letters appropriately. Johnson and Myklebust (1967) recommend helping children with problems in visual memory to revisualize letters and words. One approach to revisualization is to show the child a form, letter, or word and have him or her look at it, close the eyes and try to revisualize the form, letter, or word, and open the eyes to confirm the visual image. Children can be shown sequences of letters on chips or cards and asked to reproduce them from memory. Activities of this kind are intended to give the child practice in using visual memory with letters and words. A related activity is to have the child look and say the name of the letter or word. This is another way of strengthening visual memory, by associating the visual image with the sound of the letter or word.

The motor-kinesthetic tracing approach advocated by Fernald (1943) requires the child to trace a letter or word until he or she can write it automatically from memory. This technique uses the motor memory system to reinforce the visual memory system. As the child begins to learn a letter or word, this tracing stage is gradually eliminated and the child learns to trace the outline of unfamiliar forms with the eyes.

Remediation for letter formation

Graham and Miller (1980), after reviewing the research and literature on handwriting, suggest the following procedures for teaching letter formation.

Developmental and remedial procedures for teaching letter formation are the same for both manuscript and cursive writing. Letters are first overlearned in isolation through concentrated drill and practice, then applied within a written context. The initial formation of letters depends upon external prompts (e.g., copying, tracing) until eventually becoming internalized.

A combination of various instructional and motivational procedures is used to teach letter formation. These procedures include:

Modeling. The teacher writes the letter and names it. The student observes the number, order, and direction of the strokes.

Noting critical attributes. The teacher compares and contrasts the stimulus letter with letters that share common formational characteristics.

Physical prompts and cues. The teacher physically directs the student's hand in forming the letter. Additionally, the direction and order of strokes can be guided through use of arrows or colored dots outlining the letter shapes.

Tracing. The student forms the letter by tracing dot-to-dot patterns, dashed letters, a faded model, raised letters, or an outline.

Copying. The student copies the letter on a piece of paper or in wet sand (calling upon the tactile sense).

Self-verbalization. The student verbalizes the steps as the letter is written (using the auditory model).

Writing from memory. The student writes the letter without the aid of cues.

Repetition. The student practices forming the letter, through concentrated multisensory drills.

Self-correction and feedback. The student corrects malformed letters with the assistance of a visual aid (e.g., desk or wall alphabet chart) or under the teacher's direction.

Reinforcement. The teacher praises the student and gives primary reinforcers for correct letter formation. (p. 9-10)

There are a number of other considerations to take into account in teaching handwriting.

Speed of writing

Legible and effective handwriting depends upon more than letter formation. Fluency or speed is developed by practice. When the child learns to form the letters correctly and is able to write letters automatically, speed will increase with practice. The main consideration is to give opportunity for continual practice in correct writing.

Reversal errors

A common problem in writing is the tendency to reverse letters such as *b* and *d*. Such reversals are more common with manuscript writing than with cursive writing. One way of correcting manuscript confusions of *b* and *d* is to write the cursive letter over the printed letter— *b d* . Mather and Healey (in press) report a case of reversals that was corrected by emphasizing visual memory and imagery training in writing reversible letters.

Reversal tendencies in writing are more common in young children than in older children. Unless there is a contributing factor that results in reversals, children gradually eliminate reversals in their writing as they grow older. In some children, however, reversals persist because of poor visual imagery, as mentioned above. Others who are dominantly left-handed and have been changed in handedness continue to reverse letters. In these cases, practice in writing correctly tends to overcome the reversals. In severe persistent tendencies, a change of hand preference could be tried.

Cursive writing

The same problems of illegible letter formation that are found in manuscript writing are also found in cursive writing. When a child is having difficulties in manuscript writing, it is unwise to shift to cursive writing since cursive writing is more difficult to learn. The uppercase cursive forms, in some instances, such as the *K* and *k* , are different. In addition, there can be a problem in connecting the letters. Jordon (1972) points out that children can have a problem deciding where to stop a circular movement and when to swing back in letters such as *j, t, h*. Cursive writing requires more fine motor movements than does manuscript writing and should be introduced after the child has become more proficient in manuscript writing.

Strauss and Lehtinen (1947) advocated cursive writing because they believed it would correct reversal errors in writing. We agree that with children who show marked tendencies to reversals in writing, cursive writing helps correct the orientation problem. The main guideline is that whenever remedial systems are used, the procedure must be consistent and systematic. The child requires practice in step-by-step progression with reinforcement for correct letter formation.

A systematic VAKT procedure

In working with children with severe problems in learning to write, we have successfully used the following 12 steps. It is suggested that teachers follow the sequence below.

(1) Together with the child, establish a goal of learning to form letters legibly.

(2) After obtaining the child's attention, form the letter to be taught while the child observes the movement and the shape of the letter.

(3) Name the letter, "This is *a*," as you write it and ask the child to repeat the name. When the child repeats the name confirm it by saying, "Good, this is *a*."

(4) Rewrite the letter and discuss the formation with the child. "See, we start here, then form the letter this way."

(5) Ask the child to trace the letter with his or her index finger and name the letter. This should be repeated several times.

(6) As the child traces the letter ask the child to describe the process as you did in the fourth step.

(7) Write the letter in dots or short dashes (⟨*a*⟩) and ask the child to trace it with chalk or a pencil to form the complete letter. Repeat several times.

(8) Ask the child to copy the letter from a model. Repeat several times, being sure the child is copying legibly.

(9) When the child is able to copy the letter legibly, ask him or her to write the letter from memory, without a model.

(10) Help the child compare the written letter with the model.

(11) When the child is able to write the letter legibly, introduce another letter, such as *b*, for learning. When *b* is learned, ask the child to "now write *a*." Then alternate *a* and *b*. This allows for overlearning and avoids overloading the child with too many partially learned letters in one session.

(12) At all stages praise the child for adequate responses.

Summary

- Handwriting is a prerequisite skill to reading and spelling, as well as a tool for the motor expression of ideas.

- Two forms of writing are practiced. Manuscript writing is usually taught in the first grade while cursive writing is generally introduced in the second or third grades.

- The difficulties in handwriting stem from two sources: (1) difficulties arising from environmental and instructional factors and (2) difficulties involved with intrinsic factors or disorders of motor control, visual perception, visual memory, and hand preference.

- Left-handedness is not necessarily detrimental, but changing a left-handed child may cause some problems.

- Assessing handwriting ability includes assessment of hand preference, motor and psychological abilities, and particularly legibility of writing the letters.

- Errors that account for illegibility in handwriting are found in a small number of vowels and consonants.

- Remedial methods for handwriting include (1) practice in controlling motor patterns; (2) providing kinesthetic feedback; (3) improving visual-spatial perception, discrimination, and memory for letters and words; and (4) practice in increasing the legibility of the vowels and consonants that account for illegibility.

- Remediation of letter formation requires continuous practice in a systematic, step-by-step instructional procedure.

- Manuscript writing is the preferred procedure in initial handwriting instruction, but cursive writing may aid those children who have marked reversal tendencies.

Thought questions

1. With the current emphasis on electronic typewriters, word processors, and other aids, is the teaching of legible handwriting important? Why?

2. How did you first learn to write, by the manuscript or cursive methods? Can you evaluate the merits and disadvantages of each?

3. Of the contributing factors to handwriting disabilities, which one do you think is the most common?

4. How can you determine whether or not a child has sufficient motor control to learn to write?

5. Do you know of a child with poor motor coordination who has difficulty in writing? How would you plan a program of remediation?

6. Do you know a child who has visual-spatial problems? Can you assess his or her difficulties and plan a remedial program?

7. Do you know people whose hand preferences have been changed from left to right? Did they have problems in reading or writng?

8. How would you test a child's hand preference? Eye preference? Do you think these tests would be reliable?

9. Find a sample of an elementary child's handwriting and analyze any errors in writing. Are they similar to the illegible errors found in the research literature?

10. How can you explain the results of Lewis and Lewis, who state that the most common errors in letter forms were in letters requiring curves and vertical lines?

11. Do you agree with Strauss and Lehtinen, who advocate cursive writing with brain-injured children, or with those who advocate manuscript writing? Explain.

12. Remembering the task-process remedial method, how do you apply this approach to the remediation of a handwriting disability?

12
Spelling and written expression disabilities

Language arts specialists have stated over and over again that instruction in reading, handwriting, spelling, and written expression are intimately related. As Horn (1960) has stated,

> Spelling achievement is influenced by the student's experience in reading, handwriting, speech, and written composition in addition to what he does in periods specifically devoted to spelling. (p. 1341)

Everyone agrees that adequate written expression is essential for communication, for achievement in school, and for modern daily living. In spite of technological advances in the development of electronic typewriters, word processors, and computers, it is still necessary to learn to read, to write, and to spell.

It should be pointed out, however, that reading and spelling are different. In reading we receive; in spelling we produce. We receive new information through reading, but we express information through words whose meaning we have previously acquired. Children who have difficulty learning to read typically have difficulty in spelling (Frith, 1980). Boder (1973) and others have stated that children generally read more words than they can spell. This is not surprising since it is more difficult to produce a word than to decode it. It does not follow that if a child can read a word he or she can spell it, or vice versa, that if a child can spell a word he or she can read it.

In a series of experiments, Bradley and Bryant (1979) also found that most children could read more words than they could spell. Some children, however, did not conform to this general pattern; 29% of backward readers spelled more words than they could read. Bradley and Bryant concluded that reading and spelling are independent skills. A qualitative analysis of the errors made by the children in this experiment showed that there was a difference in the cues the children used in reading and in spelling. In spelling the children used phonological cues, but they did not rely on phonological cues in reading. Bradley and Bryant explained these findings by stating that "children can construct these words phonologically because that is how they write them, but they do not read them because they do not happen to be using a phonological code when they read" (p. 509). A repetition of the experiment with 30 children who did not have learning problems obtained the same results, again showing the independence of reading and spelling.

Studies on reading, word knowledge, and spelling with normally developing children have shown the dependence of reading and spelling on language acquisition. Beers (1980) has stated that "the child's knowledge about written words is acquired systematically, developmentally and gradually" (p. 45). In outlining three steps in teaching beginning readers to spell, Gentry and Henderson (1980) suggest that children be encouraged to write creatively, since by so doing they will discover correct spelling. Second, they discourage or *deemphasize standard spelling*. Children, they say, should not be held accountable for adult spelling. They direct the teacher to respond appropriately to nonstandard spelling. In this way the child is allowed to manipulate words so that the relationship of phonology, spelling, and meaning becomes clear. They contend that by having many opportunities, the child will gradually discover correct spelling of regular and irregular words. This philosophy may be appropriate for children developing normally but is questioned by those who deal with children with spelling disabilities. The latter are those who require special systematic instruction in spelling.

Spelling disabilities

Regardless of the general spelling methods used in the school, some children fail to learn to spell. Note the following sample of writing by a seventh-grade, 12-year-old girl, with a Wechsler IQ of 115. She was able to write several pages in an assignment. She had been promoted from year to year, was able to read, but had difficulty learning to write and spell. These are the children who are called seriously learning disabled in spelling and written expression.

Translation:
...the race but what she did not know was that someone from the rodeo was watching her. He went over to her after the race and said (Would you like a job this rodeo season) What is it? Riding on our team with your horse we need a good rider and if you would (oh yes! oh yes!) horse we practice on Saturday. I'll be there.

Most children with spelling disabilities have been taught spelling by one of three prevailing approaches.

(1) *Incidental learning.* This method hypothesizes that children can learn to spell incidentally, that they will learn to spell by reading, and that little formal instruction in spelling is needed. Peters (1967) referred to this approach as the ''caught'' method, in contrast to the ''taught'' methods below.

(2) *Learning from word lists.* This approach requires children to learn to spell from word lists. Debates in these areas center on whether children should learn hundreds of words, the words most frequently used in oral language, or words of social utility. The result is a series of word lists containing all three elements. One such word list is included in the section on remediation.

(3) *Learning to spell by generalizing.* This approach assumes that in normal development children learn generalizations that enable them to spell words that they have not previously studied. They generalize from *p-ay, st-ay, l-ay,* to *day, say,* etc. This approach has been referred to as the *inductive, discovery,* and *linguistic method.*

The three approaches have been debated by authorities in the field. In practice, however, children probably learn to spell some words incidentally, learn words by studying lists of words, and also learn by generalization from words already learned to words not included in the spelling list. The children considered in this chapter are those who have failed to learn to spell after having been given ordinary instruction in spelling in the classroom.

Factors that contribute to spelling disabilities

If a child has not learned to spell or makes excessive spelling errors after a sufficient period of ordinary instruction, teachers and parents become concerned. They wonder whether it is the instruction or developmental disabilities in the child that have kept him or her from learning to spell as other children do. In many instances the child is disabled in both reading and spelling. It is, therefore, important to consider any situations or conditions that may have contributed to a child's inability to learn to spell. Some of the physical, environmental, and developmental learning disabilities that appear to inhibit progress in spelling are described below.

Sensory deficits of vision and hearing

Sensory deficits are factors to consider. Research on the effects of visual acuity deficits on spelling achievement have found no correlation. That is, minor visual acuity problems do not seem to inhibit children's ability to learn to spell. Research results on hearing show similar results. Gates and Chase (1926) compared the spelling of deaf children with hearing children of the same reading level and found that the deaf children were superior to the hearing children in spelling. Templin (1954) repeated the study on deaf and hard-of-hearing children and found that hearing impaired children made fewer errors than did hearing children. These studies imply that peripheral sensory deficits will not inhibit children's achievement in spelling. The problem may be central rather than peripheral.

Environmental and motivational factors

These factors that hamper the learning of spelling include inadequate instruction not adapted to the strengths and weaknesses of the child, home conditions that place low value on academic success, and a lack of desire on the part of the child to learn to spell. Motivation is facilitated through spelling activities that show the child success, that reinforce the child for accomplishments, and that develop procedures that aid the child in self-evaluation.

Phonemics   As Bradley and Bryant (1979) have indicated, children learn to spell phonological words *(sat, sit, run, tap)* by using phonemic cues. Backward readers rely heavily on phonological cues to spell words. By learning the written symbols that represent sounds in the spoken word, children can translate oral words into written words. Both this approach and the generalization approach aid the child in learning to spell those words that conform to regular orthographic principles. However, because reliance on phonological cues for irregular words results in spelling *could* as *cud* or *sine* for *sign,* irregular words require other cues such as visual memory.

Visual memory   A major ingredient in learning to spell irregular words is to see a word, to visualize it when it is erased or removed, and to be able to reproduce it in writing without copying. Later the child can write the word, look at it, and remember whether or not it is correct. Children with severe visual memory problems have difficulty learning to spell irregular words. In addition to visualizing the whole word, learning to spell requires the memory of the sounds (phonemes) of the word. Learning the sound-symbol (phoneme-grapheme) relationship requires visual memory of the letters and auditory memory of the sounds. Horrocks (1966) has stated that "the learner looks sequentially at separate letters in a word and tries to memorize the visual letters in sequence." He identifies the types of imagery as:

> ...the ability to recall the sequence of letters in a word through photographic memory (visual imagery—a natural speller)
> ...the ability to learn the spelling of a new word through the intensive examination of the letters and the memorization of their sequence (visual imagery—a trained speller)
> ...the ability to write the complete word automatically and examine it to "see if it looks right" (kinesthetic imagery). (p. 2)

Perceptual   Russell (1958) studied good and poor spellers and found that visual and audi-
deficits   tory discrimination were significantly correlated with spelling ability. He noted that visual discrimination was more highly correlated with spelling than was auditory discrimination. But visual and auditory discrimination are interdependent, since they both function in identifying words (Boyd & Talbert, 1971).

Hodges (1966) stresses the point that multisensory experiences are superior to experience through one sense alone. He states:

> A child who has learned to spell a word by the use of the senses of hearing, sight, and touch is in a good position to recall the spelling of that word when he needs it in his writing because any or all the sensory modes can elicit his memory of it. (p. 39)

Schroeder (1968) confirmed Hodges' statement by conducting an experiment comparing an auditory approach to spelling with an auditory-plus-visual emphasis with children in grades four and six. He found that the auditory-plus-visual approach obtained significantly higher spelling achievement.

Speech and pronunciation

Children with articulation deficits may tend to misspell words because they mispronounce them (Furness, 1956). If a child consistently says "dum" for "drum," he or she might eliminate the *r* and spell *drum* as *dum*. A child who mispronounces "th" as "f" might spell *thumb* as *fum*. Although most children outgrow their articulatory defects by the second grade, some children retain their mispronunciations into later grades (Hull, Mielke, Willeford, & Timmons, 1976). Foreign language backgrounds and cultural deviations in pronunciation also cause spelling errors. In some cultural and socioeconomic groups, for example, word endings are sometimes dropped or added—*passed* may become *pass, came* becomes *cumbed,* and *ate* may be *eated*.

Formal assessment of spelling disabilities

There are a large number of spelling tests on the market. These tests are generally one of two kinds: a survey test or a diagnostic test.

The survey type spelling test is usually included in achievement tests such as the *Stanford Achievement Test,* the *Metropolitan Achievement Tests,* and the *Iowa Tests of Basic Skills.* These tests measure the grade level at which the child scores and give the teacher each child's relative grade or percentile level of spelling as compared to other children on which the test was standardized. Although most teachers know the spelling ability of each child (that is, equal to, above, or significantly below other children in the class), a standardized test gives a score that might verify the teacher's judgment.

The diagnostic spelling test not only measures the grade level at which the child spells but also provides a measure of discrete areas of strengths and weaknesses. These include such factors as naming sounds of the letters, writing words, spelling words orally, spelling syllables, and reversing letters in spelling, together with some of the correlates of spelling disabilities such as visual and auditory discrimination, visual memory, and speech and motor problems.

Informal teacher diagnosis

Teachers, both regular and special, observe a child's spelling and attempt to correct the errors made in spelling words. For the average child this is sufficient; he or she will learn to spell incidentally by reading, by some phonics and phonic generalization, and by the memory of how the word looks. But for children with more severe spelling disabilities, the teacher or examiner needs a more penetrating assessment. Below is an outline of the stages a teacher can pursue in analyzing the problem of spelling in children who have not learned by ordinary methods of instruction. These suggestions are adapted for spelling from the diagnostic procedures outlined in chapter 4.

Determine the disparity between potential and spelling ability

As with reading, a child's potential can be estimated by his or her comprehension of language. At what grade level does the child understand a story in a graded reading book when the story is read to the child? Has the child learned a school subject unrelated to reading, such as arithmetic? Does the child appear to have the mental maturity of other children the same age? At what level of spelling does the child perform? How much is the child below chronological age peers in spelling? The disparity between the spelling achievement and the expectancy determines the degree of retardation in spelling.

Determine spelling errors

To assess spelling errors it is necessary to observe and note the consistent errors a child makes in spelling or trying to spell words.

For young children who can spell only a few words, it is necessary to assess the child's knowledge of the sound-letter relationship. To do this, ask the child to write the first letter of a series of words like *car, man, ten, run,* and so on. Then ask the child to write the last sound of words such as *tell, ran, find,* and *man.* If the child can respond, ask him or her to write the first two letters of words with consonant clusters like *tr*ain and *cr*eep.

For children in grades two to eight, use a word list to test the child's skill in spelling. Table 12.1 presents a list by Hillerich (1976) that can be used with children to determine placement in grades two to eight. A child should be able to spell 50% of each list correctly. A child who correctly spells 50% or more of the words in Level C is considered to be at third-grade level. Likewise, a child who spells 50% or more of the words in Level F is responding like sixth-grade children. If the child cannot spell more than a few words in Level C, the child is at the level of first or second grade and requires simpler words for testing. For example, Frank could spell only the words *many* and *lock* from Level C. The teacher presented him with simpler words, some of which could be spelled phonetically, and some nonphonic words requiring a visual image of the sequence of letters. Such a test can give the teacher an insight into the level of phonics the child has mastered and what sounds or letters need to be taught.

Some questions a teacher can ask to identify the significant errors in a child's attempts at spelling are:

(1) Does the child add inappropriate letters in a word?

(2) Does the child omit any of the necessary letters in a word?

(3) Does the child reverse consonants, syllables, words?

(4) Do spelling errors reflect word mispronunciations or dialectical speech patterns?

(5) Has the child failed to generalize, spelling some words such as *me* but failing to spell *be* or *she?*

(6) Does the child make errors in consonants, vowels, or consonant clusters such as *tr*ap spelled as *tap* or *rap?*

(7) Are the child's errors primarily on irregular or demon words such as *guess, babble, half, have,* or *quite?*

(8) Has the child learned any rules in spelling?

Determine the contributing factors

Most schools screen children for vision and hearing as a standard procedure. A classroom teacher can observe whether the child is squinting at books or is showing other signs of a possible visual problem. Similarly, a teacher can,

Table 12.1
Placement
tests

Level C	Level D	Level E	Level F	Level G	Level H
clean	lady	pile	level	require	signature
write	crash	closet	account	bitter	criticism
asking	minute	beginning	flow	majority	industrial
few	shout	strike	magazine	described	endure
rain	toward	capture	restaurant	appeal	rural
third	hook	figure	include	saucers	construction
which	anyway	bull	appointment	flour	acquaintance
lock	knife	cloud	salad	editor	facilities
many	sudden	sense	equipment	possession	ability
tired	enough	honest	medicine	mischief	stationery
Mrs.	wrong	idea	troop	occurred	organize
friend	family	believed	stations	relative	interior
child	quick	proud	exciting	committee	condemn
round	I've	whom	shadow	official	commerce
catch	brain	earliest	naughty	gradually	sufficient
boxes	forgot	against	music	journal	audience
until	though	you'd	curious	appoint	doubtful
window	coin	law	principle	scratch	existence
should	whole	course	fuel	oppose	financial
Thursday	reason	joy	stranger	valued	proceed
	chase	trail	knot	interrupt	freight
	probably	receive	evil	coarse	reasonable
	threw	flood	necessary	solid	incline
	wouldn't	usually	awoke	immediate	perceive
	happen	double	gain	fortune	mathematics

Source: R.L. Hillerich, *Spelling: An Element in Written Expression.* Columbus, Ohio: Charles E. Merrill Publishing Co., 1976, p. 123. Reproduced by permission.

through a whisper test, determine whether or not the child should be referred for a hearing test.

From the history and the attitude of the child, a teacher can determine whether there are some factors in the home or school situation that have interfered with the child's learning. In these cases, reading, writing, spelling, and arithmetic may be delayed. The disability may not be specific to spelling. The attitude of the child toward learning to spell is another factor to be considered. If a child has failed repeatedly year after year, it is not surprising that he or she will be discouraged and become uninterested in learning to spell.

Visual memory has been one developmental ability that is considered crucial for learning to spell the irregular or nonphonic words. Procedures for informally evaluating visual memory have been described in the chapter on reading disabilities.

Auditory and visual discrimination and auditory memory are factors that need investigation in children with spelling disabilities. To test auditory discrimination, the teacher can stand behind the child and ask him or her to say "same" or "different" to stimulus words such as *tin–ten, tin–pin, sat–fat,* and *ran–ram.* The teacher can list a large group of similar-appearing letters and words to test children on visual and auditory discrimination.

Speech and pronunciation are evaluated by listening to a child describe an event or a picture. If a child has spelled *wun* for *run,* that is a cue that an articulation defect is interfering with spelling. The defective speech of a child is noted in responses to words such as *pitcher* for picture, *famly* for *family,* and *probly* for *probably.*

A case study

Benjamin, a 10-year-old fourth-grade child, was referred by his regular teacher because he seemed unable to learn to spell. He was examined by the school psychologist, the resource teacher, and the regular teacher. It was recommended, after an initial meeting, that the boy be placed in the fourth grade and assigned to Ms. Perkins' resource room. The examination showed that Ben was of average intelligence, was reading at the 2.8 grade level as measured by the *Wide Range Achievement Test,* and scored a spelling grade of 1.8. He was doing well in arithmetic, with a grade score of 4.2. His vision and hearing were normal. Although he had been assigned spelling lessons in spelling workbooks in the second and third grades, he did not learn to spell. He was unable to succeed in the weekly spelling tests and had become discouraged, even though he had made some progress in reading through instruction in phonics. To prepare for the IEP meeting, the resource teacher examined Ben informally.

Knowing the relative grade level of the child in spelling through the test score of 1.8 and the regular teacher's judgment that Ben spelled like a first grader, the resource teacher proceeded to assess his learning style in spelling.

The first task was to observe the errors Ben made in attempting to spell. Since he could not write stories, Ms. Perkins asked him to spell some selected phonic and nonphonic words that were included in a second-grade spelling workbook. He was able to write *sat* and *cat* accurately. He wrote *chair* as *cher.* He wrote *cake* as *kak, guess* as *ges,* etc. It was obvious from his responses that Ben relied on phonological cues in spelling.

By analyzing Ben's spelling errors, Ms. Perkins inferred that Ben had learned to read and spell through a phonic method and that he failed to spell the nonphonic sight words correctly. In checking the list of possible contributing factors to spelling, the resource teacher concluded that Ben's spelling problem was not the result of a sensory impairment, lack of opportunity to learn (environment), lack of desire to learn, or articulation errors.

Ms. Perkins proceeded to test Ben's auditory memory informally. Could he remember a sequence of words or a sequence of numbers presented auditorily? She asked him to repeat "3-7-4-6," then "5-8-3-7-2." She then asked him to repeat four words, then five words, then an eight-word sentence. Since he was able to respond adequately to this informal test, she tried auditory discrimination. Could he tell whether "ten" and "tin" were the same or different? Could he tell whether sounds /m/, /n/, /p/, /b/, and /d/ were the same or different? No basic problem was found in auditory discrimination.

Ms. Perkins then tested visual memory for words. Could he look at nonphonic words like *through, people,* and *garage* and reproduce them from memory? She wrote the word *people* on the board, told him the word, and asked him to repeat it. She then erased the word and asked him to write it from memory. It took him five trials to learn to write the word *people,* and five trials to write *through.* In other words, he was unable to remember the sequence of letters in a word long enough to reproduce it. Because Ben could spell some phonic words on the spelling test, but was unable to spell nonphonic words, the teacher hypothesized that a visual memory deficit might have inhibited Ben's ability to learn to spell irregular words.

From this informal diagnosis and Ben's school history, Ms. Perkins decided that his retardation in reading and spelling was related to a marked disability in visualization. She hypothesized that, since he was unable to remember words he saw, he had difficulty learning to read and spell. In the third grade a remedial reading teacher had tutored Ben in phonics and improved his reading from the first-grade level to high second grade. Phonics helped in spelling but it was not sufficient, since spelling requires phonics, phonic generalization, and visual memory of nonphonic words. The question was, Should she teach to the strengths by emphasizing more adequate phonics and phonic generalization, or should she emphasize memory for word wholes? She decided to use the phonics that Ben knew as a springboard for emphasizing the development of visual memory for words and phrases. These procedures will be described in the next section.

Remedial suggestions

Remediation for children with spelling disabilities utilizes many of the same teaching procedures advocated for regular classroom spelling instruction. For children who have not learned by ordinary methods, however, special programming and special emphasis is required. One of the major differences is in the diagnosis of contributing factors that are interfering with progress in spelling achievement. A child with an articulation problem, for example, who also has difficulties in auditory discrimination, will have difficulty learning unless the instruction is adapted to the child's strengths and weaknesses. In these situations a task-process teaching procedure is added to the regular skill-training procedure. Some remedial suggestions, both general and specific, are presented below.

Individualize instruction

A child who has failed in spelling in the classroom requires an individualized program. For at least the beginning of remediation, one teacher to one child in one room is recommended. A child pays more attention to the task and responds more conscientiously in an individualized situation. In addition, instruction can be better adapted to the strengths and weaknesses of the child.

Success is more assured under an individualized environment. After the child has made some progress and has developed more self-confidence, he or she can be taught with another child or in a small group.

Develop a spelling consciousness

Teach the child through practice in the spelling lesson to monitor his or her own written spelling. Valmont (1972) states that there has been a neglect in teaching spelling consciousness, "the ability to know that a word one has written is spelled either correctly or incorrectly or that one is doubtful of the spelling" (p. 1219). It is very important that a remedial spelling program include an awareness of the correct spelling of words and the habit of self-monitoring.

Organize remedial lessons to show the child success

Children become more motivated, have longer attention spans, and stay on-task longer if they are succeeding at the task at hand. It is, therefore, important to program the lessons in such a way that the child experiences success, preferably for every response. To accomplish this, begin with words with which the child can succeed and gradually increase the difficulty, building on patterns already learned. Use word families. If the child learns *oil, boil, spoil,* then add *recoil, spoiling, point.* Preparing a progress chart that can be marked every day will give a graphic presentation of the progress the child is making or the number of words learned. If the child is taught to mark this progress chart, he or she can play a game to beat the previous score. This procedure improves attention and learning.

Provide overlearning

Many spelling programs overload children with too many words and accept partial learning of each. It is advisable to teach fewer words and have children overlearn them than to partially teach many words that will be forgotten the next day. Axelrod and Paluska (1975) found that more words will be learned and maintained by teaching only six words a day. A good system is to teach word A to one correct response, then word B, then return to word A, then go to word B, and then to word C. When C is learned, go back to word B, then to word C, and then to D, etc. Continue until the child spells correctly all 5 or 6 or 10 words. Through continual and consistent review and practice, the child will overlearn and retain the words being taught.

Adapt instruction to the child's strengths and weaknesses

A major requirement in remedial spelling is to organize a spelling program that will be adapted to the child's own strengths, weaknesses, and preferred method of learning. If the child has a problem using phonemic cues in spelling, the teacher should either train the child in sound-symbol relations or use an analytic method such as asking the child to sound *cat* and write *c-a-t.* If a child's spelling problem is related to mispronunciation, enunciate the words and phrases clearly and have the child imitate. Require the child to enunciate "*r*un" if she has been spelling *run* as *wun.* If a child has a visual discrimination problem, teach visual discrimination in the spelling lesson. If the child has a memory problem, try to develop the habits of visualizing the word while studying and of remembering the visual image of the word. This is the task-process approach.

*Provide
instruction
to aid
generalization*

As indicated earlier, one of the approaches children use in spelling is generalization. Linguists have emphasized this approach. For children with severe spelling disabilities, remedial teachers must teach generalization. Instead of presenting rules, arrange the materials for study in such a way that the child will generalize. After generalization, the teacher can present the rule the child has discovered. Present *say, may, lay* in a spelling lesson and ask the child to spell *day*. If successful, ask, "How do you spell *may? Ray? Bay?"* and so forth.

*Use
multisensory
presentation
in spelling
lessons*

It was indicated earlier that a multisensory approach in teaching spelling tends to obtain the best results. This approach has the child see, hear, and feel. Luria (1966) refers to these sense modalities as the visual analyzer, the auditory analyzer, and the kinesthetic analyzer. Teach a word by having the child analyze it visually, then say and hear it (auditory analyzer), and then write it from memory (kinesthetic analyzer). When children are learning how to spell a word, they visually analyze it, vocalize it, and write it from memory.

Fernald's (1943) visual, auditory, kinesthetic, and tactile approach to reading and spelling is an example of the multisensory approach. It consists of eight steps.

(1) The teacher writes the word to be learned and says it.

(2) The child repeats the word (vocal and auditory).

(3) The child traces the word with a finger while saying the letter or word.

(4) The word is removed and the child writes it from memory.

(5) The child turns the paper over and writes the word a second time.

(6) The teacher provides the child with frequent opportunities to use the word.

(7) The teacher encourages the use of books and dictionaries to find the correct spelling of a word.

(8) The teacher organizes spelling matches that require written instead of oral responses.

*Provide
reinforcement*

During the remedial lesson, praise and encouragement are necessary. Praise or social reinforcement is sufficient for most children. For others, some material reinforcement may be necessary. When possible, provide some form of reinforcement for practice at home. This is especially effective since home practice provides rehearsal of words learned at school.

*Use words
that are in
the child's
functional
vocabulary*

It is well known that children learn and retain materials that are meaningful to them and more readily forget materials and words that are unfamiliar to them. Meaningful words learned should be applied to sentences whenever possible. A basic reading/writing vocabulary of 190 starter words supplied by Hillerich (1976) is found in table 12.2.

Table 12.2
A basic reading/writing vocabulary
190 starter words

a	do	know	our	thought
about	don't	last	out	three
after	down	left	over	through
again	each	let	people	time
all	every	like	place	to
also	find	little	play	told
always	first	long	put	too
am	for	look	right	took
an	found	made	room	two
and	four	make	said	under
another	from	man	same	up
any	get	many	saw	us
are	give	may	say	use
around	go	me	school	very
as	good	men	see	want
ask	got	more	she	was
at	had	most	should	water
away	has	Mr.	show	way
back	have	much	small	we
be	he	must	so	well
because	head	my	some	went
been	help	name	something	were
before	her	never	soon	what
best	here	new	still	when
better	him	next	take	where
big	his	night	tell	which
boy	home	no	than	while
but	house	not	that	white
by	how	now	the	who
came	I	of	their	why
can	if	off	them	will
car	in	old	then	with
children	into	on	there	work
come	is	once	these	world
could	it	one	they	would
day	just	only	thing	year
did	keep	or	think	you
didn't	kind	other	this	your

Source: R.L. Hillerich, *Spelling: An Element in Written Expression*. Columbus, Ohio: Charles E. Merrill Publishing Co., 1976. p. 57. Reprinted with permission.

Develop visualization skills in spelling

One of the most important correlates of spelling ability is visual memory; that is, the ability to visualize (see in the mind's eye), or the ability to retrieve an image of the sequence of letters in a word. Children with severe spelling and reading disabilities have great difficulty remembering what a word looks like. That is the reason they take many trials to reproduce a word. With practice, however, these children can improve their memory for words. For severe spelling disabilities, the following procedures have been used successfully.

(1) Write an unknown word to be learned on the board or on paper and pronounce it.

(2) Ask the child to look at it and to name it.

(3) Then, while looking at the word, the child should trace each letter in the air as if copying the word. Let the child label each letter (either with the sound of the letter or with the letter name). This helps the child visualize the word more accurately.

(4) Remove the word or cover it and ask the child to trace it in the air with a finger and say it while tracing it. The purpose of tracing in the air is to aid the child in visualizing the word.

(5) Repeat Step 3 if necessary.

(6) Repeat the tracing in the air and saying the word until the child is satisfied that he or she has perceived and remembered it correctly.

(7) Ask the child to write the word from memory and say it. Then compare the reproduction to the original. Repeat if necessary.

(8) Teach another word in the same way.

(9) Now ask the child to trace the first word in the air and write it from memory. If the child fails, repeat steps 2 to 7.

(10) When the child has learned to spell a word from memory and has learned other words, write the word in a progress notebook. This book of words learned can be both a progress record and a review program. It can also be used to record the number of words learned each day. Our experience indicates that the number of words learned each day will increase as the child improves in spelling skills. These improvements can be represented on a graph for motivational purposes.

(11) Use the words learned in sentences and in homework wherever possible.

Use verbal mediation

Studies by Vellutino (1978) and others have shown that saying a word aids visual memory. Earlier psychology studies have demonstrated that a person can learn words faster if he or she vocalizes the words. Vocalization is also a kinesthetic process, and thus visual memory is aided through the kinesthetic analyzer. Seeing and saying the word, writing and saying the word, and tracing the word in the air are successful techniques in spelling that use the kinesthetic analyzer.

Teach children to use a dictionary

Dictionaries are generally used to help define words but they are also used to look up word spellings. At the primary levels if the child has not learned the alphabet, the dictionary is of little use. However, as the child progresses to grades three and above, the use of a dictionary should be taught. Obviously, to use a dictionary the child must have learned the alphabet and have other prerequisite skills. Directions for teaching dictionary use can be found in many spelling workbooks and in Hillerich (1976) and Boyd and Talbert (1971).

Over the past decade, a number of "speak and spell" computing games for children that can be useful in self-instruction have appeared. The computer asks the child to spell a word and informs the child whether the word is right or wrong. The recent advent of microcomputers with programs for spelling may replace many spelling lists and workbooks. Time and research will demonstrate the usefulness of microcomputers in teaching spelling.

Written expression

One of the types of learning disabilities, according to P.L. 94-142, is *written expression*. Since this designation was made in 1975, the term *written expression* has been used to include spelling and all phases of written communication. Our concern here is not to outline the teaching of English as presented in courses in English composition, but to illustrate major difficulties children have in written communication and to present some remedial methods briefly.

Written expression refers to communicating ideas to others by means of graphic symbols. This involves having ideas to communicate, having language to express these ideas, translating the oral language into written symbols, and being able to write these symbols so that another person can understand the ideas intended.

In addition to handwriting and spelling as prerequisites to written expression, an even more important prerequisite is language development. Alley and Deshler (1979) point out that learning disabled adolescents most likely have had difficulty at earlier ages in listening, speaking, and writing. Johnson and Myklebust (1967) also emphasize the importance of auditory comprehension, oral expression, and reading for the development of written language. Phelps-Gunn and Phelps-Terasaki (1982) state that, in addition to the development of language, "the act of writing requires that a variety of visual abilities be smoothly integrated and coordinated with fine motor skills" (p. 3).

Students whose vocabulary is limited and who are poor in reading and in using grammar and syntax are prone to have difficulty organizing and formulating their thoughts in the proper form for written expression. Their written compositions tend to be short, and they seem to avoid complex ideas. Belch (1975) found that difficulties in written expression include grammatical errors, misspelled words, and errors in punctuation. Deshler, Ferrell, and Kass

(1978) found that, in monitoring their academic work, learning disabled students detected only about ⅓ of the errors they committed. They had not learned to proofread or to self-monitor their work.

As a result of these kinds of problems with written expression, students learn to compensate in different ways. They avoid writing. Learning disabled students use others' lecture notes, write essays in outline form, use tape recorders if available, and prefer to take oral examinations rather than written examinations (Alley & Deshler, 1979). These kinds of compensatory strategies, however, are of limited help to the student because they are not sufficient for meeting the many day-to-day tasks that require written expression.

Contributing factors of written language disabilities

In considering the correlates of written expression, it is necessary to understand that written expression is humanity's highest achievement and is achieved only when all the preceding levels have been established (Myklebust, 1965). A hierarchy of the components of the language arts has been proposed by Kellog (1971). It includes experience, listening, speaking, reading, and writing. Because there are so many developmental abilities and academic skills necessary for facility with written language, it is not possible to review all of them here. We will discuss four major factors that seem particularly relevant: (1) receptive oral language, (2) expressive oral language, (3) reading, and (4) motivation.

Receptive oral language

Students who have disturbances in understanding what they hear usually have difficulty in developing facility with oral expression as well as written language. These students will have difficulty comprehending because of limited vocabulary and will tend to remain at a concrete rather than an abstract level of thinking (Johnson & Myklebust, 1967). Developmental disabilities causing problems in receptive oral language also have an impact on written language.

Expressive oral language

Disturbances in oral expressive language are usually reflected in the student's written language in the form of problems with syntax and other grammatical functions, organization of words into sentences, omissions of words and word endings, misuse of verb tenses and pronouns, confused word order, sparse vocabulary, and difficulty in recalling words. Developmental disabilities affecting expressive oral language will also affect written language.

Reading

Students who have problems learning to read usually have problems in written expression. It is necessary to learn to decode written symbols before you can encode and use written symbols to express facts, ideas, and attitudes. Developmental learning disabilities that contribute to reading disabilities will also contribute to disabilities in written language.

Motivation

Students who have experienced repeated failure in attempting to express themselves through writing are said by their teachers to lack motivation. They are likely to either disdain or avoid the problem or become anxious, fearful, and frustrated. Eventually they develop feelings of helplessness and incompetence with respect to writing tasks. It is not uncommon for students to develop a "paralysis of effort" for written tasks until they are unable to express in writing thoughts that they could express verbally (Drake & Cavanaugh, 1970).

Assessment of written language

When learning disabled students enter junior and senior high school, the demands for written work increase and their plights become even more desperate. The students may try to get by as well as they can, become passive and withdrawn, or act out their frustrations with inappropriate behaviors. It is very important, therefore, that students with disabilities in written expression be identified and helped as soon as possible. In most cases, disorders of written expression are not identified until a child has progressed beyond the third or fourth grade, when difficulty with reading and spelling skills have become evident.

Gather samples of written language

The first step in assessing written language is to gather samples of written expression. This can be done by securing daily work samples, by giving the child a topic and asking him or her to write a story, or by using a standardized test. The *Picture Story Language Test* (Myklebust, 1965, 1973), for example, requires the student to look at a picture and write a story about it. The number of words and sentences, syntax, and abstract–concrete conceptual quality are assessed. The *Sequential Tests of Educational Progress* (Educational Testing Service, 1958) and the *Test of Written Language* (Hammill & Larsen, 1978b) also assess written language.

Analyze written language

The evaluation of composition or creative writing generally focuses on the following questions:

(1) How many words were used? Different? New? Inappropriate? Written per minute? Verbs? Adjectives? Nouns? Pronouns? Conjunctions?
(2) What kinds of grammatical errors were made?
(3) What kinds of punctuation errors were made?
(4) Were words capitalized properly?
(5) What was the number and average word length of sentences?
(6) Were the paragraphs appropriate in organization and content?
(7) Was the content well selected and organized?
(8) How many different points, examples, or illustrations were made?
(9) Was the purpose clear?
(10) Does the student monitor his work for errors? (Ballard & Glynn, 1975)

Assess writing deficiencies

Phelps-Gunn and Phelps-Terasaki (1982) refer to three kinds of writing problems that occur within the context of written language.

(1) Generation and elaboration of the writing act, which includes non-specific sentences, nonelaborated sentences, discrepancy between oral intent and written product, and incomplete idea formulation

(2) Lack of attention to audience, which includes lack of organization; lack of logical explanation; lack of clarity, coherence, and unity; and lack of communication to the intended audience

(3) Inadequate proofreading and error recognition, which includes inability to recognize errors in grammar, punctuation, capitalization, and sentence structure.

Assess receptive and expressive oral language

It is necessary to assess the student's development in receptive oral language, because problems in this area are often reflected in written language. However, it is possible for students who are not particularly verbal to write more fluently than they speak. In a study of fifth-grade black students who spoke nonstandard English, DeStefano (1972) found that they used more nonstandard forms in oral than in written language. Deaf students rely partly on reading to develop language and can develop written language to a more advanced stage than they can develop expressive oral language. It is, however, helpful to compare the products of written language and oral language.

Assess reading ability

When a student's ability to use written expression is not as well developed as his or her achievement in reading, it may be helpful to assess the student's reading level and compare it with the level of written expression. Many of the developmental correlates to reading disabilities will also affect written language.

Assess attitudes toward writing

Any remedial effort has a greater probability of succeeding if the student is motivated to learn and is willing to try. For this reason, it is helpful to assess students' attitudes toward their difficulties in writing. This can be done effectively by sitting down with the student, expressing your concern over his or her problems in writing, and exploring the student's concerns about the problem. This kind of interview may reveal in-depth insights into the student's attitude toward writing tasks. This information could be useful in planning remediation.

General remedial suggestions

Learning to express themselves through writing is a very difficult task for most students. Learning disabled students have an especially difficult time because of their other disabilities. Any remedial effort must be based upon the student's academic and developmental abilities and disabilities as well as general intellectual or cognitive level of functioning. There are six major objectives to consider in developing a remedial program: (1) improving oral language and reading skills, (2) improving attitudes toward writing, (3) improving ability to generate content, (4) developing adequate spelling and technical writing skills, (5) developing audience awareness, and (6) sufficiently practicing writing.

Improving oral language, handwriting, spelling, and reading skills

Because written expression is built upon receptive and expressive oral language, and upon handwriting, spelling, and reading skills, it may be necessary to provide the student with remedial procedures to develop these prerequisite skills. Remedial methods for these prerequisite skills are found in preceding chapters.

Improving attitude and motivation toward writing

Progress in writing will be greater if the student's anxiety, fears, and frustrations about writing are minimized. Irmscher (1972) emphasizes the importance of student attitude and motivation toward writing. Learning disabled students often become embroiled in the mechanics of writing; in capitalization, syntax, and so forth. For this reason, initial remedial efforts should ignore the mechanics of writing and focus on ideas (Alley & Deshler, 1979). Students should be given experiences and then the opportunity to talk about their experiences and put their ideas and thoughts on paper. The focus should be on ideas. This can be reinforced by taping their conversations and having them replayed and written down. Students should be reinforced for their efforts, and above all, their written products should be used in the classroom in a pleasant, fun way that is in itself reinforcing.

Improving ability to generate content

When learning disabled students seem to have difficulty generating ideas, they need to be taught how to select content for writing from reading, movies, discussion, experiences, television, trips, and other life experiences. They need to be taught to identify interesting and relevant topics. The what, when, where, who, and why approach of journalists can be of help in selecting topic content. Also, assignments that stimulate innovative expressions could be assignments on "unthinkable" questions, such as "What would I do if I were a bird?" "What would I do if I flew to Mars?" and other "if" questions. Or students could be assigned to write a letter to a girl or boy in Japan, China, or Borneo.

Developing technical writing skills

Alley and Deshler (1979) list a number of writing skills that need to be taught, including:

(1) Structuring paragraphs and themes
(2) Developing vocabulary
(3) Building sentences
(4) Writing questions
(5) Note taking
(6) Summarizing
(7) Monitoring written expression. (p. 124)

Developing audience awareness

Students should learn to consider the audience for whom they are writing. Writing to a child would be different from writing to a colleague or former professor. Phelps-Gunn and Phelps-Terasaki (1982) have pointed out that speakers tailor their communication to an immediate audience, to the needs of a listener. Writers must develop the ability to take the role of other persons, to take into consideration others' perspectives. The writer is required to imagine situations and to have the vocabulary and cognitive ability to communicate these ideas to someone else who is not present.

Practicing sufficiently

In order to develop facility with written expression, students have to write. It is necessary, therefore, to schedule writing activities at least three times a week (Elbow, 1973). Only through practice will writing skills improve. For writing practice to be effective, students must receive feedback and corrective instruction.

Special remedial methods

Other than the usual procedures used in elementary, secondary, and college-level English courses, few systematic remedial methods have been developed. Most approaches are adaptations of regular procedures. In discussing written language remediation, Phelps-Gunn and Phelps-Terasaki (1982) have reviewed several remedial methods that have been adapted to learning disabled students.

The Myklebust system

Myklebust (1965, 1973) has developed remedial programs for children with disorders of written expression. The first stage, according to Myklebust, is to give students experience in recognizing and developing an awareness of writing errors. This can be done by reading the written material aloud and having the students correct it or allowing them to reread their work. Children can edit their own work by reading aloud and using their oral language system as an accuracy check.

The second stage is for the students to orally organize their thoughts and ideas about what they want to communicate. Their oral language skill is used to help organize their written work.

The third stage consists of teaching the students to write at a concrete level and progress toward more complex and abstract content. Students are taught to write about subjects that are readily observable and describe them (cognitive–descriptive). Next, students learn to use their imagination about a concrete object (e.g., a knife) and then to write an expanded description such as "cut the bread into three pieces" (concrete–imaginative). The students learn to add time and sequence to their writing in order to achieve a logical sequential flow (abstract–descriptive). Picture sequences can be used to write sequential descriptions. Diaries can be effective in teaching time and sequence.

The fourth stage is to give the students an open-ended question or a single word or a topic and let them write a story. This requires instruction in ordering thoughts and preparing an outline before writing begins (abstract–imaginative). This is an important stage of the writing act. Teachers should read the students' work, make suggestions, and help students improve their ability to generate adequate writing.

The Fitzgerald Key

This system was developed in the early 1930s by Edith Fitzgerald (1966), a teacher of the deaf, for the purpose of developing written expression in deaf children. Because deaf children are unable to learn language and written expression through oral means, they need to have a written language system that can be learned through visual cues. Although this system has been widely used for many years in teaching deaf children, it has been recently adapted with some modifications to the teaching of written expression to learning disabled children.

The Fitzgerald Key (a chart) outlines the structure of a sentence from left to right to teach word order. To construct a sentence, a child follows the order in the chart. The Key is arranged to guide the child visually in the proper parts of a sentence. The sentence "I see a dog" could be written in the chart as follows:

Who	Verb Symbol =	How many	What color	What
I	= see	a		dog.
I	= see	two	brown	dogs.

The Key can also be used by children to analyze their errors in sentence structure.

The Phelps sentence guide

A systematic adaptation of the Fitzgerald Key for children having difficulties in written expression has been developed by Phelps-Terasaki and Phelps (1980), and reviewed by Phelps-Terasaki and Phelps-Gunn (1982). Like the Fitzgerald Key, it presents a sentence guide to aid the children in sentence construction. The guide consists of nine visual headings placed horizontally on a page:

(1) First? Second? Next? Then? Last? Latter, etc.
(2) Which? How many? What kind of?
(3) Who? What? How much? Which? etc.
(4) Doing? Is, are, was, were, am, have, did, does.
(5) What?
(6) For what? To what? To whom? For whom?
(7) When?
(8) Where?
(9) How? Why? It? For? Because? So that.

The Phelps system is organized to (1) develop fluency in writing simple sentences, (2) expand sentences into descriptive subjects, (3) focus on the predicate, (4) develop ability to practice editing incomplete and nondescriptive sentences, (5) develop use of verb tenses under the "when" column of the chart, (6) focus on editing errors of verb tenses, (7) develop writing of paragraphs with a series of sentences, (8) develop practice in editing paragraphs, and (9) develop the ability to create a mental picture of the content of a paragraph before writing the sentence. An example of the interaction system is presented in the following dialogue.

Teacher: Can you tell me something about this picture?

Child: He's kicking it.

T: O.K. Who is kicking it?

C: He is. (Points.) The boy is.

T: Write "The boy" in the Who column. Now, what *is* the boy *doing?*

C: He's kicking the ball.

T: Fine, write "is kicking" on the Guide here. (Points.) *What* is the boy kicking?

C: The ball.

T: Write "the ball" on the Guide. (Points to column.) Now, read the whole sentence back to me.

C: The boy is kicking the ball.

T: Good. *Who* is kicking the ball? (Points to Who column.)

C: The boy is kicking the ball.

T: *What* is the boy kicking? (Points to What column.)

C: The boy is kicking the *ball.*

T: What *is* the boy *doing* with the ball? (Points to the Doing column.)

C: The boy is kicking the ball.

T: Now, let's try to build a picture in our minds about this picture of the boy kicking the ball. How does the boy look in the picture? Close your eyes and tell me how the boy looks, where he is, and whatever else you "see" in your mind.

C: Well, he's a tall boy, and he's in the park.

T: Great! Now I know more about the picture you are describing. We'll write the new sentence right under the old one on the Guide. Where will you write "The tall?"

C: I'm not sure....

T: Well, "tall" tells you what kind of boy was kicking the ball, so write "The tall" under the What Kind Of column right here. (Points.) Then write the word "boy" under the Who column like in the other sentence.

C: Then do I write "is kicking" here again? (Points.)

T: That's right. And write *what* the tall boy was kicking in the What column. (Pauses as child writes sentence.) How about *where* the tall boy is kicking the ball? (Points to Where column.)

C: Oh, yeah. "In the park" goes there.

T: Fine. (Pauses as child finishes sentence.) Let's read the whole sentence together.

T and C: "The tall boy is kicking the ball in the park."

T: *Who* is kicking the ball in the park? (Points to Who column.)

C: *The tall boy* is kicking the ball in the park.

T: *What* is the tall boy kicking in the park? (Points to What column.)

C: The tall boy is kicking *the ball* in the park.

T: *Where* is the tall boy kicking the ball? (Points to Where column.)

C: The tall boy is kicking the ball *in the park.*

> T: What kind of boy is kicking the ball in the park? (Points to What Kind of column.)
> C: The *tall* boy is kicking the ball in the park.
> T: What *is* the tall boy *doing* in the park? (Points to Doing column.)
> C: The tall boy is *kicking* the ball in the park.
> T: You've done well. This sentence is even better than the one before. It paints a better picture in my mind when I read it.
>
> (Phelps-Gunn & Phelps-Terasaki, 1982, pp. 106-107)

Summary

- Instruction in reading, handwriting, spelling, and written expression are interrelated.

- Reading and spelling are different. Children tend to read more words than they can spell, but about ⅓ of the children can spell more words than they can read.

- Children learn to spell through incidental learning, through the use of phonetics, by visualizing the word to be spelled, and by generalizing.

- Spelling disabilities refers to difficulty in writing the appropriate sequence of alphabet letters for a spoken word.

- Difficulties in spelling may result from sensory deficits of vision and hearing, environmental and motivational factors, deficits in phonemics, deficits in visual memory, perceptual deficits, and mispronunciations.

- Informal teacher diagnosis involves determining disparity between potential and spelling, analyzing spelling errors and style of spelling, and determining contributing developmental learning disabilities.

- Suggestions for remediation involve the need for individualization, developing a spelling consciousness, organizing to show the child success, providing for overlearning, adapting instruction to the child's strengths and weaknesses, aiding generalization, and using conventional principles of learning.

- A major procedure in remedial spelling is to teach phonics and visual imagery of words through seeing, saying the word, tracing it in the air, and writing it from memory.

- Written expression refers to communicating ideas to others by means of graphic symbols.

- Written language disabilities involve deficits in auditory comprehension, oral expression, and reading. Attitude toward writing tasks is also an important aspect of problems with written language.

1. Why are reading and spelling different?

2. How do you organize a spelling method that would assist a child in spelling new words through generalization?

3. Which one of the contributing factors is most common? Explain.

4. Can you organize an informal spelling test and determine the child's level of reading and his errors and style of spelling?

5. Tabulate the suggestions for remediation and discuss the merits of the two most important methods.

6. Describe the possible difficulties a sixth-grade child can have if he or she is deficient in written expression.

7. What are the procedures you would use in analyzing the difficulties a child might have in written expression?

8. How would you motivate a child who hates to write?

9. What factors in the environment or in the child could decrease a child's interest in writing?

10. How do the special systems developed for children with difficulties in written expression differ from a high school course in English composition?

13
Arithmetic disabilities

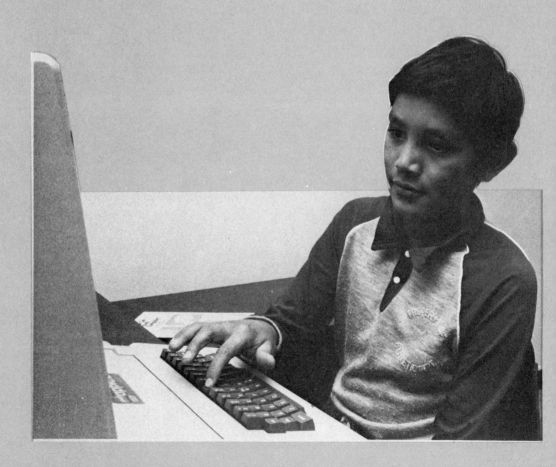

Children with arithmetic disabilities may have difficulty learning the basic skills such as addition, subtraction, multiplication, or division of whole numbers. Other students may not fail until they reach higher levels of computation with fractions or decimals, algebra, geometry, or trigonometry. Unfortunately, mastery of skills in arithmetic and mathematics has not received as much emphasis or attention as reading in American schools. Nevertheless, children with arithmetic disabilities require the same concentrated approach in diagnosis and remediation as do children with reading disabilities.

Similar to reading disabilities and language disabilities, arithmetic disabilities were first studied in adults who lost the ability to calculate as the result of brain damage. This condition was called *number blindness* or *acalculia.* Although fewer studies have been reported on children with severe arithmetic disabilities than on reading, arithmetic disabilities historically have been thought to be the result of brain damage. Kosc (1974), who has worked with children, uses the term *dyscalculia* to refer to a developmental mathematical disorder, in contrast to *acalculia,* which is defined as a postlesional mathematical deficit or a loss of an ability once acquired. He believes that damage to special centers in the brain causes disorders in mathematics abilities. In addition, there is evidence that "individuals are born with certain dispositions for mathematics" (p. 165).

This chapter will describe procedures for the diagnosis of arithmetic disabilities and present guidelines and principles for planning remediation.

Diagnostic procedures

The diagnosis of children with problems in learning arithmetic can be done by a teacher in a classroom or a resource room using informal techniques. The informal methods of diagnosis presented in this section should be used after the teacher has tried corrective teaching with no success and decided to dig deeper to discover why the child is not learning. The diagnostic procedures for arithmetic disabilities follow the same procedural format described in chapter 4, adapted to arithmetic.

Determine the achievement level in arithmetic

There are a number of arithmetic achievement tests that can be used to determine a child's level of achievement. Each school district has a battery of achievement tests used to determine every child's performance level. Once the performance level has been determined, it can be compared to a child's potential for learning arithmetic.

In the absence of test scores and in the interest of saving time, a practical approach to estimating arithmetic achievement on specific skills and concepts is to use the materials found in the classroom, particularly arithmetic workbooks written for different grade levels. Ask the child to perform a series of arithmetic tasks beginning with tasks he or she can perform successfully and gradually introduce more difficult tasks on the arithmetic hierarchy. For example,

(1) Ask the child to count by rote to 10, 25, 50, or 100.

(2) Say the name of a numeral and have the child point to the printed numeral.

(3) Ask the child to say the names of numerals.

(4) Ask the child to work whole number problems in addition, subtraction, multiplication, division, or with rational numbers in fractions or decimals.

(5) Give problems relating to time, weight, money, length, and so forth.

(6) Ask the child to work a series of word problems.

Observe the child's evidence of knowledge of basic facts, performance of arithmetic operations, and approaches to problem solving. By sampling the child's ability to perform arithmetic tasks at different skill levels, the teacher can make a rough estimate of the child's present level of arithmetic functioning, which can then be compared to the child's estimated potential for learning.

Determine discrepancies between potential and achievement

By comparing the child's achievement level to estimated potential for learning, it is possible to determine whether he or she is achieving above potential, at potential, or below potential. In grades one to three, a significant discrepancy would be achieving 1 to 2 years below potential. At any grade level above third grade, a significant discrepancy would be achieving 2 or more years below potential. A child of 9 to 10 years, for example, is generally placed in the fourth grade. His or her reading and arithmetic should be at the fourth-grade level. If the child is performing like a first- or second-grade child in arithmetic, is reading at third- or fourth-grade level, appears to be of average intelligence, and has had adequate opportunity to learn, this child could be considered disabled in arithmetic.

Determine errors in arithmetic computation and reasoning

The next step in studying failure in arithmetic is to study the child's performance on arithmetic tasks. It is helpful to determine the kinds of errors children make and the procedures they use in solving and computing arithmetic problems. Specific errors in arithmetic concepts and operations can be identified through informal techniques such as the analysis of errors on written arithmetic assignments, board work, oral questions, teacher observation, use of checklists, and teacher-made tests. Diagnostic arithmetic tests also can be helpful in determining the child's level of performance and the specific skills which have or have not yet been learned.

Children with arithmetic disabilities often tend to repeat the errors they make. Therefore it is helpful to look for patterns by analyzing the kinds of errors made during computation. The teacher should also be alert to the child's attitude, motivation, and willingness to persevere on arithmetic tasks.

Backman (1978) outlines eight categories of student work procedures and answer patterns.

(1) Arrives at a correct answer by applying appropriate arithmetic concepts and facts, using the correct procedure in the proper sequence, and recording the work appropriately.

(2) Arrives at a correct answer from a nonstandardized and often inefficient procedure devised by the student.

(3) Fails to perform a computational exercise because the child believes the problem is too difficult, does not remember how to do the problem, or lacks motivation.

(4) Makes random errors with no detectible pattern where some problems are done incorrectly and others are done correctly.

(5) Makes errors related to failure to learn concepts; confuses one concept or principle with another; fails to recognize when a concept or principle should be applied. Backman (1978) groups three kinds of conceptual problems:

(a) Errors related to the meaning or properties of an operation, such as writing an incorrect fact (e.g., 4 + 3 = 6)

(b) Errors related to the structure of the numeration system, such as ignoring place-value concepts or decimals

(c) Errors related to renaming and regrouping by failing to "rename" the digit on the left, such as

$$
\begin{array}{r} 15 \\ +\ 17 \\ \hline 22 \end{array}
\quad \text{or} \quad
\begin{array}{r} 12 \\ \times\ 5 \\ \hline 510 \end{array}
$$

(6) Makes errors related to sequencing steps within procedures because of doing the steps in the wrong order or leaving out some steps.

(7) Makes errors related to selecting information or procedures because of confusion of operations and facts. Children can do the correct procedure and know the basic facts, but confuse them. For example,

$$
\begin{array}{r} 21 \\ \times\ 5 \\ \hline 106 \end{array}
\qquad
\begin{array}{r} 54 \\ +\ 3 \\ \hline 162 \end{array}
\qquad
\begin{array}{r} 64 \\ +\ 8 \\ \hline 172 \end{array}
$$

(8) Makes errors related to recording work due to careless formation of numerals, transposition of digits, and misalignment of digits.

Identify the contributing factors

There are many reasons why children may have difficulty learning basic arithmetic skills. Chief among these are inadequate instruction, poor prerequisite skills, social maladjustment, visual and hearing impairments, emotional disturbance, physical and other health impairments, and mental retardation.

Language   Language has been found to be associated with achievement in arithmetic concepts, arithmetic operations, and algebra (Kaliski, 1962; Kosc, 1974). Children must develop a numerical vocabulary in order to understand and use concepts of magnitude, time, number, and conservation (Peterson, 1973). Children who do not develop language systems have problems organizing and categorizing information, both of which are important for learning grouping and numerical concepts. Normally, functional nonverbal concepts of magnitude seem to emerge early in cognitive development. Comparative vocabulary words, such as *littlest, middle, biggest, many,* and *more,* are mastered later.

Children with problems in auditory and visual memory who have difficulty in remembering what they hear or see often have difficulty in developing oral language. Problems in oral language are discussed in chapter 9.

Attention   Attending behavior can be disrupted by events in the child's environment or by physical conditions within the child. Inattentiveness could result from a number of causes, such as low level of visual or auditory acuity, mental retardation, inability to obtain meaning from what is heard or seen, severe emotional disturbance, hyperactivity, medication, and distractibility involving competitive stimuli in the environment.

Disabilities in attention may take several forms. These are described in chapter 5 and include hyperactivity, hypoactivity, fixation of attention, distractibility, and impulsivity or disinhibition.

In some cases, problems in attention may be related to a single sensory channel, a particular kind of task, or the conditions which precede, occur during, or immediately follow the inattentive behavior (Pysh & Chalfant, 1980). Regardless of the cause or the form inattentive behavior takes, failure to attend will impede the learning of arithmetic concepts and skills.

Visual-spatial
discrimination   A disability in visual-spatial discrimination may result in several different kinds of problems that could interfere with the learning of arithmetic and mathematics. In some cases, children may rotate numerals such as 6 or 9 because they fail to distinguish between the vertical differences between the two numerals. In other cases, children may reverse numerals (e.g., 21–12; 41–14) because they do not distinguish left-right differences. Children who do not make the distinction between left and right may make reversals in reading from right to left.

Visual-spatial difficulty can cause problems in learning place value. Luria (1966) has found that brain injury that affects visual-spatial synthesis causes difficulty in learning the concept of place value. The same digit expresses different values depending on where it is located in a numeral. For example, the 3 in 31 has a higher value than the 3 in 13. Children who do not learn the categorical structure of numbers have difficulty calculating.

Difficulty in perceiving the patterns in grouping arrangements makes it difficult to count objects in a grouping if it is not possible to touch or move the objects (Michael, Guilford, Fruchter, & Zimmerman, 1957). Spatial ability has been correlated with success in mathematics, geometry, and algebra (Smith, 1964). Children who have difficulty perceiving the relationships of lines and objects in space will have difficulty recognizing or reproducing geometric shapes and designs.

Sensory integration

Many early concepts and skills in arithmetic require children to use their hearing and vision and to touch and manipulate objects. These kinds of early learning activities are multisensory because they require input from two or more sensory channels (Belmont, Birch, & Karp, 1965).

The addition of a column of single digit numbers makes multisensory demands on the child. For example, consider:

$$
\begin{array}{r}
6 \\
5 \\
+\,9 \\
\hline
20
\end{array}
$$

First, the child looks at the 6 (visual discrimination) and says "six" (auditory memory and verbal expression). Second, he looks at the 5 (visual discrimination) and says "five" (auditory memory).

Third, he recalls the number fact (6 + 5 = 11) and says "eleven" (auditory memory). Visual memory of the symbols (6 + 5 = 11) can help learn the fact on a written symbol level without the accompanying auditory language.

Fourth, the child thinks "eleven" (auditory memory) and then looks at 9 (visual discrimination) and says "plus nine equals twenty" (auditory memory).

In teaching children with arithmetic disabilities, therefore, it is helpful to determine if a child has difficulty receiving information or responding through various combinations of the visual, auditory, and kinesthetic channels on such tasks as (1) making judgments, comparing, and matching geometric shapes, groups of objects, and numeral shapes; (2) matching number names with printed or written numerals, and (3) matching oral counting with objects.

Concept formation

There is a close relationship between mental age and the acquisition of quantitative concepts (Gesell, 1940; Gesell & Ilg, 1946). Mental age has been found to be an important factor in determining when a child learns certain concepts. Brain-injured children often are able to learn and use one concept, but have trouble shifting to a second concept (Siegel, 1957). For example, a child may learn that 1 + 2 = 3, but this same child might insist that 2 + 1 are not equal to 3. Difficulties in concept formation can be a serious obstacle to adequate performance in arithmetic.

Problem solving

One of the major correlates to successful progress in arithmetic is problem solving, which requires reasoning, inductive and deductive thinking, and the ability to handle abstractions (McTaggert, 1959). Many learning disabled children fail to use organized and systematic strategies for problem solving (Parrill-Burnstein, 1981). Learning disabled children, like younger children or children with lower mental ages, tend toward more stereotyped, perseverative, and trial-and-error approaches to solving problems (Bruner, 1973). As children become older, their problem solving becomes more systematic and their solutions more insightful (Ausubel, 1958; Elkind, 1961a, 1961b, 1961c). General intelligence has been found to be related more closely to ability in problem solving than to mechanical arithmetic calculations (Schonell & Schonell, 1958). This supports the experience of teachers who find it easier to teach children simple calculations than to teach problem-solving skills. Methods for assessing problem-solving behavior may be found in chapter 8.

Develop a hypothesis about the nature of the problem

The hypothesis provides a rationale for making decisions about the learning characteristics or learning style of the child. Knowing how a child learns best, as well as the conditions under which learning does or does not occur, gives the teacher a logical rationale for selecting appropriate instructional objectives and matching teaching procedures and materials to the child's needs and abilities.

A teacher can develop a hypothesis by integrating the data and information obtained during the diagnosis. The child's level of arithmetic achievement, his or her intellectual level, the discrepancy between achievement and potential, the kinds of errors made in arithmetic, and the status of the child's developmental abilities should be analyzed to determine the nature of the problem.

A task-process approach to remediation

Remediation for children with specific learning disabilities in arithmetic requires more than the usual developmental techniques of instruction. When the diagnosis has been completed and a hypothesis about the nature of the problem formed, the teacher must individualize a remedial program for the child. This section will present guidelines for individualizing remedial instruction for children with arithmetic disabilities.

The task-process approach to the remediation of arithmetic disabilities is concerned with the arithmetic portion of the elementary school curriculum as well as the developmental disabilities that may be contributing to failure.

Select instructional objectives

The first step in developing a remedial plan from the results of the diagnosis is to select appropriate instructional objectives at the child's skill level. This requires knowing exactly which skills the child has and has not mastered on the hierarchy of arithmetic skills. The instructional objectives should be written so explicitly that the teacher knows when each one has been achieved. The written objective has three major components:

(1) The behavior the child must perform to achieve the objective (e.g., the child can add a column of five one-digit numbers)
(2) The condition under which the child must perform (e.g., written on a worksheet both vertically as well as horizontally)
(3) The standard for having achieved the objective (e.g., with 100% accuracy)

The entire objective would be written as follows:

The child can add a column of five one-digit addition problems written on a worksheet both vertically and horizontally with 100% accuracy.

Break the objective down into operational subskills

Second, each instructional objective on the arithmetic hierarchy has prerequisite skills or subskills. For example, adding two one-digit numbers has at least six subskills:

(1) Say number names by rote.
(2) Count forward to nine by rote beginning with any number.
(3) Indicate the numerical value of any numeral (e.g., 3 = / / /).
(4) Establish numeral-number correspondence (e.g., 5 = five).
(5) Add a column of one-digit numerals.
(6) Recall and write the correct numeral for the answer.

A child may fail to add a column of one-digit numbers because of failure in any one of these six substeps. In teaching an instructional objective, the teacher should do a task analysis of the skill to determine which subskills are required. It is a simple matter to determine which prerequisite skills or subskills a child can or cannot do.

Determine which developmental learning abilities are involved in the task

Third, task analysis will help determine which developmental learning abilities are involved in a particular task. Table 13.1, for example, schematically presents five arithmetic tasks and indicates which developmental learning abilities are primarily involved in these tasks (squares) and which abilities may be secondarily involved (small circles). Neither the skills nor the developmental learning abilities in table 13.1 are intended to be exhaustive. The sensorimotor skills, for example, are not included for the sake of simplicity.

Table 13.1 simply represents five examples of how a task in arithmetic or in mathematics can be analyzed in terms of the developmental learning abilities involved. For example, reading numerals makes demands primarily on concept formation, language, auditory-visual association, and auditory and visual memory.

Table 13.1
Developmental learning abilities involved in arithmetic and mathematical skills

Tasks	Problem solving	Concept formation	Language	Integration & association	Memory		Discrimination		Attention	
					Auditory	Visual	Auditory	Visual	Auditory	Visual
1. Comparison of sets		■	■					■	■	■
2. Rational counting	•	■	■	■	■		■	•	•	•
3. Reading numerals	■	■	■	■	■	■	•	•	•	•
4. Arithmetic operations	■	■	•	•	■	■	•	•		•
5. Story problems	■	■	■	•	•	•	•	•	•	•

Consider develop-mental disabilities in organizing instruction

Fourth, having ruled out the more common correlates to failure in arithmetic, such as poor instruction, sensory impairment, low intelligence, and lack of motivation, and having identified a developmental learning disability, the teacher should consider the impact of the disability on the various arithmetic tasks that are to be taught. Knowledge of the disability combined with an analysis of the arithmetic tasks makes it possible to predict the kinds of difficulties a child will experience on those tasks involving the ability. This information is helpful in making decisions about the most appropriate way to present new concepts, facts, and operations to the child in order to facilitate learning.

Examples of the task-process approach

This section illustrates how a teacher may approach arithmetic remediation through a task-process approach. Five arithmetic tasks that have been analyzed in terms of the developmental abilities required to perform the task (see table 13.1) are presented. These tasks include (1) comparison of sets, (2) rational counting, (3) reading numerals, (4) arithmetic operations, and (5) story problems.

It should be noted that books on teaching mathematics by Bley and Thornton (1981), Reisman and Kauffman (1980), Johnson (1979), and others provide excellent and much more detailed suggestions for remediation.

Comparison of sets

During the early number program, children must learn to compare sets of objects to determine whether they are equivalent or if one set involves "same," "more," or "fewer" than another. There are five kinds of developmental disabilities that might interfere with the comparison of sets. These are concept formation, language, visual discrimination, and visual and auditory attention.

If a child does not understand the basic concepts of same, more, or less, it is necessary to point out the one-to-one correspondence between two sets and emphasize that both sets have the "same" number of objects; for example,

Thus, the teacher is accomplishing concept learning and language learning simultaneously. An example of task-process remediation is presented for each of the four major disabilities that could cause difficulty in comparing sets.

(1) "More" and "less" can be taught by providing one set of three objects and one set of objects with either four or two objects. Expressions such as "more" and "less" are used to describe the comparison. Many children learn these concepts and vocabulary incidentally, but when a learning disabled child does not learn incidentally, remedial language instruction must be deliberate.

(2) If the child has problems in visual discrimination or visual attention, it is helpful to use identical objects in all equivalent sets to be matched. For example, provide a set of three green blocks and ask the child to make another set to match the original set of green blocks. Emphasize one-to-one correspondence.

(3) Disturbances in visual figure-background discrimination can be reduced by keeping the extra blocks in a sack and giving them to the child one at a time as requested until the set has been matched. Later, introduce irrelevant characteristics in the materials used. For example, provide a set of three green blocks and have the child match it with yellow blocks, or nickels, or paper clips. This will help the child ignore irrelevant dimensions and concentrate on the one-to-one correspondence.

(4) In teaching "more" and "less" to children who have visual attention or discrimination differences, begin with matching sets where large differences occur. Children should be asked to touch those objects in a set that cannot be matched one-for-one to the elements in another set. Matching objects can then be changed to matching pictures.

Rational counting

Rational counting refers to the counting of objects rather than merely reciting number names in sequence. Children are taught to move each object as it is counted so they do not skip objects or count some objects twice. There are five major disabilities that often cause difficulty in learning to count.

(1) Children who have conceptual and language problems may not grasp the "one number–one object" idea. The child must be taught that a number name is given to each object counted. This can be taught by demonstrating the "touch-say" concept. The teacher touches each object, saying "one, two, three," etc. This counting procedure can be done by the teacher and the child in unison until the child understands the basic idea of one number–one object.

(2) A disability in oral expressive language might prevent the child from saying the number names appropriately. A child with an oral expressive language problem must be taught to say the number names in sequence. This can be done using rhymes, songs, and rhythmic activities.

(3) A problem in visual-vocal-motor integration might result in failure to see, touch, and say the name of each object. In these cases, the teacher must begin with small groups of objects (e.g., two, three, or four) and (a) direct the child's eyes toward the first object, (b) have the child touch the ob-

ject, and then (c) say the number word. These three steps can be accelerated until they occur simultaneously and are integrated.

(4) Problems in memory can interfere with counting of objects. For example, children must remember that when they associate a number name with the last object in a set of five objects, that number name tells how many objects are in the set. A slightly different skill is involved in counting five objects from a set containing more than five objects. The child has to remember and listen for the number name during the act of counting and stop when he or she hears it.

(5) Children with a problem in auditory discrimination may have difficulty discerning the differences in the sounds of the numeral names such as "sixteen" and "sixty." This could affect the development of both the understanding and use of number names. Remediation for this kind of problem should be focused on auditory discrimination training in which the child is taught to differentiate between spoken numbers. A common procedure for auditory discrimination training is to give the child practice in hearing numeral names, present two numeral names and ask if they are the same or different, and have the child repeat the numeral names. Activities using objects can be used to help children learn to differentiate and identify numeral names which they hear.

Reading numerals

Reading numerals is an important part of the arithmetic readiness curriculum. There are three basic patterns of reading numerals to be mastered (1–12, 13–19, and 20–99). Children must learn to look at the numeral (e.g., 5) and say the numeral name (e.g. "five") and hear the numeral name and point to the appropriate numeral symbol. These tasks require the child to attend and discriminate auditorily and visually, but failure to read numerals is most often the result of a conceptual problem, sensory associations, or auditory or visual memory problems. (See table 13.1.) Suggestions for remediation follow.

(1) If the child has a conceptual problem, remediation should be directed toward teaching the child that the number symbol (e.g., 5) stands for a particular number of objects (e.g., • • • • •). This can be accomplished by repeatedly displaying the numeral together with the set of five objects. Practice should be given by having the child match numerals with sets of objects in which the spatial arrangements vary.

(2) If the child has a disability in associating the visual symbol (e.g., 5) and the numeral name (e.g., "five"), make the initial presentation through the preferred or most intact modality. For example, if a child functions most effectively through the visual channel, present the numeral to be learned visually (e.g., 5) and then tell the numeral name (e.g., "five"). Children with visual discrimination problems can trace numerals on the chalkboard, on sandpaper, or in wet sand. Their hands can be guided using verbal prompts such

as "the seven goes across and down." The child might be asked to close the eyes to concentrate on the direction and shapes of the numerals being taught. Each time a child looks and traces a numeral he or she should say the numeral name. These kinds of multisensory activities reinforce both auditory and visual memory for symbol-name correspondence.

(3) When the child has been taught to associate two or three numerals with their names, it is helpful to provide the opportunity to practice recognizing or recalling numerals or numeral names. For example, present with three numerals (e.g., 4, 5, and 6) and ask the child to point to "six," "four," or "five." This requires the child to recognize the appropriate symbol visually. Asking the child to write a "four," "five," or "six" requires visual recall. Practice may be given in auditory recall by asking the child to say the names of various numerals. Auditory recognition can be practiced by presenting a numeral (e.g., 4) and asking if this is a "two, five, or four?"

Arithmetic operations

Procedures for computing pencil-and-paper arithmetic problems follow a step-by-step progression for each operational sequence the student must master. The procedure for task-process analysis of arithmetic operations presented here can be used for addition, subtraction, multiplication, division, and other operations. This kind of analysis is helpful in identifying the kinds of developmental abilities involved in an operation. Information of this kind provides direction for identifying potential developmental disabilities and for planning remediation. The procedure for task-process analysis of arithmetic operations is illustrated in the following two examples.

(1) *Addition.* A task-process analysis of the arithmetic operation for adding whole numbers in the two-digit addition below requires five major developmental abilities: problem solving, concept formation, visual discrimination, visual memory, and auditory memory. For example, when learning to add two-digit numerals, the child first models each addend using an appropriate manipulative such as bundles of 10 sticks and single sticks.

The first step of the operational sequence is to look at the arithmetic problem and remember to read from the right.

$$\begin{array}{r} 25 \\ + \ 17 \\ \hline \end{array}$$

Visual attention and visual-spatial memory are required to perform this task. Spatial direction is important, or the child will read in the wrong direction.

Second, the child should look at 25 and say "twenty-five." Number recognition requires visual discrimination and visual memory. To say "twenty-five" requires auditory recall memory.

Third, the child looks at 25 and recognizes that he or she needs to show two bundles of ten sticks and five single sticks.

```
                   Tens        Ones
        25
      + 17
```

This requires understanding the concepts of number, counting, and place value. Visual discrimination and visual memory are involved in manipulating and placing the bundles of sticks in the tens or ones columns.

Fourth, the child repeats the second and third operations for the numeral 17.

```
                   Tens        Ones
        25
      + 17
```

Fifth, the child then counts the 12 single sticks in the ones column. He or she must decide to group 10 together to form another group of ten. This new bundle is placed with the other tens. The remainder (2 sticks) are counted and recorded in the problem.

```
                   Tens        Ones
       ¹25
      + 17
        2
```

This requires the child to understand the concept of rational counting, the concept of number, the concept of place value, and use visual-spatial memory for recording the answer.

Sixth, the child then counts the bundles of 10 and records this number in the problem.

```
       ¹25
      + 17
        42
```

Concepts of number, place value, counting, and visual-spatial memory for recording the answer are required.

It is extremely important in this developmental stage that the child relates what he or she is doing with the sticks or other manipulatives to the steps in completing the written problem. This is accomplished by recording the results of each step of the procedure immediately, as was described in the example.

(2) *Multiplication.* In teaching multiplication, it is a good idea to begin with a story. For example, "Jack has two fish tanks. In each tank he has 26 fish. How many fish does he have?" During the initial teaching of this problem, children must have a grasp of the multiplication facts, place value, and distributive property, and be able to multiply multiples of 10 by a one-digit number.

The first step is to show 26 by placing two bundles of tens and six ones. This should be done twice:

Tens   Ones

Major developmental abilities for this task include visual discrimination, visual-spatial memory, concepts of number, counting, and place value.

Second, count the single sticks (12) and record in the problem:

$$\begin{array}{r} 26 \\ \times\ 2 \\ \hline 12 \leftarrow \end{array}$$

Developmental abilities include the concepts of rational counting, number, place value, and visual-spatial memory for recording the answer.

Third, count the groups of 10 (4) and ask what number is four tens? The answer (40) is recorded in the problem.

$$\begin{array}{r} 26 \\ \times\ 2 \\ \hline 12 \\ 40 \leftarrow \end{array}$$

Developmental abilities for this task include visual discrimination, visual-spatial memory, and concepts of number, counting, and place value.

Fourth, add 12 and 40 and record the answer in the algorithm.

$$\begin{array}{r} 26 \\ \times\ 2 \\ \hline 12 \\ 40 \\ \hline 52 \leftarrow \end{array}$$

Developmental abilities include the concepts of rational counting, counting, and place value; and visual and auditory memory for adding and recalling and writing the correct numerals in the answer.

(3) *Remedial application.* Regardless of which arithmetic operation is being taught (addition, subtraction, multiplication, or division), the task-process analysis can help teachers pinpoint the specific arithmetic subskill where the child is having difficulty and the developmental abilities involved. The examples of addition and multiplication demonstrate how the operations may be analyzed. Remediation is directed at the operational subskill and the developmental disabilities that may be contributing to the problem.

For example, if a child has difficulty adding a two-digit multiplication problem,

$$\begin{array}{r} 26 \\ \times\ 12 \\ \hline 52 \\ 26 \\ \hline \end{array}$$

a number of remedial cues might be used. Cues for visual-spatial memory should be used to remind the child to begin adding in the right-hand column. Color codes, arrows, or a verbal self-reminder such as "add right down" might be used. Similar cues could be used for regrouping, etc. If the child has difficulty remembering number facts (e.g., 5 + 6 = __), number cards with the problems written on one side and the answers on the other may be used to provide drill with visual and auditory memory.

Word or story problems

One of the most important goals in elementary school mathematics is to help children become proficient problem solvers. Although there are many types of problem-solving activities in arithmetic, we have chosen textbook word problems in subtraction to illustrate the task-process approach to problem-solving difficulties in arithmetic. The story problem is used to give the child the opportunity to extract the basic information of a problem, translate this information into mathematical form, and apply previously learned concepts to derive a solution.

Larson (1982) demonstrates how complex a simple subtraction problem can be (e.g., 5 − 2 = __) when expressed as a word problem in different types of situations. Subtraction situations are presented in figures 13.1 and 13.2 to illustrate the task-process approach to the remediation of word or story problems.

**Figure 13.1
Take away**

This is the first meaning of subtraction that is usually taught children. In a take-away situation, the number of objects in a set is given, and then some of the objects are physically removed. Children are asked to find the number of objects that is left over (remain).

Example:
Paul had five kittens. He gave two to Jeff. How many kittens does Paul have left?

Solution using concrete materials:
(1) The child gets five kittens.
(2) The child removes two kittens.
(3) The remainder are then counted to find the answer.

Solution using a number sentence:
5 − 2 = ☐

Courtesy of C. Larson, 1982.

Figure 13.2
Comparison

In this situation the child is asked to find the difference between two sets. The children are given the number of objects in two disjoint sets and asked: "How many more are in Set A than in Set B?" Or they are asked the harder question: "How many fewer are in Set B than in Set A?"

Example:
Paul has five kittens. Jeff has two kittens. How many more kittens does Paul have than Jeff?

Solution using concrete materials:
(1) The child gets two sets of kittens, one with five kittens and one with two kittens.
(2) The child places the two sets in one-to-one correspondence.
(3) The kittens without a partner are counted to find the answer.

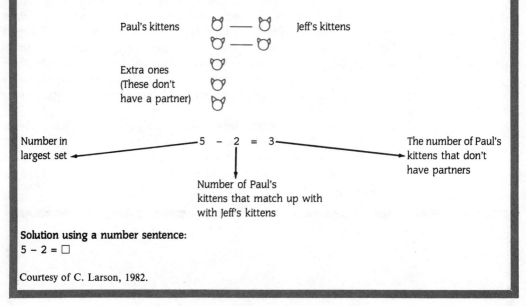

Solution using a number sentence:
5 – 2 = □

Courtesy of C. Larson, 1982.

The story problems in figures 13.1 and 13.2 require children to apply previously learned skills. Knowing a basic arithmetic skill does not insure that the child understands when and how to use it in another context. The processes of attention, discrimination, memory, and integration are all involved in problem solving, but the three major disabilities that create the most severe problems with story problems are oral language, concept formation, and problem solving.

Children with problems in oral language may have difficulty in either reading story problems or understanding spoken story problems. If the child has a deficit in the vocabulary of story problems, remediation should be directed toward understanding, using, and reading vocabulary that has not been learned. Children should be taught to repeat the problem, repeat it in their own words, and verbalize and act out the problem situation with manipulables. It is helpful to teach children to translate oral story problems into written form as well as to translate a written story problem to a mathematical sentence.

If the child has not been taught or has not mastered the basic arithmetic concepts or operations, he or she will have difficulty determining whether the solution of word problems requires addition, subtraction, multiplication, or division. In these cases it is necessary to teach those concepts or operations. For example, with children who are still at the concrete level, the use of manipulable objects may help associate the numbers in the story problem with the mathematical sentence. These children may have difficulty in determining which operation (addition, subtraction, multiplication, division, or another operation) may fit the story problem.

It is important to use situations within the child's experience, background, reading level, and mathematical experience. Practice in writing mathematical sentences is very helpful in teaching a child to recognize patterns in selecting the correct operation. Having the child create a story problem for computational exercises also helps children recognize operation patterns.

Programs for teaching arithmetic skills

There are a number of instructional programs that are often used for children who have difficulty learning arithmetic. Some of the programs were designed for children with learning problems, and others were developed for use with normal children. All of these programs are adaptable for use with learning disabled children. Some programs which might be useful are:

(1) The Computational Arithmetic Program (Smith & Lovitt, 1982)

(2) Structural Arithmetic (Stern, 1965)

(3) Project Math: Levels 1 and 2 (Cawley, Fitzmaurice, Goodstein, Lepore, Sedlack, & Althouse, 1976a, 1976b)

(4) DISTAR (Engelmann & Carnine, 1970, 1972, 1975)

(5) Montessori materials (Montessori, 1964, 1965a, 1965b)

(6) Cuisenaire rods (Davidson, 1969)

(7) The Greater Cleveland Mathematics Program (Science Research Associates, 1963)

(8) Programmed Math (Sullivan, 1968)

(9) Mathematics in Action (Kane & Deans, 1969)

(10) Seeing Through Arithmetic (Van Engen, 1963).

Looking to the future, the development of microcomputer technology holds great promise for arithmetic programming. The structure of arithmetic and mathematic operations can be sequenced and programmed for systematic instruction. The computer capability to present forms, objects, number problems, and word problems and to reinforce the student visually in a highly prescriptive, systematic fashion may replace many of the instructional methods used today.

As microcomputers become more widely used in the schools, the instructional role of the teacher in arithmetic will probably change. Less emphasis will be placed on direct instruction and more emphasis will be placed on assessing individual program needs, performing task-process analysis, selecting individualized programs, monitoring, and assisting individual children.

Children may have difficulty solving story problems because of a disability in the problem-solving process. It is helpful to teach the child a procedure for solving story problems. Bley and Thornton (1981) and Krulik and Reys (1980) review suggestions for teaching problem solving in mathematics. Children need to be taught how to progress through the stages in solving a word-story problem. For example:

(1) Read or listen to the story problem and try to comprehend the situation.

(2) Use manipulables and concrete materials to act out the problem.

(3) Relate the story problem to the mathematical operations. The word problem must be associated with the correct number sentence (e.g., $5 - 2 = \_$).

(4) Compute the answer.

(5) Check the answer.

Summary

- Historically, neurologists first directed attention toward disorders of calculation (acalculia) in adults who had suffered brain injury.

- The diagnosis of arithmetic disabilities involves determining if a discrepancy exists between a child's potential and achievement in arithmetic, determining the kinds of errors the child makes in arithmetic computation and reasoning, identifying the correlates to the arithmetic disability, developing a hypothesis about the nature of the problem and organizing a remedial program.

- Some of the major contributing factors of arithmetic disabilities include language, attention, visual-spatial discrimination, sensory integration, concept formation, and problem solving.

- The task-process approach to remediation of arithmetic problems includes (1) selecting instructional objectives, (2) breaking objectives down into operational subskills, (3) determining which developmental learning abilities are involved in the task being taught, and (4) considering developmental disabilities in organizing instruction.

- There are a number of arithmetic instructional programs that have been devised for handicapped and for normal children. Many of these programs can be adapted for use with learning disabled students.

- The development of microcomputers may affect the future instruction of arithmetic and mathematics in the schools as well as the role of the teacher.

1. If there is such a condition as *dyscalculia,* a developmental mathematical problem, what would this mean to a child's progress during remediation? How would the progress of this child differ from a student whose problems originated from lack of instruction?

2. Which correlates of arithmetic disability do you believe occur most frequently? Least frequently? Why?

3. Explain why the task-process approach to remediation can be used with any instructional program in arithmetic.

4. How would a disability in visual discrimination affect a child learning to compare sets? How would you teach this child?

5. If a child has a severe memory problem, what would you do to teach rational counting?

6. Children must learn to read numerals. How is this different from reading letters? How are reading numerals and letters the same?

7. Conduct a task-process analysis for $32 \times 4 =$ ____. What are the arithmetic subskills? What are the developmental abilities for this task?

8. What developmental abilities are required for success in working word problems? How would you remediate these problems?

9. Microcomputers are being used more each year. Do you believe children with developmental disabilities would be able to work microcomputers? Why or why not?

10. With the use of pocket computers, should arithmetic computation skills be deemphasized in the schools? Modified? In what ways?

part 4
major issues

14

Self-esteem, social behavior, and delinquency

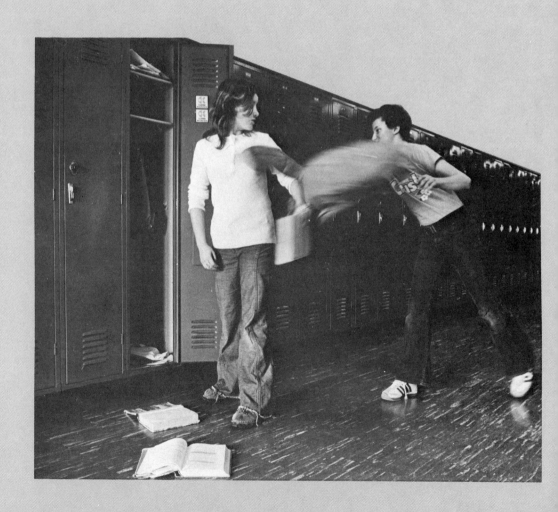

Does a learning disability in a child negatively affect his or her self-esteem or social behavior, or lead to conduct disorders or delinquency? As in other areas, there are many children who have learning disabilities who are not so affected. On the other hand, many authorities find that some children with learning disabilities have low self-esteem and interact inadequately with their teachers and classmates. Cartledge and Milburn (1978) point out that when a child develops an expectation of failure, he or she no longer tries to learn. In these cases, the child may become inattentive, fail to follow directions, or not work independently or in groups. Minskoff (1982) and Smith (1981) also state that difficulties in communication often result in the development of social behavior patterns that are disruptive to learning disabled children and to their classmates.

This chapter will discuss three problems that may be found in learning disabled students: (1) reactions to failure, (2) social perceptions, and (3) delinquency. Parents and teachers should be aware that these problems may arise in some children and that they should be identified and treated as soon as possible.

Reactions to failure

A child who believes that he or she has no control over the outcome of events may demonstrate a behavior pattern Seligman (1975) refers to as *learned helplessness*. It is characterized by (1) low expectation of success, (2) insufficient time in persisting on tasks, and (3) the belief that failures are caused by personal deficiencies and successes are due to external events beyond the child's control. Negative self-attitudes and low self-esteem often result from these beliefs (Abramson, Seligman, & Teasdale, 1978; Diener & Dweck, 1978; Dweck, 1975; Dweck & Reppucci, 1973).

Richard, a second grader, had difficulty learning to read. Although his estimated level of intelligence was in the normal range he had nearly stopped trying to read because he expected to fail. Richard persisted only a few seconds when attempting to decode a word before he would stop trying. On those occasions when he successfully decoded a word, Richard attributed his success to luck. He believed he was not very smart and that caused his failure in reading. When diagnosed, Richard was found to have a learning disability in visual memory and auditory discrimination which had caused his initial failure in reading. The impact of his subsequent academic failure created a second problem—the learned helplessness syndrome.

This section will discuss three of the major characteristics of children's reactions to failure.

Expectations for success or failure

How well a child expects to do on a task seems to influence how well the child actually performs. A history of failure on a particular task may lead a person to expect little success or failure on similar tasks in the future (Weiner, 1979). There is some question about the extent to which children's expectancy for success or failure is *specific* to a particular task such as reading, baseball, or arithmetic or *generalized* to other kinds of tasks. Learning disabled children whose success expectation is specific may say, "I don't read very well, but I'm pretty good at math." Children who present a generalized failure expectation make statements such as "I'm not good at anything."

Butkowsky and Willows (1980) found that poor readers expected to do less well on both academic-like tasks (anagrams) and nonacademic-like tasks (line drawings) than did average or good readers. Their study suggests that poor readers have a generalized expectation of failure. In contrast, Pysh (1982) found that learning disabled boys did not generalize a lower expectancy of success on academic-like tasks (anagrams) to nonacademic-like tasks (line drawings). Pysh's results suggest that feelings of low expectancy for success were not generalized but were task-specific.

Pysh suggests that the differences in the results of the two studies might be explained by differences in the research population, basic ability, achievement, and background of the subjects. None of the subjects in Butkowsky and Willow's research group had been diagnosed or placed in special education programs. On the other hand, all of Pysh's research group had been diagnosed, placed in special education, and received remediation. Perhaps the learning disabled children in Pysh's study had learned the task-specific nature of their problems from their remedial teachers and, therefore, avoided the overgeneralization of expected failure.

More study is needed to determine the conditions under which learning disabled children develop a generalized expectation of success or failure and which conditions contribute to a task-specific expectancy for success or failure. It is important for teachers to try to help learning disabled children decrease the effects of failure on future performance. This can be done by starting to teach children where they are and progressing gradually to more difficult tasks. Programmed instruction also helps reduce the frequency of failure.

Persistence time

Everyone needs to spend a certain amount of time to master new tasks. Children who believe they will be successful tend to persist on task. Unfortunately, many learning disabled children have little confidence in their ability to learn, have no confidence in their problem-solving abilities, or view tasks to be learned as too difficult for them. This negative attitude may lead learning disabled children to be unable or unwilling to persist on a task long enough to understand or complete it (Andrews & Debus, 1978).

Pysh (1982) found the amount of time learning disabled boys persisted was significantly less than that of normally achieving boys in an experiment using both anagram and line-drawing tasks. Many learning disabled children prefer not trying rather than trying and risking failure.

Since persistence is a prerequisite to any learning, it is important, therefore, to increase the amount of time learning disabled children persist on learning tasks. This may be done by initially reinforcing the child for increased persistence time rather than for the correctness of work. After the child has increased the amount of time on task, the teacher can then emphasize accurate or appropriate responses.

Beliefs about the causes of success or failure

When children repeatedly succeed or fail on a particular task, they attempt to explain the causes of their successes or failures. These explanations about the causes of behavior are called *attributions* (Bar-Tal, 1978). Children's beliefs about what causes them to succeed or fail may be attributed to causes originating within the child, *internal* causes, or to causes originating from the environment, *external* causes (Heider, 1958; Rotter, 1966). Their explanations may be *stable* and unchangeable—for example, intelligence, knowledge, personality, attitudes affecting performance, or task difficulty. Other attributed causes may be *unstable* and changeable—for example, effort or luck (Frieze, 1981; Weiner, Heckhausen, Meyer, & Cook, 1972). Pysh (1982) adapted the theoretical model of Weiner, Frieze, Kukla, Reed, Rest, and Rosenbaum (1971) in order to categorize the children's explanations for success or failure on tasks. (See figure 14.1.)

Beliefs about the causes of success or failure appear to affect children's future performance. If a child believes his failure is caused by personal (internal) factors that cannot be changed (stable), then the child will expect to fail

Figure 14.1
Attributional categories

	Stable	Unstable
Internal (within the person)	1. Ability 2. Performance expectation	3. Effort 4. Mood
External (outside the person)	5. Task difficulty 6. Experience	7. Luck
	8. I don't know.	

Source: M.V. Pysh, *Learning Disabled and Normal Achieving Children's Attributions and Reactions to Success or Failure.* Unpublished doctoral dissertation, Northwestern University, 1982, p. 91. Used with permission.

again. Similarly, if a child believes his success is caused by events outside himself (external) that are changeable (unstable), the child also will expect to fail again. In contrast, children who believe their own personal knowledge and ability (internal) are stable will expect their success to continue. Those children who believe external changeable factors cause failure tend to attribute their failure to a fluke. As Frieze (1981) stated,

> Those who expect to do well will continue to have high expectations and those who have low expectations will maintain them regardless of how they actually perform. (p. 58)

Reasons for failing

Several studies have found that learning disabled boys tend to attribute their failure to circumstances or reasons beyond their control. Therefore, they feel this failure cannot be changed (Butkowsky & Willows, 1980; Frieze & Weiner, 1971; Pysh, 1982).

Nancy, a ninth-grade learning disabled student, for example, believed that she did not have the mental ability to succeed in school. She believed her mental ability would never improve. Tim, a fifth grader, attributed his failure to task difficulty. Nancy's reason for failure (mental ability) was *stable* and *internal.* Tim's reason for failure (task difficulty) was also *stable,* but was *external.* In both cases, Nancy and Tim believed that the reason for their failure was beyond their control. In both cases, continued failure and helplessness tended to lower their self-esteem.

Pysh (1982) also found a small subgroup of learning disabled elementary school boys who explained their failure in terms of their lack of effort or mood. These are *unstable* and *internal* factors. Failure was said to be their personal responsibility. Each of these boys believed that he could change failure to success provided he was given another opportunity to complete the task. Dweck (1975) has referred to children who exhibit this response to failure as being *mastery oriented.* Determining if children believe the origin of their failure is within themselves (internal) and cannot be changed (stable) or is within themselves but can be changed (unstable) helps teachers plan how to teach the child to cope with failure.

Tollefson, Tracey, Johnsen, Borgers, Buenning, Farmer, and Barke (1980) point out that "attributions are affected by the expectancy of task outcomes (success and failure) and tend to act as a confirmation of one's self-image" (p. 8). Table 14.1 presents a cycle for a learning disabled child with a negative initial expectation, as described by Pysh (1982).

Reasons for success

Success in school might be defined as responding appropriately to questions, being correct in working problems, or mastering different skills as they are taught. Individuals, however, perceive the reasons for their successes in different ways. Normally achieving boys, for example, mentioned personal effort (internal–unstable) to explain their success (Pearl, Bryan, & Donahue, 1980). Good readers also took more personal credit for success than poor

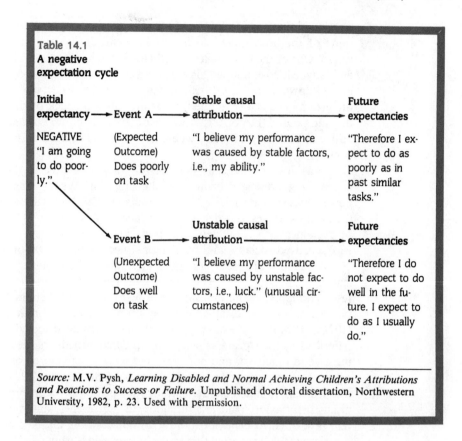

Table 14.1
A negative expectation cycle

Initial expectancy ——→ Event A ——→ Stable causal attribution ———————————————→ Future expectancies

NEGATIVE "I am going to do poorly."

(Expected Outcome) Does poorly on task

"I believe my performance was caused by stable factors, i.e., my ability."

"Therefore I expect to do as poorly as in past similar tasks."

Event B ——→ Unstable causal attribution ———————————————→ Future expectancies

(Unexpected Outcome) Does well on task

"I believe my performance was caused by unstable factors, i.e., luck." (unusual circumstances)

"Therefore I do not expect to do well in the future. I expect to do as I usually do."

Source: M.V. Pysh, *Learning Disabled and Normal Achieving Children's Attributions and Reactions to Success or Failure.* Unpublished doctoral dissertation, Northwestern University, 1982, p. 23. Used with permission.

readers (Butkowsky & Willows, 1980). In contrast, learning disabled boys were found to attribute their success on anagram tasks to task ease (external-stable). Pearl et al. (1980) found that non-school-identified but learning disabled students also mentioned task ease as an explanation for success. Similarly, Hallahan, Gajar, Cohen, and Tarver (1978) and Chapman and Boersma (1979) found that learning disabled students attributed success less to personal and internal factors than did normal children. It appears, therefore, that learning disabled boys tend to attribute their success to task ease, an external factor, rather than the personal or internal ability mentioned by normally achieving boys.

Social perceptions

Joshua, a learning disabled eighth grader, had suffered brain injury in an automobile accident at age 3. His intellectual potential was borderline. Although Josh was usually ignored or rejected by his classmates, they sometimes gave him attention by laughing at his failures, playing jokes on him, or treating him as a class clown. At a Sunday night football game, for example, some of the boys waved Josh to join them. Josh was pleased to join the group. One of the boys talked quietly to Josh while the rest of the boys smiled and laughed. Josh nodded his head and was given a box of popcorn. Then he moved down 10 rows, sat behind a girl in a red sweater, and looked back at the group. The leader nodded, so Josh pulled the back of the girl's sweater out and poured the popcorn down her back. The group howled with glee and Josh ran back to join them, where he was congratulated and slapped on the back.

Was Josh not socially perceptive? Was he unable to discriminate between the goodness or badness of the situation? Was he unable to perceive how he was viewed socially by his classmates? Did Josh willingly comply with the group's wishes in order to achieve acceptance? Or could Josh's behavior be explained as a combination of poor social perception of the act, how he was perceived socially, and his personal need for approval or acceptance?

A number of researchers have attempted to determine the effects of a learning disability on personality and personal adjustment. The usual research report compares a sample of learning disabled children with a sample of non-learning disabled children on one or more characteristics. Bryan (1974a, 1974b), for example, found that learning disabled students were described by their peers as being unpopular, worried, frightened, never having a good time, sad, and not neat, and were often ignored or rejected more often than were non-learning disabled students. Bryan (1974a) also found that learning disabled children seemed to spend less classroom time on task-oriented behavior, paid less attention to the teacher, and were involved in non-task-oriented behavior more than non-learning disabled children.

Strag (1972) reported that parents described learning disabled children as clinging, unable to receive affection, having little impulse control, being uncontrolled in emotional and motoric expression, and being inconsiderate.

Many kinds of contributing factors have been proposed to explain social perception difficulties. Johnson and Myklebust (1967) define *social perception* as the ability to immediately recognize and interpret the meaning and significance of the behavior of others. The reasons why learning disabled children, and many other handicapped children, have social perception problems are not clear.

London (1978) and Bruininks (1978a) believe that a low self-concept can affect social perception. Disorders in verbal communication in which children do not understand what is said or have difficulty expressing themselves may also cause social perception problems (Bryan & Bryan, 1978; Pearl & Cosden, 1982; Spekman & Roth, 1982).

Hyperactivity (a condition in which children lack attention), impulsivity, and motor restlessness have been mentioned as contributing factors (Douglas & Peters, 1980). Visual-spatial recognition problems might cause difficulty in perceiving facial expressions, bodily gestures, and other visual nonverbal cues meant to convey a message to the learning disabled child (Bryan, 1977). The need to achieve peer popularity because of rejection may cause children to want to perceive the behavior of others more positively than the behavior actually is meant to be (Bruininks, 1978b).

Disabilities in thinking have also been proposed as causes of poor social perception. Lack of understanding of both verbal and emotional expressions (Gerber & Zinkgraf, 1982) and difficulty in making inferences about people's emotions or intentions (Pearl & Cosden, 1982) have been cited as contributing factors. A low level of social problem-solving skill was also found to detract from social perception and adjustment (Hazel, Schumaker, Sherman, & Sheldon-Wildgen, 1982). In some instances learning disabled children may be able to learn social skills, but may not always know when to apply them in daily situations (Schumaker & Ellis, 1982). Not being capable of considering the feelings of others is another possibility (Enright & Lapsley, 1980). Adelman and Taylor (1982) believe that the lack of motivation to learn or use social perceptual skills should be considered.

Many learning disabled students may not have acquired or have been taught social information that is important in both social behavior and social perception. Minskoff (1980a, 1980b, 1980c, 1982) has discussed the need to develop social skills such as (1) adjusting language to different people and situations, (2) analyzing the sensitivity or degree of formality in different situations, (3) knowing when to listen and when to talk, (4) understanding facial and body cues, (5) not standing too close, staring, eavesdropping, or touching excessively, (6) understanding the significance of voice pitch, volume, and tempo, and (7) recognizing the symptoms of impatience, anger, tolerance, and other emotions. Learning disabled children may need to be taught these kinds of perceptual skills.

In conclusion, we should point out that not all learning disabled children have any or all of these characteristics. In a review of factors contributing to peer-interaction patterns, Bruck and Hebert (1982) questioned the popular generalization that learning disabled children have social disabilities. They concluded that these generalizations are not accurate characterizations of all learning disabled children, but may be problems for many.

Juvenile delinquency and learning disabilities

When Neil was 11, he was caught shoplifting. At 13 he was apprehended with two older boys breaking and entering a store. At 14 he was arrested for reckless driving without a license and possession of marijuana. Neil had been diagnosed as learning disabled at age 9. He had a history of failure in school and had been placed for 2 hours each day in a resource room where he received assistance with his oral language and with conceptual problems that interfered with his learning to read. Neil's father had left the family when Neil was 2 years old. At present, Neil lived with his grandmother and mother, who had difficulty controlling him.

Neil's self-esteem was low. As he grew older, he had become increasingly more argumentative and aggressive. He had tried to run away from home on two occasions. Following his arrest, Neil was placed in a half-way house. He attended the local high school and received counseling in addition to his resource room program.

Neil's case raises several interesting questions. What is the relationship between learning disabilities and juvenile delinquency? Did Neil's delinquent behavior originate from his intrinsic learning disabilities, which in turn contributed to his academic failure, loss of self-esteem, and severe social problems? Was Neil's delinquent behavior due to extrinsic factors in his environment? Or was the delinquency caused by a combination of factors?

At the present time there seems to be a question concerning the link between learning disabilities and juvenile delinquency. There are two major studies which summarize the various points of view on this issue. The first study was conducted by the American Institutes for Research (Murray, 1976). The second study was conducted by the Association for Children with Learning Disabilities (ACLD) and the National Center for State Courts (NCSC) (Dunivant, 1982). These studies were funded by the National Institute for Juvenile Justice and Delinquency.

The American Institutes for Research study

This report summarized the current theory and knowledge concerning the link between learning disabilities and juvenile delinquency. The principal author of this report, Charles Murray (1976), reached two conclusions. His first conclusion was "the existence of a causal relationship between learning disabilities and delinquency has not been established; the evidence for a causal link is feeble" (p. 65). Murray pointed out that, though most of the quantitative studies can be criticized with respect to design, the studies that have been done persistently suggest a pattern of learning handicaps.

Murray's second conclusion is that "the cumulation of observational data reported by professionals who work with delinquents warrants further, more systematic exploration of the learning handicaps of delinquents" (p. 68).

Murray pointed out three research design needs that should be implemented in studying this problem:

(1) A longitudinal study to compare the development of a group of learning disabled children with non-learning disabled children

(2) A study to demonstrate that the average delinquent is more likely to suffer from learning disabilities than his or her nondelinquent counterpart

(3) A common definition and a determination of the incidence of learning disabled delinquents and nondelinquents.

The ACLD and NCSC study

The results of the research project conducted by the Association for Children with Learning Disabilities (ACLD) and the National Center for State Courts (NCSC) were reported by Dunivant (1982).

This report summarizes the results of a research project designed to investigate the relationship between learning disabilities (LD) and juvenile delinquency and to evaluate the effectiveness of academic remediation in improving the educational achievement and reducing the delinquency of learning-disabled delinquents. A cross-sectional study of 1,943 adolescent males sampled from public schools, juvenile courts, and corrections facilities found that learning disabilities and delinquency were significantly related. This relationship remained significant even when differences between learning-disabled and non-learning-disabled youths in sociodemographic backgrounds and tendencies to give socially approved responses were statistically controlled. The boys with LD reported significantly higher rates of general delinquent behavior. Their tendencies to engage in violence, substance abuse, and school disruption were especially greater than those of the non-learning-disabled boys. The likelihood of arrest and adjudication was also substantially higher for the teenagers handicapped by learning disabilities. Somewhat surprisingly, this was true even when the probabilities of arrest and adjudication for similar offenses were compared. A longitudinal investigation of 351 officially nondelinquent boys assessed the development of delinquency over a two-year period. The results of this research were generally consistent with those from the cross-sectional study. The learning-disabled adolescents evidenced greater increases over time in self-reported and official delinquency than their non-learning-disabled counterparts. The evaluation of an academic treatment program demonstrated that remedial instruction was effective in improving the academic skills and decreasing both the self-reported and official delinquency of learning-disabled youths who had been officially adjudicated. The degree of effectiveness, however, depended upon the amount of remediation received and upon certain intellectual and social characteristics of the participants. Implications for public policy and future research are discussed. (p. 46)

Contributing factors

Dunivant (1982) discusses five possible hypotheses that might explain the relationship between learning disabilities and juvenile delinquency.

(1) *The school failure hypothesis.* This hypothesis maintains that learning disabilities produce academic failure. This failure in turn results in more academic failure. Students may feel frustrated with their failure, which may result in aggression. Learning disabled students may be labelled as problem students and grouped with students who have behavior problems. This labelling and grouping eventually leads them to engage in socially troublesome behavior. Active rejection or uncaring attitudes by teachers and administrators may contribute to student withdrawal and commitment to socially unacceptable behavior. Learning disabled teenagers may turn to delinquency as a source of income and attribute blame for their problems to others and not themselves.

(2) *The susceptibility hypothesis.* Learning disabled students may engage in delinquent activities because of certain cognitive and personality characteristics such as lack of impulse control, failure to anticipate the consequences of future actions, poor perception of social cues, irritability, suggestibility, and the tendency to act out feelings.

(3) *The differential arrest hypothesis.* Learning disabled students are more apt to be apprehended by the police because they lack the abilities to plan strategies to avoid detection or to conceal their true intentions, activities, and feelings when they encounter the police. Also, deficiencies in social interaction, abrasiveness, and general demeanor while talking with police could be a factor in determining whether students are apprehended or not.

(4) *The differential adjudication hypothesis.* Delinquents with learning disabilities who have been charged with violations may run a greater risk of adjudication following arrest than non-learning disabled adolescents. Intake and probation officers, defense attorneys, prosecuting attorneys, or judges may make more severe decisions because of the learning disabled adolescent's lack of self-control, irritability, or social abrasiveness. Because they do not understand the legal proceedings, they are unable to communicate effectively and lack social perception about the importance of events or questions. Thus, learning disabled people may be unable to present themselves and their stories in a favorable light.

(5) *The differential disposition hypothesis.* Because of the reasons cited above, learning disabled delinquents may have a higher probability of receiving a more severe disposition from the Juvenile Court, such as commitment to a training school or some other correctional facility, than do non-learning disabled delinquents.

Dunivant also points out that those who believe that learning disabilities do not have a causal effect on delinquency present two major arguments.

(1) *The sociodemographic characteristics* point of view states that differences in delinquency between learning disabled and non-learning disabled juveniles should be attributed to the characteristics of different populations such as parent education, financial ability, cultural differences, and language spoken in the home.

(2) *The response bias hypothesis* alleges that learning disabled delinquents do not conceal as much of their antisocial behavior as do the non-learning disabled when being interviewed. The learning disabled, therefore, are not proficient in giving the socially desirable response or making the correct impression during interviews.

Conclusions On the basis of the two studies reported in this section, it seems obvious that the link between learning disabilities and juvenile delinquency has not been clearly delineated. It is difficult to establish such a link because of the different kinds of learning disabilities, the differences in severity, and the wide variance in the environmental backgrounds of the subjects.

It *is* clear, however, that the large majority of delinquents are educationally retarded. This fact, however, does not establish a cause-and-effect relationship. It is also known that a large number of internal and external problems may contribute to delinquency. The question here is whether one of these contributing factors is a learning disability. Fortunately, *the large proportion of learning disabled children are not delinquent.*

Although the studies are not clear-cut, a learning disability may be one factor that combines with other conditions to precipitate delinquency. It is possible that a child who is predisposed to delinquency may become delinquent if untreated school failure leads to truancy and antisocial conduct. These conclusions become more obvious from studying single cases than from relying on large group studies.

Summary

- Many children with developmental and academic learning disabilities have difficulty with their self-esteem and social behavior.

- Children who believe they have no control over the outcome of events may develop a behavioral pattern of learned helplessness and stop trying to cope with difficult problems.

- Many learning disabled children have low expectations of success. In some cases, expectancy for success or failure may be specific to a particular task. In other cases, learning disabled children may generalize their low expectations of success or failure to other kinds of tasks.

- Children who have little confidence in their abilities to learn or cope sometimes develop a negative mental set and do not persist on a task long enough to understand or complete it.

- Some learning disabled children attribute their reasons for failing to circumstances beyond their control, which they believe cannot be changed. These circumstances might be either internal reasons such as lack of ability or external reasons occurring within their environment.

- When learning disabled children are successful, they usually attribute their success to task ease (an external-stable factor) rather than to personal or internal reasons, as do most normally achieving children.

- Many learning disabled children are not socially perceptive. It may be inaccurate, however, to characterize all learning disabled children as not being socially perceptive.

- Learning disabled children are often rejected by their peers and teachers. This rejection may be caused by many different factors, such as problems in verbal and nonverbal communication, hyperactivity, thinking, applying social skills, learning social skills, or controlling their emotions.

- The precise link between learning disabilities and juvenile delinquency is not clear, but there is some evidence that a learning disability does contribute to delinquency in some cases.

1. Can you describe a personal situation in which you demonstrated learned helplessness?

2. In what circumstances do you usually expect to be successful? In what kinds of situations do you expect failure? How did you form these expectations?

3. How would you plan to increase a child's persistence time in working arithmetic problems?

4. You believe that if you could change a child's beliefs about the reasons for his success or failure, his performance in school would improve. What kinds of strategies would you use to bring about a change in the child's beliefs?

5. What strategies can be used in a group of students to increase everyone's social perceptiveness?

6. How would you try to change rejection of a learning disabled child by his or her peers to peer acceptance? What strategies would you employ with the learning disabled child? With the peer group?

7. What characteristics would you include on a checklist for describing poor social perception?

8. What factors would you include in a formula to predict juvenile delinquency among learning disabled adolescents?

9. What arguments would you give to indicate that learning disabilities are *not* linked to juvenile delinquency?

10. What kind of research project would you develop to study learning disabilities and juvenile delinquency in your community?

15
Providing educational services

Children with learning disabilities receive special educational services because of a series of events that occurred over a period of nearly 200 years. As indicated in chapter 2, the initial impetus came from neurologists who studied the relationship of brain disorders and behavior. The study of language and reading disorders led to the development of test and remedial programs. During the three decades from 1930 to 1960, private and university clinics studied the symptoms of various kinds of learning disabilities and refined tests and remedial methods. Private schools sprang up specializing in helping children who were "neurologically impaired" or "perceptually handicapped."

Because of parents' persistent requests for public school services for their handicapped children, state and federal government became involved in the 1950s. Traditionally, education had been the responsibility of the states. In 1957 the federal government first appropriated funds for educational research and later for teacher training. In 1963 the federal government, in Public Law 88-164, expanded its provisions from support for mentally retarded and deaf students to all handicapped children. Research and teacher training for learning disabilities was not direct, but received meager support under "Crippled and Other Health Impaired Requiring Special Education."

It was not until 1969 that a special bill for learning disabilities, the *Learning Disabilities Act of 1969,* was passed. It was at this time that a federal definition was formulated and federal funds were provided for extended research and personnel preparation. The landmark legislation to provide education to *all* handicapped children was enacted in 1975 (Public Law 94-142). It required the public schools to provide services for all handicapped children, including the learning disabled.

This chapter reviews the educational services resulting from the federal legislation to meet the needs of learning disabled children. These include:

(1) Identification of learning disabled students
(2) Individual evaluation
(3) Eligibility conference
(4) Individualized education program conference
(5) Education program alternatives
(6) Related services
(7) Transition between program levels
(8) Parent communication
(9) Impartial due process hearings.

Together, these procedures and programs comprise the kinds of services that should be available to most learning disabled students and their parents in the nation's schools. A more detailed review of these procedures may be found in *The Compliance Manual* (Chalfant & Pysh, 1980).

The identification of learning disabled students

If a learning disabled child is to reach his or her full intellectual, social, emotional, and academic potential, he or she must be identified as soon as possible. Figure 15.1 presents a series of stages that may be followed to identify any high-risk student who may have learning problems that require individual evaluation (Pysh & Chalfant, 1978). Let's examine each stage of the model.

Identification

Schools identify high-risk students who are having or might have difficulty in school through screening and referral procedures. Public schools use a variety of screening techniques and methods to examine the entire school population

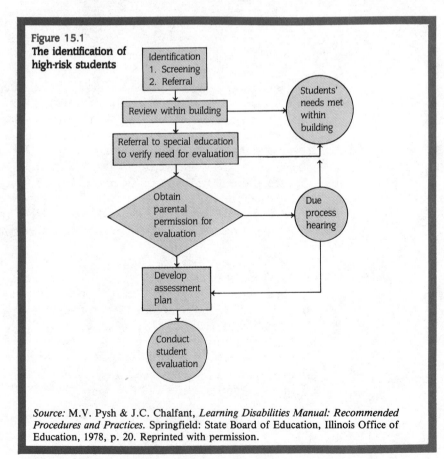

Figure 15.1
The identification of high-risk students

Source: M.V. Pysh & J.C. Chalfant, *Learning Disabilities Manual: Recommended Procedures and Practices.* Springfield: State Board of Education, Illinois Office of Education, 1978, p. 20. Reprinted with permission.

and to identify those students who might be expected to have difficulty in school. Helpful screening procedures include:

(1) Hearing and vision screening

(2) Speech and language screening

(3) School staff screening through report card checks, observation, group tests, and records

(4) Motor performance screening

(5) Perceptual and cognitive screening

(6) Social and emotional screening

(7) Health status

(8) Screening of information collected by parents

(9) Annual review of children who were previously referred and are not currently being served.

Screening should include preschool children from ages 3 to 5. This requires the cooperation of parents, social service agencies, medical facilities, nursery schools, and day care centers. School-aged students should be screened annually for physical problems such as visual or hearing impairments. At the junior and senior high school level, initial reading and written language screening for each student is often done by the English department. Reports of academic counselors, advisers, and homeroom teachers also help identify high-risk students during the transition from junior to senior high school. Developing a comprehensive screening program requires coordinating the school staff, scheduling the various screening approaches, and collating the information.

A referral is a formal request for a comprehensive individual examination. Referral systems are based on the assumption that those who come into contact with a student and believe the student needs help will forward his or her name and problem to those who are responsible for taking appropriate action. A referral can originate with teachers, principals, parents, outside agencies, or the students themselves. For best practice, a single referral-processing system and a single referral form should be used within a school system.

Review referrals within building

Many schools have established a procedure for reviewing referrals to special education services within the building to insure that all pertinent data have been included. In some cases, it may be necessary to return the referral form to the teacher for more information. In other cases, a review could result in deciding to meet the child's needs with resources within the building rather than recommending that the child be tested.

Referral to special education

Referrals received by special education staff are screened to determine their validity. If the need for a comprehensive case study evaluation is questionable, classroom observations might be recommended or a teacher conference scheduled to obtain more information. If the special education staff decides that a comprehensive evaluation is not necessary, the referring party is informed of the reasons for that decision and suggestions are made for program modification, changes in teaching method, new grouping arrangements, and so forth.

Obtain parental permission for evaluation

If the need for evaluation is verified, the first step is to obtain parental permission. The child's parents should always be included in the decision-making process. If a child is referred to special education, the parents must be informed in their native language and they must give written permission before the child can be evaluated. It is best to contact the parents personally in a meeting or on the telephone before sending a letter of explanation. The parents should have the opportunity to ask questions. If they will not get involved or refuse to consent to have their child evaluated, state regulations govern the procedures the public agency uses to override a parent's refusal to consent. A due process hearing (explained later) may be scheduled to resolve the conflict.

Develop an assessment plan

In conducting a comprehensive case study evaluation, it is important to coordinate the efforts of everyone involved to avoid omission of relevant areas of assessment or duplication of effort. The coordination may be accomplished by selecting a case manager from the assessment team or by conducting a multidisciplinary team assessment conference to:

(1) Select specific assessment objectives
(2) Select assessment procedures that are as efficient as possible
(3) Assign responsibility for assessment
(4) Generate a time line so that the case study evaluation will be completed within 60 school days. (*Federal Register,* 1977a)

The individual evaluation

The individual evaluation of a child is the foundation for all educational planning. Before a learning disabled child can be placed in a special education program, an individual evaluation must be conducted to (1) identify specific areas of educational need, (2) accurately reflect the child's aptitude for achievement, and (3) identify other factors that might be interfering with school performance. (See figure 15.2.)

The evaluation is conducted by a team called a *multidisciplinary team* because each member makes a special contribution during the evaluation. The team should include at least one teacher or other specialist with knowledge in the area of suspected disability. In evaluating a child suspected of having a specific learning disability, each public agency shall include on the multidisciplinary team:

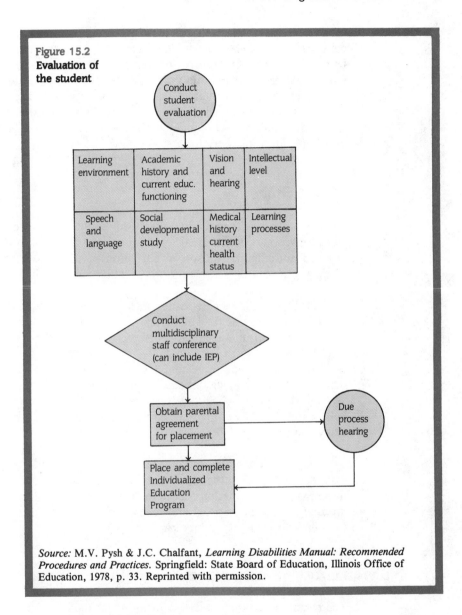

Figure 15.2
Evaluation of the student

Source: M.V. Pysh & J.C. Chalfant, *Learning Disabilities Manual: Recommended Procedures and Practices.* Springfield: State Board of Education, Illinois Office of Education, 1978, p. 33. Reprinted with permission.

(a) (1) The child's regular teacher, or

(2) If the child does not have a regular teacher, a regular classroom teacher qualified to teach a child of his or her age; or

(3) For a child of less than school age, an individual qualified by the State educational agency to teach a child of his or her age; and

(b) At least one person qualified to conduct individual diagnostic examinations of children such as a school psychologist, speech language pathologist, or remedial reading teacher. (*Federal Register,* 1977a, 121a.540)

The tests that are used should provide a valid estimate of the child's true aptitude level, achievement level, or any other factors that are purported to be measured. For this reason, children must be evaluated in their native language, and testing and evaluation materials and procedures should be selected and administered so as not to be racially or culturally discriminatory. The child should be evaluated in all areas related to the suspected disability. No single procedure should be used as the sole criterion for determining an appropriate educational program.

The eligibility conference

After completing the individual case study evaluation, the multidisciplinary team convenes to determine whether or not the child in question is learning disabled and eligible for special education programs and related services. There are five major purposes for the multidisciplinary eligibility conference:

(1) To establish a composite understanding of the child's problem

(2) To determine the child's unique educational needs

(3) To determine eligibility for special education programs and related services

(4) To determine the extent a child's needs can be met in the regular school program or in special education programs

(5) If need and eligibility for service are arrived at quickly, the second half of the eligibility conference could be used for writing the individualized education program (IEP).

The membership of the multidisciplinary team should vary from case to case, depending upon the nature and complexity of the child's problem and the amount of information needed to determine eligibility and to write the individualized education program. The parents are always given an opportunity to attend the eligibility conference.

The individualized education program (IEP) conference

The results of the individual examination are the basis for planning for the educational needs of the child. For this reason, it is helpful to complete testing before decisions are made about the child's individualized education programs. Public agencies are responsible for initiating the meetings to develop the individualized education program within 30 calendar days after the multidisciplinary team determines that a child needs special education or related services (*Federal Register,* 1977b, 121a.343).

The mechanism for planning is the individualized education program (IEP). The IEP is a written statement of the child's educational needs and the manner in which special education and related services will be provided. The IEP should include:

(1) A statement of the child's present levels of educational performance

(2) A statement of annual goals, including short-term instructional objectives

(3) A statement of the specific special education and related services to be provided and the extent to which the child will be able to participate in regular educational programs

(4) The projected dates for initiation and anticipated duration of services

(5) Appropriate objective criteria and evaluation procedures and schedules for determining, at least annually, whether the short-term instructional objectives are being achieved.

The people at the IEP conference should include someone from the public agency who is qualified to provide for or supervise special education services. The child's teacher should be present, and at least one of the child's parents. In some cases the child should be present as well. Other individuals who can contribute to a well-rounded program plan should be invited. It is very helpful to have members from the evaluation team present. If this is not possible, then someone who is knowledgeable about the evaluation procedures and the results should attend.

The parents are invited to participate in the meeting and to help develop the child's IEP. Written parental approval must be obtained before a learning disabled child can be placed in a special education program and the IEP initiated.

A child's individualized education program should be reviewed at least once annually and an evaluation should be conducted every 3 years or more frequently if the conditions warrant or if the child's parents or teacher request an evaluation.

Educational program alternatives

Decisions related to the specific placement of an individual student must be based on the results of the comprehensive evaluation and the multidisciplinary conference. The extent of services recommended for a child should be based on individual needs.

Because of the many different kinds of learning disabilities, which may range from mild to severe, it is important that a range of services and placement alternatives be provided. Figure 15.3 is a model that presents the different levels of service (Pysh & Chalfant, 1978). Beginning with preventive intervention, each level of the model represents an increasing amount of special education service. Conversely, as the service becomes more specialized, the

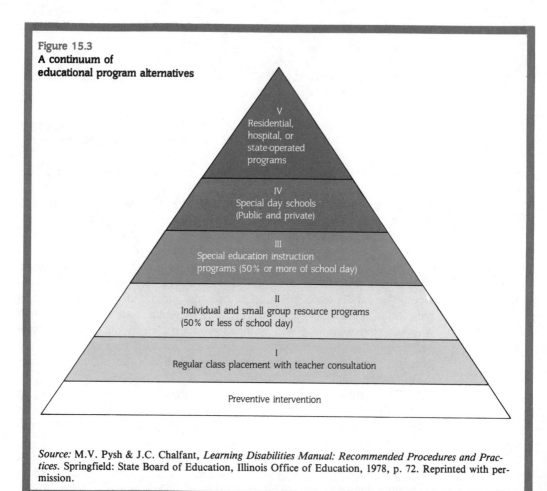

Figure 15.3
**A continuum of
educational program alternatives**

V
Residential,
hospital, or
state-operated
programs

IV
Special day schools
(Public and private)

III
Special education instruction
programs (50% or more of school day)

II
Individual and small group resource programs
(50% or less of school day)

I
Regular class placement with teacher consultation

Preventive intervention

Source: M.V. Pysh & J.C. Chalfant, *Learning Disabilities Manual: Recommended Procedures and Practices.* Springfield: State Board of Education, Illinois Office of Education, 1978, p. 72. Reprinted with permission.

number of students needing the service at that level decreases. The tapered design of the model indicates that fewer students need residential programs (Level V) than regular classroom placement with teacher consultation (Level I).

The concept of placing students in programs appropriate to their needs, removed as little as possible from the regular classroom, is referred to as the "least restrictive alternative" (Kaufman & Morra, 1978). One of the goals of special education is to move the student to the next lower level of service presented in figure 15.3, until the child is once again in the regular classroom.

**The
Teacher
Assistance
Team**

When a child begins to develop learning and behavior problems, it is natural for a teacher to refer him or her for diagnosis. This tendency has caused a great deal of work for diagnostic teams, because many of these children do not have severe enough problems to be eligible for special education. To help the teachers cope with these problems, Chalfant, Pysh, and Moultrie (1979) developed a Teacher Assistance Team model, which is effective in reducing the number of inappropriate referrals and resolving the problems of many children in the classroom.

The Teacher Assistance Team model is designed to help classroom teachers cope with students who have learning and behavior problems. The team consists of three elected teachers plus the teacher who is asking for assistance. Parents or other persons can be invited to serve on the team as needed. In requesting assistance, the teacher provides the team with the following information:

(1) What would the teacher like the student to do?

(2) What does the student do (assets) and what does the student not do (deficits)?

(3) What has the teacher done to help the student cope with his or her problems?

(4) What other background information might be helpful?

The team and the teacher requesting assistance conceptualize the student's difficulties and conduct a 30-minute problem-solving meeting. Procedures in group dynamics are applied by team members to (1) negotiate specific objectives with the teacher, (2) brainstorm alternative suggestions for intervention, (3) select intervention suggestions, (4) refine the suggestions when necessary, and (5) plan follow-up activities. When the teacher leaves the meeting, he or she has a carbon copy of the recommendations. A mandatory follow-up meeting is held in 2 to 6 weeks to determine whether or not the suggestions are working.

The Teacher Assistance Team model was evaluated in Arizona, Nebraska, and Illinois during a 2-year national demonstration project sponsored by the Bureau of Education for the Handicapped, Department of Education (Chalfant, 1980). Data were gathered during the 2nd year of the project from 15 teams in the three demonstration states. During the 1979–1980 academic year, teachers who normally would have referred 200 students to special education services for testing had an opportunity to use their Teacher Assistance Teams for help. (See table 15.1.) Of the 200 students concerned, the teams were able to help the classroom teacher resolve the problems of 133 students, or 66.5%. The teams helped the teachers cope with 103 of the 116 students who were educationally underachieving (88.7%). Among the 200 children in the study, 30 were placed in resource rooms in special education and were also assigned part-time to regular classrooms. Although they created problems for the regular teachers, the Teacher Assistance Teams helped resolve the problems of all 30 children.

The teams were not successful in helping teachers cope with 54 students. When these students were referred to special education for testing, all 54 students were found to be eligible for special education services.

In comparison to this record of no false referrals, contrast schools without Teacher Assistance Teams had approximately 50% or more false refer-

Table 15.1
**Effectiveness of
Teacher Assistance Teams**

Target population	Number staffed	Number helped within building	Number referred to special education	Percentage of referrals helped within building
Educationally under-achieving and problem students	116	103	0	88.7
Mainstreamed handicapped students	30	30	0	100
Students referred to special education	54*	0	54	0
Total	200	133	54	66.5

*All 54 children referred to special education for assessment were found to be eligible for services.

rals. In these schools, the cost for assessing children ranged from $300 to $1600 per child, depending upon the extent of the evaluation. Schools with Teacher Assistance Teams cut their costs for diagnosis by approximately 50%.

The Teacher Assistance Team provides (1) an alternative program for teachers with educationally underachieving and problem students, (2) a means for helping teachers support mainstreamed handicapped students, (3) an opportunity for teachers to share their competencies, (4) a way to include parents in educational planning for their child before special education becomes an issue, and (5) a reduction in staff time and money by reducing inappropriate referrals to special education.

**Level I—
Regular
class place-
ment with
teacher
consultation**

Many learning disabled students with mild or moderate disabilities can be maintained in the regular classroom, with the regular teacher implementing the student's individualized education program. In these cases, special education services consist of consultation with the regular classroom teacher. In junior and senior high schools, learning disabled students can benefit from small classes taught by subject matter specialists in English, science, mathematics, and so on. Although these small classes are identified with the departments offering the classes, the learning disabilities teacher works with the academic teacher in planning and implementing the student's program.

Regular classroom placement with teacher consultation seems to be a simple and inexpensive way of serving mildly learning disabled children. To be successful, regular classroom placement with teacher consultation requires certain conditions, as identified by Pysh and Chalfant (1978):

(1) The classroom teacher must have the expertise and desire to attempt to individualize instruction in the classroom setting.

(2) A lower student-teacher ratio and a low incidence of special education placements in a single classroom may be needed for teachers to give more attention to individualizing instruction.

(3) Additional instructional materials and equipment should be made available to the regular teacher on request to meet the needs of learning disabled students. Special adapted materials such as recorded books and large print materials should be available.

(4) Cooperation of regular teachers and administrators and special educators is necessary to make successful and appropriate curriculum modifications.

(5) The learning disabilities consultant must be able to:

(a) Provide inservice training to regular classroom teachers and other personnel through consultation on individual cases and/or group sessions

(b) Develop or modify curriculum, methods, and materials for regular classroom teachers and other personnel

(c) Demonstrate specific instructional methods and strategies in the classroom as the need dictates

(d) Assess learning problems and make appropriate recommendations to the regular teacher. (pp. 76-77)

This alternative avoids placing mildly learning disabled children in special classes. Although the mildly handicapped or mildly educationally retarded may benefit from a consultative model, many moderately to severely learning disabled children require more individualized instruction than can be provided within the regular classroom (Meyen & Lehr, 1980).

Level II— Individual and small group resource programs (50% or less)

Learning disabled children with problems of moderate severity may need either individual or small group instruction to supplement the regular classroom program (Wiederholt, Hammill, & Brown, 1978). Resource rooms are designed to provide instruction in those areas in which students are having difficulty and not progressing in the regular classroom. Students may spend up to half of the school day in a resource room receiving remedial development of basic skills or tutorial supportive work in academic skills. The regular classroom teacher has responsibility for the student's education. The special education resource room teacher has the responsibility for implementing specialized services as designated on the student's IEP. Students might be scheduled for two, three, or even five 30-minute periods a week or for several periods totaling less than 50% of the school day.

Level III—
Special
education
instruc-
tional
programs
(50% or
more)

There are some learning disabled students whose needs cannot be met in a regular classroom setting because they have severe problems, multiple handicaps, emotional instability, lack of social awareness, or a poor self-concept. Self-contained classrooms are useful in helping those students gradually adjust to the demands of the school setting, providing structure, teaching basic skills necessary for success in the regular classroom, and providing intensive support to parents. Class size is usually kept between 10 and 15 students. Some students can take part in the regular school program in one or more academic courses. Other students may take part in nonacademic classes such as art, music, industrial arts, home arts, or physical education for at least part of the school day.

Level IV—
Special day
schools:
Public and
private

When the problems of learning disabled students are so severe and so complex that they cannot be maintained in special classes in public schools, the children may be placed in special day school programs. Day school services may be provided by the school district or may have to be purchased from private schools that specialize in those problems. Private day schools can sometimes provide a more protected and totally structured environment for severely disabled students. The total school population is usually small, and the whole day can be designed for a specific population of students with special needs. Students in special day schools should be returned to the less restrictive public school programs as soon as their progress permits. The major disadvantages of special day schools are the high expense to maintain them, the lack of socialization with nonhandicapped children, and the distances usually involved in traveling to the site.

Level V—
Residential
schools

A residential school setting providing 24-hour care is needed by only a very small number of learning disabled students whose problems are so profound, complex, or unique that no public or private day school programs can meet their needs. Emotional disturbance, delinquency, social maladjustment, or harsh home situations may lead to residential placement.

Related services

Related services are the developmental, corrective, or supporting services necessary to maintain a handicapped child in an educational setting. These include:

(1) Speech services
(2) Audiology
(3) Psychological services
(4) Physical therapy
(5) Occupational therapy
(6) Recreation

(7) Early identification and assessment

(8) Counseling

(9) Medical services for diagnostic or evaluation purposes

(10) School health services

(11) Social work services.

The area of related services provides wide latitude for interpretation. This latitude can lead to controversy if parents and educators disagree about the need and appropriateness of a particular related service. Many parents and teachers are confused by the difference between a necessary service and one that may be "helpful" to their child but is not necessarily essential to maintain the child in school.

Transition between program levels

One of the goals of special education is to serve learning disabled students in the least restrictive alternative. Guidelines are needed for helping children make the transition to another placement at either a higher or lower level (see figure 15.3). For example, if Alan has benefitted from a Level II resource room placement for 50% or less of the school day, the multidisciplinary team should consider placing him in a Level I service—regular classroom placement with teacher consultation. Criteria for these decisions should include such factors as (1) the extent to which the student will continue to benefit from the present placement; (2) current academic, social, emotional, or physical needs; (3) the extent to which either the current or proposed environment can be modified to meet the student's needs; (4) a comparison of the student's performance with other students in the present or proposed placement; and (5) the need for further evaluation in making the decision. Similarly, students who are not progressing in their present placements should be moved to more comprehensive programs at higher levels. To have any kind of transitioning system work, there must be on-going monitoring and evaluation of the student's progress.

Parent communication

It is very important that parents support, participate in, and understand the entire special education effort for their learning disabled child. Parents should be kept informed about and participate in all decisions concerning their child, beginning with identifying the child, participating in the multidisciplinary conference, planning the IEP, and making placement decisions. They should be apprised of their child's progress throughout the year.

Many parents are anxious and worried about their child's condition, progress or lack of progress in school, and social and emotional problems.

Parents need an opportunity to ask questions and become informed about their child's progress in school. This can be done through periodic parent-teacher conferences. With particularly anxious or hard-to-reach parents, a home visit can often be a way to begin positive communication. Parent groups can be organized that meet monthly and sponsor informative programs, followed by large and small group discussions.

Teachers must be trained to use effective communication skills for talking with parents, because some parents go through a great deal of stress and tension in attempting to cope with their learning disabled child's problems. Teachers of learning disabled children must learn to use the principles of good communication in order to be effective. These include listening, observing, and interpreting what parents are saying; coping with their own emotional responses to parents; deciding what to say; and deciding how to say it (Chalfant & Pysh, 1980). Many schools establish parent groups. Sometimes other parents or parent groups can be more successful in communicating with parents than school personnel.

Impartial due process hearing

When the parents disagree with the school personnel about the appropriate educational program for their child, a due process hearing may be called. The purpose of an impartial due process hearing is to resolve differences concerning the identification, evaluation, or educational placement of the child in a program providing special education or related services (*Federal Register, 1977b*).

There are several procedures suggested by Chalfant and Pysh (1980) that can be used to help avoid the need for a due process hearing. The first is continuous contact with parents. Parental anger and requests for hearings often result from anxiety about what is or is not happening to their child in school. Parents need to have time to ask questions about their child and his or her problems, to be involved in planning their child's educational program, and to be kept informed through personal contacts, telephone calls, notes, or visits.

Day-by-day grievance procedures for parents should be established, beginning with the teacher, and then involving the principal, special education supervisor, director of pupil personnel, or superintendent. The vast majority of parental concerns can be handled at these levels.

Teachers and administrators should prepare for parent contacts. Parents need to be told the purpose of the meetings before they occur. Agendas should allow time for parents to ask questions, explain concerns, and comment on what is being said. Parents have the right to expect confidentiality and to request, inspect, review, and copy educational records. Educators must make every effort to use accurate, specific, and understandable language in both their conversation with parents and their written reports.

Ultimately, the Board of Education may become involved. If the Board of Education is unable to resolve the problem, then mediation or a due process hearing may be in order. In many states, mediation is used as an intervening step before the formal due process hearing. The mediation can be conducted by a member of the state educational agencies or a professional who was not previously involved in the case. Mediation can lead to the resolution of differences between parents and agencies without resorting to the stress of a formal hearing.

A due process hearing may be initiated by either the parents or the public educational agency. The hearing is usually conducted by the state educational agency or the public agency directly responsible for the education of the child in accord with state statutes, regulations, or written policy. The public agency informs the parents of any free or low-cost legal and other relevant services available in the area.

When a parent requests a hearing, it must be completed within 45 days after the request for a hearing is received (*Federal Register,* 1977b, 121a.512). However, the hearing or reviewing officer may grant specific extensions of time beyond the mandatory time limits. Each hearing and each review involving oral arguments must be conducted at a time and place that is reasonably convenient for the parents and the child involved.

Individuals involved in these hearings have the right to:

(1) Be accompanied and advised by counsel and by individuals with special knowledge or training with respect to the problems of handicapped children

(2) Present evidence and confront, cross-examine, and compel the attendance of witnesses

(3) Prohibit the introduction of any evidence at the hearing that has not been disclosed to that party at least 5 days before the hearing

(4) Obtain a written or electronic verbatim record of the hearing

(5) Obtain written findings of fact and decisions. (After deleting any personally identifiable information, the public agency shall transmit those findings and decisions to the state advisory panel.)

If a hearing is conducted by a public agency other than the state education agency, any party aggrieved by the findings and decision in the hearing may appeal to the state educational agency, which will conduct an impartial review of the hearing. All parties have the right to continue to be represented by counsel at the state administrative review level. A detailed account of what is involved in a formal due process hearing may be found in *A Primer on Due Process* (Abeson, Bolick, & Hass, 1975).

The future of programs for learning disabled children

There are three major issues that professionals in education must resolve if the public schools are to continue to support programs for learning disabled students.

First, professionals who are working in the field of learning disabilities must arrive at a consensus concerning criteria and procedures for identifying learning disabled children. The problems and concerns about identification of learning disabled children have been presented again and again during the past decade. It is time to stop reminding ourselves of the problems in the field and to begin developing effective solutions to those problems.

Professionals in research, training, and service must coordinate their efforts to reach a consensus about the major issues in the field. It is time for people with different philosophies to sit down together in a positive spirit of problem solving and try to achieve a consensus through open discussion. Research efforts must be undertaken to improve the instruments and procedures used for identification, diagnosis, and remediation.

Second, regular education must begin to develop alternative programs or services for children who are educationally underachieving, but who are not eligible for learning disabilities services or other special education programs. At present, many children who are not learning disabled and who are educationally underachieving for many reasons other than learning disabilities are being placed in programs for the learning disabled. Children who lack motivation to learn, who have received inadequate instruction, who are economically or culturally disadvantaged, or who have conduct problems are often placed in services for the learning disabled, because there are no other educational programs for them.

Alternative approaches might include smaller classes for these children, teacher aides, summer programs, a tutorial system of volunteers, consultant help to regular teachers, and innovative methods for grouping students in regular classrooms according to their needs, ability level, and learning characteristics.

If the indiscriminate placement of children in learning disabilities programs continues, the role of the learning disabilities teacher will simply be that of a tutor for children who need help in the basic and daily assignments. If this occurs, the truly learning disabled students will not receive the specialized training they need for maximum learning to occur.

Third, institutions of higher education must modify existing teacher-training curricula to prepare personnel to meet the needs of the educationally underachieving in the public schools. Similarly, public schools must provide inservice training for teachers working in the schools. That training would include special methods for individualizing instruction and systems for grouping children for instruction.

It is critical to the future of this field that these three issues be resolved. The learning disabilities teacher's role should be that of a diagnostic-prescriptive remedial specialist for children with developmental and academic disabilities. The unique contribution of the learning disabilities teacher should be to contribute to the differential diagnosis of learning disabled children, provide specialized instruction for individual students or small groups, and serve as a consultant for regular classroom teachers.

Summary

- Programs for learning disabled children and adults have evolved over a period of 200 years. They began with neurologists studying individuals who had lost the ability to read, write, spell, compute arithmetic, or use language because of brain injury.

- Learning disabled students are identified through (1) screening the school population to identify those students who present major problems in learning and (2) referring children for diagnosis.

- The individual evaluation is the basis for all educational planning and is accomplished by an interdisciplinary team. The team determines whether or not the student is eligible for learning disabilities services.

- The individualized education program (IEP) conference is a mechanism by which school personnel and parents develop a written statement of the student's present level of educational performance and an instructional plan for meeting the student's needs.

- Public schools should provide a range of educational programs for learning disabled children, to serve children with disabilities ranging from mild to severe. The programs would include consultation for regular teachers who have learning disabled children in their classes, resource rooms, and special classrooms for the severely learning disabled.

- Related services by other disciplines should be available to provide the support services necessary to maintain a learning disabled child in an educational setting. These services include counseling, social work services, psychological services, and so forth.

- Schools should develop a monitoring system that helps determine whether or not a child's program placement should be altered. Criteria are needed to facilitate the transition of learning disabled students from one program level to another. This will help prevent children's programs from becoming static and ineffective.

- Teachers must be prepared to communicate effectively with parents in explaining children's problems, the results of individual testing, the instructional program, the child's progress in the program, and so forth.

- When the school and the parents have differences of opinion concerning a particular child, the impartial due process hearing is used to resolve those differences.

- The frequency of due process hearings can be reduced by establishing grievance procedures for parents and maintaining communication with parents through parent–teacher groups.

Thought
questions

1. You have been asked to establish a system for identifying learning disabled students. What are your recommendations for identifying learning disabled students in the primary, intermediate, junior high school, and senior high school levels?

2. What kinds of individuals would you place on a multidisciplinary team for diagnosing learning disabled children?

3. Marie received an individualized evaluation and was found not to be learning disabled. She was not eligible for any kinds of special education services. What responsibility does the school and the team have to help Marie?

4. Both parents disagree with the school, which says their child should be removed from the regular classroom for 1 hour a day for remedial work. How would you justify this placement to the parents?

5. Matt is in the second grade. His receptive and expressive oral language is low. He can read sight words, but with limited meaning. His IQ is 85, and he is at least 1 year behind in his skills. What kind of placement is most appropriate for a problem of this kind? Why?

6. When should learning disabled children be placed in services for 1 hour a day? For 50% or more of the school day?

7. You are a special education supervisor. A learning disabled student from one of your resource rooms is being placed in the regular classroom full-time. What kinds of arrangements do you make prior to, during, and after the transition?

8. You are the learning disabilities teacher in Lincoln School. What would you do to maintain communication with the parents of your children?

9. The parents of one of your children are extremely unhappy with the placement and individual program their child is receiving. The parents have demanded a due process hearing. As the child's learning disabilities teacher, what kinds of information should you prepare for the hearing?

10. The president of the United States has given you five million dollars to plan and organize for the future of learning disabilities in the U.S. How do you think this money can be used most effectively?

16

The relationship of developmental learning disabilities to academic disabilities

This text assumes that developmental learning disabilities (inattention, poor memory, weak perception, inadequate thinking, and underdeveloped language) tend to interfere with or inhibit a child's achievement in academic subjects. This assumption is in concert with the definitions of *learning disabilities* reported in chapter 1. The federal definition refers to disorders in "basic psychological processes which manifest themselves in imperfect ability to listen, think, speak, read, write," and so forth. The National Joint Conference on Learning Disabilities notes that "these disorders are intrinsic to the individual and presumed to be due to central nervous system dysfunction." Most definitions can be interpreted to assume that (1) there exists a neurological or organic condition, (2) which leads to a disorder in a psychological process (developmental learning disability), (3) which in turn affects the child's ability to perform academically in school.

The question that is legitimately raised is, What is the relationship of developmental learning disabilities to academic disabilities? How valid are the assumptions that a visual memory or auditory memory deficit can result in a reading disability or a language disability? Does spatial disorientation result in a mathematical disability? Do attention, language, problem solving, and other developmental learning disabilities interfere with achievement in reading, writing, spelling, or arithmetic?

Clinicians and teachers continually report that they find children who are educationally underachieving because of related psychological disabilities. This opinion has been supported by a number of surveys. Arter and Jenkins (1979) questioned teachers about their opinions on this matter; 95% of learning disability teachers believed the research supported their own experience that developmental learning disabilities must be taken into consideration with children with academic disabilities. Kirk, Senf, and Larsen (1981), in a questionnaire study with 1500 professionals, found that 80 to 90% of them believed that they should pay attention to psychological processes, including modality preference.

Researchers for the last 50 years have been trying to identify the apparent relationship between developmental learning disabilities and academic achievement. They have sometimes found what seem to be differences between some research results and clinical experience and among research results themselves.

To help clarify some of these differences, we will review and analyze the contradictory research studies that have dealt with the relationship of developmental learning disabilities and academic achievement. No attempt will be made to review all of the studies, but we will concentrate on a representative group of research studies. The purpose of this review is to delineate the reasons why some of the studies contradict each other and seem to be at variance with clinical practice, teacher experience, and common sense.

Most of these studies have been concerned primarily with the relationship of developmental learning disabilities and the process of learning to read. The focus of our review will be on (1) the relationship of visual perception to academic achievement, (2) the relationship of auditory perception to academic achievement, and (3) the studies on modality preference.

Visual perception

Among developmental learning disabilities, problems of visual perception have received the greatest attention. Questions concerning the relationship of visual perception deficits and reading disability have flourished for years.

Visual perception includes not only details of form and color but also spatial and directional orientation, figure-ground perception, visual memory, visual discrimination, and other related problems. All of these have been considered in studying the causes and correlates of learning disabilities, especially of severe reading disabilities.

As indicated in chapter 2, Hinshelwood (1917) explained a reading disability as resulting from a visual-perceptual deficit caused by brain damage. Orton (1928) also developed theories of visual-perceptual deficits to explain children's disabilities in reading. Since the 1920s, because of these theories, many experiments have attempted to explain reading disabilities by demonstrating a deficit in one or more of the perceptual processes. The results of research have been contradictory and equivocal, resulting in major controversies about what has become known as the *perceptual deficit hypothesis*.

One of the leading critics of the hypothesis that perceptual deficits are related to reading disabilities is Vellutino. After many years of research, he published his criticism and comments in a book entitled *Dyslexia* (1979). He reviewed the numerous studies comparing poor readers with normal readers on visual-motor abilities. Vellutino concluded that tests of visual-motor integration will in most instances tell us little of the etiology of reading disability.

In addition to reviewing the studies on visual-motor abilities, Vellutino reviewed studies on trace duration, spatial and directional orientation, mirror writing, figure-ground and pattern perception, speed of perceptual processing, spatial redundancy, and visual memory. In his own research, he designed a series of studies comparing good with poor readers on memory for Hebrew letters and words. From these experiments, Vellutino concluded that the good and poor readers did not differ on visual memory except when visual-verbal tasks were employed. He concluded that reading disabilities may be due to a dysfunction in some aspects of visual-verbal learning and not to intersensory or intrasensory learning involving nonverbal stimuli. He explains a reading disability as a result of a deficit in linguistics or verbal mediation (another developmental disability) rather than in visual memory. In one report Vellutino dramatized the issue by entitling an article "Has the Perceptual Deficit Hypothesis Led Us Astray?" (Vellutino, Steger, Harding, Moyer, & Niles, 1977). Fletcher and Satz (1979) countered with an article subtitled "Has Vellutino Led Us Astray?" They claimed that verbal mediation is important in visual memory but that deficits in both visual memory and linguistic processes may underlie reading disabilities. This latter view is the one supported by most learning disability specialists.

It would be unproductive to review the many contradictory studies on the relationship of visual-perceptual deficits to reading disabilities. The usual group research experiment on visual memory and reading disability is to test the visual memory of a group of poor readers and compare them with the visual memory of a group of good readers, controlling for such factors as intelligence and age. Some of these studies show a relationship between visual memory and reading disability, while some do not.

In clinical practice, we sometimes find a child with a reading deficit who is unable to reproduce in writing words presented to him or her. One 11-year-old reading disabled child took 12 trials to reproduce the word "horse" from memory. Another 9-year-old child, who had a WISC IQ of 140 and was unable to read at the first-grade level, took seven trials on the same task.

Why are there discrepancies among research studies? In trying to answer this question, Mather (1983) has undertaken the task of finding the factors that can explain the discrepancies in research studies. In her review, Mather delineates six reasons that could explain the contradictions.

(1) *The fallacy of assuming a unitary factor.* Research that studies a single factor such as speed of perception, discrimination, or memory fallaciously assumes that a single factor might cause all reading disabilities. When we select a group of poor readers and compare them with a group of good readers, we are testing whether that unitary factor is *in and of itself* the cause or correlate of the reading difficulty. Over 50 years ago, Monroe (1932) reported that no one factor was present in all of her 415 reading disability subjects; and Malmquist (1958), after studying reading failures in first-grade children, warned that it was useless to attempt to isolate a single factor to explain all reading failures. If 3 out of 100 reading disability subjects had a severe visual memory problem, those few subjects would not be sufficient to obtain statistically significant differences between a group of good and poor readers. The fact that 97 out of 100 poor readers had other problems does not indicate that visual memory could not have been a contributing factor in the other 3 cases. In other words, according to Doehring (1978), a single research paradigm obscures the results of other significant factors.

In any group of poor readers there will be a number of subtypes. Denckla (1972) found, for example, that among 190 clinic cases, 15% of her reading disabled subjects have language disabilities, 10% had a "dyscontrol syndrome," and 5% had specific visual-spatial difficulties. The remaining 70%

had a mixture of syndromes. It is obvious from these data that group designs on one factor tend to cover up and obscure frequently occurring types of reading disabilities. The significance of one factor such as a deficit in visual perception may not be detected (Gross & Rothenberg, 1979; Guralnick, 1978). These infrequent contributing factors show up in clinical practice but not in group studies. This may explain the discrepancy between clinical observation and group studies, and contradictions between group studies.

(2) *Task difficulty.* Another factor noted by Mather as affecting research inconsistency is the difference in task difficulty. Samuels and Anderson (1973) found that in a paired associate task there were no differences between children with low visual memory and those with superior visual memory when the task was easy. When the task became more difficult and complex, however, children who scored low on a test of visual recognition memory had difficulty. Lahey and McNees (1975) also found that there was no difference between good and poor readers on a simple task of discriminating single letters and matching them to a sample. When the match-to-sample consisted of several letters, Lahey and Lefton (1976) found that poor readers made more errors than good readers.

(3) *Methodological differences.* Another major factor that could account for discrepancies in research results is the methodology used, including the deviation used in differentiating good from poor readers. Spring and Capps (1974) used a discrepancy of 2 years below grade placement, while Macione (1969) and Torgesen and Goldman (1977) used a half year below grade. Some authors used tests while others (Lahey & Lefton, 1976) used the number of workbooks completed.

Another factor in methodology that can account for differences in results is the level of intelligence of the subjects. Torgesen and Dice (1980) found that only 24% of the studies had samples of children with average IQs for both groups. In many of the studies no level of intelligence was reported.

(4) *Age-related factors.* Still another discrepancy can be explained by age-related factors. A number of investigators (Fletcher & Satz, 1979; Gibson & Levin, 1975; Senf & Freundl, 1971) have pointed out that the importance of perceptual skills recedes with age. Young children, ages 6 and 7, made more errors in visual-perceptual tasks while a delay in conceptual-linguistic skills was more typical in older children (Satz & van Nostrand, 1973). Swanson (1977) explains some of these differences by stating that older children tend to use mediational functions and strategies in short-term memory tasks, while younger ones use mediation less. Fletcher and Satz (1979) indicate that beyond age 8, group measures of visual perception tend to attenuate or plateau. This could explain why such studies as that of Olson (1966) found no difference between good and poor readers on the Frostig perceptual tests when used with children in the third grade. These results are expected, since the third graders reached the top of the norms of the Frostig tests, thus resulting in no differences.

(5) *Correlational studies.* Another major problem in studying the relationship of visual perception to reading is the use of correlations. Larsen and Hammill (1975) reviewed 50 studies that used correlational methods. They concluded that the relationship between visual perception and reading is minimal. In a more recent review of studies, Hammill and McNutt (1981) set a standard of a correlation of .30 as a criterion for "practical usefulness." Their study showed an average correlation of .29. They concluded that for practical purposes the relationship of .29 could not be used for predictive validity. Kavale (1982), using meta-analysis on similar data, concluded that visual perception is an important correlate of reading achievement.

In view of the contradictory results and interpretations, we can ask whether correlational studies help us to diagnose or treat children. Can we improve our diagnostic procedures by noting that the correlation is 25, 30, or 40? If we have 5% of poor readers who have visual memory problems, how are these 5 out of 100 children going to affect the degree of correlation? How can we identify the five children by using correlational studies? Are correlational studies adding to our knowledge or confusing us?

(6) *The null hypothesis.* Another factor that has led some authors to reject the perceptual deficit hypothesis is the misinterpretation of the null hypothesis. The null hypothesis states that there is no difference between two sample populations. If a researcher finds no difference between a group of poor readers and a group of good readers on a test of memory for digits, that finding cannot be used to deny the contribution of an auditory memory deficit to a reading disability in individual cases. All one can say from such a no-difference result is that in the sample population studied there was no difference. Going beyond this conclusion is unscientific. Fletcher and Satz (1979), referred to earlier, criticized Vellutino and his colleagues for extrapolating beyond the null hypothesis. Although Vellutino, they stated, found no difference between his groups of good and poor readers on tasks of visual memory, his findings do not negate the possibility of visual memory sometimes being a contributing factor to reading disabilities; nor do the no-difference results indicate that reading disability is due *solely* to a deficit in verbal mediation. In other words, it is unscientific to conclude from null findings that there is no relationship between visual or auditory perception and reading ability. *Evidence of absence does not mean absence of evidence.*

Auditory perception

So far, we have concentrated on the relationship of visual perception deficits to reading disability. Similar research has been conducted on the relationship of auditory perception (especially memory) to reading disabilities. This research has generally found a relationship between poor auditory sequential memory and reading disability. Auditory memory in the research studies includes short-term memory as well as long-term memory. Short-term memory is tested by digit repetition, word repetition, or phrase and sentence repetition.

While reviews by Rugel (1974), Torgesen (1978, 1979), and Kavale (1981b) found a significant relationship between auditory sequential memory and learning disabilities, Hammill and Larsen (1974b), after reviewing selected studies, concluded that the relationship between auditory perceptual skills and reading was not sufficient for "practical purposes."

Hammill and Larsen (1974b) reviewed 33 studies of the relationship of auditory perceptual skills to reading disability and found a positive correlation between a number of auditory perceptual skills and reading achievement. The average correlation between reading and auditory memory was less than .35. This correlation, though positive, was not considered sufficient for predictive purposes. Kavale (1981b) conducted a meta-analysis of 106 studies on the relationship of reading to auditory perceptual skills. He concluded that auditory perceptual skills are important correlates of reading ability.

Many studies relating sound blending to learning to read have been conducted. These studies, reviewed by Harber (1980), also show discrepancies in results. As we noted when discussing visual perception, methodological factors contribute to these discrepancies. In general, however, it appears that children who enter school with strong sound-blending ability, all other factors equal, learn to read better than those children who have inadequate sound-blending ability. At the third-grade level, however, sound-blending ability does not differentiate good and poor readers.

The major concentration of studies on auditory memory has been on attempts to analyze the factors responsible for the poor performance of learning disabled children on auditory memory tasks. Ring (1976) and Richie and Aten (1976) conducted studies on good and poor readers. They found that the poor readers were inferior on a large number of meaningful and nonmeaningful auditory sequential memory tasks. In analyzing the results, they found that learning disabled children were able to use mnemonic or problem-solving strategies to aid their auditory sequential memory. Torgesen and Goldman (1977) and Torgesen and Houck (1980) found that learning disabled children perform below non-learning disabled children on sequential memory tasks and tend to use less rehearsal and other strategies.

It is common knowledge that auditory dysfunctions caused by peripheral hearing deficits interfere with the development of language. Other than deafness or near deafness, some children appear to have a deficit in the functions of the brain (a central auditory dysfunction), rather than in the ear. Studies of auditory central process dysfunction in relation to reading and language suffer the same problems as studies of visual memory in children with reading disabilities. The studies of Willeford (1976) and Willeford and Billger (1978) used tests designed for adults and found little relationship between these tests of auditory processing and their sample of learning disabled children. As with tests of visual perception, it was not found that such tests could differentiate learning disabled students from non-learning disabled students. Because learning disabled students are a heterogeneous group, it should not be expected that such tests would differentiate the groups.

Modality preference

Common sense and clinical observation tell us that deaf or severely hard-of-hearing people learn primarily through the sense of vision, while the blind or severely visually defective learn primarily through the auditory and haptic channels. This is referred to as *modality preference,* which refers to the sense avenue or channel through which a child learns best. Practitioners have tried to determine the best modality for learning so that instruction can be adapted to the preferred modality. The bulk of the research literature, on the other hand, indicates that using modality preference in learning to read is not important.

Kampwirth and Bates (1980) reviewed the research on modality preference and teaching methods. They conclude that "there is little research supporting the efficacy of matching children's auditory and visual preferred modalities to teaching approaches" (p. 604). Tarver and Dawson (1978) reviewed 15 studies investigating the interaction between modality preference and method of teaching reading. Out of the 15 studies only 2 showed an interaction. The reviewers concluded that "modality preference and method of teaching reading are not aptitude-treatment variables which can be matched effectively" (p. 27).

The conclusions from research studies are contrary to the opinions of many individuals working with learning disabled children. Shall we believe teachers and clinicians who find that some children can learn better through one modality, or should we believe the group research results?

Our opinion is that, in a very small proportion of children, modality preference is important for teaching and that the research reported could have been inadequately designed or not sufficiently sensitive to ferret out this rare phenomenon. This generalization is made on the basis of the experience reported by numerous teachers and our own clinical experince. Consider an example.

We examined a girl with mild cerebral palsy, age 5½, who had tested low on an intelligence test. We found on the ITPA that her visual abilities on tests of visual memory, visual closure, and visual association were markedly inferior to her comparable auditory abilities. The parents were informed that this child might have difficulty learning to read because of the visual modality deficit. Six months later the father informed the examiners that the prediction was wrong and that the girl had already learned to read 30 words. He had typed 30 words on cards and taught her to read the words by presenting the card visually and spelling the word to her simultaneously. To illustrate his claim, he demonstrated her performance as follows.

He showed her a word and said, "You know this word—*c-a-t*" (spelling it). When he spelled it for her, she would say "cat." He proceeded to show that by this method the child learned to recognize all 30 words. The father was asked to shuffle the cards and present them to her visually without the auditory cues of spelling each word. By this visual mode of presentation, she responded correctly to only a few words. She was then presented the words by spelling them out without the visual presentation. She named all of the words when they were presented auditorily. The father was surprised to note that he was presenting the words through two senses simultaneously but that the child was learning by only one modality. It was obvious that his child had a clear-cut auditory modality preference.

Children with such an extreme auditory-perceptual deviation are rare. Probably 99% of our children have the minimal amount of auditory perceptive ability necessary for learning to read. There is a continuum of perceptual abilities, but there is a point on this continuum below which a modality preference is important for learning. Deaf and severely hearing impaired students learn primarily through the visual channels, and the blind and severely visually handicapped learn primarily through the auditory and haptic channels. These central handicaps show up in clinics or in schools. Such rare cases do not show up in the statistics in studies that compare groups that test slightly below average on visual or auditory abilities. If 1, 2, or even 3 children in 100 had a visual or auditory modality preference, no significant difference would be found between good and poor readers on statistical tests. The few children with a central visual or auditory modality preference can only be identified by case analysis.

We might take an example from physics. Suppose it takes x amount of strength to lift a 2-gallon pail of water, and suppose we find that a 4-year-old can barely lift the pail of water. If we test school-aged children of 6, 7, or 8 years of age on lifting the pail of water, and if they all succeed equally, this would not allow us to conclude that strength is not necessary to lift a 2-gallon pail of water. This conclusion is similar to those reached from the studies on modality preference.

If we could measure modality strengths more accurately and could determine at what point in the continuum a modality strength is needed to learn to read, we might come closer to the truth. Is it possible that in the studies mentioned, the samples did not include enough children with severe weakness in the modality being tested to show a statistically significant difference? Perhaps the visual or auditory modality preferences were not different enough to interfere with reading. Should we neglect the one or two children in a hundred who need to have teaching methods altered to match their modality preference, or should we strive to identify and assist those rare children who require help? Aptitude-instructional interaction requires a determination of the degree of aptitude deficit that will interfere with learning a particular task.

Concluding remarks

One of the most important considerations among diagnosticians and teachers working with learning disabled children is to determine what contributing factors or correlates are involved when a child has an academic disability. As reviewed in this chapter, the results of group research studies have been equivocal and have not given us definitive answers. One can ask, To what extent does information obtained from group studies actually help us in the diagnosis, identification, prediction, and treatment of *individual* learning disabled children and adults?

Maybe we are not asking the right questions with the right group when we compare good and poor readers in a classroom on developmental learning disabilities. Instead of comparing good and poor readers on perceptual deficits, perhaps we should compare children with and without severe perceptual handicaps with their later academic performance. In so doing, we would be asking, "What is the probability of childen with perceptual deficits becoming academic failures?"

If we were to compare a group of educable mentally retarded children with a group of normal children on Downs syndrome or PKU, we might find no statistically significant difference between the groups simply because Downs syndrome and PKU are rare in a random sample of mildly retarded children. If we disregard the significance of the null hypothesis, as has been done with some studies reported here, we would conclude erroneously that Downs syndrome and PKU are not factors in mental retardation. This is what we have done with studies when we compare good and poor readers on a unitary factor like visual memory or visual discrimination or modality preference or auditory processing. As with Downs syndrome or PKU, there may be only a few children in a hundred or in a thousand who have Downs syndrome or PKU or a significant problem in one or more of the developmental learning disabilities.

In the field of developmental learning disabilities, it is necessary to ask the right questions about the right children. It is essential to find children who have severe developmental learning deficits and ask the right question, i.e., "What is the probability of these children becoming learning disabled at a later age?"

What we need are studies that find the rare cases of severe developmental learning disabilities and determine whether or not these children become academically disabled at a later age. Such studies are not conducted because of the difficulty of this kind of research. It will require the examination of several thousand children to find a sample of 10 to 15 children whose disability is severe. It will then require a waiting period to determine whether the deficit affects later school achievement.

Children with developmental learning disabilities are being neglected because of questionable studies that deny the existence of the relationship of developmental learning disabilities to academic disabilities. Teachers and clinicians working with individual children have insisted that these developmental learning disabilities *do* exist and *do* interfere with academic learning. The opinions of the teachers and clinicians may be closer to the facts than some group studies on questionable populations asking the wrong questions. Future research should concentrate on the identification of children with rare severe developmental learning disabilities. Instead of asking, Do poor readers have a visual-perceptual problem? we should ask, Do children with a visual-perceptual problem have difficulty learning to read? Questions like this may reveal for us the exact nature of the relationship between developmental learning disabilities and academic disabilities.

References

Abeson, A., Bolick, N., & Hass, J. *A primer on due process*. Reston, Va.: The Council for Exceptional Children, 1975.

Abramson, L.Y., Seligman, M.E.P., & Teasdale, J.D. Learned helplessness in humans: Critique and reformulation. *Journal of Abnormal Pyschology*, 1978, *87*, 49-74.

Adelman, H.S., & Compas, B.E. Stimulant drugs and learning problems. *The Journal of Special Education*, 1977, *11*, 377-415.

Adelman, H.S., & Taylor, L. Enhancing the motivation and skills needed to overcome interpersonal problems. *Learning Disability Quarterly*, 1982, *5*, 438-446.

Adler, S. Behavior management: A nutritional approach to the behaviorally disordered and learning disabled child. *Journal of Learning Disabilities*, 1978, *11*, 651-656.

Agranowitz, A., & McKeown, M.R. *Aphasia handbook for adults and children*. Ann Arbor, Mich.: Edwards Brothers, 1959.

Alley, G., & Deshler, D. *Teaching the learning disabled adolescent: Strategies and methods*. Denver: Love Publishing, 1979.

American Psychiatric Association. *Diagnostic and statistical manual of mental disorders* (3rd ed.). Washington, D.C.: Author, 1980.

American Speech and Hearing Association. Public school speech and hearing services. *Journal of Speech and Hearing Disorders*, Monograph Supplement 8, 1961.

Andrews, G.R., & Debus, R.L. Persistence and the causal perception of failure: Modifying cognitive attributions. *Journal of Educational Psychology*, 1978, *70*, 154-166.

Arter, J.A., & Jenkins, J.R. Examining the benefits and prevalence of modality considerations in special education. *The Journal of Special Education*, 1977, *11*, 281-298.

Arter, J.A., & Jenkins, J.R. Differential diagnosis–prescriptive teaching: A critical appraisal. *Review of Educational Research*, 1979, *49*, 517-555.

Atkinson, R.C., & Shiffrin, R.M. The control of short-term memory. *Scientific American*, August, 1971, *225*, 82-90.

Ausubel, D.P. *Theory and problems of child development*. New York: Grune & Stratton, 1958.

Ausubel, D.P. *The psychology of meaningful verbal learning*. New York: Grune & Stratton, 1963.

Axelrod, S., & Paluska, J. A component analysis of the effects of a classroom game on spelling performance. In E. Ramp & G. Semb (Eds.), *Behavior analysis: Areas of research and application*. Englewood Cliffs, N.J.: Prentice-Hall, 1975.

303

Backman, C.A. Analyzing children's work procedures. In M.N. Suydam & R.E. Reys (Eds.), *Developing computational skills, 1978 yearbook.* Reston, Va.: National Council of Teachers of Mathematics, 1978.

Ballard, K.D., & Glynn, T. Behavioral self-management in story writing with elementary school children. *Journal of Applied Behavioral Analysis,* 1975, *8,* 387-398.

Bangs, T.E. *Language and learning disorders in the pre-academic child.* New York: Appleton-Century-Crofts, 1968.

Bannatyne, A. *Language, reading and learning disabilities.* Springfield, Ill.: Charles C Thomas, 1971.

Barkley, R.A. Predicting the response of hyperkinetic children to stimulant drugs: A review. *Journal of Abnormal Child Psychology,* 1976, *4,* 327-348.

Barkley, R.A. A review of stimulant drug research with hyperactive children. *Journal of Child Psychology and Psychiatry and Allied Disciplines,* 1977, *18,* 137-165.

Barrett, T. Visual discrimination tasks as predictors of first-grade reading achievement. *Reading Teacher,* 1965, *18,* 276-282.

Barsch, R. *Achieving perceptual-motor efficiency: A space-oriented approach to learning.* Seattle: Special Child Publications, 1967.

Bar-Tal, D. Attributional analysis of achievement related behavior. *Review of Educational Research,* 1978, *48,* 259-271.

Bauer, R.H. Memory processes in children with learning disabilities: Evidence for deficient rehearsal. *Journal of Experimental Child Psychology,* 1977, *24,* 415-430.

Becker, W.C., & Engelmann, S. Analysis of achievement data on six cohorts of low income children from 20 school districts in the University of Oregon Direct Instruction follow through model. *Follow Through Project, Technical Report #76-1.* Unpublished manuscript, University of Oregon, 1976.

Beers, J.J. Developmental strategies of spelling competence in primary school children. In E.H. Henderson & J.J. Beers (Eds.), *Developmental and cognitive aspects of learning to spell.* Newark, Del.: International Reading Association, 1980.

Belch, P. The effect of verbal instructions and instructions combined with point loss on the writing behavior of students. *School Applications of Learning Theory,* 1975, *8,* 27-33.

Belmont, I., Birch, H.G., & Karp, E. The disordering of intersensory and intrasensory integration by brain damage. *Journal of Nervous and Mental Diseases,* 1965, *141,* 410-418.

Benton, A.L. *Right-left discrimination and finger localization.* New York: Hoeber-Harper, 1959.

Berger, N.S. Why can't John read? Perhaps he is not a good listener. *Journal of Learning Disabilities,* 1978, *11,* 633-638.

Berlyne, D.E. Attention as a problem in behavior theory. In D.I. Mostofsky (Ed.), *Attention: Contemporary theory and analysis.* New York: Appleton-Century-Crofts, 1970.

Berry, M.F., & Eisenson, J. *Speech disorders: Principles and practices of therapy.* New York: Appleton-Century-Crofts, 1956.

Berry, M.M. *Language disorders of children: The basis and diagnosis.* New York: Appleton-Century-Crofts, 1969.

Betts, E. *Foundations of reading instruction.* New York: American Book, 1946.

Binet, A. L'education de l'intelligence. In *Les idees modernes sur les enfants.* Paris: Ernest Flammarion, 1911.

Birch, H.G., & Lefford, A. Intersensory development in children. *Monograph of the Society for Research in Child Development,* 1963, *28* (5, Serial No. 89).

Bley, N.S., & Thornton, C.A. *Teaching mathematics to the learning disabled.* Rockville, Md.: Aspen, 1981.

Bloom, L., & Lahey, M. *Language development and language disorders.* New York: John Wiley, 1978.

Boder, E. Developmental dyslexia: A diagnostic approach based on three atypical reading-spelling patterns. *Developmental Medicine and Child Neurology,* 1973, *15,* 663-687.

Boll, T. Conceptual vs. perceptual vs. motor deficits in brain-damaged children. *Journal of Clinical Psychology,* 1972, *28,* 157-159.

Borys, S., & Spitz, H.H. Effect of peer interaction in problem-solving behavior of mentally retarded youths. *Journal of Mental Deficiency,* 1979, *84,* 273-279.

Bower, G.H. A selective review of organizational factors in memory. In E. Tulving & W. Donaldson (Eds.), *Organization of memory.* New York: Academic Press, 1972.

Bower, G.H., & Hilgard, E.R. *Theories of learning.* Englewood Cliffs, N.J.: Prentice-Hall, 1981.

Boyd, G.A., & Talbert, E.G. *Spelling in the elementary school.* Columbus, Ohio: Charles E. Merrill, 1971.

Bradley, L., & Bryant, D. Independence of reading and spelling in backward and normal readers. *Developmental Medicine and Child Neurology,* 1979, *21,* 504-514.

Broden, M., Hall, R.V., & Mitts, B. The effect of self-recording on the classroom behavior of two eighth-grade students. *Journal of Applied Behavior Analysis,* 1971, *4,* 191-199.

Brown, A.L. Knowing when, where, and how to remember: A problem of meta-cognition. In R. Glaser (Ed.), *Advances in instructional psychology.* Hillsdale, N.J.: Erlbaum Associates, 1978.

Bruck, M., & Hebert, M. Correlates of learning disabled students' peer-interaction patterns. *Learning Disability Quarterly,* 1982, *5,* 353-362.

Bruininks, V.L. Actual and perceived peer status of learning disabled students in mainstream programs. *The Journal of Special Education,* 1978, *12,* 51-58. (a)

Bruininks, V.L. Peer status and personality characteristics of learning disabled and nondisabled students. *Journal of Learning Disabilities,* 1978, *11,* 484-489. (b)

Bruner, J.S. *Beyond the information given.* New York: W.W. Norton, 1973.

Bryan, T. An observational analysis of classroom behaviors of children with learning disabilities. *Journal of Learning Disabilities,* 1974, *7,* 26-34. (a)

Bryan, T. Peer popularity of learning disabled children. *Journal of Learning Disabilities,* 1974, *7,* 621-625. (b)

Bryan, T. Learning disabled children's comprehension of nonverbal communication. *Journal of Learning Disabilities,* 1977, *10,* 501-506.

Bryan, T.H., & Bryan, J.H. *Understanding learning disabilities.* Port Washington, N.Y.: Alfred Publishing, 1975.

Bryan, T., & Bryan, J. Social interactions of learning disabled children. *Learning Disability Quarterly,* 1978, *1,* 33-38.

Butkowsky, I.S., & Willows, D.M. Cognitive-motivational characteristics of children varying in reading ability: Evidence for learned helplessness in poor readers. *Journal of Educational Psychology,* 1980, *72,* 408-422.

Cartledge, G., & Milburn, J.F. The case for teaching social skills in the classroom: A review. *Review of Educational Research,* 1978, *48,* 133-156.

Cawley, J.F., Fitzmaurice, A., Goodstein, H., Lepore, A., Sedlack, R., & Althouse, V. *Project Math* (Level 1). Tulsa: Educational Development Corp., 1976. (a)

Cawley, J.F., Fitzmaurice, A., Goodstein, H., Lepore, A., Sedlack, R., & Althouse, V. *Project Math* (Level 2). Tulsa: Educational Development Corp., 1976. (b)

Chalfant, J.C. A Teacher Assistance Model: Inservice training for teachers and administrators. *Final Report: Grant No. G007801745.* Washington, D.C.: U.S. Department of Education, Bureau of Education for the Handicapped, 1980.

Chalfant, J.C., & Flathouse, V.E. Auditory and visual learning. In H.R. Myklebust (Ed.), *Progress in learning disabilities* (Vol. 2). New York: Grune & Stratton, 1971.

Chalfant, J.C., & Foster, G. Identifying learning disabilities in the classroom. *Slow Learning Child,* 1974, *21,* 3-14.

Chalfant, J.C., & King, F.S. An approach to operationalizing the definition of learning disabilities. *Journal of Learning Disabilities,* 1976, *9,* 228-243.

Chalfant, J.C., & Pysh, M.V. *The compliance manual: A guide to the rules and regulations of the Education of All Handicapped Children Act P.L. 94-142.* Mount Kisco, N.Y.: Pathescope Educational Media, 1980.

Chalfant, J.C., Pysh, M.V., & Moultrie, R. Teacher Assistance Teams: A model for within building problem solving. *Learning Disability Quarterly,* 1979, *2*(3), 85-96.

Chalfant, J.C., & Scheffelin, M.A. *Central processing dysfunctions in children: A review of research.* (NINDS Monograph No. 9). Washington, D.C.: U.S. Department of Health, Education and Welfare, 1969.

Chall, J.S., & Mirsky, A.F. (Eds.). *Education and the brain: The seventy-seventh yearbook of the National Society for the Study of Education.* Chicago: University of Chicago Press, 1978.

Chapman, J.W., & Boersma, F.J. Learning disabilities, locus of control and mother attitudes. *Journal of Educational Psychology,* 1979, *71,* 250-258.

Chomsky, N. *Aspects of the theory of syntax.* Cambridge, Mass.: MIT Press, 1965.

Clark, E. Some aspects of the conceptual basis for first language acquisition. In R.L. Schiefelbusch & L.L. Lloyd (Eds.), *Language perspectives: Acquisition, retardation, and intervention.* Baltimore: University Park Press, 1974.

Cratty, B.J. *Developmental sequences of perceptual-motor tasks: Movement activities for neurologically handicapped and retarded children and youth.* Freeport, N.Y.: Educational Activities, 1967.

Cratty, B.J. *Perceptual motor behavior and educational processes.* Springfield, Ill.: Charles C Thomas, 1969.

Cravioto, J., & DeLicardie, E. Environmental and nutritional deprivation in children with learning disabilities. In W.M. Cruickshank & D.P. Hallahan (Eds.), *Psychoeducational practices: Perceptual and learning disabilities in children. Volume 2: Research and theory.* Syracuse, N.Y.: Syracuse University Press, 1975.

Critchley, M. *The dyslexic child* (2nd ed.). London: Heinemann Medical Books, 1970.

Cruickshank, W.M. *Concepts in learning disabilities: Selected writings* (2 vol.). Syracuse, N.Y.: Syracuse University Press, 1981. (a)

Cruickshank, W.M. Learning disabilities: A definitional statement. In *Concepts in learning disabilities: Selected writings* (Vol. 2). Syracuse, N.Y.: Syracuse University Press, 1981. (b)

Cunningham, C.E., & Barkley, R.A. The role of academic failure in hyperactive behavior. *Journal of Learning Disabilities,* 1978, *11,* 274-280.

Damron Reading-Language Kit. New York: McGraw-Hill, 1978.

Davidson, J. *Using the Cuisenaire rods.* New Rochelle, N.Y.: Cuisenaire of America, 1969.

Davis, G.A. *Psychology of problem solving: Theory and practice.* New York: Basic Books, 1973.

Dechant, E.V. *Improving the teaching of reading* (3rd ed.). Englewood Cliffs, N.J.: Prentice-Hall, 1982.

Decker, S.N., & DeFries, J.C. Cognitive abilities in families of reading disabled children. *Journal of Learning Disabilities,* 1980, *13*(9), 517-522.

DeFries, J.C., & Decker, S.N. Genetic aspects of reading disability: A family study. In R.N. Malatesha & P.G. Aaron (Eds.), *Reading disorders: Varieties and treatments.* New York: Academic Press, 1982.

de Hirsch, K. Differential diagnosis between aphasic and schizophrenic language in children. *Journal of Speech and Hearing Disorders,* 1967, *32,* 3-10.

Delacato, C.H. *Neurological organization and reading.* Springfield, Ill.: Charles C Thomas, 1966.

DeLoach, T.F., Earl, J.M., Brown, B.S., Poplin, M.S., & Warner, M.M. L.D. teachers' perceptions of severely learning disabled students. *Learning Disability Quarterly,* 1981, *4,* 343-358.

Denckla, M.B. Clinical syndromes in learning disabilities: The case for "splitting" vs. "lumping." *Journal of Learning Disabilities,* 1972, *5,* 401-406.

Denckla, M.B. Minimal brain dysfunction. In J.S. Chall & A. Mirsky (Eds.), *Education and the brain: The seventy-seventh yearbook of the National Society for the Study of Education* (Part II). Chicago: University of Chicago Press, 1978.

Deno, E. Special education as developmental capital. *Exceptional Children,* 1970, *37,* 229-237.

Deshler, D.D., Ferrell, W.R., & Kass, C.E. Error monitoring of schoolwork by learning disabled adolescents. *Journal of Learning Disabilities,* 1978, *11,* 401-414.

DeStefano, J.S. Productive language differences in fifth-grade students syntactic forms. *Elementary English,* 1972, *49,* 552-558.

de Villiers, P.A., & de Villiers, J.G., Early judgements of semantic and syntactic acceptability by children. *Journal of Psycholinguistic Research,* 1973, *1*(4), 299-310.

Dewey, J. *How we think.* New York: D.C. Heath, 1933.

Dewey, J. *Logic: The theory of inquiry.* New York: Holt, 1938.

Diener, C.T., & Dweck, C.S. An analysis of learned helplessness: Continuous changes in performance, strategy and achievement cognitions following failure. *Journal of Personality and Social Psychology,* 1978, *36,* 451-462.

Doehring, D.G. The tangled web of behavioral research on developmental dyslexia. In A.L. Benton & D. Pearl (Eds.), *Dyslexia: An appraisal of current knowledge.* London: Oxford University Press, 1978.

Douglas, V.I. Stop, look, and listen: The problem of sustained attention and impulse control in hyperactive and normal children. *Canadian Journal of Behavioral Science,* 1972, *4,* 259-282.

Douglas, V.I., & Peters, K.G. Toward a clearer definition of the attentional deficit of hyperactive children. In G. Hale & M. Lewis (Eds.), *Attention and the development of cognitive skills.* New York: Plenum Press, 1980.

Drake, C., & Cavanaugh, J.A. Teaching the high school dyslexic. In L.E. Anderson (Ed.), *Helping the adolescent with the hidden handicap.* Belmont, Calif.: Fearon, 1970.

Dunivant, N. *The relationship between learning disabilities and juvenile delinquency: Executive summary.* Williamsburg, Va.: National Center for State Courts, 1982.

Dunn, L.M., Smith, J.O., et al. *Peabody Language Development Kits.* Circle Pines, Minn.: American Guidance Service, 1967, 1968, 1969, 1982.

Durrell, D. *Durrell Analysis of Reading Difficulty.* New York: Harcourt, Brace & World, 1937, 1955.

Dweck, C.S. The role of expectations and attributions in the alleviation of learned helplessness. *Journal of Personality and Social Psychology, 1975, 31,* 674-685.

Dweck, C.S., & Licht, B.G. Learned helplessness and intellectual achievement. In J. Garber & M.E.P. Seligman (Eds.), *Human helplessness: Theory and applications.* New York: Academic Press, 1980.

Dweck, C.S., & Reppucci, N.D. Learned helplessness and reinforcement responsibility in children. *Journal of Personality and Social Psychology, 1973, 25,* 109-116.

Dykman, R.A., Ackerman, P.T., Clements, S.D., & Peters, J.E. Specific learning disabilities: An attentional deficit syndrome. In H.R. Myklebust (Ed.), *Progress in learning disabilities* (Vol. 2). New York: Grune & Stratton, 1971.

Edmark Associates. *Edmark reading program: Teacher's guide.* Seattle. Author, 1972.

Education for All Handicapped Children Act, Public Law 94-142, 94th Congress, S.6. November 29, 1975. 89 Stat. 794.

Educational Testing Service. *Sequential Tests of Educational Progress: English.* Princeton, N.J.: Educational Testing Service, Cooperative Tests and Services, 1972.

Elbow, P. *Writing without teachers.* New York: Oxford University Press, 1973.

Elkind, D. The development of quantitative thinking: A systematic replication of Piaget's studies. *Journal of Genetic Psychology, 1961, 98,* 37-46. (a)

Elkind, D. Children's discovery of the conservation of mass, weight and volume: Piaget replication study II. *Journal of Genetic Psychology, 1961, 98,* 219-227. (b)

Elkind, D. Quantity conceptions in junior and senior high school students. *Child Development, 1961, 32,* 551-560. (c)

Elkins, J. *Some psycholinguistic aspects of the differential diagnosis of reading disability in grades I and II.* Unpublished doctoral dissertation, University of Queensland, Australia, 1972.

Elkins, J. The use of the revised ITPA with some Queensland children. *Australian Psychologist, 1974, 9*(3), 71-77.

Engelmann, S., & Bruner, E.C. *DISTAR reading I: An instructional system* (2nd ed.). Chicago: Science Research Associates, 1974.

Engelmann, S., & Carnine, D. *DISTAR: Arithmetic I, II and III.* Chicago: Science Research Associates, 1970, 1972, 1975.

Engelmann, S., & Carnine, D. *Theory of instruction: Principles and applications.* New York: Irvington Publishers, 1982.

Enright, R.D., & Lapsley, D.K. Social role-taking: A review of the constructs, measures, and measurement properties. *Review of Educational Research, 1980, 50,* 647-674.

Faas, L.A. *Children with learning problems: A handbook for teachers.* Boston: Houghton Mifflin, 1980.

Farr, R. *Reading: What can be measured?* Newark, Del.: International Reading Association, 1969.

Federal Register. Assistance to states for education of handicapped children: Procedure for evaluating specific learning disabilities. Part III. Thursday, December 29, 1977. (a)

Federal Register. Education of handicapped children: Implementation of part B of the Education of the Handicapped Act. Part III. Tuesday, August 23, 1977. (b)

Federal Register. Procedures for evaluating specific learning disabilities, *42*(250), Section 121a.541. Washington, D.C.: U.S. Department of Health, Education and Welfare, Office of Education, December 29, 1977. (c)

Feingold, B.F. *Why your child is hyperactive.* New York: Random House, 1975.

Feldhusen, J.F., & Treffinger, D.J. *Teaching creative thinking and problem solving.* Dubuque, Iowa: Kendall/Hunt, 1977.

Fendrick, N. Visual characteristics of poor readers. *Teachers College Contributions to Education, No. 656.* New York: Columbia University, Teachers College, 1935.

Fernald, G.M. *Remedial techniques in basic school subjects.* New York: McGraw-Hill, 1943.

Fernald, G.M., & Keller, H. The effect of kinaesthetic factors in the development of word recognition in the case of non-readers. *Journal of Education Research,* 1921, *4,* 355-377.

Feuerstein, R., in collaboration with Y. Rand & M.B. Hoffman. *The dynamic assessment of retarded performers: The learning potential assessment device, theory, instruments, and techniques.* Baltimore: University Park Press, 1979.

Fitzgerald, E. *Straight language for the deaf.* Washington, D.C.: The Volta Bureau, 1966.

Flavell, J.H. Developmental studies of mediated memory. In H.W. Reese & L.P. Lipsitt (Eds.), *Advances in child development and behavior* (Vol. 5). New York: Academic Press, 1970.

Flavell, J.H. What is memory development the development of? *Human Development,* 1971, *14,* 272-278.

Flavell, J.H., & Wellman, H.M. Metamemory. In R.V. Kail, Jr., & J.W. Hagen (Eds.), *Perspectives on the development of memory and cognition.* Hillsdale, N.J.: Erlbaum Associates, 1977.

Flesch, R. *Why Johnny can't read.* New York: Harper & Bros., 1965.

Fletcher, J.M., & Satz, P. Unitary deficit hypothesis of reading disabilities: Has Vellutino led us astray? *Journal of Learning Disabilities,* 1979, *12,* 155-159.

Fraenkel, J.R. *Helping students think and value: Strategies for teaching the social studies.* Englewood Cliffs, N.J.: Prentice-Hall, 1973.

Frieze, I.H. Children's attributions for success and failure. In S. Brehm, S. Kassin, & F. Gibbons (Eds.), *Developmental social psychology.* New York: Oxford University Press, 1981.

Frieze, I.H., & Weiner, B. Cue utilization and attributional judgments for success and failure. *Journal of Research in Personality,* 1971, *39,* 591-606.

Frith, U. Unexpected spelling problems. In U. Frith (Ed.), *Cognitive processes in spelling.* New York: Academic Press, 1980.

Frostig, M. The needs of teachers for specialized information on reading. In W.M. Cruickshank (Ed.), *The teacher of brain-injured children.* Syracuse, N.Y.: Syracuse University Press, 1966.

Forgus, R.H., & Melamed, L.E. *Perception: A cognitive-stage approach.* New York: McGraw Hill, 1976.

Frostig, M., & Horne, D. *The Frostig Program for the Development of Visual Perception.* Chicago: Follett, 1967.

Frostig, M., Maslow, P., LeFever, D., & Whittlesey, J. *The Marianne Frostig Test of Visual Perception: 1963 Standardization.* Palo Alto, Calif.: Consulting Psychologists Press, 1964.

Furness, E. Mispronunciation, mistakes, and method in spelling. *Elementary English,* 1956, *33,* 508-511.

Gaddes, W.H. *Learning disabilities and brain function: A neuropsychological approach.* New York: Springer-Verlag, 1980.

Gadow, K.D. Effects of stimulant drugs on attention and cognitive deficits. *Exceptional Education Quarterly,* 1981, *2*(3), 83-93.

Gagné, R.M. (Ed.). *Learning and individual differences: A symposium of the Learning Research and Development Center: University of Pittsburgh.* Columbus, Ohio: Charles E. Merrill, 1967.

Gagné, R. *The conditions of learning.* New York: Holt, Rinehart & Winston, 1970.

Gates, A.I., & Chase, E.H. Methods and theories of learning to spell tested by studies of deaf children. *Journal of Educational Psychology,* 1926, *17,* 289-300.

Gates, A., & McKillop, A. *Gates-McKillop Reading Diagnostic Tests.* New York: Teachers College Press, 1962.

Geldard, F.A. *The human senses.* New York: John Wiley, 1953.

Gentry, J.R., & Henderson, E.H. Three steps to teaching beginning readers to spell. In E.H. Henderson & J.J. Beers (Eds.), *Developmental and cognitive aspects of learning to spell.* Newark, Del.: International Reading Association, 1980.

Gerber, P.J., & Zinkgraf, S.A. A comparative study of social-perceptual ability in learning disabled and nonhandicapped students. *Learning Disability Quarterly,* 1982, *5,* 374-378.

Gerstmann, J. Fingeragnosie: Eine umschriebene Storung der Orienterung ameigenen Korper. Wien: Klin. Wchn-Schr., 1924, *37,* 1010-1012. Cited in A.L. Benton, *Right-left discrimination and finger localization.* New York: Hoeber-Harper, 1959.

Gesell, A. *The first five years of life: A guide to the study of pre-school children.* New York: Harper Brothers, 1940.

Gesell, A., & Ilg, F. *The child from five to ten.* New York: Harper Brothers, 1946.

Getman, G.H. The visuo-motor complex in the acquisition of learning skills. In B. Straub & J. Hellmuth (Eds.), *Learning disorders* (Vol. 1). Seattle: Special Child Publications, 1965.

Gibson, E.J., & Levin, H. *The psychology of reading.* Cambridge, Mass.: M.I.T. Press, 1975.

Gillespie, P., Miller, T., & Fielder, V. Legislative definitions of learning disabilities: Roadblocks to effective service. *Journal of Learning Disabilities,* 1975, *8,* 660-666.

Gillingham, A., & Stillman, B.W. *Remedial work for reading, spelling, and penmanship.* New York: Hackett and Wilhelms, 1936.

Gillingham, A., & Stillman, B.W. *Remedial training for children with specific disability in reading, spelling and penmanship.* Cambridge, Mass.: Educators Publishing Service, 1973.

Glass, G.G. *Teaching decoding as separate from reading.* Garden City, N.Y.: Adelphi University Press, 1973.

Glynn, E.L., & Thomas, J.D. Effect of cueing on self-control of classroom behavior. *Journal of Applied Behavior Analysis,* 1974, *7,* 299-306.

Glynn, E.L., Thomas, J.D., & Shee, S.K. Behavioral self-control of on-task behavior in an elementary classroom. *Journal of Applied Behavior Analysis,* 1973, *6,* 105-113.

Goldberg, H.K., Shiffman, G.B., & Bender, M. *Dyslexia: Interdisciplinary approaches to reading disabilities.* New York: Grune & Stratton, 1983.

Goldstein, K. *Language and language disturbances: Aphasic symptom complexes and their significance for medicine and theory of language.* New York: Grune & Stratton, 1948.

Gordon, W.J. *Synectics.* New York: Harper and Row, 1961.

Graham, N.C. Short-term memory and syntactic structure in educationally subnormal children. *Language and Speech,* 1968, *11*(Part 4), 209-219.

Graham, S., & Miller, L. Handwriting research and practice: A unified approach. *Focus on Exceptional Children,* 1980, *13*(2), 1-16.

Gray, B., & Ryan, B. *A language program for the non-language child.* Champaign, Ill.: Research Press, 1973.

Grey, J.A., & Wedderburn, A.I. Grouping strategies with simultaneous stimuli. *Quarterly Journal of Experimental Psychology,* 1960, *12,* 180-184.

Gross, K., & Rothenberg, S. An examination of methods used to test the visual perceptual deficit hypothesis of dyslexia. *Journal of Learning Disabilities,* 1979, *12,* 670-677.

Guralnick, M.J. The application of single subject reseafch design to the field of learning disabilities. *Journal of Learning Disabilities,* 1978, *11,* 415-421.

Hagen, J.W. Some thoughts on how children learn to remember. *Human Development,* 1971, *14,* 262-271.

Hallahan, D.P., Gajar, A.M., Cohen, A.B., & Tarver, S.G. Selective attention and locus of control in learning disabled and normal children. *Journal of Learning Disabilities,* 1978, *11,* 231-236.

Hallahan, D.P., Kauffman, J.M., & Ball, D.W. Selective attention and cognitive tempo of low achieving and high achieving sixth grade males. *Perceptual and Motor Skills,* 1973, *36,* 579-583.

Hallahan, D.P., Lloyd, J., Kosiewicz, M.M., Kauffman, J.M., & Graves, A.W. Self-monitoring of attention as a treatment for a learning disabled boy's off-task behavior. *Learning Disability Quarterly,* 1979, *2,* 24-32.

Hallgren, B. Specific dyslexia (congenital word-blindness): A clinical and genetic study. *Acta Psychiatrica et Neurologica,* 1950, Supplementum 65, 1-287.

Halstead, W.C. *Brain and intelligence.* Chicago: University of Chicago Press, 1947.

Hammill, D.D., & Larsen, S.C. The effectiveness of psycholinguistic training. *Exceptional Children,* 1974, *41,* 5-14. (a)

Hammill, D.D., & Larsen, S.C. The relationship of selected auditory perceptual skills and reading ability. *Journal of Learning Disabilities,* 1974, *7,* 429-435. (b)

Hammill, D.D., & Larsen, S.C. The effectiveness of psycholinguistic training: A reaffirmation of position. *Exceptional Children,* 1978, *44,* 402-414. (a)

Hammill, D.D., & Larsen, S.C. *Test of Written Language.* Austin, Tex.: Pro-Ed, 1978. (b)

Hammill, D.D., Leigh, J.E., McNutt, G., & Larsen, S.C. A new definition of learning disabilities. *Learning Disability Quarterly,* 1978, *4,* 336-342.

Hammill, D.D., & McNutt, G. *The correlates of reading.* (Pro-Ed Monograph #1.) Austin, Tex.: Pro-Ed, 1981.

Harber, J.R. Auditory perception and reading: Another look. *Learning Disability Quarterly,* 1980, *3*(3), 19-29.

Harris, A.J., & Sipay, E. *How to increase reading ability* (6th ed.). New York: David McKay, 1975.

Harrison, E.M. The brain-damaged child and writing problems. In J. Arena (Ed.), *Building handwriting skills in dyslexic children.* San Rafael, Calif.: Academic Therapy Publications, 1970.

Haskins, R., & McKinney, J. Relative effects of response tempo and accuracy in problem solving. *Child Development,* 1976, *47,* 690-696.

Havertape, J.F., & Kass, C.E. Examination of problem solving in learning disabled adolescents through verbalized self-instructions. *Learning Disability Quarterly,* 1978, *1,* 94-103.

Hazel, J.S., Schumaker, J.B., Sherman, J.A., & Sheldon-Wildgen, J. Group training for social skills: A program for court-adjudicated, probationary youths. *Criminal Justice and Behavior,* 1982, *9,* 35-53.

Head, H. *Aphasia and kindred disorders of speech* (Vols. 1, 2). New York: Macmillan, 1926.

Healey, W.C., Ackerman, B.L., Chapell, C.R., Perrin, K.L., & Stormer, J. *The prevalence of communicative disorders: A review of the literature* (Final report). Rockville, Md.: American Speech-Language-Hearing Association, 1981.

Heckelman, R.G. The neurological impress method of remedial reading instruction. *Academic Therapy,* 1969, *4,* 277-282.

Hegge, T.G., Kirk, S.A., & Kirk, W.D. *Remedial reading drills.* Ann Arbor, Mich.: George Wahr, 1936.

Heider, F. *The psychology of interpersonal relations.* New York: John Wiley, 1958.

Hermann, K. *Reading disability: A medical study of word-blindness and related handicaps.* Springfield, Ill.: Charles C Thomas, 1959.

Hewett, F.M. A hierarchy of educational tasks for children with learning disorders. *Exceptional Children,* 1964, *31,* 207-214.

Hildreth, G. *Learning the three R's.* Minneapolis: Educational Publishers, 1936.

Hillerich, R.L. *Spelling: An element in written expression.* Columbus, Ohio: Charles E. Merrill, 1976.

Hinshelwood, J. *Congenital word blindness.* London, H.K. Lewis, 1917.

Hodges, R.E. The psychological basis of spelling. *Research on handwriting and spelling.* Champaign, Ill.: National Council of Teachers of English, 1966.

Holborow, P., Elkins, J., & Berry, P. The effect of the Feingold diet on "normal" school children. *Journal of Learning Disabilities,* 1981, *14,* 143-147.

Hook, P.E., & Johnson, D.J. Metalinguistic awareness and reading strategies. *Bulletin of the Orton Society,* 1978, 62-78.

Horn, E. Spelling. In C.W. Harris (Ed.), *Encyclopedia of educational research* (3rd ed.). New York: Macmillan, 1960.

Horrocks, E.M. *Guidelines for spelling.* Boston: Ginn, 1966.

Hull, F.M., Mielke, Jr., P.W., Willeford, J.A., & Timmons, R.J. *National speech and hearing survey.* Washington, D.C.: U.S. Department of Health, Education and Welfare, Office of Education, Bureau of Education for the Handicapped, 1976.

Hulse, S.H., Egeth, H., & Deese, J. *The psychology of learning* (5th ed.). New York: McGraw-Hill, 1980.

Hunter, E. *Memory: Facts and fallacies.* Baltimore: Penguin Books, 1957.

Irmscher, W.F. *The Holt guide to English.* New York: Holt, Rinehart & Winston, 1972.

Itard, J.M.G. *[The wild boy of Aveyron.]* (Trans. G. Humphrey & M. Humphrey). New York: Appleton-Century-Crofts, 1932.

Jackson, J.H. On the physiology of language. *Brain,* 1915, *38,* 59-64.

Johnson, D.J., & Myklebust, H.R. *Learning disabilities: Educational principles and practices.* New York: Grune & Stratton, 1967.

Johnson, M., & Kress, R. *Informal reading inventories.* Newark, Del.: International Reading Association, 1965.

Johnson, N.F. Chunking: Associative chaining versus coding. *Journal of Verbal Learning and Verbal Behavior,* 1969, *8,* 725-731.

Johnson, W.W. *Arithmetic and learning disabilities: Guidelines for identification and remediation.* Boston: Allyn & Bacon, 1979.

Jordon, D.R. *Dyslexia in the classroom.* Columbus, Ohio: Charles E. Merrill, 1972.

Kagan, J. Reflection-impulsivity and the general dynamics of conceptual tempo. *Journal of Abnormal Psychology,* 1966, *71,* 17-24.

Kaliski, L. Arithmetic and the brain-injured child. *The Arithmetic Teacher,* 1962, *9,* 245-251.

Kampwirth, T.J., & Bates, M. Modality preference and teaching method: A review of research. *Academic Therapy,* 1980, *15,* 597-605.

Kane, R.B., & Deans, E. *Mathematics in action.* New York: American Book, 1969.

Karnes, M. *GOAL: Language development.* Springfield, Mass.: Milton Bradley, 1972.

Karnes, M. *Karnes early language activities (GEM).* Champaign, Ill.: Generators of Educational Materials, 1975.

Karnes, M. *Learning language in the home.* Reston, Va.: Council for Exceptional Children, 1977.

Karnes, M., Zehrbach, R., & Teska, J. The Karnes preschool program, rational curricular offerings and followup data. In S. Ryan (Ed.), *A report on longitudinal evaluations of preschool programs* (Vol 1). Washington, D.C.: Office of Child Development, Children's Bureau, 1974. (DHEW Pub. No. (OHD) 77-24.)

Kass, C.E. Psycholinguistic disabilities of children with reading problems. *Exceptional Children,* 1966, *32,* 533-539.

Kaufman, M.J., & Morra, L.G. The least restrictive environment: A major philosophical change. In E.L. Meyen (Ed.), *Exceptional children and youth: An introduction.* Denver: Love Publishing, 1978.

Kavale, K. Functions of the *Illinois Test of Psycholinguistic Abilities* (ITPA): Are they trainable? *Exceptional Children,* 1981, *47,* 496-510. (a)

Kavale, K. The relationship between auditory perceptual skills and reading ability: A meta-analysis. *Journal of Learning Disabilities,* 1981, *14,* 539-546. (b)

Kavale, K. Meta-analysis of the relationship between visual perceptual skills and reading achievement. *Journal of Learning Disabilities,* 1982, *15,* 42-51.

Kellog, R.E. Listening. In P. Lamb (Ed.), *Guiding children's language learning* (1971). Dubuque, Iowa: William C. Brown, 1971.

Kephart, N.C. *The slow learner in the classroom.* Columbus, Ohio: Charles E. Merrill, 1971.

Kephart, N.C. The perceptual motor match. In W.M. Cruickshank & D.P. Hallahan (Eds.), *Perceptual and learning disabilities in children: Psychoeducational practices* (Vol. 1). Syracuse, N.Y.: Syracuse University Press, 1975.

Kingsley, H.L. & Garry, R. *The nature and conditions of learning* (2nd ed.). Englewood Cliffs, N.J.: Prentice Hall, 1957.

Kirk, S.A. *Manual of directions for use with the Hegge-Kirk-Kirk remedial reading drills.* Ann Arbor, Mich.: George Wahr, 1936.

Kirk, S.A. *Educating exceptional children.* Boston: Houghton Mifflin, 1962.

Kirk, S.A. Behavioral diagnosis and remediation of learning disabilities. In *Proceedings of the Conference on Exploration into the Problems of the Perceptually Handicapped Child.* Evanston, Ill.: Fund for Perceptually Handicapped Children, 1963. [Reprinted in S.A. Kirk & J. McCarthy (Eds.), *Learning disabilities: Selected ACLD papers.* Boston: Houghton Mifflin, 1975.]

Kirk, S.A., & Elkins, J. Characteristics of children enrolled in the child service demonstration centers. *Journal of Learning Disabilities,* 1975, *8,* 630-637.

Kirk, S.A., & Gallagher, J. *Educating exceptional children* (4th ed.). Boston: Houghton Mifflin, 1983.

Kirk, S.A., & Kirk, W.D. How Johnny learns to read. *Exceptional Children,* 1956, *22,* 158-160.

Kirk, S.A., & Kirk, W.D. *Psycholinguistic learning disabilities: Diagnosis and remediation.* Urbana: University of Illinois Press, 1971.

Kirk, S.A., & Kirk, W.D. Uses and abuses of the ITPA. *Journal of Speech and Hearing Disorders,* 1978, *43,* 58-75.

Kirk, S.A., Kliebhan, Sr. J.M., & Lerner, J.W. *Teaching reading to slow and disabled readers.* Boston: Houghton Mifflin, 1978.

Kirk, S.A., & Lord, F.E. (Eds.). *Exceptional children: Educational resources and perspectives.* Boston: Houghton Mifflin, 1974.

Kirk, S.A., McCarthy, J.J., & Kirk, W.D. *The Illinois Test of Psycholinguistic Abilities* (rev. ed.). Urbana: University of Illinois Press, 1968.

Kirk, S., Senf, G., & Larsen, R. Current issues in learning disabilities. In W.M. Cruickshank & A.A. Silver (Eds.), *Bridges to tomorrow.* Volume 2: The best of ACLD. Syracuse, N.Y.: Syracuse University Press, 1981.

Kneedler, R.D., & Hallahan, D.P. Self-monitoring of on-task behavior with learning disabled children: Current studies and directions. *Exceptional Education Quarterly,* 1981, *2*(3), 73-82.

Kohler, W. *The mentality of apes.* New York: Harcourt Brace, 1925.

Kornetsky, C. Minimal brain dysfunction and drugs. In W.M. Cruickshank & D.P. Hallahan (Eds.), *Psychoeducational practices: Perceptual and learning disabilities in children. Vol 2: Research and theory.* Syracuse, N.Y.: Syracuse University Press, 1975.

Kosc, L. Developmental dyscalculia. *Journal of Learning Disabilities,* 1974, *3,* 164-177.

Krulik, S., & Reys, R.E. *Problem solving in school mathematics: 1980 Yearbook.* Reston, Va.: National Council of Teachers of Mathematics, 1980.

Krupski, A. An interactional approach to the study of attention problems in children with learning handicaps. *Exceptional Education Quarterly,* 1981, *2*(3) 1-11.

Lahey, B.B., & Lefton, L.A. Discrimination of letter combinations in good and poor readers. *The Journal of Special Education,* 1976, *10,* 205-210.

Lahey, B.B., & McNees, M.P. Letter discrimination errors in kindergarten through third grade: Assessment and operant training. *The Journal of Special Education,* 1975, *9,* 191-199.

Langford, K., Slade, K., & Barnett, A. An explanation of impress techniques in remedial reading. *Academic Therapy,* 1974, *9,* 309-319.

Larsen, C.C. Teaching beginning writing. In J. Arena (Ed.), *Building handwriting skills in dyslexic children.* San Rafael, Calif.: Academic Therapy Publications, 1970.

Larsen, S.C., & Hammill, D.D. The relationship of selected visual perceptual abilities to school learning. *The Journal of Special Education,* 1975, *9,* 281-291.

Larson, C. Personal correspondence. University of Arizona, Tucson, 1982.

Lee, D.M., & Rubin, J.B. *Children and language.* Belmont, Calif.: Wadsworth, 1979.

Lenneberg, E.H. *Biological foundations of language.* New York: John Wiley, 1967.

Lerner, J.W. *Learning disabilities: Theories, diagnosis, and teaching strategies* (3rd ed.). Boston: Houghton Mifflin, 1981.

Lerner, J., Mardell-Czudnowski, C., & Goldenberg, D. *Special education for the early childhood years.* Englewood Cliffs, N.J.: Prentice-Hall, 1981.

Levine, M.A. *A cognitive theory of learning: Research on hypothesis testing.* Hillsdale, N.J.: Erlbaum Associates, 1975.

Lewis, E., & Lewis, H. An analysis of errors in the formation of manuscript letters by first-grade children. *American Educational Research Journal,* 1965, *2,* 25-35.

Lewis, M. The development of attention and perception in the infant and young children. In W. Cruickshank & D. Hallahan (Eds.), *Perceptual and learning disabilities in children: Research and theory* (Vol. 2). Syracuse, N.Y.: Syracuse University Press, 1975.

London, P. *Beginning psychology.* Homewood, Ill.: Dorsey Press, 1978.

Lucas, E.V. *Semantic and pragmatic language disorders.* Rockville, Md.: Aspen, 1980.

Luick, A., Kirk, S., Agranowitz, A., & Busby, R. Profiles of children with severe oral language disorders. *Journal of Speech and Hearing Disorders,* 1982, *47,* 88-92.

Luria, A.R. *Higher cortical functions of man* (B. Haigh, trans.). New York: Basic Books, 1966.

Lund, K., Foster, G.E., & McCall-Perez, F.C. The effectiveness of psycholinguistic training: A reevaluation. *Exceptional Children,* 1978, *44,* 310-319.

Macione, J.R. *Psychological correlates of reading disability as defined by the Illinois Test of Psycholinguistic Abilities.* Unpublished doctoral dissertation, University of South Dakota, 1969.

Madison, B.D. A kinesthetic technique for handwriting development. In J. Arena (Ed.), *Building handwriting skills in dyslexic children.* San Rafael, Calif.: Academic Therapy Publications, 1970.

Maker, J.C. Problem solving: A general approach to remediation. In D.D. Smith (Ed.), *Teaching the learning disabled child.* Englewood Cliffs, N.J.: Prentice-Hall, 1981.

Malmquist, E. *Factors related to reading disability in the first grade of the elementary school.* Stockholm: Almquist and Wiksell, 1958.

Mann, L. *On the trail of process.* New York: Grune & Stratton, 1979.

Martin, H. Nutrition, injury, illness, and minimal brain dysfunction. In H. Rie & E. Rie (Eds.), *Handbook of minimal brain dysfunction—A critical review.* New York: John Wiley, 1980.

Masland, M.W., & Case, L.W. Limitation of auditory memory as a factor in delayed language development. *British Journal of Disorders in Communication,* 1968, *3,* 139-142.

Mather, N. *Visual perception and reading achievement: The conflict between clinical practice and group research.* Paper presented to Arizona CEC Annual State Convention, Phoenix, February, 1983.

Mather, N., & Healey, W. The efficacy of a memory strategy for eliminating reversal behavior. *Journal of Learning Disabilities* (in press).

McGinnis, M.A. *Aphasic children.* Washington, D.C.: Alexander Graham Bell Association for the Deaf, 1963.

McTaggert, H.P. *A factorial study of the problem-solving ability of fifth grade girls.* Washington, D.C.: Catholic University Press, 1959.

Meier, J. Prevalence and characteristics of learning disabilities found in second grade children. *Journal of Learning Disabilities,* 1971, *4,* 6-21.

Menyuk, P. Comparison of grammar of children with functionally deviant and normal speech. *Journal of Speech and Hearing Research,* 1964, *7,* 109-121.

Meyen, E.L., & Lehr, D.H. Least restrictive environment: Instructional implications. *Focus on Exceptional Children,* March 1980, *7,* 1-8.

Michael, W., Guilford, J., Fruchter, B., & Zimmerman, W. The description of spatial-visualization abilities. *Educational and Psychological Measurement,* 1957, *17,* 185-199.

Minskoff, E.H. *Teaching essential language skills.* Ridgefield, N.J.: Educational Performance Associates, 1979.

Minskoff, E.H. Developing social skills in resource classes for the learning disabled. *Learning disabilities: An audio journal for continuing education,* 1980, *4*(3). (a)

Minskoff, E.H. A teaching approach for developing non-verbal communication skills in students with social perception deficits: Part I. *Journal of Learning Disabilities,* 1980, *13,* 118-124. (b)

Minskoff, E.H. A teaching approach for developing non-verbal communication skills in students with social perception deficits: Part II. *Journal of Learning Disabilities,* 1980, *13,* 203-208. (c)

Minskoff, E.H. Training LD students to cope with the everyday world. *Academic Therapy,* 1982, *17,* 311-316.

Minskoff, E.H., Wiseman, D., & Minskoff, J.G. *The MWM Program for Developing Language Abilities.* Ridgefield, N.J.: Educational Performance Associates, 1972.

Minskoff, E.H., Wiseman, D., & Minskoff, J.G. *The MWM Program for Developing Language Ability.* Ridgefield, N.J.: Educational Performance Associates, 1975.

Monroe, M. *Children who cannot read.* Chicago: University of Chicago Press, 1932.

Montessori, M. *[The Montessori method: Scientific pedagogy as applied to child education in "the children's houses"]* (A.E. George, trans.). New York: Frederick Stokes, 1912.

Montessori, M. *The Montessori method.* New York: Schocken Books, 1964.

Montessori, M. *Dr. Montessori's own handbooks.* New York: Schocken Books, 1965. (a)

Montessori, M. *The Montessori elementary material.* Cambridge, Mass.: Robert Bentley, 1965. (b)

Mortinger, G.J. Use of specific instructions to modify several aspects of creative writing. *The Directive Teacher,* 1979, *1,* 7-23.

Mulford, R. *Prototypicality and the development of categorization.* Paper presented at the Boston University Conference on Child Language, 1977.

Murray, C.A. *The link between learning disabilities and juvenile delinquency.* Prepared for the National Institute for Juvenile Justice and Delinquency Prevention, Office of Juvenile Justice and Delinquency Prevention, Law Enforcement Assistance Administration, Washington, D.C. 1976.

Myklebust, H.R. *Auditory disorders in children.* New York: Grune & Stratton, 1954.

Myklebust, H. *The psychology of deafness* (2nd ed.). New York: Grune & Stratton, 1964.

Myklebust, H. *Development and disorders of written language: Picture Story Language Test* (Vol. 1). New York: Grune & Stratton, 1965.

Myklebust, H. *Development and disorders of written language: Studies of normal and exceptional children* (Vol. 2). New York: Grune & Stratton, 1973.

Myklebust, H.K., & Boshes, B. *Minimal brain damage to children* (Final report, Contract 108-65-142, Neurological and Sensory Disease Control Program). Washington, D.C.: U.S. Department of Health, Education and Welfare, 1969.

National Advisory Committee on Handicapped Children. *First Annual Report, Subcommittee on Education of the Committee on Labor and Public Welfare, U.S. Senate.* Washington, D.C.: U.S. Government Printing Office, May, 1968.

Newland, E. An analytical study of the development of illegibilities in handwriting from the lower grades to adulthood. *Journal of Educational Research,* 1932, *26,* 249-258.

Nielsen, J.M. *Agnosia, apraxia, aphasia: Their value in cerebral localization* (2nd ed.). New York: Hafner Publishing, 1962.

Olson, A.V. School achievement, reading ability, and specific visual perception skills in the third grade. *The Reading Teacher,* 1966, *19,* 490-492.

Orton, S.T. Specific reading disability—Strephosymbolia. *Journal of the American Medical Association,* 1928, *90,* 1095-1099.

Orton, S. *Reading, writing, and speech problems in children.* New York: W.W. Norton, 1937.

Osburn, A.F. *Applied imagination* (3rd ed.). New York: Scribner's, 1963.

Otto, W., Askov, E., & Cooper, C. Legibility rating for handwriting samples: A pragmatic approach. *Perceptual and Motor Skills,* 1967, *25,* 638.

Otto, W., McMenemy, R., & Smith, R. *Corrective and remedial teaching* (2nd ed.). Boston: Houghton Mifflin, 1973.

Parrill-Burnstein, M. *Problem solving and learning disabilities: An information processing approach.* New York: Grune & Stratton, 1981.

Patton, B.R., & Griffen, K. *Problem solving group interaction.* New York: Harper and Row, 1973.

Pavlov, I.P. *[Lectures on conditioned reflexes.]* (W.H. Gantt, trans.). New York: International Publishers, 1928.

Pearl, R., Bryan, T., & Donahue, M. Learning disabled children's attributions for success and failure. *Learning Disability Quarterly,* 1980, *3,* 3-9.

Pearl, R., & Cosden, M. Sizing up a situation: LD children's understanding of social interactions. *Learning Disability Quarterly,* 1982, *5,* 371-373.

Pelham, W.E., Schnedler, R.W., Bologna, N.C., & Contreras, J.A. Behavioral and stimulant treatment of hyperactive children: A therapy study with methylphenidate probes in a within-subject design. *Journal of Applied Behavior Analysis,* 1980, *13,* 221-236.

Penfield, W., & Roberts, L. *Speech and brain mechanisms.* Princeton, N.J.: Princeton University Press, 1959.

Peters, M.L. *Spelling: Caught or taught.* New York: Humanities Press, 1967.

Peterson, D. *Functional mathematics for the mentally retarded.* Columbus, Ohio: Charles E. Merrill, 1973.

Phelps-Gunn, T., & Phelps-Terasaki, D. *Written language instruction.* Rockville, Md.: Aspen, 1982.

Phelps-Terasaki, D., & Phelps, T. *Teaching written expression: The Phelps sentence guide program.* Novato, Calif.: Academic Therapy Publications, 1980.

Piaget, J. *The language and thought of the child* (3rd ed. rev.). London: Routledge and Kegan Paul, 1959.

Piaget, J. *The child's conception of the world.* Patterson, N.J.: Littlefield, 1969.

Piaget, J., & Inhelder, B., in collaboration with Sinclair-DeZwart, H. *[Memory and intelligence.]* (A. Pomerans, trans.) New York: Basic Books, 1973.

Pick, A.D., Christy, M.D., & Frankel, G.W. A developmental study of visual selective attention. *Journal of Experimental Child Psychology,* 1972, *14,* 165-175.

Pysh, M.V. *Learning disabled and normal-achieving children's attributions and reactions to success and failure.* Unpublished doctoral dissertation, Northwestern University, 1982.

Pysh, M.V., & Chalfant, J.C. *Learning disabilities manual: Recommended procedures and practices.* Springfield: State Board of Education, Illinois Office of Education, 1978.

Quiros, J.B., & Schrager, O.L. *Neuropsychological fundamentals in learning disabilities.* San Rafael, Calif.: Academic Therapy Publications, 1978.

Rapp, D.J. Food allergy treatment for hyperkinesis. *Journal of Learning Disabilities,* 1979, *12,* 608-616.

Raschke, D., & Young, A. A comparative analysis of the diagnostic-prescriptive and behavioral-analysis models in preparation for the development of a dialectic pedagogical system. *Education and Training of the Mentally Retarded,* 1976, *11* 135-145. (a)

Raschke, D., & Young, A. The dialectic teaching system: A comprehensive model derived from two educational approaches. *Education and Training of the Mentally Retarded,* 1976, *11,* 232-246. (b)

Raths, L., Wassermann, S., Jonas, A., & Rothstein, A. *Teaching for thinking: Theory and application.* Columbus, Ohio: Charles E. Merrill, 1967.

Reeves, W. *An investigation of conceptual functioning in learning disabilities, schizophrenic, and normal children.* Unpublished doctoral dissertation, Northwestern University, 1972.

Reid, D., & Hresko, W. *A cognitive approach to learning disabilities.* New York: McGraw-Hill, 1981.

Reisman, F., & Kauffman, S. *Teaching mathematics to children with special needs.* Columbus, Ohio: Charles E. Merrill, 1980.

Reitan, F.M., & Davidson, L.A. *Clinical neuropsychology: Current status and application.* Washington, D.C.: Winston, 1974.

Richardson, S.O. Voice and speech disorders of mental and emotional origin. In S.S. Gellis & B.M. Kajan (Eds.), *Current pediatric therapy*. Philadelphia: W.B. Saunders, 1968.

Richie, D., & Aten, J. Auditory retention of nonverbal and verbal sequential stimuli in children with reading disabilities. *Journal of Learning Disabilities*, 1976, *9*, 312-318.

Richter, D. (Ed.). *Aspects of learning and memory*. London: Heinemann Medical, 1966.

Rie, H., & Rie, E. (Eds.). *Handbook of minimal brain dysfunction—A critical review*. New York: John Wiley, 1980.

Ring, B. Effect of input organization on auditory short term memory. *Journal of Learning Disabilities*, 1976, *9*, 591-595.

Roach, E., & Kephart, N.C. *Purdue Perceptual Survey Rating Scale*. Columbus, Ohio: Charles E. Merrill, 1966.

Robinson, H.M. *Why pupils fail in reading*. Chicago: University of Chicago Press, 1946.

Rotter, J.B. Generalized expectancies for internal versus external control of reinforcement. *Psychological Monographs: General and Applied*, 1960, *80*(1), 1-28.

Ross, A.O. *Psychological aspects of learning disabilities and reading disorders*. New York: McGraw-Hill, 1976.

Ross, A.O. *Learning disability: The unrealized potential*. New York: McGraw-Hill, 1977.

Rugel, R.P. WISC subtest scores of disabled readers. *Journal of Learning Disabilities*, 1974, *7*, 57-64.

Russell, D.H. Auditory abilities in achievement in spelling in the primary grades. *Journal of Educational Psychology*, 1958, *49*, 315-319.

Samuels, S.J., & Anderson, R.H. Visual recognition memory, paired-associate learning, and reading achievement. *Journal of Educational Psychology*, 1973, *65*, 160-167.

Satz, P., & van Nostrand, G.K. Developmental dyslexia: An evaluation of theory. In P. Satz & J. Ross (Eds.), *The disabled learner: Early detection and intervention*. Rotterdam, The Netherlands: Rotterdam University Press, 1973.

Schiff, W. *Perceptions: An applied approach*. Boston: Houghton Mifflin, 1980.

Schonell, F., & Schonell, F.E. *Diagnosis and remedial teaching in arithmetic*. Edinburgh: Oliver and Boyd, 1958.

Schroeder, H.H. *An analysis of the use of visual and auditory perception in spelling instruction*. Unpublished doctoral dissertation, University of Iowa, 1968.

Schuell, H. Auditory impairment in aphasia: Significance and retraining techniques. *Journal of Speech and Hearing Disorders*, 1953, *18*, 14-21.

Schumaker, J.B., & Ellis, E.S. Social skills training of LD adolescents: A generalization study. *Learning Disability Quarterly*, 1982, *5*, 409-414.

Science Research Associates. *Greater Cleveland Mathematics Program*. Chicago: Science Research Associates and the Educational Research Council of Greater Cleveland, 1963.

Scott, K.G. Engineering attention: Some rules for the classroom. *Education and Training of the Mentally Retarded*, 1966, *1*, 125-129.

Seguin, E. *Idiocy: Its treatment by the physiological method*. New York: William Wood, 1866.

Seligman, M.E.P. *Helplessness: On depression, development and death.* San Francisco: Freeman, 1975.

Senf, G.M. An information-integration theory and its application to normal reading acquisition and reading disability. In N.D. Bryant & C.E. Kass (Eds.), *Leadership Training Institute in learning disabilities: Final report* (Vol. 2). Tucson: University of Arizona, 1972.

Senf, G.M., & Freundl, P.C. Memory and attention factors in specific learning disabilities. *Journal of Learning Disabilities,* 1971, *4,* 94-106.

Sharp, E.Y. The relationship of visual closure to speechreading. *Exceptional Children,* 1972, *38,* 729-734.

Shulman, L.S. Seeking styles and individual differences in patterns of inquiry. *School Review,* 1965, *73,* 258-266.

Siegel, S. Discrimination among mental defective, normal schizophrenic and brain-damaged subjects on the visual-verbal concept formation test. *American Journal of Mental Deficiency,* 1957, *62,* 338-343.

Sigel, I. Concept formation. In J.J. Gallagher (Ed.), *The application of child development research to exceptional children.* Reston, Va.: Council for Exceptional Children, 1975.

Skinner, B.F. *Verbal behavior.* New York: Appleton-Century-Crofts, 1957.

Slingerland, B.H. *A multi-sensory approach to language arts for specific language disability children.* Cambridge, Mass.: Educators Publishing Service, 1974.

Smith, D.D. *Teaching the learning disabled.* Englewood Cliffs, N.J.: Prentice-Hall, 1981.

Smith, D.D., & Lovitt, T.C. *The Computational Arithmetic Program (CAP).* Austin, Tex.: Pro-Ed, 1982.

Smith, E.E., Shoben, E.J., & Rips, L.J. Structure and process in semantic memory: A featural model for semantic decisions. *Psychology Review,* 1974, *81,* 214-241.

Smith, I.M. *Spatial ability.* San Diego: Knapp, 1964.

Smith, J.O. Effects of a group language development program upon psycholinguistic abilities of educable mentally retarded children. *Special Education Monograph 1.* Nashville, Tenn.: George Peabody College for Teachers, 1962.

Smith, S. *Genetic studies and linkage analysis of specific dyslexia: Evaluation of inheritance in kindreds selected for the parent autosomal dominant transmission.* Unpublished doctoral dissertation, Indiana University, 1978.

Soroky, D.L.A. *Comparative effectiveness of three instructional delivery systems utilized for identifying aphasic children within the Los Angeles Unified School District.* Unpublished doctoral dissertation, University of Northern Colorado, 1979.

Spache, G.D. *Diagnostic Reading Scales* (rev. ed.). Monterey: California Test Bureau, 1972.

Spearman, C. *The nature of intelligence and the principles of cognition.* London: MacMillan, 1927.

Spekman, N.J., & Roth, F.P. An intervention framework for learning disabled students with communication disorders. *Learning Disability Quarterly,* 1982, *5,* 429-437.

Sprague, R.L., & Sleator, E.K. Effects of psychopharmacological agents on learning disorders. *Pediatric Clinics of North America,* 1973, *20,* 719-735.

Spring, C., & Capps, C. Encoding speed, rehearsal, and probed recall of dyslexic boys. *Journal of Educational Psychology,* 1974, *66,* 780-786.

Stanovich, K.E. Individual differences in the cognitive processes of reading II: Text level processes. *Journal of Learning Disabilities,* 1982, *15,* 549-554.

Stark, J., Poppen, R., & May, M. Effects of alterations of prosodic features on the sequencing performance of aphasic children. *Journal of Speech and Hearing Research,* 1967, *10,* 849-855.

Stern, C. *Structural arithmetic.* Boston: Houghton Mifflin, 1965.

Sternbach, R.A. Congenital insensitivity to pain: A critique. *Psychological Bulletin,* 1963, *60,* 252-264.

Sternbach, R.A. *Pain: A psychophysiological analysis.* New York: Academic Press, 1968.

Stone, C.A. *Reading disorders in learning disabled adolescents.* St Lucia, Queensland, Australia: University of Queensland Press, 1981.

Strag, G.A. Comparative behavioral rating of parents with severe mentally retarded, special learning disability, and normal children. *Journal of Learning Disabilities,* 1972, *5,* 631-635.

Strauss, A.A., & Kephart, N.C. *Psychopathology and education of the brain injured child. Volume 2: Progress in theory and clinic.* New York: Grune & Stratton, 1955.

Strauss, A., & Lehtinen, L. *Psychopathology and education of the brain injured child* (Volume 1). New York: Grune & Stratton, 1947.

Sullivan, M.D. *Programmed Math.* New York: McGraw-Hill, 1968.

Swanson, H.L. Nonverbal visual short-term memory as a function of age and dimensionality in learning disabled children. *Child Development,* 1977, *48,* 51-55.

Swisher, L., & Matkin, A. Specific language impairment: The method of L. Swisher and A. Matkin. In *Current Therapy of Communication Disorders.* New York: Thieme-Stratton, 1983.

Talland, G.A., & Waugh, N.C. *The pathology of memory.* New York: Academic Press, 1969.

Tarver, S.G., & Dawson, M.M. Modality preference and the teaching of reading: A review. *Journal of Learning Disabilities,* 1978, *11,* 5-17.

Tarver, S.G., Hallahan, D.P., Kauffman, J.M., & Ball, D.W. Verbal rehearsal and selective attention in children with learning disabilities: A developmental lag. *Journal of Experimental Child Psychology,* 1976, *22,* 375-385.

Taylor, J. (Ed.). *Selected writings of John Hughlings Jackson.* New York: Basic Books, 1958.

Templin, M.C. Phonic knowledge and its relation to spelling and reading achievements of fourth-grade pupils. *Journal of Educational Research,* 1954, *47,* 441-454.

Terman, L.M., & Merrill, M.A. *Measuring intelligence.* Boston: Houghton Mifflin, 1937.

Thurstone, L., & Thurstone, G. *Primary Mental Abilities Test (PMA).* Chicago: Science Research Associates, 1965.

Tollefson, N., Tracey, E., Johnsen, P., Borgers, S., Buenning, M., Farmer, A., & Barke, C. *An application of attribution theory to developing self-esteem in learning disabled adolescents.* Paper presented to The Institute for Research in Learning Disabilities, University of Kansas, Lawrence, January, 1980.

Torgesen, J.K. Memorization processes in reading-disabled children. *Journal of Educational Psychology,* 1977, *69,* 571-578. (a)

Torgesen, J.K. The role of nonspecific factors in the task performance of learning disabled children: A theoretical assessment. *Journal of Learning Disabilities,* 1977, *10,* 27-34. (b)

Torgesen, J.K. Performance of reading disabled children on serial memory tasks: Selective review of recent research. *Reading Research Quarterly,* 1978, *1,* 57-87.

Torgesen, J.K. Factors related to poor performance on memory tasks in reading disabled children. *Learning Disability Quarterly,* 1979, *2*(3), 17-23.

Torgesen, J.K., & Dice, C. Characteristics of research on learning disabilities. *Journal of Learning Disabilities,* 1980, *13,* 531-535.

Torgesen, J.K., & Goldman, T. Verbal rehearsal and short term memory in second grade reading-disabled children. *Child Development,* 1977, *48*(1), 56-61.

Torgesen, J.K., & Houck, D.G. Processing deficiencies of learning disabled children who perform poorly on the digit span test. *Journal of Educational Psychology,* 1980, *72,* 141-160.

Traub, N., & Bloom, F. *Recipe for reading.* Cambridge, Mass.: Educators Publishing Service, 1970.

Treisman, A.M. Monitoring and storage of irrelevant messages in selective attention. *Journal of Verbal Learning and Verbal Behavior,* 1964, *3,* 449-459.

Turnbull, A.P., & Schulz, J.B. *Mainstreaming handicapped students: A guide for the classroom teacher.* Boston: Allyn & Bacon, 1979.

Valmont, W.J. Spelling consciousness: A long neglected area. *Elementary English,* 1972, *49,* 1219-1222.

Van Engen, H. *Seeing through arithmetic.* Chicago: Scott, Foresman, 1963.

Vellutino, F. Toward an understanding of dyslexia. In A.L. Benton & D. Pearl (Eds.), *Dyslexia: An appraisal of current knowledge.* London: Oxford University Press, 1978.

Vellutino, F.R. *Dyslexia: Theory and research.* Cambridge, Mass.: MIT Press, 1979.

Vellutino, F.R., Steger, B.M., Harding, C.J., Moyer, S.C., & Niles, J.A. Has the perceptual deficit hypothesis led us astray? *Journal of Learning Disabilities,* 1977, *10,* 375-385.

Vygotsky, L.S. *Thought and language.* Cambridge, Mass.: MIT Press, 1962.

Wallace, G., & Kauffman, J.M. *Teaching children with learning problems* (2nd ed.). Columbus, Ohio: Charles E. Merrill, 1978.

Wallach, M.A., & Kogan, N. *Modes of thinking in young children.* New York: Holt, Rinehart, & Winston, 1965.

Wallas, G. *The art of thought.* New York: Harcourt, Brace and World, 1926.

Waugh, R.P. Relationship between modality preference and performance. *Exceptional Children,* 1973, *39,* 465-469.

Wechsler, D. *Wechsler Intelligence Scale for Children–Revised.* New York: Psychological Corporation, 1974.

Weiner, B. A theory of motivation for some classroom experiences. *Journal of Educational Psychology,* 1979, *71,* 3-25.

Weiner, B., Frieze, I., Kukla, A., Reed, L., Rest, S., & Rosenbaum, R.M. *Perceiving the causes of success and failure.* New York: General Learning Press, 1971.

Weiner, B., Heckhausen, H., Meyer, W., & Cook, R.E. Causal aspirations and achievement behavior: Conceptual analysis of effort and reanalysis of locus of control. *Journal of Personality and Social Psychology,* 1972, *21,* 239-248.

Wender, P.H., & Wender, E.H. *The hyperactive child and the learning disabled child: A handbook for parents.* New York: Crown, 1978.

Wepman, J.M. Auditory discrimination, speech and reading. *Elementary School Journal,* 1960, *3,* 325-333.

Wepman, J. Auditory perception and imperception. In W. Cruickshank & D. Hallahan (Eds.), *Perceptual and learning disabilities in children: Research and theory* (Vol. 2). Syracuse, N.Y.: Syracuse University Press, 1975.

Wernicke, C. The symptom-complex of aphasia. In A. Church (Ed.), *Diseases of the nervous system.* New York: Appleton-Century-Crofts, 1908.

Wiederholt, L., Hammill, D., & Brown, V. *The resource teacher.* Boston: Allyn & Bacon, 1978.

Wiig, E., & Semel, E. *Language assessment and intervention for the learning disabled.* Columbus, Ohio: Charles E. Merrill, 1980.

Willeford, J.A. Central auditory function in children with learning disabilities. *Audiology and Hearing Education,* 1976, *2,* 12-20.

Willeford, J.A., & Billger, J.M. Auditory perception in children with learning disabilities. In J. Katz (Ed.), *Handbook of clinical audiology* (3rd ed.). Baltimore: Williams & Wilkins, 1978.

Wissink, J., Kass, C., & Ferrell, W. A Bayesian approach to the identification of children with learning disabilities. *Journal of Learning Disabilities,* 1975, *8,* 36-44.

Wittrock, M.C. Education and the cognitive processes of the brain. In J.S. Chall & A.F. Mirsky (Eds.), *Education and the brain: The seventy-seventh yearbook of the National Society for the Study of Education* (Part II). Chicago: University of Chicago Press, 1978.

Woodcock, R.W., & Clark, C.R. *Peabody rebus reading program.* Circle Pines, Minn.: American Guidance Service, 1969.

Ysseldyke, J., & Salvia, J. Diagnostic-prescriptive teaching: Two models. *Exceptional Children,* 1974, *41,* 181-185.

Zeaman, D., & House, B. The role of attention in retardate discrimination learning. In N. Ellis (Ed.), *Handbook of mental deficiency.* New York: McGraw-Hill, 1963.

Name index

Subject index